Environmental Damage and Liability Problems in a Multilevel Context

Energy and Environmental Law & Policy Series
Supranational and Comparative Aspects

VOLUME 22

Editor

Kurt Deketelaere

Professor of Law, University of Leuven, Belgium,
Honorary Chief of Staff, Flemish Government
Honorary Professor of Law, University of Dundee, UK
Secretary – General, League of European Research Universities (LERU), Belgium

Editorial Board

Dr Philip Andrews-Speed, Associate Fellow, Chatham House
Professor Michael Faure, University of Maastricht
Professor Günther Handl, Tulane University, New Orleans
Professor Andres Nollkaemper, University of Amsterdam
Professor Oran Young, University of California

The aim of the Editor and the Editorial Board of this series is to publish works of excellent quality that focus on the study of energy and environmental law and policy.

Through this series the Editor and Editorial Board hope:

- to contribute to the improvement of the quality of energy/environmental law and policy in general and environmental quality and energy efficiency in particular;
- to increase the access to environmental and energy information for students, academics, non-governmental organizations, government institutions, and business;
- to facilitate cooperation between academic and non-academic communities in the field of energy and environmental law and policy throughout the world.

Environmental Damage and Liability Problems in a Multilevel Context

The Case of the Environmental Liability Directive

Sandra Cassotta

Wolters Kluwer

Law & Business

Published by:
Kluwer Law International
PO Box 316
2400 AH Alphen aan den Rijn
The Netherlands
Website: www.kluwerlaw.com

Sold and distributed in North, Central and South America by:
Aspen Publishers, Inc.
7201 McKinney Circle
Frederick, MD 21704
United States of America
Email: customer.service@aspenpublishers.com

Sold and distributed in all other countries by:
Turpin Distribution Services Ltd.
Stratton Business Park
Pegasus Drive, Biggleswade
Bedfordshire SG18 8TQ
United Kingdom
Email: kluwerlaw@turpin-distribution.com

Printed on acid-free paper.

ISBN 978-90-411-3830-9

© 2012 Kluwer Law International BV, The Netherlands

Printed and Bound by CPI Group (UK) Ltd, Croydon, CR0 4YY.

To the Memory of my Adored Mother and Franco

Table of Contents

Foreword

On 21 April 2004, the Council of Ministers and the European Parliament adopted the European Directive (2004/35/EC) on Environmental Liability with regard to the Prevention and Remedying of Environmental Damage (ELD) which entered into force at EU level on 30 April 2004. Member States had until 30 April 2007 to bring these provisions into force at national level. A first evaluation of the implementation process is now possible, and maybe even necessary.

For this purpose, it must be recalled that the ELD of 2004 is the result of a long process. For more than 18 years, the European Commission had studied and debated the notion of an EU-wide legislative scheme, establishing the basic criteria for environmental clean-up and liability. From the Green Paper of 1993, to the White Paper of 2000, the Proposal of 2002 to – finally – in 2004 the text of the ELD.

The Text of the ELD is – in many aspects – the result of different compromises: at political level and, also, at a more substantial level. The issue of legal terminology in the ELD should not be underestimated, especially if we bear in mind that the goal of the ELD was and still is to harmonise the law in this field. The text of the ELD is very diplomatic, is not very explicit, not even on some core focal points of the whole new liability regime that it wanted to introduce, like the strict liability issue.

Thus, it is possible to find evidence of this compromise in the language of the ELD, in the legal terminology used in it.

Hence, by using a much generic or a non-technical legal terminology at European level, there is a risk of leaving a too wide space for interpretation at national level, putting at stake – from the very beginning – the result wanted to be achieved which is the one of harmonising the rules. This is the case for the definition of 'damage', included in Article 2, which according to the ELD means 'a measurable adverse change in a natural resource or measurable impairment of a natural resource service which may occur directly or indirectly'.

Although whereas n. 5 states: 'Concepts instrumental for the correct interpretation and application of the scheme provided for by this Directive should be defined especially as regards the definition of environmental damage. When the concept in question derives from other relevant Community legislation, the same definition should be used so that common criteria can be used and uniform application promoted', the text of the ELD and its various linguistic versions is full of traps to this aim. Article 3 of the ELD, dedicated to define the scope of the ELD – for example – states that the Directive shall apply to:

(a) Environmental damage caused by any of the occupational activities listed in Annex III, and to any imminent threat of such damage occurring by reason of any of those activities.

(b) Damage to protected species and natural habitats caused by any occupational activities other than those listed in Annex III, and to any imminent threat of such damage occurring by reason of any of those activities, whenever the operator has been at fault or negligent. By consequence, it should be noted that 'fault and negligence' become in the English version important to define the liability regime of the ELD. Nonetheless, these concepts become in the German and in the Italian version criteria that include the malicious intent of the operators, having being translated into German with 'vorsätzlich oder fahrlässig', and into Italian with 'comportamento doloso o colposo'. In the French version the text seems the exact translation of the English one, stating that the operator must have committed 'une faute ou une négligence'.

Given these difficulties, in future years, it will be auspicable and urgent to understand how the legal framework of the ELD of 2004 has been put into work and has become 'law in action', and above all it has reached the result of harmonising the liability regime as far as environmental damages are concerned. The book of Sandra Cassotta, which goes back to the entire decision-making process of the development phase of the Liability Directive until the present legal text of the ELD, offers a rich variety of instruments in order to operate this analysis, which goes beyond the surface of black letter rules into the depth of the various implementation processes.

Barbara Pozzo,

November 2011

Acknowledgements

In finalising my PhD Dissertation which has formed the base of the work of this book, and concluding a 'Chapter' of my life which has offered me an extraordinary and stimulating experience, I am delighted to record my sincere appreciations to the work of many, who have made contributions.

First of all, I would like to express my deep gratitude to my advisor, Birgitte Egelund Olsen, from the Department of Law, Aarhus University Business and Social Sciences, for the profound influence she had on me, in both scholarly and personal experiences. She is a real mentor and a model, who taught me so much, and with such a rare capacity to transmit to scholars the passion for the job of researcher.

My gratitude also goes to the 'giant experts' of the focal topic of this study: Barbara Pozzo, from the Università degli Studi di Milano – Facoltà di Giurisprudenza, Ellen Margrethe Basse, from the Department of Law, Aarhus University Business and Social Science who patiently helped me to improve the scientific quality of this book, and Nicolas de Sadeleer from the Université de St Louis of Brussels. My gratitude goes also to Jan Darpö, Uppsala Universitet for his brilliant and pungent suggestions during my PhD Defence which I have incorporated in this book. I was extremely lucky to benefit from their advice, long experience and expertise recognised nationally and internationally at the highest level of academic research. To all of them, goes my gratitude for the very stimulating observations and comments during my presentations of parts of this work.

I would like also to express my warmest thanks to both Amin Alavi and Matthew Elsmore from the Department of Law, Aarhus University, Business and Social Science for their contributions in commenting on some parts of the draft chapters.

I thank the DASTI (Danish Agency for Technologies and Innovation, numbers of granting 09061777 and 645060345) for having made possible the granting of this three-year project and which I have been extremely proud to benefit from.

Acknowledgments

My final words must be addressed with heartfelt thanks to the secretaries and the IT staff of the Department of Law, Aarhus University, Business and Social Science both for their professionalism and for having contributed to make me feel comfortable at work.

Thanks also, of course, the whole Department of Law of Aarhus University, Business and Social Science for the encouragements in my research during the 'coffee-breaks'.

Thank you also to my husband, Cino, and my little son Francesco for their patience.

Sandra Cassotta

Aarhus, 31 October 2011

Part I

'What' and 'How' in the Multilevel Environmental Liability Regime

Chapter 1

Setting the Field: Environmental Law and Policy on Environmental Damage and Liability Problems

1.1   INTRODUCTION AND STATEMENT OF THE PROBLEM

Since the 1970s, the EU Member States have started to feel the need for harmonising national legislations by setting up liability regimes for environmental damage. The point of using liability as an element in solving the legal problems of environmental harm soon became more than an issue of national and EU level's affair. It involved international law and international politics and thus, should be perceived as an expression of an international regional cooperation between sovereign States and International Organisations and Non-Governmental Environmental Organisations (NGOs). At the end of 2000, it become apparent that those who were interested in an environmental liability regime were not only official actors of the EU institutions, the international level and the Member States, but also the so-called 'non-official actors' (groups of interest, such as, the business sector, environmental organisations, NGOs, chemical industries, insurances, and banks, etc.).

Today, environmental damage and environmental liability is a multi-dimensional problem as it involves three-levels (EU, international and national) moving through the entanglement of both political and legal components. The parallel regimes at the EU, international and national levels, regulating environmental issues requires an understanding of the interplay which exists between different legal systems and decision-levels of the law-making process. The role of international institutions, and international actors, and the new developments of international law and practices, exercise a certain exogenous 'pressure' on national legal systems which are prone to adopt a more precise environmental legislation, which is stringent in terms of implementation and control of international obligations.

The study aims at explaining why the process of implementation of the Environmental Liability Directive, called 'ELD'[1] was not successful in most of the Member States, and also why the ELD manifests a very limited harmonising effect.

The phenomenon of harmonisation is evaluated in relation to those conventions and treaties which are strictly connected with the legal and political problems of the ELD and the book enquiry on the evaluation of the optimal level of harmonisation. The ELD was not only adopted in order to harmonise legal systems, but also to fully implement the Polluter-pays principle.

The implementation of the ELD plays a pivotal role between the Europeanisation and the European Integration process. Under the Europeanisation phenomenon, depending on the national regimes already in place, Member States will have to adjust or to set up new laws; implement new policies; interact with the EU institutions, internal groups, non-official actors, agencies; and set-up new policy coordination in a top-down and bottom-up approach. Under the process of European integration (formation of policy areas, formation and introduction of principles of law, treaties, directives, and sources of law), the environmental liability regime seems to present respectable preliminary potentials which will in the future run in parallel to other regulations from international laws and international agreements.

The focus on the ELD and most importantly, on the development phase of the Environmental Liability Directive, is relevant as it offers an innovative analytical perspective as the ELD represents a sort of 'complement' and 'integrates' the conventions and treaties on environmental damage, especially where the reparation of the damage is not fully recovered.

This latter observation, explains why such kinds of analysis will also be strongly beneficial for international law, as it highlights the situation of overlap and integration between EU sources of law and international sources of law. However, the study on the ELD also sheds light on the changes occurring in the system of the 'orthodox hierarchy of sources of law' as it paves the way for a new area in the design of the legal system undertaken by the EU.

---

1. In the long *iter* of the law-making process of an EU legal act including the EU proposed legislation which precedes the adoption of a legal act (regulation, directive or decisions), in order to distinguish between the past from the present, two distinct expressions will be used in the book. When the book refers to the 'past' which refers to the development phase of the Environmental Liability Directive, or its gestation process, the expression 'Environmental Liability Directive' or 'Liability Directive' will be used *per esteso*. Whilst when referring to the 'present' which refers to the period of time up to the adoption of the ELD ahead, or until the current days, period of which is corresponding to the present legal text of the Environmental Liability Directive 2004/35/EC with regards to the Prevention and Remedying of Environmental Damage as adopted by the European Parliament and of the Council on the 21 April 2004, the abbreviated expression 'ELD' will be used along the book.

Hence, the question of research for this project consists, firstly, in assessing the ELD's capacity to achieve its goals and ambitions in terms of environmental protection, and, secondly, what the optimal level of harmonisation is.

The book reveals a new analytical perspective in solving the problems of effectiveness of the EU environmental law and policy with particular emphasis on a problem-solving approach centred on the weakness in the effectiveness of environmental directives. In parallel, it considers the impact of the international dimension and the international law on the national level *via* the EU level of intermediation.

In light of the statement of the problem formulated in the question of research of the study, four hypotheses are elaborated and validated throughout the book:

- Hypothesis 1: the study into the advancement and regression of the Environmental Liability Directive in a three-level triangular perspective (EU, international and domestic) sheds light on the important relationship existing between the EU Law and international law and offers, at the same time, the possibility of solving the low level of effectiveness of EU environmental law.
- Hypothesis 2: the Environmental Liability Directive represents a type of complement or integration to the international conventions/treaties on the environmental damage, or vice versa, the international convention/treaties can integrate the EU law especially when the reparation of the damage is not fully covered.
- Hypothesis 3: the existence of a relationship between the role of the EU as an external actor in external environmental relations and the effectiveness of the Environmental Liability Directive, and if more leadership from the Commission would have rendered the European environmental liability regime more effective.
- Hypothesis 4: the lessons which can be learned from the analysis of ELD in terms of advancement and regression analysed under the impact of the international dimension are representing a source of inspiration both for the Member States and the EU as a legislator.

The book's analytical task aims at finding common solutions to common problems and requires an interdisciplinary approach combining and integrating law and political science. In that sense, there are serious motives justifying as to why an interdisciplinary approach is necessary in order to address the question of research of this book.

In primis, the effectiveness of EU environmental law is a question of law, policy, politics and theory, and is concerned with the structure of the EU and the relationship between Member States and the EU. The double nature of the obstacles of implementation, enforcement, impact and compliance of EU environmental law consists of the existence of both legal and politico-institutional barriers and the need of analysing them in a bottom-up and top-down approach.

Secondly, the double advantage offered by a study conducted with a legal and political approach: (1) political side: understanding the reason for the malfunctioning and the reason for the weakness of environmental directives; (2) legal side: understanding the EU environmental rules and the procedural aspects concerning the law-making process, which can only be provided by an interdisciplinary legal and political eye perception.

Thirdly, an interdisciplinary approach is necessary if the phenomenon under scrutiny is a multi-causal phenomenon, and in that sense, the environmental damage is a multi-level political and legal multi-causal problem caused by different factors and within different intersectional levels.

Fourthly, given the existence of different areas or levels involving the study of the ELD and the possible interactions and overlap between the different sources of law in the three-level perspective – EU, international and national – more order has to be established. In other words, the reparation of the damage needs a theoretical approach conducted in a systematic fashion. The environmental harm and the problems of responsibility have always had a practical and concrete character often issued by necessities and emergency situations (i.e., Chernobyl; Seveso I; and II; Erika and the Prestige's cases etc.). The environmental liability regime is therefore an 'empiric law' developed by tragic events and intersecting a range of issues not belonging to environmental law but protected by it and laying in a *chaotic status*.

Therefore, there is an urgent need for identifying, ordering, and systematising in a theoretical manner the problems and potentials of the Environmental Liability Directive's law formation process concerning the reparation and prevention of the damage at a global level. This can be done only by tracing the contour of an integrated international law framework able to investigate both the political and legal perspective of the ELD's process of implementation in a multilevel global dimension, and 'reconstruct', theoretically, the environmental liability regime caused by the environmental harm.

With regards to the study's delimitation of the time and spatial dimensions, for the first dimension, the study covers the period of time from the 1976 until the present days. The reason for the choice of this starting date is because the birth of the environmental liability regime can be traced back to the 1970s' when the Commission submitted to the Council the 1976 First Directive's Proposal focusing on the Waste Sector.

Thereafter, the development of the environmental liability regime is intertwined with several EU actions, treaties and conventions regarding the environmental liability regime which started after the mid-1990s. Specifically, the Lugano Convention, the Basel Convention and Protocol, the Aarhus Convention, the Commission's Green Paper and White Paper on environmental liability, until the changes introduced by the enforcement of the recent Treaty of Lisbon. The end date is not really 'delimited' as the implementation of the ELD is still an ongoing process that has to be observed from the 31 April 2007, the official deadline imposed on the Member States for the transposition of the ELD into national law. The spatial dimension is delimited only to the Western Countries due to the progress in unification of trade, policy and law in those countries. A western system of law, consisting of Civil Law and Common Law will be discussed with regards to selected case examples. All of the focal issues treated in the conventions, treaties, EU sources of law and policy or national provisions, are selected as they are strictly interconnected with those covered by the ELD.

The book includes a comparative approach,[2] chosen in order to analyse how different national rules at EU level and at international level try to solve common problems on environmental harm and liability issues and the importance of dialogue between different systems of law. On the national level, the focus on civil law is mostly directed to the conditions of Italy and the German example. The comparison between the Italian and German legal systems on environmental damage and liability problems is very representative for explaining the existing legal models protecting natural resources at the EU level. A third country, the US, has been selected as a Common Law legal historical comparative model since some of the instruments chosen to protect the environment at the EU level have already been experienced in the past within US law.

Additionally, along with the traditional way of comparing, the study includes and makes use of another innovative comparative approach consisting of comparing in a 'non-traditional way', the EU sources of law and policy, with international law and domestic law through using the 'interactions' among the zones of overlap among the different spaces of sources of law and policy.

1.1.1   THEORETICAL FRAMEWORK

Theoretically, the analysis of environmental law is uncertain as there is a lack of theories of environmental governance.[3] Furthermore, there are no studies which examine the problems concerning the prevention and reparation of the damage on a global scale with reference to the public and private levels and in light of the competition, overlap, and integration existing between EU sources of law and international sources of law. There is a gap in the literature on liability in cases of environmental damage perceived also as 'trans-boundary damage', and in relation to specific conventions, treaties and EU actions. Also, in general, research has focused on the emergency situations of environmental damage.[4] However, as pointed out by Biermann, International Relations (IR) research on environmental regimes has provided a number of useful insights into the factors which could make a regime more influential on state's actions.[5] Moreover, in the realm of

---

2. On the use of the comparative approach together with an innovative comparative approach, or 'non-traditional comparative approach', see the next paragraph as well as the next sub-section 1.1.3.1 of the present chapter.
3. Young, O.R., *'Why is there No Unified Theory of Environmental Governance?'* Essay for the 9th Biennial Conference of the International Association for the Study of Common Property, 2002, II EG/Darthmoth College.
4. See List, Rittberger, Young and also the work on epistemic communities as influential factors in regime creation in Haas.
5. Biermann, F., Brohm, R., and Dingewerth, R., *'Global Environmental Change and the Nation States – Proceedings of the 2001 Berlin Conference on the Human Dimension of Global Environmental Change'*, 2002, Potsdam: Potsdam Institute for Climate Impact Research, pp. 1–9.

environmental damage, it is worth noting that the crucial point of convergence between the theoretical discourse on international environmental policy and legal concerns was, and still remains, focusing on the problem of the effectiveness of environmental regimes.[6]

For the International Relation (IR) community, environmental regimes lack a definition of effectiveness.[7] From a political point of view, environmental rules manifest a certain difficulty in achieving environmental protection goal achievements. From a legal point of view, it is well known that environmental rules present a weak degree of efficacy and a weak degree of social justice with an insufficient involvement and participation of citizens of the regulation protecting environment.

From a theoretical point of view, the point of departure of this study develops a political **three-level triangular theory** (Cassotta, 2011) upon which other legal theories are integrated and merged in order to propose a whole 'integrative international law framework of analysis combining political science and law'.

The book proposes a **three-level triangular theory** (Cassotta, 2011) because the environmental liability regime is a multi-dimensional problem. The environmental damage concerns three-levels (EU, international and national) of decision-levels of law-making and levels of sources of law and policy. The process of implementation of the ELD is not independent from the international level, and what happens at the EU level reverberates at the international level and at the domestic level and vice versa in a triangular relationship between the EU, international and domestic levels. In that sense, a brief overview of the transposition process in Member States shows how the most contentious elements of the EU decision-making during the law-making process reverberates at national level.[8] The kernel of the three-level triangular theory is that the EU, situated in the middle of the EU bargaining interplay between the international level and domestic level (EU capacity to enter into international negotiation agreements) acts as a sort of 'intermediate', revealing the dynamism of its dual nature as an international organisation and as an actor-player in the external world. The theory explains also that not only the official actors, such as the EU Commission, the EU Council, or the EU Parliament are important in the decision-making law process, but also the so-called 'non-official actors' matter and interact with the EU decision-making.

The three-level triangular model explains that negotiations and debates are not linear as they occur simultaneously at all levels of interplay reflecting each other,

---

6. The manner in which legal science and political science treats effectiveness conceptually will be object of analysis in Chapter 4.
7. The pioneer in approaching the study of effectiveness of law and who combined political science with law is Francis Snyder. See Snyder, F., '*The Effectiveness European Community Law: Institutions, Process, Technique, Tools and Techniques*', 1993, The Modern Law Review, Vol. 56, No. 1, pp. 19–54.
8. Coroner, F., '*Environmenental Liability Directive: How well are Member States Handling Transposition?*', Environmental Liability, 2006, Lawtext Publishing, Vol. 14, Issue 6, November – December, pp. 226–229; De Smedt, K., '*Is Harmonisation always Effective'? The Implementation of the Environmental Liability Directive*', 2009, European Energy Environmental Law Review.

and that the three-level triangular strategy is important in order to produce an effective environmental law in terms of environmental protection goal achievements and optimality of harmonisation. In that sense the proposed theory offers the possibility of understanding the right *formula* for reaching environmental protection. In fact, the theory traces a multidisciplinary framework of analysis which individualised seven common core factors determining the concept of environmental liability, the respect of the sequential order of which determine environmental effectiveness and success in terms of environmental protection goal achievements. These factors, called 'focal points', represent the points of intersection between the political and legal contexts of the multilevel dimension to be treated in a systematic chain of logical sequences which must be respected in their sequential order since the change of the first factor can determine variation of the last factor. This 'domino' or 'reverberating effect' can determine advancement in terms of environmental effectiveness and the success in terms of environmental protection goal achievements.

The theory is interlaced with the methodology employed in the research of this study, as these same focal points are also maintained throughout the book as tools of systematisation and comparison in the zones of overlap between the EU, international and domestic levels of environmental sources of law and policy, and the US model.

Nevertheless, the three-level triangular theory presents certain weak points.

Firstly, the model does not explain the role of its main negotiator (the EU Commission), its influence, and the limits of its powers during negotiations. The question of competence to negotiate on both external agreements and external mixed agreements is not clearly laid down in the TFEU.[9] In that sense, sometimes the Commission has exclusive competence in conducting external negotiations, i.e., in the trade of agricultural goods which are part of the exclusive competence of the EU (Article 218 of the TFEU which corresponds to the 'old' Article 300 of the TEU). However, it can happen that the Commission can in practice, and in cases of the conclusion of agreements, also be accompanied by the EU Member States'

---

9. The question of competence of the EU to negotiate on external negotiations was not even clearly laid down in the EC Treaty. Prior to the enforcement of the Treaty of Lisbon, in order to avoid possible confusions in linguistic terminology in any study concerning the institutional system of the EU there was a clear distinction that had to be maintained between the term EC (European Community) and the term EU (European Union). The EC (and not the EU) was competent in the field of international external relations. The EC was part of the EU but the EC solely had international personality in *strictu sensu*, not the EU. The EU was not a member of international organisations and did not negotiate. It was only the EC that had such an international legal personality. Therefore, prior to the TFEU, the EU lacked any legal personality preventing it from acceding into Treaties and agreements. Subsequent to the enforcement of the Treaty of Lisbon, Art. 46 of the TFEU, provides that the EU shall have legal personality, which should enable the EU to enter into treaties and agreements on behalf of Member States. However, even though the enforcement of the Treaty of Lisbon solves the confusions in linguistic terminology and supposes a stronger EU, it does not solve the question of competence of the EU to negotiate in external negotiations, particularly in the case of mixed environmental agreements which still remain as a pending question.

government representatives. This same ambiguity in the question of competence to negotiate applies also to the capacity of the EU to conclude mixed environmental agreements, as the environmental field is one of the 'shared competencies' that the EU has to share with Member States. It is not only the Commission, but also the Council which can conclude agreements. However, there is still an important *enigma* as to who is competent to negotiate: the Member States or the EU?

Secondly, the notion of 'intermediation' of the EC between the international level (top level) and domestic level (low level) has not been developed. The concept of intermediation lacks investigation into the context of a 'structural systemic theory' within a three-level analysis. The three-level triangular theory does not clarify the relationship between the levels in terms of their possible 'interactivity' and does not consider the possibility of using the theory as a 'structural theory' by comparing the three-levels, since the levels can also be analysed in terms of systems.

In the light of the above critiques[10] of the developed three-level triangular theory, it is clear, as *per* the first *lacuna*, that the analysis of the ELD and its developing phase, is interlaced with the configuration of the system of the EU or the institutional choice chosen for the international organisation, the relationship between the EU and the Member States, and the external environmental relations. What is decided at an intermediate level (EU Level) is reflected at a top level (international level) and is mirrored at a lower level (domestic level).

Nevertheless, clarification of the role of the EU (intermediate level) should be resolved because it allows the question of competence between the EU and the Member States to emerge, outlining the role of its main negotiator (the Commission). In other words, it should be considered whether more competence should be left at the domestic level both for the success of environmental policy achievements and for a better efficacy of environmental rules, or rather, whether it is the role of its main negotiator, the Commission, which should be strengthened in order to obtain the same result in terms of environmental effectiveness of environmental policy and law, and optimality of the level of harmonisation.

In addition, the importance of the 'interactivity' of the levels of analysis described in the second *lacuna* is relevant because the analysis of the environmental liability regime is not immerged in a single order. Environmental damage and the liability regime are not immerged in a single order. Environmental damage and the liability regime are regulated by a patchwork of different rules, (EU supranational law, international law, European organisation law, international principles of law and customs, national legislations) in what is called 'normative pluralism', but also by 'cultural pluralism' (different regulatory powers to local communities). Therefore, it is important to understand and systematise the interactivity between the different levels of regulations. By consequence, it is possible to study the interactions of different 'legal spaces' and compare the EU law, the international

---

10. The term 'critique' here, can be interchanged with the term '*lacuna*'.

law, the EU Member States' laws, or the law of other international organisations, in 'terms of systems' through examining as to whether there is a link or bridge-force between the levels aspect, the latter, still unexplored both by the legal and political theorists, especially by the scholars dealing with rational choice theories.

With regards to the first three-level triangular theory's lacuna, **Vervey's theory** (2004)[11] is able to address the critique. Vervey's theory explains the influence of the EU international treaty-making power practice and international legal relations on the development of international law. Both Vervey's theory and the proposed three-level triangular theory enquire into the *enigma* regarding who is competent to negotiate. Vervey upgrades more the question of who was responsible for political arrangements between the EU, EC, its Member States and the 'third parties'. Furthermore, Vervey's theory goes further than the proposed three-level triangular theory as its theory is able to complement the three-level triangular theory as it advocates the possibility of enhancing cooperation and coexistence between the EU and the Member States. Vervey explains that Member States have not lost their sovereignty or legal personality, but rather, have transferred part of it into the EU. He offers the explanation of the legal implications and the role of its main negotiator, and supports the choice for an EU Federal Constitutional system since this would enhance legitimacy and transparency in the law-making process. The three-level triangular theory refers, without developing it, to the power of 'intermediation' of the EU. Vervey suggests the manner of how to balance this power in order to have more effective legal results.

In substance, a political scientific analysis based on the proposed three-level triangular theory, combined with a legal scientific theory based on a legal analysis of the EU international treaty-making power, reverberates at the national level and can potentially lead to increase environmental effectiveness, and consequently to overcome barriers to the process of implementation of the EU.

As to the second *lacuna* of the three-level triangular theory, the theoretical approach based on **Polycentrism and Legal pluralism** (1995),[12] offers an important tool in explaining the interconnections and comparisons of the legal spaces. Pluralism is a modern legal theoretical approach which challenges both the old legal monistic approach and the hierarchical order of the legal sources of law. The main arguments for pluralists are that the sources of law are interactive and not hierarchical.[13]

According to Pluralism and Legal Polycentrism, there is a simultaneous existence within a single order of different rules of law to identical situations. When different rules can solve in various ways, the same situation, it is defined as a

---

11. Vervey Delano, R. *'The European Community, the European Union and the International Law of the Treaties – As a Comparative Legal Analysis of Community and Union's External Treaty-making practice'*, 2004, Cambridge University Press.
12. Petersen & Zahle *'Legal Polycentricity: Consequences of Pluralism in Law'*, 1995, Dartmouth Publishing Company.
13. Arnaud, A.J., *'Legal Pluralism and the Building of Europe'*, in Petersen & Zahle, *'Legal Polycentricity: Consequences of Pluralism in Law'*, 1995, Dartmouth Publishing Company, pp. 149–169.

situation of pluralism.[14] Legal pluralism complements the theoretical gap in the three-level triangular theory regarding the absence of explanation on the interactivity of the levels, and shows how the levels could integrate and overlap each other.

Polycentrism and Legal Pluralism is applied in situations of clashes or confrontations between laws placed at national level and laws placed at supranational level. The theory explains that what is important in EU law is not the demand of national legislation to be in harmony rather to recognise spaces where legislations could usually give its place up to another type of regulation other than law. Polycentrism explains that the three-level spaces could be analysed in terms of systems, and that a confrontation and comparison of EU law, international law and Member States' laws can be achieved in terms of legal spaces.[15] In other words, Pluralism explains what the three-level triangular theory cannot explain: how the levels of the structure should be used. On the other side, Polycentrism neglects the role of the groups of interest, a gap that can be covered by the three-level triangular theory.

A last theoretical component supports the two legal theories (Vervey's theory and Polycentrism) and increases the explanatory power of these two legal theories: Lindross and Meheling's the theory on the end of the 'self-contained regimes'. **Lindross and Meheling's theory** (2005)[16] reinforces the advantages of Pluralism and helps to promote order in situations of divergences and fragmentation of legal systems as in the case of the environmental damage and liability regime.

The environmental liability regime is immerged in 'civil law, administrative law, private law, public law, EU law, international law, criminal law, and, international private law', and the Lindross and Meheling's theory squares well with its analysis since it is a 'non-traditional way' or a 'non-orthodox' way in which to approach the subject, given the peculiarity of the environmental liability regime and the impossibility of analysing it in a more traditional manner. The theory shows a new way of analysing into environmental law, known by legal experts, as being an atypical area of specialisation of the international law.

To recapitulate, the theoretical framework proposed by this book is composed of four theories complementing each other in a manner in which to trace the contours of an integrated international law and policy framework. The framework of analysis is called 'integrative' since it integrates and combines in 'synthesis':[17] (1) the proposed political science theory, the *three-level triangular theory* of

---

14. Arnaud, A.J., '*Legal Pluralism and the Building of Europe*',1995, Dartmouth Publishing Company, page 149.
15. Santos De Sousa expressly sees 'the existence of three-simultaneous and interactive legal spaces – local, national, world legal –, as a central feature for world legality' in Wilhelmsson, T., '*Legal Integration and Disintegration of National Law*', in '*Legal Polycentricity*', 1995, page 129.
16. Lindross, A., and Mehling, M., '*Dispelling the Chimera of Self-Contained Regimes' International Law and the WTO*', 2006, European Journal of International Law, pp. 857–877.
17. For an understanding of the use of 'theoretical synthesis' in theory-building, see Helleman, G., '*The Forum: Are Dialogue and Synthesis Possible in International Relations?* Institut für Vergleichende Politikwissenschaft und Internationale Beziehungen, Johann Wolfgang Goethe-Universität Frankfurt am Main, 2003, International Studies Review, 5, pp. 123–153.

Cassotta of 2011 with (2) the legal *theory on the EU Treaty-making power* of *Vervey of* 2004, and with (3) the legal theory of *Polycentrism and Legal Pluralism* of Petersen, Zahle, Arnaud *et al* of 1995; supported by a (4) fourth last legal theory on '*the end of the self-contained regimes*' of Lindross and Meheling of 2005.

The theoretical integrative framework of international law and policy (Cassotta, 2011), combining law and policy, is used as an interdisciplinary framework of analysis throughout the whole book and presents five characteristics:

(1) Reliance on systemic theoretical structure since it involves three spaces (of rules) which integrate a methodology and place the law into a 'multi-level context'.

(2) Dynamic (non-static) and predictive since it can also be employed in conditions of exogenous changes or changing situations (i.e., the relationship between EU law and international law and the change of hierarchy of legal sources of law, the changes in international law, and the change of the level of optimality of harmonisation or the change of the concept of harmonisation).

(3) Interdisciplinary since it combines political science with legal science.

(4) Multi-causal model of analysis.

(5) Presents the characteristic of being a 'middle ground theory' as it combines in 'theoretical synthesis bits of information in provenance from two different disciplines (political science and law) in a theoretical space where dialogue and pluralism amongst the theories is possible.

The theoretical dialogue amongst the theories gives birth to a cross-paradigmatic model of -EU law, international law, national legal orders-, mixed with political science, and elements of the decision-making law process combined with an international relation perspective.

1.1.2   OPERATIONALISING THE THEORETICAL INTEGRATIVE FRAMEWORK
          OF INTERNATIONAL LAW AND POLICY

The study applies the proposed *theoretical integrative framework of international law and policy* (Cassotta, 2011) to the empirical case which consists of both the development phase of the Environmental Liability Directive since its origins, to the current legal text of the ELD and to selected examples of legal models of environmental protection such as Italy, the German example and the US. Each theory of the framework is applied to some specific arguments of the environmental damage and liability problems of the developing phase of the Environmental Liability Directive and to the current situation of the ELD. This manner of operationalising enables the testifying of the combination 'in synthesis' of the theories contained in the framework, especially the combination between the political and legal components. The means of matching theories with facts is through selecting 'key debates' or 'key arguments' which makes sense in order to explain the legal barriers or potentials of the decision-making process of the ELD and the implementation phase of the

ELD, in relation to the international level. The impact of the EU level on the international level enables the ineffectiveness of EU environmental law to be approached in a predictable way.

In that sense, effectiveness is defined as the point of conjunction and dialogue between the two disciplines, and where and when policy and law applies, is also considered in the operationalising phase of the framework, as developed in Chapter 4.

In order to facilitate the application of the developed *theoretical integrative framework of international law and policy* (Cassotta, 2011) to the empirical case study, the *three-level triangular theory* (Cassotta, 2011) is corresponded to the analysis of the environmental damage and the liability arguments and problems, keeping in mind, contemporaneously, the integrative theories, especially when the three-level triangular theory's *lacuna* arises. This allows combining instantaneously political components with legal elements only where it is necessary, and with the extent of weight of information that is needed for the validation of the hypotheses exposed in the introduction and for the achievements of the study's objective.

With regards to the *three-level triangular theory* (Cassotta, 2011) the three-levels of the structure are investigated from both the political and legal perspectives where the necessity emerges. The proposed model, treated as a 'structural theory', allows the identification of the interactions between levels, a comparison of the levels, and facilitates the combination of the information contained in the two disciplines.

In the first stage of the operationalising phase, the combination of the two disciplines is achieved in a balanced fashion by individualising and investigating the points of intersection of the framework of analysis between policy and law, as developed in Chapter 2. In the second stage of the operationalising phase, the two disciplines are combined and integrated in a way in which to provide a stronger preponderance to the legal components and legal aspects involved in the development phase of the Environmental Liability Directive, as exposed in Chapter 3. This second phase is also the phase containing the analysis of the selected examples (Italian and German), and the US Model as well, as an example of how Europeans have been inspired by the American experience when dealing with the environmental damage and liability obstacles. This phase is also the phase where hypothesis 1, formulated in the introduction,[18] is validated positively.

With regards to *Vervey's theory* (2004) and its contributions, this approach is applied in Chapter 4, especially to the role played by the main negotiator of the EU, the EU Commission, during the external negotiations of mixed environmental negotiations of the decision-making process of the law-formation process of the environmental liability regime.

---

18. Hypothesis 1: the study into the advancement and regression of the ELD in a three-level triangular perspective (EU, international and domestic) sheds light on the important relationship existing between EU law and international law and offers, at the same time, the possibility of solving the low level of effectiveness of EU environmental law.

This is because what is decided at an intermediate level (EU level) with the involvement of certain key actors, impacts not only at a top level (international level) and on the development of international environmental law, but also downwards in the legal systems of the EU Member States (domestic level) in what is the implementation phase of the ELD. The contributions identified in Chapter 4, are the empirical part of where hypothesis 3, formulated in the introduction,[19] is validated positively.

As to the theory of *Polycentrism and Legal Pluralism* treated by Petersen, Zahle, Arnaud, *et al.* (1995), the theory is operationalised where the ELD complements international law and the environmental treaties and conventions, and vice versa, in order to gain deep insight and identify the overlaps, integrations, and, entrenchments between the EU sources of law and policy and the international sources of law, as demonstrated in Chapters 3 and 5. The latter are also the chapters where hypothesis 2,[20] formulated in the introduction, is validated positively.

The *theory regarding the end of the existence of the 'self-contained regimes'* formulated by *Lindross and Meheling* (2006) is applied throughout Chapters 3 to 5 to support the set of legal theories especially where the question of the relationship between the ELD and the general environmental law is faced. The model is employed and applied to the liability regime taken in its global dimension, in order to establish its 'non-self contained *status' en tant que* regime. In that sense, the theory is applied in Chapters 3 and 5, and the latter chapters, also validates, positively, hypothesis 4,[21] formulated in the introduction.

1.1.3   METHODOLOGY AND RESEARCH DESIGN

1.1.3.1   Methodology

The comparative methodology is the crucial tool for 'reconstruction' of the environmental damage and liability problems from a legal, political and theoretical perspective. The comparative approach is not only referred to in the 'traditional sense', or understood as the 'traditional way' of comparing legal systems.[22]

---

19. Hypothesis 3: the existence of a relationship between the role of the EU as an external actor in external environmental relations and the effectiveness of the Environmental Liability Directive, and if more leadership from the Commission would have rendered the European liability regime more effective.
20. Hypothesis 2: the Environmental Liability Directive represents a type of complement or integration to the international conventions/treaties on the environmental damage, or *vice-versa*, the international conventions and treaties can integrate the EU law especially when the reparation of the damage is not fully covered.
21. Hypothesis 4: the lessons which can be learned from the analysis of the ELD in terms of advancement and regression analysed under the impact of the international dimension are representing a source of inspiration both for the Member States and the ELD legislator.
22. See Zweigert K. & Kötz H., *'An Introduction to Comparative Law'*, last Edition, Calderon Press; Gambaro S. & Sacco R., *'Trattato di Diritto Comparato – Sistemi Giuridici Comparati'*, last edition, UTET; David R. & Spinosi Jauffret C., *'I grandi sistemi giuridici contemporanei'*

Normally, what it is compared or what lawyers or legal scholars specialised in comparative law are used to observing is, for example, the comparison of a given legal system belonging to a certain legal family with another legal system belonging to another legal system of the same family[23] or with a legal system belonging to different families.[24] This book makes use of the comparative methodology in the 'traditional sense' or in the 'orthodox way', by comparing legal systems, where it compares, for example, the Italian legal system in protecting natural resources with the German law or when it compares the provisions of the ELD with the provisions of the implementing law of Italy or with the US model.

The book also proposes another means of comparison which could be called a 'non-traditional way' or 'non-orthodox' method of comparing the law, not of legal orders, but in terms of the levels of different systems, such as, for example comparing the EU level, with the international level and the domestic level of sources of law and policy. In that sense, it is a study of the interactions of the different levels of legal spaces and legal traditions, and a comparison of the rules of the different levels (EU, international and national levels); the examination of the links between the levels and what types of bridge forces there are between these regulatory levels such as the role on the official and non-official actors, represents a new method of investigation into the environmental liability regime. This is a non-traditional method of approaching the problems of environmental damage. This approach is justified since the environmental liability is characterised by intersecting ranges of issues not belonging to environmental law, rather protected by it and laying in a *chaotic status*.

Therefore, a 'non-traditional approach' is required in order to extract the potentials amongst the levels of sources of law, and reinsert them in the process of updating and improvement of environmental regulations. The use of the comparative methodology in a systemic structure, allows the introduction of order and systematisation in the phenomenon under observation.

The method demands an incorporation of elements deriving from exogenous factors from 'level spaces' to 'level spaces' within a three-level structure of the three-level triangular theory. The comparison between different legal orders strongly accommodates the dialogue between legal science and political science, and, therefore, strongly welcomes the interdisciplinary approach.

The comparative methodology in a systemic structure relies on a comparison of legal sources of law at EU, international and domestic levels of spaces. In the comparison of these three-levels of legal spaces, special attention is dedicated to the 'general principles of international environmental law'.

---

last edition, CEDAM; Merryman, J.H., '*The Civil Law Tradition. An Introduction to the Legal System of Western Europe and Latin America*', last edition, Standford University Press, Stanford, California; Gandolfi M.L., '*Profili del Trespass to land – il torts e gli improvements del trespasser*', Studi di diritto comparato, 1979, Pubblicazioni della Facoltà di Giurisprudenza della università di Pisa, Milano-Giuffré Editore.

23. For example comparing French law with Spanish or Italian law; or Danish Law with Swedish law.
24. For example comparing French law with Russian law or Danish law with US or Chinese law.

The general principles of international environmental law emerged in the international law as typical examples of 'soft-laws' aimed at realising a certain *consensus* at a global level (i.e., in cases of trans-boundary damage, the green house effect, and the climate change). These principles are becoming more important than ever.[25] The relevance of these principles emerges both at regional supranational level and at Member States' level on specific environmental law.[26] The force of the general principles of environmental law is becoming so strong today that there is a common belief in defining the international environmental law as 'the law of the general principles'[27] which are 'behind' all legislation.

The general principles of environmental law are part of the methodology of this book as they are the rings of conjunctions between the levels of sources of law and policy and they are ordered, balanced and systematised, especially in their functions as unifying (or bridge) forces between the three legal spaces.

The study's methodology also relies on a legal-political comparison of the two cases of Italy and the German example, and the US Model taken as historical comparative model of analysis since they all represent different key typologies of patterns in protecting legally natural resources.

The cross-fertilised confrontation and comparison between the legal systems at all of the levels is based on the use of seven focal points. In that sense, the methodology in the present study, matches in an ideal way, the research design of the theory-building, as the book lays down a framework of analysis based on the focal points of intersection between the legal and political contexts of the multilevel dimensions. These are to be treated in a systematic chain of logical legal sequences which must be respected in its sequential order, and stresses that the notion of environmental damage is the capital problem. The seven focal points are (1) definition of environmental damage, (2) scope of application, (3) problem of who is entitled to claim for environmental damage, (4) compensation for environmental damage, (5) choice of the type of liability, (6) causality link, and (7) insurance mechanism.

The book outlines and concludes that, the notion of environmental damage, in the ELD should change in order to achieve success in terms of environmental protection goal achievements.

The comparative methodology, both in the traditional and non-traditional forms, is used as a tool permitting the development of a common platform of research aimed at developing a new scheme of analysis valuable in a multilevel context. Specifically, the method offers a means of analysing a certain number of

---

25. Sand, P., *'Principles of International Environmental Law'*, 2007, Cambridge University Press; Birnie, P., Boyle A., Redgwell C., *'International Law & the Environment'* 2009, Oxford; de Sadeleer N., *'Environmental Principles*, 2007, Oxford; Louka, E., *'International Environmental Law – Fairness, Effectiveness and World Order'*, 2006, Cambridge University Press; Amirante, D., *'Diritto ambientale italiano e comparato – Principi'*, 2003, Quaderni della rivista Diritto e gestione dell'ambiente della seconda universtità degli studi di Napoli, Jovine Editore.
26. Prieur, M., *'Droit de l'environnement'*, 2001, Paris.
27. Amirante, D., *'La forza normativa dei principi e il contributo del diritto ambientale alla teoria generale'*, 2006, Jovine Editore, pp. 93–156.

problems related to environmental harm from an ontological perspective which are analysed and compared predominantly at three-levels and in the selected legal systems, with a cross comparative technique. The same method is maintained all throughout the book, when analysing cases of law, sources of law and policy at all of the levels, with the purpose of reaching a certain degree of homogeneity, consistency and coherency in the architecture of the research design of this book, especially in maintaining the linkage between the research question, the proposed framework of analysis, and the methodology.

The final purpose in explaining such a linkage, between the question of research, the framework and methodology which all together are forming what is defined the research design[28] of the present book, is to suggest how to increase the effectiveness in the EU environmental liability regime. Nevertheless, is it not always easy, neither for political scientist, nor for a legal scholar to 'define' the concept of effectiveness in environmental law. With that respect, Chapter 4 of the present book adds a further peace into the difficult puzzle on how to increase effectiveness in the EU environmental liability regime, by merging into a sole definition, both the political and legal science perspective when defining effectiveness.

The purpose of defining and understanding how to render the environmental liability regime more effective rely on the necessity to find the optimal level of harmonisation.

The historical background in the case of the US model's experience on environmental issues has been chosen as a case study since it provides a useful example in several respects. The issue of environmental liability in that country fully emerged in the 1980s, when several environmental-pollution cases were recorded and, at the same time, a number of small enterprises entered risky sectors.[29] In the 1980s Congress accordingly issued the Comprehensive Environmental Response Compensation and Liability Act of 1980 (CERCLA) in order to cope with the 'decontamination' of sites subject to environmental risks, through charging the reimbursement of the clean-up costs to the liable parties and through creating a public fund, the 'Superfund'.[30] Thus, the US law has been faced with problems of effectiveness, efficiency and predictability considerably earlier than at the EU level.

The environmental liability regime at the EU level is based on the Principle of precaution, the Principle of prevention and the Principle of correction at the source of damage caused to the environment, as well as on the Polluter-pays principle.[31]

---

28. The research design of this book will be treated in the next sub-section.
29. Ringleb, A., Wiggings S., '*Liability and Large-Scale, Long-Term Hazards*', Journal of Political Economy, June, 1990, pp. 574–595.
30. The Superfund allows decontaminating the sites included in a national list, the National Priority List (NPL), with money being primarily collected from taxes on oil and oil-derived products
31. Article 174 of the EC Treaty and the '*White Paper on Environmental Liability*', COM(2000) 66 final, Brussels, February 9, 2000. See also Kramer, '*EEC Treaty and Environmental Protection*', London, and also '*Commentaires de l'Acte Unique Européen en matière de l'environnement*' in Revue Juridique de l'Environnement, 1988, Revue juridique de l'environnement,

In the 1990s, several initiatives from the Commission started to elaborate a European framework of civil liability, taking into consideration the different national situations.[32] The Commission started to evaluate several options for the regulation of the issue.[33] However, in contrast to the US experience, the EU environmental liability system does not set up a public fund, as had been the case in the US which provides for a Superfund. The EU insists on another point of view which is the proper and smooth functioning of the internal market.

In substance, the fact that there are various environmental liability regimes in the different EU Member States raises the question as to whether this jeopardises not only the environment but also the free competition amongst companies within the single internal market. Hence, it may be argued that the Commission accentuates the need for a 'lower common denominator' amongst different Member States, and thus emphasises the importance of examining the *pros* and *cons* of different criteria for imputability.

In all Member States of the EU, there are provisions on civil liability for personal injury and property damage. However, only rarely do they cover damage done to the environment. National regimes providing for compensation to be paid for damage to the environment are the exception to the rule.

Overall, the research material is based on a qualitative analysis of selected data based on: (1) primary resources, comprehensives of a first sub-distinction between primary resources of 'hard law' and primary resources of 'soft law'; and (2) secondary resources, comprehensive of second sub-distinction between 'academic' and 'non-academic material'.

Specifically, the primary resources comprehends hard law, such as provisions of relevant treaties, conventions and agreements, cases law, law texts; and soft law, including material, such as, inventory of relevant documentation on the policy and the implementation process, policy papers, guide-lines, and declarations.

The secondary resources comprehends academic material, such as books, articles, and material of seminars on the topic; and non-academic material, such as, reports, minutes of meetings, newsletters, press releases, and reports from NGOs.

1.1.3.2 Research Design

The combination of the selected four theories contained in the *theoretical integrative framework of international law and policy* (the three-level triangular theory; the theory on the EU legal treaty-making power and its influence on international

---

pp. 75 ss, and Meli, *'L'origine del principio chi inquina paga da parte della CEE'*, 1998, Rivista Giuridica dell'Ambiente.

32. Pozzo, B., *'Toward Civil Liability for Environmental Damage in Europe: The White Paper of the Commission of European Communities'*, 2001, Vol.1, Issue 2, Article 2, Global Jurist Topics, pp. 1–34.

33. The question was already very controversial between those who wanted a directive and those who strongly supported the use of a regulation as explicated by Hartkamp *et al*, in *'Toward a Civil Code'*, 2004, Kluwer Law International, pp. 677–695.

law; the Polycentrism theory; and the theory about the end of the self-contained regimes) is chosen from among four possible options of combination of theories proposed by a study on research design.[34] In a first stage, the theories are not evaluated against the reality of the empirical phenomenon of the environmental damage. Instead, each theory is evaluated against another theory and serves to explicate part of the same phenomenon. Consequently if a theory is not able to explain part of the phenomenon in a satisfactory way, another theory intervenes and complements it with a stronger explanatory power, what the other theory has not explicated. This neither entails the elimination of the previous theory nor that the helping theory act as a substitute of the previous one. Rather, the theories 'coexist' and share the same structure in a relationship based on complementarity.

A research design characterised by this type of combination of theories is defined a 'Zero Competitive Model of Dialogue' based not on competitive theories (zero competitively), but rather on complementary theories. In a second stage, the theories are evaluated against the reality and the framework is tested against the empirics of the environmental damage and liability problems both on the development phase and the current *status* of the ELD. Each theory is 'carrier' or vehicle of elements of politics or law that are injected in a whole theoretical framework giving birth to a new integrated international law model characterised by theories susceptible of being: compared, complemented, interconnected and interactivated. Each theory contains elements of both politics and law that are sometimes strong and sometimes weak. However, it is evident that in a political science theory, the political information is stronger, and that in legal theories the legal elements are, without any doubt more accentuated. Therefore, each theory adjusts the weakness of the other theory adding more or less political force or more or less legal force. The four theories operate 'in synthesis' and suggests a definition of a new concept of environmental law that need to lie on a theoretical ground.

The middle ground of theories is the point of agreement/overlap and departure of the four theories, the interaction of which led to the formulation of a new concept of environmental law. The effectiveness of environmental law and a new concept of environmental law should lie on a theoretical discourse which is a mixture of law, politics, political science and theory. The combination of the four theories also suggests not only a new concept of effective environmental law but also a new concept of optimisation of the level of environmental harmonisation.

The relationship between EU law and international law and vice versa, in a three-level triangular strategy, help to tackle the obstacle of environmental ineffectiveness of the EU environmental law and policy and to achieve a better environmental law and policy outcome by sorting out a better law in terms of environmental protection goal achievements.

The interdisciplinary approach of this book makes possible that each bits of political or legal information presented in the different theoretical reasoning

---

34. Jupille, J., Caporaso, J., Checkel, J.T., *'Integrating Institutions – Rationalims, Contructivism and the Study of European Union';* Comparative Political Studies, Vol., 36 No. ½, February, March, pp. 1–40.

'coexists' in a whole theoretical integrative framework of international law and policy and are incorporated from 'theory' to 'theory' in a way of creating a 'common-theoretical-ideal-space' where law and policy coexists sharing common values. The new theoretical zone is the space of optimisation of harmonisation and where a new *area* in the design of the EU legal system occurs.

1.2   VALUE ADDED OF THE BOOK

The motive for writing this book is not to find a universal solution on how to find the way to halt environmental damage magically by sorting out from a gold Pandora kit, the genial *formula* on how to make the world community liable for environmental damage. Rather, more humbly, the purpose of writing this book is to present a new approach from a global perspective in solving problems of effectiveness of EU environmental law. In that sense, this book offers a new approach to some of the elements of information for experts which are essential to the understanding of what the right *formula* for reaching environmental protection is, and how the optimal level of harmonisation in terms of environmental protection can be achieved. In fact, it is not by causality that the study proposes a framework of analysis based on the factors determining the concept of environmental liability, the respect of the sequential order of which determines the success in terms of environmental protection goal achievements.

These factors, called focal points, can be the object of a common simultaneous enquiry not only by legal experts when investigating the law of liability, but also by economists interested, for example, in costs-effective analysis; political scientists involved in understanding the political compromises and trade-offs behind the formulation of the ELD provisions; insurance law specialists who have to be aware of the problems in the ELD when they issue insurance policies, and finally, natural scientists, constantly involved in the difficult task of participating in the formulation of the chameleonic definition of the term 'environmental damage'.

Currently, a book on how to improve and update the ELD is relevant as now days we are immersed in a reality where the international community is trying to implement the aims of the sustainable development on issues of a certain magnitude, such as the damaging effects of climate change, the polluting effects of CO_2 emissions and the advancing loss of biodiversity. More specifically, more than ever, a book on how to update the ELD is highly topical as the ELD will be the object of a procedure of revision for possible amendments and redrafting of its provisions prior to 30 April 2014.

Hence, the study contributes with the proposal for amendments through individualising the precise shortcomings of the ELD which should be addressed by the EU legislator. The book concludes with some proposals for amendments to the ELD.

Commencing at the EU level dimension, progressing toward the international level, and finally reaching the national dimension of the law, the title of this book is 'Environmental Damage and Liability Problems in a Multilevel Context: the Case of the Environmental Liability Directive'. Thus, the title is explicative by it-self of the potential and possibility to use the proposed theoretical framework linked to the methodology of this study and generalised it not only to the 'ELD case' but also to other 'cases'[35] susceptible to be analysed in a multilevel perspective, and to other environmental directives[36], and thus, it is supposed of generating, in that sense, further research to improve environmental law and policy and identify the optimal level of harmonisation.

The value added from the present book, is to lay down a new analytical perspective in solving the ineffectiveness of environmental policy and the weaknesses in the effectiveness of the EU environmental directives. In parallel, it considers the interactions and synergies between EU law, international law and national law *via* the EU level of intermediation. Therefore, it is not only an analytical and accurate description of the current parallel regimes at EU, international and national level.

In that sense, the purpose of this book is to go further than a meticulous state-of-the art of the environmental liability law in Europe, even though the latter case would be a perfectly respectable and a high level research task. In addition, neither is it the intent of this book to present an exhaustive political-legal *panorama* of the process of implementation in 27 Member States, which would certainly be a valuable work as well. Additionally, the book is not delimiting the analysis of the ELD and its context through a sole discipline or with approaches based on the classical combination of law and economics, which have been useful and widely explored in the past in explaining problems of environmental civil liability.

At least but not last, another value of this book is also to provide with an example of 'law in context' as it observes how the ELD developed and the multi-level context where it finds it-self embedded. The reader is guided from the very first start at the inception of the Environmental Liability Directive until the present and projected in three dimensions into the multidimensional context of the law formation process of the environmental liability regime whereby the ELD developed. The book is projected also into the future, as drawing back into the past, in such a way, it uses the historical comparative part as a tool to explain the present problems in the ELD by using the past to avoid of committing the same mistakes in future.

---

35. Examples of other interesting cases which can be analyzed in a multilevel context and where it is possible to apply the same framework and methodology of the present research, are the cases of 1) the movement of hazardous waste; and 2) the building of regulatory frameworks for a new generation of environmental damages caused by the use of nanotechnology in renewable energy products and processes (i.e., in solar photovoltaic panels or wind energies mills), and also in batteries and fuel burning processes using nano-materials. The movement of hazardous waste; and the 'new generation of nano-environmental damages' are examples of other types of politico-legal topical issues requiring a 'multi-layered approach' with international, EU and national regulations interacting simultaneously.
36. Other environmental directives susceptible to be analyzed with the same framework and methodology of the present research are: Directive 2008/EC on Waste and Repealing certain Directives, and Directive 2009/28/EC on Promotion of the Use of Energy from Renewable Sources.

This study lay down a framework of analysis based on the focal points of intersection between the legal and political contexts of the multilevel dimensions to be treated in a systematic chain of logical legal sequences that must be respected in its sequential order, and stresses that the notion of environmental damage is the capital problem. The book outlines and concludes that, the notion of environmental damage, in the ELD should change, in order for the ELD to achieve success in terms of environmental protection goal achievements.

1.3   TOWARDS AN UNTRADITIONAL
            INTERDISCIPLINARY FRAME ON THE
            'COEXISTENCE BETWEEN PUBLIC LAW
            AND PRIVATE LAW APPROACH'

This book is the result of a research project that was not focused on discrediting the use of a public law approach compared to private law approach in the environmental protection rules. Rather, the approach of this book is that both public law and private law approaches coexist. Thus, in the ELD, it is not necessary to adduct that public law is 'better' than private law in protecting natural resources or vice versa. The two approaches coexist in a space where also the way to perceive the law is important in such a space of coexistence.

Thus, it is not the intention, in this book, to reject a public law system and it is neither the intention of the author of this book to conduct a classical comparative law research for all the due respect for the previous work of comparative law on what is the classical debate of a public approach *versus* a private approach or 'if it is better a private approach system than a public law system'. Rather, the objective of this book is to shift the debate to a different new perspective.

Having said that, the command & control regulations, a part from being a valid and respectable instrument for environmental protection do not always seems to represent a liability *stimulus* or incentive for potential polluters who tend to just comply with standards level without valid encouragement to search for new clean or green technologies or lesser polluting products. That is not to discredit the role of public law on environmental matters. Not at all, on the contrary, public law had and still has fundamental importance on the environmental protection.

However, problems emerge when, for example, it is a question to exercising a certain control over some kind of public law obligations (i.e., environmental standards) where often some kinds of different bureaucratic mechanisms enter into play. Then, sometimes, a public law approach can (and it is not said that it does) reinforce administrative bureaucratic mechanism rather than provide a real protection of the environment. Furthermore, even though private law cannot ensure the preventative action against the environmental damage, such as public law obligations are able to do, it can still offer some instruments that are able to play an important role.

The opinion of the author of this book is that they should both coexists, public law and private law approaches. In different legislations it has been possible to observe some kind of adaptation of pre-existing regulation presents in national legal systems, with new rules of private law (i.e., emissions and civil responsibility of public law coexisting with private law) such as occurred in the US or in Italy, as it will be explained in the following chapters.

Liability as a consequence of environmental damage can be regulated with a public law approach and a private law approach and the public law approach could be a problem if this perspective does not cover certain situations and if the public administrations never receive the money covering the costs of restoration. In the private law approach, the State or the public administration is regarded as the injured party in a tort law manner in relation to the polluter.

The public authorities have the right to be compensated for the damage caused by unlawful acts. Public law and private law may provide different answers to questions such as for example the legal basis for liability (choice of the type of liability, if *culpa* or strict based and the time limits). An important question is what happens if the public law approach does not cover certain situations.

The main existing legislations which have as an object to establish environmental civil liability as a consequence of environmental damage are aimed at regulating private relationships leaving to the latter, the choice to be entitled to exercise a right. On the contrary, public law is aimed at protecting the environment and at regulating not only State organisation and public authorities' activities but also actors' behaviour of private actors and private relationships of natural and legal persons which are all obliged to respect public law, especially when they carry on activities with potential environmental impact. Therefore, it is not possible to consider or separate the different aims of public and private law as both aspects are part of environmental protection law and they overlap and interact constantly. There is an undeniable dualism between the modern environmental law where both environmental protection and public interests (collective interests) coexists with environmental protection of individual interests (private interests). Hence, it is not possible to advocate that a private approach is better than a public approach when protecting legally the environment. Rather, it is the message of this book that only a holistic view based on a multilevel and multidisciplinary approach can help to solve problems of liability as a consequence of environmental damage.

1.4   A NEW HOLISTIC PERSPECTIVE OF THE LAW

Legal science and comparative law are not the only methods to solve normative problems, there are other methods. In order to fully grasp the perspective of this study, it is also important to understand what the aim and the way to perceive the law are. How the law is perceived.

The book regard comparative law in 'terms of systems' so it is very much related to the way the law is perceived and on how legal science is perceived. Thus, legal science represent not only a technique of interpreting texts, principles, rules and standards but also the discovering of theoretical models for preventing and solving social conflicts in a way in which this will facilitate a study on several ways of regulating situations in different systems or in terms of systems. This path will enable the researcher to gain valuable knowledge or most importantly to understand the relevant legal function.

Thus, the perspective of this book depends on the way the law is perceived and used as an instrument by seeking to compare different functions in different systems in a way to use the law as a 'tool' to ensure the implementation of political goals.

The 'holistic vision' of the law, in the present analysis, is an amalgamation of a multitude of cultural aspects. The law has to be analysed and understood in 'context'. Even if and when legislators at different levels (EU, international and national) have tried in different ways to harmonise legislation or to introduce a foreign construction, it will inevitably be reformulated within the local culture. This understanding of the law means that the law can never be extricated from its culture, historical and political context. If the law is perceived 'in context', from that perspective, contextual excursions and even theoretical legal excursions are always permitted including non-legal studies material. They are permitted and never sufficient.

This perspective can be used to refresh in a new and promising way the legal discourse at EU, international and national level, which consists in perceiving the law in a pluralistic approach or 'law in pluralism'. The pluralistic perspective or the pluralistic understanding of what look the same in black letter law may have the same origins (environmental conventions or environmental agreements) and may be analysed in a new perspective. In that sense, also a non-normative law can be of importance as the law does not always fully describe the politico-cultural *substratum* of the society.

People also subject them-self to rules other than legal ones which is why the present study tries to build a framework based upon comparison by systematising parts, politico-legal parts of the problem under investigation and trying to find a solution by comparing the focal points not only by observing the differences and similarities of these focal points of the existing parallel regimes regulating environmental liability but also by looking on how the focal points could have been integrated and complemented. The results of such a way of comparing different levels of sources of law and policy are presented in a scientific manner according to the functional role of the different solutions. The final purpose of this non-orthodox comparison is to make the law effective.

One of the mayor problems has been and still is to identify and measure effectiveness since effectiveness is part of an immense and complicated picture and it has to do with law, policy, and theory and with systematisation and logic where not only rules and legal acts are evaluated but also non-legal rules, soft-regulations, administrative practices, hidden procedural aspects and voluntary agreements which have all to be considered. This is because factors other than black letter law play a role and there are also politico-legal and economical elements which have to be taken into account which is why, a multidisciplinary approach in this research, is vital.

1.5   TERMINOLOGY

Along the study, several different terms related to 'civil liability', 'environmental civil liability' or 'environmental liability', are employed. Therefore, it appears useful for the reader to have some basic terminologist guidance as to the precise meaning and the appropriate use of such a terminology.

In that sense, it is necessary to clarify the differences and similarities in respect to terms, such as (1) civil liability; (2) environmental civil liability; (3) environmental liability; (4) criminal environmental liability (which is the only liability excluded in this study but explained for the sake of the entire picture composing the different types of existing 'environmental liabilities' used in environmental law); and finally (5) administrative environmental protection legal model of liability.

The present section aim at furnishing a basic exposition on the different terminology in relation to the above five terms, as more explanations regarding the precise use and application of these terms, will follow along the chapters of this book. The aforementioned terms are developed and find their proper meaning and full identity all along the legal and historical comparative analysis of the development phase of the environmental liability regime in Europe and in the US which collides also with the development of the industrial society and the new environmental risks, as it will be explained in Chapter 3.

The term 'civil liability' appears in different sectors, since environmental law and environmental damage is only one of the possible areas of law where this term is used. Civil liability is the liability or legal obligation that anyone has, to repair a wrong (or a tort) or a breach inflicted to another where for example subject x commits a damage to y and subject x is obliged to compensate according to law or regulations which can be contained in civil codes or in the jurisprudence. There are two main prerequisites for liability: (1) the existence of the causality link, which is the *nexus* between the author of the damage and the event; and (2) the existence of the subjective element of *culpa*. Therefore, the classical archetypal that it is found in all civil codes is: 'subject x causes damage to subject y, subject x must repair. However, the problem comes when this archetypal is applied in environmental law and to environmental damage, problem the latter which lead straight a way to the second definition of the term 'environmental civil liability'.

This is because civil liability, when applied to environmental law or environmental damage is completely disrupting this archetypal because, as it will be explained more in details in Chapter 3, section 3.1.1.1 of this book, frequently, the goods belonging to 'subject y' (which is in this case the environment that has been damaged) does not belong to anyone as it has no owners. Therefore, the term 'civil environmental liability' compared to the term 'civil liability' *tout-court*, is really putting into trouble the use of civil liability when applied to environmental damage.

In a nutshell, the problems that all legislators, at EU, international and national and also in the US model had and still have, is how to make it fit 'civil liability' into environmental damage and from a legal point of view, how this fitting could be operationalised in the light of the solutions of the seven focal points which have been identified in this book, and which are still pending to be solved by all legislators, at all the levels and at any time (past, present and future).

However, the term 'environmental civil liability' refers to the means of helping to recover the costs of damages that occurs either in violation of existing environmental standards or as a result of wrongful (or tort) behaviours inflicted to others where the unique peculiarity compared to the other terminological mentioned formulations resides in the meaning to provide solutions to recover the damage from those responsible for pollution, in line with the core principle of environmental law which is the Polluter-pays principle.[37] The Polluter-pays principle in the means of the term 'environmental civil liability' prevents and repair the damages caused to the environment where with the tem 'environment' it is meant the ensemble of *media* such as the water, soil, air, flora and fauna. On one hand, environmental civil liability is applicable to certain kinds of professional activities that can be explicitly enumerated by legislators at all the levels (EU, International and national).

On the other hand, the same terminological expression, is applicable when the behaviour of an actor commit a wrongful damaging situation act and therefore through environmental civil liability, environmental legislation attempt to regulate the behaviour of actors where 'actors' can be defined as potential polluter(s) or 'operator'(s) as it is defined by the EU Law in the ELD, and where environmental legislators, attempts to regulate this behaviour of actors by making fit liability into environmental damage by trying to solve the problems related to the seven focal points.

The term 'environmental liability' overlaps with the term 'environmental responsibility' where the latter refers to the duty to prevent the damage whilst 'environmental liability' is more applied to explain the idea that in case of environmental damage, there is a duty to compensate and to establish the situation of the *status quo ante* and re-establish the previous situation before that the damage occurred which is called '*restitutio ad integrum*'.

In case of environmental liability a wrongful act is not needed as the existence of the environmental damage trigger liability and the term 'liability' refers to the distributions of costs for environmental damaging situations including violations of environmental rules by the behaviour of actors which are usually punishable through administrative schemes or even criminal sanctions.[38]

Therefore administrative schemes and criminal sanctions are two different legal ways to enforce environmental legislation. Criminal sanctions refers to another kind of liability described with the term 'environmental liability law' or 'criminal liability' which is the type of liability that this study excludes as the ELD neglected the impact of environmental crime on the victim of that crime which is rather the object of another Directive adopted by the EU which is Directive 2008/99/EC on the protection of the environment through the criminal law.[39]

---

37. The Polluter-pays principle will be explained and analyzed in several part of this book, especially in Chapter 3, section 3.1.1.4 and Chapter 5, section 5.4.1.
38. Larsson M.L., '*The Law of Environmental Damage*', 1999, Kluwer Law International-The Hague, page 35.
39. Directive 2008/99/EC of the European Parliament and the Council of 19 November 2008 on the Protection of the Environment through Criminal Law, O.J.L 328, 6.12.2008.

Finally, the expression 'administrative environmental protection legal model', it is referred to the role of public authorities consisting in 'taking care' of the environment by making sure that the potential polluter(s) or the operator(s) responsible for environmental pollution take the self necessary measures (i.e., clean-up) of prevention or ensures the payment of the costs of restoration of the environmental damage in accordance with the Polluter-pays principle. This entails that in an administrative environmental protection legal model, the competent authorities have a role in safeguarding the implementation and enforcement. In the substance an in 'an administrative environmental liability perspective' the public authorities detains an administrative environmental power to protect 'legally' natural resources against environmental damaging situations. At first glance, administrative liability can be considered to be an issue under public law as involving the exercise of public authorities by administration towards citizens.

Environmental damages to public natural resources (*res communes*) can occurs both on public and private land and in terms of environmental effectiveness the public must have access to a remedy reacting private land. Hence, the administrative environmental protection liability cannot certainly be analysed in an exhaustive way through using a frame perspective of public law *versus* private law but rather in a frame of coexistence between a public law approach and private law approach which explain why the ELD is based on a public law approach 'supplemented' by a private law approach.

Part II

Matching Theory with Facts: Building the Framework

Chapter 2
In Search for a Framework of Analysis: The Focal Points at the EU, International and Domestic Levels

2.1   WHY THE NEED TO IDENTIFY THE FOCAL POINTS
     AND HOW TO TREAT THEM

In the light of the context where the concept of EU environmental liability has being developing, as it will be explained in the next chapter,[40] and on the basis of different legal studies dealing with environmental liability, it is possible to identify the focal points existing at all the levels. Some of the focal points are also similar to key legal issues that the US model had to face when involved in liability problems as a consequence of the environmental damage.[41] The existence of these crucial focal points in the parallel regimes explains why it is so difficult to protect 'legally' natural resources. In the present chapter, it is discussed, if the order of exposition and consideration of these focal points is not casual, and if they can be considered partly as being key factors of the concept of environmental liability for their importance in ensuring that the goals of an environmental liability regime are reached.

From a holistic vision, an analysis of the parallel regimes in a three-level perspective involved in the mechanism of multilevel interplay is concerned with:

(1) Definition of environmental damage
(2) Scope of application
(3) Problem of who is entitled to claim for environmental damage

---

40. The context where the ELD has being developing, will be analyzed in the next Chapter 3.
41. The US Model and the way the US approaches the similar focal points, will be shown further on, in sub-section 3.1.5 of the next Chapter 3.

(4) Compensation for the environmental damage
(5) Choice of the type of liability regime
(6) Causality link
(7) Insurance mechanism.

An analysis of each of the above mentioned focal points, is necessary, in order to fully grasp the development and the problems of the European environmental liability regime in the multilevel context of the parallel regimes.[42] Thus, it is assumed that the order of exposition of these focal points is such as it is found a systematic interrelation in terms of logical legal sequence from 'focal point' to 'focal point'.

In such a way, for example, if the definition of the environmental damage, which is the capital problem, is problematic or change, all the other focal points placed in the chain of sequential order will vary, as will be shown in the following sections, 2.1.1 to 2.1.7.

2.1.1   DEFINITION OF ENVIRONMENTAL DAMAGE

The first capital problem is the legal definition of environmental damage. This definition is crucial since it determines the type, the extent, and the intensity of liability and, consequently, also, the sanctions inflicted on the polluter. The act of qualifying and determining what is environmental damage is a very difficult task due to the ambiguous character of the concept of ecological damage, susceptible of covering both damage caused to *res propriare*, to *res communes*, or *res nullus*.[43] Thus, once the concept of environmental damage is defined, the EU legislator or the drafter of a Convention or the domestic legislator has to face another problem strictly connected to the previous capital problem which is to define the object, or the scope of application, of environmental protection.

2.1.2   SCOPE OF APPLICATION

The problem of the scope of application of environmental protection is strictly interlaced with the definition of the environmental damage. In other words, what is it that the legislators, or the drafters of conventions, decide to define, and/or include as the object of legal protection? What needs to be protected (is it the water, the land, the landscape, or all at once?), only damage to natural resources, or also damage caused by environmental pollution to individual rights (personal injuries, property damage, and health)?

---

42. The parallel regimes refers to the EU, international, national, and US Model.
43. De Sadeleer, N., '*Les Responsabilité environnementales dans l'espace européen – Point de vue Franco-Belge*', 2006, Brulant- Bruxelles, page 742.

This second problem explains for example why the choice in having a 'broad definition' of environmental damage,[44] as in the Lugano Convention,[45] or instead a restricted definition[46] since that the definition of environmental damage and the problem of the scope of application are two facets of the same legal problem.

By implication, the scope of application[47] depends not only on what the legislator decides to include/not to include in the notion of environmental damage but also on how the notion of environmental damage is designed and formulated.[48]

2.1.3   PROBLEM OF WHO IS ENTITLED TO CLAIM
             FOR ENVIRONMENTAL DAMAGE

Depending on the chosen definition of environmental damage, the third difficulty is the problem of ownership. The question is who owns natural resources? In other words, who is entitled to claim for compensation? The determination of the criteria of accusation in charge depends on the definition of environmental damage. The problem of the entitlement has been treated differently in the legal systems. For example, some countries have preferred to confer the right of compensation on the governments, or representative agencies, to recover on behalf of the collectivity compensation for harm to natural resources. In the US, the difficulty has taken shape in the problem of the public goods, and has been concerned with the diffuse interests.[49]

---

44. A 'broad definition' of environmental damage is inclusive not only of damages to natural resources, but also individual traditional damages.
45. In particular, by accentuating the different meanings of the term 'environment' as it will be shown in the sub-section 3.1.3 dedicated to the Lugano Convention, specifically, in the sub-section 3.1.3.1 titled 'Definition of Environmental Damage'.
46. A 'restricted definition' of environmental damage includes environmental damage to natural resources but not individual traditional damages.
47. The scope of application of the environmental liability rules is the object of environmental protection and includes 'the field' or 'the activities' that determine environmental damage and need to be protected by environmental regulations. The scope of application indicates what is, that it is exactly covered by the environmental liability regulations and determines where the environmental regulations have to be applied, the extent and intensity of liability as a consequence of the environmental damage. The scope of application is therefore determined by what it is chosen or not to be considered 'as a environmental damage' or 'within' the notion of environmental damage, and by implication, the scope of application depends on how the definition of environmental damage is formulated.
48. In the formulation of the definition of environmental damage it is also considered the linguistic and stylistic aspect which has a considerable impact in the scope of application of the environmental rules and the degree of intensity of liability as it will be explained in further details in section 5.12.1 of Chapter 5.
49. Which will be treated in sub-section 3.1.5 focusing on the US as a historical-comparative approach, in the next Chapter 3.

2.1.4   Compensation for Environmental Damage

The fourth problem is the difficult task of defining compensation for environment as a good subject to a market price. The most difficult obstacle when quantifying the environment is the formulation of specific numbers of quantification sufficiently developed to be able to influence the potential polluters into a finite number of polluters.[50]

The criteria of quantification of the damage are very important as they have a direct incidence on the preventive function of civil liability.[51] The prevention of the quantification of the damage has in turn, another importance for the insurers. In fact, the insurers have to take into account the quantification of the damage when they have to deliver an insurance policy.[52]

2.1.5   Choice of the Type of Liability

The choice of the type of civil liability regime to put into functioning in legislations is a very difficult task. The EU legislation, the international instruments protecting natural resources, and the domestic legislation, have all being concerned with the difficult task of addressing the problem of the choice of the type of liability. This was of course a pre-existing problem in most of the modern legislation. The question which still remains is which type of liability appears to be the most appropriate to discipline environmental damage: fault liability, or strict liability? What are the criteria to choose? The general trend has demonstrated the preference for the strict liability regime.

Hence, it appears with firm evidence that fault based liability regime was not, and would not have been, suitable to solve and satisfy legal demands and justice problems in a wide range of cases, where the damage is caused by the enterprise's activities.[53]

---

50. Pozzo, B., *'Danno Ambientale ed imputazione della Responsabilità'*, 1996, Milano Giuffré Editore, pp. 188–195, and all the US bibliography on CERCLA and on the US DOI Regulations (US Department of Interior Regulations). In 1986, the DOI, promulgated some rules, the so-called 'Assessment of Damage for Natural Resources Injuries establishing criteria for the quantification of the environmental damage' that established criteria for the quantification of the damage with costs-benefits analysis. See for that point Brighton, W.D., and Askman, D.F., *'The Role of Government Trustee in Recovering Compensation for Injury to Natural Resources'*, in Wettersteins *'Harm to the Environment – the Right to Compensation and the Assessment of Damages'*, 1997, Clarendon Press, Oxford, pp. 193–195.
51. Pozzo, B., *'Responsabilità per i danni all'ambiente: valutazioni giuridiche ed economiche'*, 2003, Quaderni Crasl, S10/finale, page 14.
52. Canadian, *'Responsabilià civile e assicurazione'*, 1993, Milano; and Gambaro, A., Pozzo, B., *'Responsabilità delle imprese in campo ambientale,'* pp. 88–140.
53. The general trend based on the preference for a strict liability regime in Europe will be explained in the sub-section 3.1.1 titled 'The Main Existing Liability Criteria Divided into Groups' in the next Chapter 3.

2.1.6   Causality Link

The identification of the causality link, or 'causation', is also one of the main problems and it is strictly connected with the previous difficulty of the choice of the type of liability regime to implement (fault based liability v. strict liability). Causality link simply means when it is possible to establish a link between the author of the damage and the event. This task is aggravated in environmental law. This means that environmental damage is a sector where ordinary rules targeted to regulate the causality link have proved to be insufficient for achieving positive results, since its application is problematic.[54]

Basically, there are two main obstacles for the identification of causation:

(a) The problem of the time factor, or the so-called 'remoteness of the damage'. This problem is concerned with the manifestation of the environmental damage.

     For example, in case the damage appears, or emerges, at the surface several years after the verification of the damaging actions, with the related difficulties of demonstrating the relationship between the damaging actions and the damaging events.

(b) The problem emerging in case the damage is not a consequence of a single damaging situation: this is what it is known as 'cumulative emissions', or 'diffuse pollution'. This is in other words the problem of the identification of the author of the damage where the legislator has to face the problem of determining what the percentage of responsibility is for each polluter to the polluting activity. A significant example of this latter problem is in cases of the identification of the authors of the acid rain, where the result of the pollution caused by rain reverberates at a long distance to the location where the loss of the substance provoked damage, with the consequent difficulty in determining the author of the damage.

The solutions adopted in the field of the causality link, such as those addressing the above described obstacles (a) and (b) which are typical in determining causation, cannot be detached from the problem of the choice of the type of liability as they have to be 'in line' with the type of liability regime which has been chosen. This is the reason why, very often, there is more logic in analysing strict liability rather than fault liability for environmental damage when observing the problems which the causality link entails once applied in environmental law.

2.1.7   Insurance Mechanism

The use of the concept of liability, together with growing public opinion in the environmental field, ecological disasters and the risk management dynamic, or the

---

54. Pozzo, B., '*Responsabilità per i danni all'ambiente: valutazioni giuridiche ed economiche*', 2003, Quaderni Crasl, S10/finale, pp. 22–31.

so-called ecological damage, pushed the argument of liability toward another 'hot debate' focusing on what exactly the role of insurance should be.[55] In substance, the main task which an insurance system has to conduct in environmental law is how to manage the environmental risk. The problem of how to link, in the best way insurance and civil liability in the environmental field, turned out to also be a constant and common concern at the EU, international, and at the domestic level.

The problem of insurability had appeared in the US prior to appearing in Europe, and there is a considerable body of literature on the topic, especially concerning the number of difficulties which the US market system encountered. In particular, the crisis of the US market system has been outlined by several authors.[56] Hence, from the mistakes which the American system encountered, it is possible to learn how to improve the relationship between insurance and civil liability, and not to reproduce the same failures.

For example, the most difficult task which the Americans had to tackle was how to manage the risk. This is, first and foremost, due to the peculiarities of the functioning of the insurance system when applied in cases of environmental damage.

The two major problems in risk management of the environmental insurance market are the lack of information, and the asymmetry of information.[57] The lack of information simply means that there is a lack of data spreading uncertainties for the insured (who suffer the environmental damage) and the insurer (who assumes the risk of the contingency in consideration of payment of premium). These uncertainties reflect negatively in the calculation, the extent and frequency of the environmental damage, which in turn makes it very difficult for insurers to predict environmental damage.[58]

The 'asymmetry of information' is the phenomenon by which insurers dispose of less information compared to the people willing to be insured, or vice versa. This unilateral phenomenon gives birth to what is called 'adverse selection'. In the cases of environmental damage it is very difficult to predict the variations of the level of the risk of the environmental damage for the insured.

Once the insured is covered by an insurance contract for environmental damage, they could reduce, or relax their defences against environmental damage, and give birth to another phenomenon which is called 'moral hazard'.[59] These two

55. Monti, A., '*Environmental Risk: a Comparative Law and Economics Approach to Liability and Insurance*', 2001, European Review of Private Law, pp. 51–79.
56. Abraham, K., '*Environmental Liability and the Limits of Insurance*', 1988, Col. L. R, Vol. 88, page 942; Pfennigsdorf, '*L'assicurazione r.c Danni da inquinamento*' – *Considerazioni politiche per gli assicuratori*, in Ass, 1991, page 48.
57. Abraham, K.S., '*Environmental Liability and the Limits of Insurance*', 1988, Columbia Law Review, Vol. 88, page 946.
58. Pozzo, B., '*Liability Insurance and Environmental Risk*', 2000, Revue Hellénique de Droit International, Athens, Vol.1, pp. 1–25; and Porrini, D., '*Financial Internalisation of Environmental Damage: Legal Framework for Economic Solutions*', 2003, University of Siena Faculty of Economics, Goodwin, R.M.
59. Shavell, S., '*Economic Analysis of Accident Law*', 1987, Harvard University Press, Cambridge.

phenomena are the most dangerous problems causing an erroneous, or distorted functioning of the insurance market.

The distortion of the functioning of the insurance market is mainly due to the fact that the insurers, who move in a field where they are aware that they could take advantage from the moral hazard, will tend to raise the price of the insurance policies and distort, in this way, the insurance market. The distortion of the market, will in turn affect the insurance contract for the subjects having a low degree of risk, as they would bear, without any reasons, a high insurance *premium*.[60]

Therefore, the main problem at all the levels in the environmental insurance scheme is to make it fit into the mechanism of civil liability without that the insurance coverage is transformed into a 'legal certificate of pollution' (how to pollute 'legally'), and render the insurance system a serious working instrument aimed at preventing environmental damage. In addition, the huge amount of money which often needs to be cash in case of sudden accidents represents an enormous problem, at all the levels.

Insurance, in case of environmental damage, could, eventually, be extremely costly and often there is a need of high maximal coverage.

In the substance, all the focal points can be considered as key factors which, make, partly vary the dependent variable, which is civil liability as a consequence of environmental damage. The focal points are important because they ensure that the goals for an environmental civil liability regime are reached. This is because these factors can determine changes and variations in the concept of environmental civil liability legislation which could be positive, or negative for the effectiveness of the law in terms of environmental goal achievements. In addition, all of these factors are also placed in a chain of logical sequence, in a way that if one factor is not functioning, or is changing, it will immediately affect the others, in what it could define being as a 'domino effect'. This means, for example, that if the definition of the environmental damage is problematic, or too vague, then this will affect the scope of application, and the determination of who owns natural resources, which will in turn create difficulty in choosing the appropriate type of liability (fault or strict), which will in turn render difficult to establish compensation and the causality link, which will reflects on the functioning of the insurance mechanism, and so on.

The frame based on the focal points which are common to the three-levels is necessary to explain *ceteri paribus*, the reasons for having a Directive in the area of environmental liability but also to show that the definition of the environmental damage is the crucial and most sensitive of the focal points.

In this chain of logical sequence, the definition of environmental damage is the first key problem which reverberates over all the other factors in sequence.

---

60. Monti, A., *'Environmental Risk and Insurance. A Comparative Analysis of the Role of Insurance in the Management of Environmental Related Risks'*, 2002, Environmental Risks and Insurance, OECD Report; and Porrini, D., *'Financial Internationalisation of Environmental Damage: Legal Framework for Economic Solutions'*, Simple 9/03, pp. 1–16.

The focal points of this chain of logical sequence are to be considered not only as the key points of the environmental civil liability legal problems but also as the object of negotiations which are at stake at all the three decision-levels, and are therefore, also the sensitive points of intersection between the legal and political dimension, as it will be proved in the next chapter.

Chapter 3

The Liability Directive from an Historical-Comparative Perspective

3.1   INTRODUCTION: THE CONTEXT OF THE LIABILITY
                 DIRECTIVE – THE STRUCTURE OF THE
                 HISTORICAL-COMPARATIVE CHAPTER

The aim of this chapter is to contextualise the Environmental Liability Directive in the analytical frame of the EU, international and national level dimension of regulations and trace the development of the Environmental Liability Directive since its inception. The chapter combines aspects of environmental law, liability law and insurance issues, starting from the EU level, to the international level and reaching more specifically the domestic dimension of the issues regulating environmental liability. The historical analysis of liability resulting from environmental damage, in a multilevel-comparative perspective, will illustrate the *pros* and *contras* of the different solutions regulating environmental liability problems that were adopted at all the levels.

Although the ELD is adopted now, the story of the ELD has not been closed yet. The difficult negotiations of the development phase of the Environmental Liability Directive caused several problems that are mirrored in the legal text of the final decision of the ELD and are reflected in crucial focal points of the liability regime. That is why there is the need to identify, select and analyse these focal points of the Environmental Liability Directive that have created in the past problems in the decision-making.

In the EU law making decision-process, debates on crucial focal points reflected and delayed the adoption of the ELD's legal act. The adoption of the ELD's legal act, still render today, problematic the transposition and make differs the implementation of the ELD. These focal points are the particular crucial difficulties to which the law-makers at EU, international and national levels are confronted to.[61] These focal points are at the same time, not only key factors of the concept of environmental liability but also, the object of the past negotiations, at EU, international, and national decision-making levels and often the way that these focal points are designed it is a result of a political compromise more based on obvious trade-offs.

Hence, the plan for this chapter is to trace the development of the Environmental Liability Directive by presenting initially, in its first sub-section (3.1.1), some general aspects of environmental liability in the existing context of the levels. In particular there are three main existing civil liability regimes that are present at EU, international and national level. This typology is characterised by liability based on fault, strict liability, and absolute liability.

The subsequent core sub-section is focussed on the EU level and particularly on the origins and inception of the European Community initiatives in the field of environmental liability (section 3.1.2).

Community action was in this area, first and foremost justified by the fact that different national liability schemes would interfere with the functioning of the internal market, since they created unequal conditions for competition. In this sense, it is worth noting that the inception of Community interest into environmental liability originally emerged in the waste sector and culminated with the current ELD. The analysis of different EC legal proposals, directives and legal papers related to the Environmental Liability Directive, demonstrates that the red line, in the development of the law formation process, was the functioning of the internal market in conjunction with a high level of environmental protection. The EU level is therefore leading the environmental liability regime compared to the international level given that at international level, regulations are not in force and in that sense the international level represent an unsuccessful example. The EU level shows that it has given the first impulse for the existence of an environmental liability interest not only in Europe but also at the international level and that this effort, even though it was contentious, had produced a regulation which is at least in force.

On the other hand, the international level is used in this chapter, in order to explain how the ELD has developed and to evaluate partly the result of harmonisation of the environmental liability in Europe. The international level is used as a tool because it is the mirror where the current European situation is reflected and reverberate, which in turn also is reflected in the implementation phase of the ELD. However, the lack of *consensus* and the insufficient required ratifications of the main treaties regulating the issue of environmental liability impede their enforcement.

Even though regulations and Conventions on environmental liability are not in force at the international level they are still part of the context where the ELD has developed. Namely, the 1993 Lugano Convention and the 1999 Basel Protocol

---

61. As identified and explained in the previous chapter, and as it will be demonstrated in the following chapters of this book.

which serve as evaluating tools, are presented and analysed in sections 3.1.3 and 3.1.4 in the light of the similar focal points identified in Chapter 2.

The choice of the selection in relation to these two cases from international law is justified by the fact that the issues of regulation are parallel and overlap with the similar issues of regulation and the focal points existing at the EU level. In fact, the motive for having selected these two specific environmental treaties is also due to the reason that they have important overlaps with EC legal acts, directives, proposals, and debates as exposed in the previous sections. In the Basel Protocol case, as it will be examined in the next chapter, the overlap is more visible after the year 2000.

Special attention, in section 3.1.5 is given to the US experience when regulating environmental damage which demonstrates solutions but from a different perspective for the similar problems emerging from the focal points existing at the EU, international and national levels. Therefore, the US experience is used as a historical-comparative approach. The US experience is not part of the international level but part of the context where the ELD has developed.

The US Model, as it is examined in this section, is part of the history of the European environmental liability, having already been considered by the European law-makers as a source of inspiration that has been taken into account during the European environmental liability law-making process.

In the following sub-section, it is analysed deeper the legal background of the ELD (section 3.1.6) by discussing and comparing, in the final three sub-sections of this legal comparative historical chapter (sections 3.1.6.1, 3.1.6.2 and 3.1.6.3), approaches implementing options produced by the EU policy papers (the Green and the White Papers) and compare them in the light of the key focal points of the CERCLA, the Lugano Convention and the Basel Convention and Protocol.

In the last sub-section, rather than present an overview of the different experiences in regulating environmental damage and liability problems at national level, just a short picture of the examples of Germany and Italy is offered in order to provide the reader with an idea of the kind of problems existing in the different pre-existing types of environmental liability at the domestic level (section 3.1.6.4) which is the situation existing at the national level before the adoption of the ELD. In fact, the two cases are exemplificative to show that not all the countries have the same approaches to environmental legal protection but also to explain partly the reason why there was a necessity of harmonising the area of environmental liability at the EU level.

Some preliminary conclusions are drawn to close the discussion of this chapter, in the last section (3.2).

3.1.1   THE MAIN EXISTING CIVIL LIABILITY CRITERIA FOR
          ENVIRONMENTAL DAMAGE DIVIDED INTO GROUPS

Since the beginning of the 1980s, most modern legislations focusing on environmental protection have had to face the possibility of using civil liability for environmental damage.[62] As a result of this trend, most European countries have incorporated civil liability into environmental statutes, a phenomenon which concerned both Civil Law and Common Law countries.[63]

In most European countries, and also in the US, three main types of civil liability criteria as a consequence of environmental damage are 'used': (1) fault-based liability, (2) strict liability and (3) absolute liability. These three criteria are not independent variables. Their order in terms of sequences provides a true understanding of the way in which environmental civil liability has developed in Europe. In fact, prior, to the growth of industrialisation, in the last century, the European countries had a type of liability prominently based on fault. With the development of the industrial *era* this type of liability, within certain sectors, was no longer functioning, and there was a clear necessity to 'correct' the fault based liability criteria. This is the reason why most countries started to design their environmental legislations utilising the strict liability criteria.[64]

Prior to industrialisation, the principle of 'no liability without fault' was, in practice, the pre-eminent factor within the legal systems of Europe, which meant that there was no liability in cases where there was no fault by the wrongdoer of the environmental damage. Therefore, the damages laid where they occurred in case where there was no fault to justify their transfer to their wrongdoers, or 'to another'.[65] This trend that was based on the conviction that the shifting of the loss from the victim to the wrongdoer was possible only if the wrongdoer was at fault (*culpa*), was a common trait both for Civil Law and Common Law countries.[66] This approach led to the understanding that before the growth of an automated society, the problem of the choice of the criteria for the assignment of liability was not fault liability *versus* strict liability, but rather fault based liability versus 'nothing'.

The passage from fault liability into strict liability took place in both Common Law and Civil Law countries. However, in the Common Law countries, the shift occurred in a different way in comparison to the Continental Civil Law tradition.[67]

This was a result of the fact that in the Common Law countries, environmental civil liability originated from the tort system, and thus, founded environmental liability more on the existence of the causality link between the potential

---

62. Just to mention some significant examples, see the previously mentioned US law CERCLA (Comprehensive Environmental Liability Act) adopted in 1980; the Italian Law no. 349 adopted in 1990; the Portuguese Environmental Law adopted in 1987; the German Law on Civil Liability for Environmental Damage (Umwelthaftungsgsets) adopted in 1990.

63. Pozzo B, '*Danno ambientale ed imputazione della responsabilità. Esperienze giuridiche a confronto*', 1996, Milano.

64. Calabresi G., '*The Cost of Accidents. A Legal and Economical Analysis*', 1970, New Haven, Yale University Press; Trimarchi P., '*Rischio e responsabilità oggettiva*', 1961, Milano, Giuffré; Ponzanelli G., '*La responsabilità civile-profili di diritto comparato*', 1992, Bologna, Il Mulino.

65. Pozzo B., '*Danno ambientale ed imputazione della responsabilità*', 1996, Milano, page 251.

66. Ponzanelli G., '*American Tort Process*', 1992, Pisa.

67. In the Continental tradition, the concept of fault had been evolving for centuries out of the Roman sources of law.

wrongdoer of the damage and the event rather than on fault.[68] Therefore, the passage from fault liability into strict liability occurred in a different way in the Common Law countries as it meant a clear break with the previous system which was based on the systems of torts.

With the change into an industrialised *era*, the society had to face new problems and new types of dangerous activities, for example those originating from mining, building construction and railways. The accidents related to those activities started to have greater and different dimensions. The legal systems had two types of reaction: on one hand, the protection of the victims of these accidents, and on the other hand, less protection for the victims. Faced with this new situation, strict liability seemed more adequate to face the new risks of industrialisation.

Both Civil Law and Common Law countries had to change their views of conceiving the legal thinking of the system of civil liability, and use it not only as an instrument to shift the environmental damage from one side to the other (shifting the loss), but also as an instrument to distribute the damage among all the members of the society (spreading the loss).[69] In the latter case, civil liability becomes an instrument of the distribution of the environmental costs, as the enterprise shifted onto the other subjects the costs of accidents in a way to render all the users of the product paying for the costs of accidents. The only risk of this approach was that it would have increased the price of the products and would have rendered such products not competitive when compared with other similar products produced by other enterprises. This was the main point of attack by those who criticised the strict liability criteria.

In order to solve this possible inconvenience and defend the appropriateness of strict liability *versus* fault liability as a better criterion to assign liability for environmental damages, an argument was starting to be used: the setting up of an insurance system.[70] The insurance system is able to distribute the risk of a given activity among the users, or all the subjects, that are involved in the same type of activity. This practice broke with the general idea that strict liability was too costly and burdensome for the wrongdoer of the environmental damage.

By implication, it appeared with firm evidence, that the fault based liability regime was not, and would not have been, suitable when used to solve and satisfy legal demands and justice problems in a wide range of issues, especially where the environmental damages were caused by the enterprises' activities.

Thus, all over Europe and North America, the jurists had to face a new reality based on the shift into an industrial civilisation and had to recognise the process of effectiveness of strict liability *versus* fault based liability in cases of environmental damages. After the establishment of this new industrial civilisation's reality, the deterrent function of strict liability was acknowledged also by the court praxis,

---

68. Jones B., '*Deterring, Compensating, and Remedying Environmental Damage: The Contribution of the Tort Liability*' in Wettersteins '*Harm to the Environment – the Right to Compensation and the Assessment of the Damage*', 1997, Clarendon Press, Oxford, pp. 11–27.
69. Calabresi G., '*The Cost of Accidents. A Legal and Economic Analysis*' 1970, New Haven, Yale University Press; Fleming J.C., '*The Law of Negligence in Modern Tort Law*', 1985, Oxford.
70. Calabresi, G., '*The Cost of Accidents. A Legal and Economic Analysis,*' 1970, New Haven, Yale University Press.

since the judges tried to offer adequate solutions based more on equity compared with those offered by the traditional statues based on fault liability, especially in the field of industrial accidents.[71]

In substance, the trend at the domestic level is that most European countries have incorporated environmental liability into environmental statutes: typically public law instruments containing references to liability.

Thus, after having respected the historical sequence of the legislative events, as previously described, thereafter follows an analytical presentation of the main types of the different existing civil liability criteria for environmental damage divided into three groups: fault-based, strict-based and absolute liability.

3.1.1.1   Fault-Based Liability

Under the fault-based liability standard, the defendant is liable only for the environmental damage caused by intentional or fault (negligent or reckless) conduct where negligence is defined as a general standard of due care, namely the due diligence standard taken as a behavioural rule.

However, a precise definition showing the difference between fault liability and strict liability is not easy to formulate in clear terms, given that the border between the two criteria may not be very clear, particularly in the events assuming the *res ipsa loquitur* principle.[72]

The typical classical situation where fault liability applies is when subject x damages subject y with the existence of the subjective element of *culpa*, and x must repair it. However, it is important to note that in environmental law, civil liability, when applied to the environmental damage, is completely disrupting this typical classical situation.

This is mainly due to the fact that frequently the good belonging to subject y (in our case the environment that has been damaged) is not susceptible to be the object of any ownership, as it is simply not belonging to anyone as it is *res commune* and a public good.

In cases of fault liability, the injured parties (y) of the environmental damage are not facilitated since they must prove the *culpa* of the potential wrongdoer (x) in order to be compensated for the damage. By implication, compensation as a consequence of the damages is difficult for the injured parties to obtain. Under a fault based liability criteria, regime compensation[73] can be obtained if the injured

---

71. Fleming, J.G., '*An Introduction to the Law of Torts*', 2nd ed, 1985, Oxford Calderon Law Series.

72. *Res ipsa loquitur principle* is a principle of Roman law which means that the evidence of facts in itself can relieve victims of the burden of proof. Applied in the *culpa* based regime, this principle implies that the polluter is assumed to be liable for environmental damage unless he/she/it can prove that the environmental damage was not the result of a careless or reckless conduct from his part and that the same damaging result could have been caused by other events.

73. There is a distinction between two main forms of compensation for environmental harm. One is the compensation for environmental damage including also damage to things and persons which derives from environmental pollution and that can be in the form of 1) pure economic loss for

parties proves that the potential wrongdoer failed to comply with a legal and established standard of due care (or due diligence).[74]

The levels of care, and the level of activity of the potential polluter, are important factors determining the probability that an accident will take place. Also the frequency with which a certain activity is carried out is a factor determining the probability that an accident will take place.[75] The concept of level of care, assumes a particular importance if it is considered the environmental damage as being the damage as an unilateral accident, which means a direct damage to natural resources caused only by the behaviour of the potential wrongdoer.

Whilst, the same concept, is not considered as relevant in cases of damages caused by pollution to individual property and physical injury as other rules would apply in those kinds of damages.[76]

If it is still considered the damage as being the direct damage to natural resources (excluding the damage caused to individual propriety and physical injury), what y would have to do, in order prove the fault of x, is to demonstrate that x has violated the standards of due diligence.[77] Nevertheless, the criteria of fault based regime present certain limitations and gaps, as it is no longer functioning in certain cases and types of activities.

In addition, according to the analysis of Shavell on the criteria for assigning civil liability, the level of care is not the only factor determining the probability that an accident will take place. Also the level of activity and the frequency with which a certain activity is carried out are important factors.[78] This is because, the fault

---

harm to plaintiff's financial well being, 2) bodily injury (physical injury/illness/pain emotions), 3) harm to property (land)/or reduction of the enjoyment of such a property. The other form of compensation, is more linked to the ecological dimension (direct damage to natural resources) and is the consequence of an ecological damage where compensation has the meaning of repair (or remediate) or, replace or, restore (where the costs of remediation, or replacement, or restoration, determine the amount, in monetary terms of the payment of the compensation). The term restoration, for example, means to bring the natural resources to the *status quo ante* and can include also historical or cultural values. In that sense, it is important to note that 'remediation' does not necessary include in its meaning restoration or full restoration. See for that point Jones., B., *'Deterring, Compensating, and remedying Environmental Damage: The Contribution of Tort Liability'* in Wettersteins *'Harm to the Environment'- the Right to Compensation and Assessment of the Damage'*, 1997, Calderon Press, Oxford, pp. 11–27.

74. The level(s) of care or the standard(s) of care (or due diligence) are criteria of tolerability, such as, for example, maximum values allowed of concentration and emissions into the environment of polluting substances that one should respect and keep under control. In other words, the levels of care are the levels, that one should take into account when for example exercising a given activity, and that fixes values that have to be respected in order to avoid to transform such an activity in a polluting activity or and environmental damaging activity.
75. Shavell, S., *'Economical Analysis of Accident law'*, 1987, Harvard.
76. As for example those which consider the contributory negligence on the subject that has been damaged. See for that point, Pozzo, B., *'Danno Ambientale ed Imputazione della Responsabilità- Esperienze giuridiche a contronto'*, 1966, Milano, page 276, footnote n. 111.
77. An *vice-versa*, if the potential polluter (x) wants to be exempted of being considered at fault, and therefore, not considered liable, he/she/it has to prove that he/she/it did not violate the level of care, or that he/she/it has exercised its activity without exceeding these levels criteria.
78. Shavell, S., *'Economical Analysis of Accident Law'*, 1987, Harvard.

based liability regime in not sufficient to cover situations where there is a high risk of accidents (high level of activity) and activities carried on with a certain frequency. In these mentioned situations, actually, the probability that an accident would take place is not dependent from the level of care of a subject, and a fault-based regime, in those cases, would be inefficient, as the judge, would not examine the level of activity or frequency with which an activity is carried on, but the due diligence level only.

An element that can be used to grasp the difference between fault and strict liability lies in their respective goals' emphasis. The main goal of the fault based liability standard is deterrence[79] and, thus, the prevention of the environmental damage.

The main goal of strict liability regime is also deterrence,[80] but the strict liability regime, emphasises more, in its goal, the compensation of the environmental damage.

3.1.1.2   Strict Liability

Under a strict liability regime the victims of the environmental damage are facilitated since they do not have to prove *culpa* of the potential wrongdoer in order to receive compensation. The important advantage of this regime is that it relieves the victim from the burden of proof. Strict liability is generally adopted in cases involving activities likely to have harmful consequences even if conducted with due care, or due diligence, or in respect of the normal criteria for standards or tolerability. In that sense, the choice of strict liability is the more appropriate of the two to be applied in the cases of the classical situation where a given subject x damages subject y without the subjective element of guilt, or without faulty behaviour or in absence of negligence.

This is the situation when, for example, an industrial activity, conducted by an enterprise, damages in absence of fault, and where the victim, in order to get compensation, only is obliged to demonstrate the causality link, which is the link between the wrongdoer of the damage and the event.

Therefore, in cases of strict liability, the victim of the damage does not have to demonstrate that the normal level of due care or tolerability has been violated in order to be compensated, solely the causality link. The main goal of strict liability is to provide the victims with adequate compensation for environmental harm both in cases of activities which present a high risk of danger, as well as activities which, although involving a low degree of danger, are defined as 'hazardous'.

---

79. It thus creates the incentive to refrain from damage causing-activities and practice better risk management.

80. In fact, under the strict liability regime, the responsible party will pay damages every time that the accident occurs, and he will be induced to take into consideration, not only the level of care, but also the effects that an increased level of activity will produce on the expected accident losses. See for that point Pozzo, B. '*Danno Ambientale ed imputazione della responsabilità*', 1996, Milano, page 278.

Some authors have linked strict liability with the environmental risk and advanced the notion that since it is the industrial enterprise which profits from environmental risk of pollution when conducting a dangerous activity, it is then the same enterprise that should bear the costs associated with such a risk.[81]

Another aspect sustaining a better appropriateness of a strict liability regime compared to a fault based regime, is the one which is related to the situation where civil liability is interlaced with international law and public law. In this case, for example, civil liability often related to the cases where it is necessary to set up standards of due care at international level.

The standards of due care in international environmental law are not very well established, and vary according to the circumstances, the nature (if it is an industrial, mechanical or dangerous activity) and the dimension of the polluting activity.[82]

The public law can fix environmental standards or normal criteria of tolerability such as maximum values allowed by regulations for both of concentration of and emissions into the environment, of polluting substances, which will certainly have an effective deterrent effect on environmentally harmful activities. Even though these standards facilitate the work of the lawyers and legislators on one hand, and that of the management on the other, the update and the control of these standards is not always easy since it is often depends on the public administrations and their capacity to work quickly, efficiently, independently from any political pressures, and on the availability of economic financial resources. In that sense, given that these standards are difficult to be established in case of environmental pollution, strict liability and compensation can often constitute a tool of last resort in order to avoid a 'no liability' situation in cases of failure to establish standards.

Strict liability admits certain exemptions from liability if it is possible to invoke a certain number of circumstances precluding wrongfulness, namely an act of God, distress, *force majeure*, unforeseeable event, state of necessity and, where expressly provided by a legal instrument or rule, intentional or negligent conduct on the part of the victim.

---

81. Calabresi, G., '*The Costs of Accidents. A Legal and Economical Analysis*', 1970, New Haven, Yale, University Press; Trimarchi A, '*Rischio e Responsabililtà Oggettiva*', 1961, Milano.
82. If an environmental damage is a consequence of a wrongful act, the case would be regulated applying a fault based liability regime. Instead, in case the environmental damage is not the result of an intentional act by the author of the environmental damage but it is the result of a) an action which was permitted, according to the state of scientific and technical knowledge of the time when it was committed but for which it turned out that it was damaging for the environment, only after that this action was committed, or b) situations like for example the damage caused by toxic loss or hazardous discharges due to an accident occurring during the processing phase of a permitted and lawful activity that it is sometimes authorized by a public administration, then there is less logic in applying a fault based criteria to a) and b), given that in both cases, there is no intentional guiltiness by the author of the damage.

3.1.1.3 Absolute Liability

The obligation of an actor to pay for the damage regardless of any lack of care is sometimes referred to as 'absolute liability'. This type of liability is very similar to the strict liability; however, it differs from it in the degree of stringency involved, given that it does not permit any type of defence and there are no exemptions compared with strict liability. An example can be found in the 1972 Convention on International Liability for Damage Caused by Space Objects, which provides for liability for damage caused on the surface of the earth, or aircraft in flight.[83] This group of liabilities is not particularly relevant to the Environmental Liability Directive since there are no indications, amongst its provisions, for this type of liability. Nevertheless, the reason for mentioning absolute liability is to provide the reader with a full picture of the main existing civil liability criteria. Table 3.1 will sum up the typology of civil liability as a consequence of environmental damage.

Table 3.1   Existing Typology of Civil Liability Used As a Consequence of Environmental Damage

	Causation	*Proximity Cause/ Adequacy*	*Fault*
Fault Liability (1)	Requires proof of causation – The burden of proof is on the plaintiff	The plaintiff has to prove that the act of the defendant played a substantial part in causing the injury	Require proof of negligence – the plaintiff has the burden of proof
Strict Liability (2)	Requires proof of causation	Reasonable imputation of damage	Not relevant
Absolute Liability (3)	Not relevant	Not relevant	Not relevant

3.1.1.4 Environmental Liability and the Polluter-Pays Principle

Another level of further development of civil liability as a consequence of environmental damage is when it is connected to the Polluter-pays principle.

---

83. Kiss A. & Shelton D., '*Strict Liability in International Environmental Law*', 2007, The George Washington University Law School Public Law and Theory Working Paper No. 345, Legal Studies Research Paper No. 345, page 1136 (the paper can be downloaded at http://ssrn.com/abstract=1010478).

Environmental civil liability is also a concretisation of the Polluter-pays principle introduced at the EU level in 1973.[84] The linkage between liability and this principle determines the further development of the way in which to conceive liability. The theoretical debate introduced at the EU Level on the relationship existing between civil liability and the Polluter-pays principle has been important for its connection with the economic aspects of environmental protection.[85]

The positive aspects emerging from the relationship between the civil liability and the Polluter-pays principle have been highlighted by several authors whom have defined the Polluter-pays principle as a good instrument operating as an incentive to lower pollution in a way in which it is not the tax-payer whom has to pay rather the polluter.[86] Jans pointed out that the EC Community must, especially, ensure standards and environmental liability schemes, in which it is the persons who are responsible for the pollution who shall bear the costs.

Kramer defines the Polluter-pays principle as being 'firstly an economic principle belonging to the public sphere, and has to be understood as expressing the costs of environmental impairment, damage and clean-up that should not be borne via society's taxes, but by those persons who caused the pollution.'[87]

However, there are some difficulties in the relationship between the Polluter-pays principle and the sphere of civil liability, i.e.: who the polluter is, what the damage is, or how much compensation should be paid. Another problem of the Polluter-pays principle when applied to civil liability is that it is not legally binding *en tant que* principle since it is not enforceable. When applied to liability, the Polluter-pays principle is aimed at generating reparation of the damage but its application is not automatic. In fact, normally, it is the public authorities which provides for the reparation of the environment and it is the same public authorities which have to make sure that the clean-up costs are recovered.

In addition, when using civil liability, the application of the Polluter-pays principle faces the difficulty of having to face the determination of the causality link.[88]

---

84. By the First Action Programme concerning the environment of the 22 November 1973 and by the Recommendation of the Council of the 3 March 1975 regarding the awarding of the cost and the intervention of public powers in the branch of environmental law.

85. Several references to the principle can be found in secondary legislation. An example is: Directive 75/422 (which is no longer in force), Art. 15 where 'the costs of disposal of waste must be borne by 1) the holder who has waste handled by a waste collector or by an undertaking authorized to carry out waste disposal activities or 2) the previous holders or producer of the product from which the waste came.'.

86. Jans J.H., '*European Environmental Law*', 2008, European Law Publishing, page 43; Kramer, L., '*EC Environmental Law*', 2007, Thomson Sweet & Maxell, pp. 27–29; Carpentier, R.,'*Environment et industrie*', 1974, RMC, pp. 235–239.

87. Kramer L., '*EC Environmental Law*', 2007, Thomson Sweet & Maxell, pp. 27–28.

88. This could be explained with two examples: of diffuse pollution and cumulative emissions. The diffuse pollution is the phenomenon where it is difficult to establish the causality link between the author of the damage and the event. We have cumulative emission, for example when the damage is not a consequence of a single damaging situation and the difficulty lies in the problem of identifying the author of the damage and defining what percentage of

The choice of the type of liability (whether it is fault-based or strict) it is important in relation to the concretisation of the Polluter-pay principle. The choice of strict liability facilitates the application of this principle.

In a fault based regime, there is a need to demonstrate fault which is an obstacle to the victims of the damages as they must prove *culpa* of the potential wrongdoer (if *culpa* is not proved, the principle is not applied). Therefore, a strict liability choice coupled with the Polluter-pays principle ensures that victims can obtain compensation from polluters and square well with the main goal of strict liability in environmental damage which is compensation.

Environmental rules, as described previously, are important tools which apply civil liability and the Polluter-pays principle at the EU and national levels but also internationally. Basically, civil liability originated from the national legal systems and it is an instrument of private law which is being increasingly used for public purposes, both from the EU level and from the International level. In fact, environmental Conventions also employ civil liability with the express purpose of protecting a public asset: the environment.[89] The international Conventions try to apply these tools concretely in practice.

At the international level, the general trend of environmental Conventions is to channel liability to the person who is in control of the environmentally damaging activity.[90]

A common concern of all the levels is the lack of a robust insurance market or compensation funds willing to provide coverage for such types of activities, and the diffuse character of these activities. Pollution comes from many diffuse sources and practically all industries today pollute. One thing is certain, that nowadays, an advanced industrialised society working without polluting absolutely cannot realistically be imagined. In addition, in cases where an environmental legislation initiates a compensation fund, the eternal enigma consisting of whom (which industry) will contribute to such a fund, will still be pending a solution at all levels.

---

responsibility each of the polluter has in the polluting activity. A representative case is the phenomenon of 'acid rains' which fully explains the problem of the Polluter-pays principle when applied to civil liability because we do not know who really are the polluters or who is the wrongdoer(s) of the damage (who is the wrongdoer of the acid rains) and by consequence who must pay.

89. Wetterstein, P., '*Recent Trends in the Development of International Civil Liability*', page 32; Berkgamp '*Liability and Environment: Private and Public Law Aspects of Civil Liability for Environmental Harm in an International Context*', 2001, The Hague-London-New York.

90. For example, in cases of oil pollution and sea transfer of hazardous substances the person in control is the *ship-owner*. In cases of nuclear pollution, it is the *operator of the nuclear power plant*. In cases of dangerous activities as the general Lugano Convention holds, it is the *operator* liable for incidents resulting from dangerous activities. In cases of carriage of dangerous goods (as in the Basel Convention), it is *the person who gives notification to the country of destination*. In cases of waste transport, *the person who gives notification to the country of destination that a waste transfer is to take place* is the person who is liable until the disposer takes control of the waste, and so forth. In '*International Environmental Law*', Louka, E., 2006, Cambridge University Press, pp. 448–451.

3.1.2   THE ORIGINAL IDEA OF HARMONISING ENVIRONMENTAL LIABILITY

The gestation of the development phase of the Environmental Liability Directive was a long and protracted process, of more than thirty years, before reaching the point, where there was 'finally' a Directive designing a civil liability regime at the EU Level.

Since the development phase of the Environmental Liability Directive, the mechanism through which the decision-making process, under which the first legal acts attempting to create a Directive occurred, was through simultaneous inter-action with other decision-making *fora*. As a result of this mechanism of political-legal interaction between multilevel *arena*, provisions contained in sources of international environmental law (Lugano and Basel), US law (CERCLA) and domestic level of Member State legislations (such as the German law and the Italian law) interact simultaneously and synergistically with the sources of EU law and policy (legal proposals, directives and policy papers inherent to the developing phase of the Environmental Liability Directive). The simultaneous synergistic inter-actions of the different sources of law and policy occurred, in some of their respective issues of regulation and legal provisions regulating sensitive focal points of the environmental liability regime and in a biunique direction (EU law integrates and complements international environmental law on the environmental damage and vice versa, international environmental law integrates and complements EU law).[91]

Before such a mechanism of multilevel interplay took place, the first impulse to launch the new idea of creating a harmonised environmental liability regime had appeared first, from the EU level rather than from the international level.

In fact, prior to the development phase of the Environmental Liability Directive, the very first impulse behind the EC interest in giving birth to the idea of creating a harmonised civil liability regime for environmental damage can be traced back to the early 1970s. The idea of adopting a Directive on the prevention and remedy of the environmental damage has been concerning the EC Institutions, especially the Commission, since the 1970s.[92] In the same period, the EC started to become involved with environmental politics.

The idea of adopting a legal act, regulating in a harmonised way, the different environmental civil liability regulations of the Member States, found also, at the EC level, a certain propitious fertile political ground. In fact, it was also during and subsequently to the 1970s, that the Heads of State and Governments in Paris asked the EC institutions to prepare the first Environmental Action Programme. The programme adopted the EC environmental principles – the Polluter-pays principle and the Principle of Prevention, as guiding EC Principles.[93]

---

91. As will be shown in the next following sections and sub-sections of the present chapter.
92. Before the starting of the Lugano and Basel negotiations, and before that the mechanism of interactions between the parallel EU/international environmental law regimes in biunique directions occurred.
93. Krämer, L., '*The Single European Act and Environmental Protection*', 1987; n. 24 CMLR, pp. 659–688.

The concretisation of the legal idea of harmonising civil liability for environmental damage, took shape in the enactment of the first proposal for a directive on civil liability as a consequence of environmental damage in the waste sector. This proposal can be traced back to 1976, when the Commission submitted to the Council the 1976 First Proposal focusing on the Waste Sector, and included joint and several liabilities of any holder of toxic, or dangerous, waste responsible for unauthorised disposal as well as an explicit reference to the Polluter-pays principle.[94] The proposal noted in the first paragraph of the preamble that 'diverging national liability schemes cause unequal conditions of competition and interfere with the functioning of the internal market'. Harmonisation of national liability schemes was thus necessary. However, this first step toward the creation of a civil liability regime did not result in a Community action until much later, as the EC was in an explorative phase in which to examine the different types of liability and in which sector to apply them. This was a very initial phase where the concept of environmental liability, at the EU level, was not so defined.

The preparatory works in secondary EU legislation aimed at improving the regime of civil liability in the waste sector started at the end of the 1980s. The 1984 EC Directive on the Transfrontier Shipment of Hazardous Waste[95] mentioned again the concept of environmental liability.

This was the second time that this concept appeared; however, it was the first time that it was contained in a directive and not in a proposal for a directive.

In the preamble of the text of the directive, there is an explicit reference to the fact that 'any difference between the provisions on disposal of hazardous waste may distort the conditions of competition and, thus, directly affect the functioning of the internal market.' Therefore, the preamble of this directive reaffirms the same motives of existence of the 1976 First Proposal focusing on the Waste Sector.[96] The directive was based on the concretisation of the concept of *cradle-to-grave* registration of hazardous waste, on the basis of which hazardous wastes can be traced back to their sources. The progress in the regime of civil liability as a consequence of the environmental damage in the waste sector was made with Article 11 of this directive, which gives the producer of waste the responsibility

---

94. Proposal for a 'Council Directive on Toxic and Dangerous Wastes' (OJ 1976 C 194/2).
95. Directive on the Transfrontier Shipment of Hazardous Waste (OJ L 13.12.84, 326/31). This directive was replaced by regulation 259/93 on the supervision and control of shipments of waste within, into and out of the European Community. Regulation 259/93 was replaced again by another regulation, which is regulation 1013/2006 referred as the 'Basel regulation'. However, this regulation was an extremely complicated piece of legislation, and one of the reasons for this, is that it serves to implement not only the Community's own objectives in the waste sector, but also several of its international obligations amongst which those committed with the 1989 Basel Convention. The Community is itself a party to the 1989 Basel Convention in addition to the Member States. See for that point Jans, J.H., '*European Environmental Law*', 2008, European Law Publishing, pp. 438–439. The 'Basel regulation' of 2006 was once again replaced by regulation 1418/2007. Today, this last regulation 2007 has been amended by Regulations 2008 cited as 'the Transfrontier Shipment of Waste (Amendment) Regulations 2008', and come into force on 5th February 2008.
96. See second paragraph of the previous page.

to take 'all necessary steps to dispose of, or arrange for the disposal of, waste so as to protect the quality of the obligations established in paragraph 1' (the obligation of the producer of waste).[97]

The directive also contained the intention to determine a system of insurance; however, nothing was made possible due to the difficulties of the Council in fulfilling the obligation to establish further progressive provisions regarding liability for environmental damage. Article 11 of this directive also stated a deadline where the Council itself must have determined, no later than 30 September 1988, 'the conditions for implementing the civil liability of the producer in the case of damage or that of any other person who may be accountable for the said damage and shall determine a system of insurance.'

In 1989, a year after the above mentioned deadline stated in the aforementioned directive on the Transfrontier Shipment of Hazardous Waste, where the Council (within one year of time) must have determined the conditions for implementing civil liability in the waste sector, the Commission submitted another directive's proposal which is the 1989 First Proposal for a Directive on Civil Liability for Damage caused by Waste.[98] The Commission proposed this directive as a result of the necessity to harmonise national liability rules for environmental damage caused by waste. Once again, the motive for the proposal for a directive on civil liability for damage caused by waste was to eliminate, distortion on competition for enterprises, thus, ensuring the free movements of goods within the future internal market, and reproach national legislations in a way of avoiding differences in the level of protection of health, property and environment.

A prime objective of the proposal of the directive was to apply the Polluter-pays principle in order to achieve the goal of completing the internal market. The proposal is preceded by a COM-document with explanatory purposes under the name of 'Explanatory Memorandum'.[99] The eight pages of the Explanatory Memorandum of the proposal of this directive, which is included and precedes the proposal, states that: 'the aim of the directive is to establish a uniform system of liability within the Community, by ensuring firstly, that the victim of the damage caused by waste receives fair compensation, and, secondly, that industry waste-related costs resulting from environmental damage are reflected in the price of the product, or service, giving rise to waste. The occurrence of differences among national laws regarding the designation of the person liable (producer, holder) and the absence of converted development of notions such as the definition of environmental damage and injury to the environment covered by liability, the causality link, the limitations of liability, etc., would lead to unequal conditions for competition among Member States and, thus, to artificial currents of investments and of wastes to those countries where conditions are less stringent for the

---

97. OJ L 13.12.84, 326/31.
98. Proposal for a Council Directive on Civil Liability for Damage caused by Waste (COM(89) 282 final – SYN 217, (OJ C 4.10.89, 251/3).
99. The Explanatory Memorandum is inserted and precede the Proposal for a Council Directive on Civil Liability for damage caused by Waste (COM(89) 282 final SYN 217, pp 1–8.

operators and most disadvantageous to the victims. The current differences in national provisions on the civil liability of the producer for the damage and injury to the environment caused by waste are liable to distort competition, giving rise to differences in the level of protection of health, property and the environment.'[100]

The novelty of the proposal (also called 'the First Proposal') consisted of not only having connected liability rules with the establishment of the internal market, but also with the choice of liability, the type of reparation, the *locus standi*[101] for the non-official actors – the groups of interest, and the legal basis of the directive.

With regards to the type of liability chosen in its Article 3, the proposal for the directive chooses strict liability for damages caused by waste and states that 'the producer of waste shall be liable under civil law for the damage of, and injury to, the environment caused by the waste irrespective of fault on his part.'

As to the type of compensation, different options are exposed in Article 4 and include the prohibition of the act causing the damage, the reimbursement of expenditure arising from measures to prevent damage, or to compensate for damage. In addition, Article 4 paragraph 4 determines that the groups of interest may bring an action as plaintiff, if they have standing under national law.

Other relevant aspects emerging from this Memorandum are related to what is considered included, or not included, in the notion of environmental damage, and the legal basis of the proposal for this directive.

The Memorandum states that it does not consider only the environmental damage to natural resources caused by waste as being damage, but also the damage to health and property.[102] This is related to the motive of the proposal which is the completion of the internal market to be achieved by eliminating the differences in national provisions on the civil liability of the producer of waste, in order to avoid obstacles in the free movement of goods, and to avoid differences in the legislations in the fields of health protection, property and environment. Therefore, it was clear that the existence and persistence of these differences in these three sub-mentioned fields would have had a direct effect on the establishment of the internal market. That is the logical reason explaining as to why, in this same document, it is specified, at point 11,[103] that the legal foundation for this legal proposal lies in Article 100 A (became Article 95 EC and corresponding to the current Article 114 of the TFEU) and not in Article 130 R and Article 130 S (became Articles 175 and 176 EC and corresponding to the current Articles 192 and 193 of the TFEU). In fact, Article 100 A (current Article 114 of the TFEU) is used as a legal basis related to

---

100. In the page 1 and 6 of the Explanatory Memorandum inserted and preceding the Proposal for a Council Directive on Civil Liability for damage caused by Waste (COM(89) 282 final SYN 217.
101. *Locus standi* is the right to start a legal action as an active subject in law or to be heard, a sufficient interest, or the legal capacity to challenge some decision.
102. Page 3 of the Memorandum, where 'environmental damage' is not only to natural resources but is also connected to the damage to the property of the individuals, and to the individuals (health).
103. Page 6 of the Memorandum.

the establishment of the internal market, whilst Article 130 R and Article 130 S (current Articles 192 and 193 of the TFEU) are employed as measures which do not have a bearing on the functioning of the internal market, and contain the principles and objectives of the EC Environmental policy.

The choice of the Article 100 A (current Article 114 of the TFEU) was, therefore in line with the double goals of the proposal for this directive, which were not only environmental-oriented protected (render liable as a consequence of the environmental harm caused by waste), but also connected to the functioning of the internal market (including, in the latter, also the protection of health and property).

However, the question of the justification of the choice between the two articles as legal foundations for legal acts was not so evident. In general, the problem of the choice of on which legal basis to attribute to legal acts was not new.[104] There was uncertainty, and reluctance, due to the existence of disagreements between the Commission and the Council on which legal basis to use in certain proposed directives.[105]

The problem was that even though the two articles were concerned with environmental protection, the borderline between the two spheres of application of the two articles was not totally clear. On one hand, sometimes, the objectives of these two articles could be cumulated and overlap. On the other hand, they provided different objectives and different degrees of legal-bounding for the Member States' legislations. For these reasons, there were still doubts as to the legal foundations to be used in this legal proposal. In fact, the Economic and Social Council proposed to modify the proposal of this directive and together with the European Parliament, a suggestion to change the legal basis for the proposal of this directive from Article 100 A (current Article 114 of the TFEU) of the EC Treaty to

---

104. At that historical time, the problem was even more evident because previous to the Amsterdam Treaty, the choice between the two articles entailed different decision-making procedures: Art. 100 A required a decision made by majority vote with the EP, the so-called cooperation procedure while Art. 130 S asked for a decision by unanimity vote at the Council. After the Amsterdam Treaty, the decision-making procedure is the same which is the co-decision procedure with the approval of the Council deciding by qualify majority of voting. That it is why, at the present time, given that the decision-making procedures are the same, it is possible to combine the two articles. See for the latter point Jans, H.J., '*European Environmental Law,*' – in section 'The question of the dual legal basis', Europa Law Publishing, 2000, page 55 and for a reiteration and updating of the same point see also Jans, H.J., '*European environmental Law*'- in section re-titled as 'Article 175 EC or Art 95 EC?', 2008, Europa Law Publishing, page 69.
105. The disagreements between the Commission and the Council regarding the appropriateness of the use of one article rather than another was mitigated with a judgment of the ECJ giving an extensive interpretation of Art. 100 A. The ECJ formulated an extensive interpretation for Art. 100 A leaving little room to application for Art. 130 S only in cases involving both environmental protection and internal market. The Court stated that the objective of environmental protection can be effectively pursued by measures based on the solely Art. 100 A given that it obliges, in para. 3, the Commission to take as a base a high level of environmental protection and that also high level objectives of environmental protection can be achieved by Art. 100 A. See for that point, the Judgment of the Court of 11 June 1991, Case 'The Commission *versus* the Council,' Case C-300/89.

Article 130 R and 130 S, (current Articles 192 and 193 of the TFEU) was rejected.[106] In that sense, given that the proposal of this directive was double oriented and not only internal market goal achievement-oriented, the use of Article 130 R and 130 S alone[107] would have been inappropriate because the objectives of the proposal were not only to protect the environment with EC principles and objectives but also to ensure the smooth functioning of the internal market.

Since it was not possible to combine the two articles, at that time period, the choice of the legal basis was Article 100 A also because the other option (especially Article 130 S) asked for decisions to be taken by unanimity voting which would have rendered the decision-making too slowly and too dependent on complex political debates at the Council of the EU.

Another proposal to modify the proposal for this directive in relation to the possibility of extending liability for waste to the carrier of waste, or the person having actual control of waste, was rejected.[108]

The proposal for this directive was too weak, and did not allow it success in terms of environmental goal achievements corresponding to the original goals of the proposal for the directive to achieve both environmental protection and completing the internal market. The weaknesses in terms of environmental goal achievements were due, partly, as a result of the directive's proposal not being preceded by an important political debate. In that sense, the Commission find difficulties in justifying and convincing in a powerful manner, why there was the need to have a regime on the issue-area of environmental liability as a consequence of the waste damage.

The Commission should have had a stronger role in justifying the necessity to have a shift from Member States rules to the EU level and directs towards a more severe civil environmental liability regime. In addition, also the fact that there was a weak participation of the role of the non-official actors, such as the groups of interest, created obstacles in elaborating a proposal allowing succeeding in term of environmental goal achievements.[109]

The European environmental civil liability regime started to change and became more effective, only with the second proposal (the so-called 'Second Draft'), the 1991 Proposal of the Commission for the Council Directive on Civil liability for Damage caused by Waste.[110] The proposal for this directive

---

106. For this proposition (change of the legal basis) to modify the proposal of this directive, see CES (90), Opinions and Reports, 28 February 1990, pp. 2–3.
107. The two articles not coupled with Art. 100 A but standing alone.
108. For this proposition (extension of liability to the carrier of waste or the person having actual control of waste) to modify the proposal of this directive, see CES (90), Opinions and Reports, 28 February 1990, pp. 2–3.
109. The proposal was widely criticized by industry, which felt that it was being unfairly single out. See Clarke, C., '*The proposed EC Liability Directive: Half-Way through Co-decision*', 2003, RECIEL, page 255.
110. The Commission proposal to the Council for a Directive on Civil liability for Damage caused by Waste, COM(91) 219 final – SYN 217, OJ C 23.7.1991, 192/5.

was trying to impose a uniform system of liability to pay for the clean-up of environmental waste and to adopt the Polluter-pays principle.

The European Parliament and the Economic and Social Council proposed several amendments to this proposal such as the replacement of the phrase 'injury to the environment' by 'impairment of the environment'. Article 2 described impairment as 'any significant physical, chemical, or biological, deterioration of the environment insofar, as this is not considered to be damage to property.'[111] The scope of application of the proposal of the directive is described in its Article 1 where it states that, 'This directive shall concern civil liability for damage and impairment of environment caused by waste in the course of an occupational activity from the moment it arises.' This proposal was definitely much more severe than the concept of liability previously proposed since it also extended liability to the eliminator of waste. In fact, Article 2 paragraph 1(f) extended liability to the eliminator of waste and identified him as the person who carries out any of the operations listed in the Annex IIA or IIB to Council Directive 75/442/EEC.[112]

This person is liable only if he is not able, within a reasonable period of time, to identify the producer. The latter provision is, therefore, in line with the so-called *cradle-to-grave* registration of hazardous waste prescribed by the directive of 1984 on the Transfrontier Shipment of hazardous Waste. On the basis of this registration waste materials can be traced back to their source. In cases where it would be difficult to compensate i.e.: when liability occurs during transportation, or storage of waste, liability should be attributed irrespective to fault (Article 3 paragraph 1).

Advancement, in this second proposal of 1991, was made with regards to the *locus standi* of the non-official actors in Article 4, if it is compared it with the first proposal, where the groups of interest could act as plaintiff, but only if their national laws attributed this right to them. Whilst in this second proposal of 1991, Article 4 paragraph 3 frees them from this prerequisite and states that

> common interests groups, or associations which have as their objective the protection of nature, and the environment shall have the right either to seek any remedy under paragraph 1(b) or to join in legal proceedings which have already been brought. The conditions under which the groups of interest, or associations, defined in the previous sentence may bring action before the competent authority shall be established by national legislation.

Another element of advancement in this Second Proposal of 1991 is concerned with a provision concerning the insurance mechanism. In the amended proposal of this second proposal,[113] in the preamble, it is stated that 'the liability of the producer and the eliminator of waste must be covered by insurance or other financial

---

111. See Amended Proposal for the Commission Proposal to the Council for a Directive on Civil Liability for Damage caused by Waste, COM(91) 219 final – SYN 217, Art. 2, letter (d).
112. The Framework Waste Directive, which is Directive 75/442, OJ, 1975, L 194/47 as amended by Directive 91/156, OJ 1991 L 78/32.
113. See Amended Proposal for the Commission Proposal to the Council for a Directive on Civil Liability for Damage caused by Waste, COM(91) 219 final – SYN 217.

security' and moreover, in Article 3 paragraph 2 of this same amended proposal, it can be noticed that 'the producer shall include in his annual report the name of its insurers for civil liability purposes.' This new amended proposal was therefore trying to set up a European Fund of Compensation for Damage and Impairment of the Environment caused by Waste.[114]

The 1991 Second Proposal on liability connected to waste was trying to address the problem of how the sites would be cleaned-up and who would pay for this. The advancement of this proposal compared to the First of 1989, consisted of the policy approach established in the Treaty of Rome which asks for economic integration and the establishment of the internal market together with an elevated degree of environmental protection. In addition, the law appeared more effective, not only for the extended *locus standi* to the groups of interest and for the above mentioned 'double' integrated approach, but also since civil liability become more interlaced with a public policy and societal steering approach.

However, the 1991 Second Proposal directive on liability, connected once again with waste and proposing a stronger regime, was neither examined nor adopted by the Council of the EU.[115] The proposal remained in a deadlocked situation for several years in the same way which all of the previous proposals focusing on the attempt to initiate a European environmental liability regime in the waste sector were.[116]

The failure of the 1991 Second Proposal was due mainly to political barriers.

Firstly, the European attitude was not sufficiently interested and motivated towards the creation of an environmental liability regime as a consequence of the environmental waste damage, even though the first original idea to create a har-monised environmental liability regime in this sector was launched by the Com-mission. Under the mechanism of multilevel interplay, the Commission was not strong enough to take advantage of the interactions, draw the attention of the Member States to the focal points of the environmental liability regime and mit-igate the divergence of interests.

Especially, as a result of the strong opposition of some Member States, in particular the UK, and the lack of interest of other Member States, the situation exacerbated. The UK considered that domestic legislation was sufficient to

---

114. See Amended Proposal for the Commission Proposal to the Council for a Directive on Civil Liability for Damage caused by Waste, COM(91) 219 final – SYN 217, Art. 11, para. 2.
115. Krämer, L., '*Focus on European Environmental Law*', 1997, London, page 143; and de Sadeleer, N., '*Les responsabilité environnementales dans l'espace européen*'. Point de vue Franco-Belge, 2006, Brulant, Bruxelles, page 731.
116. This 1991 second proposal disappeared completely from the agenda by the end of 1991, without any official explanations. After this proposal there are no signs of similar official documents dealing with the matter, except an unpublished document circulating at the beginning of 1992 which was written by a lawyer with a North American Common Law background whose use of key terms like 'liability' or 'civil' and 'damage' differed signifi-cantly from the interpretation put on them by most Civil Law countries of the Continental Tradition. For this point see Clarke, C., '*The proposed EC liability Directive: Half-Way through Co-decision*' 2003, RECIEL, page 256, footnote n. 15.

guarantee appropriate environmental protection, and there was no need to devolve this task by creating European environmental rules.

Secondly, there was a total absence from the EC to consider and meet the requirements of the concept of subsidiarity which already existed at that time.[117] The definition of subsidiarity, without being expressly related to the Subsidiarity principle, was present in Article 130 R (4) of the Single European Act where it is stated that:

> The Community shall take action relating to the environment to the extent to which the objective referred to in paragraph 1 (i) to preserve, protect and improve the quality of the environment; (ii) to contribute towards protecting human health; (iii) to ensure prudent and rational utilisation of natural resources can be attained better at Community level than at the level of the individual Member States. Without prejudice to certain measures of a Community nature, the Member States shall finance and implement the other measures.[118]

In that sense, in the light of the existing liability regimes that were already in place at the national levels, and at the international level, the EC failed to consider and to interpret the concept of subsidiary such as described in the aforementioned EC provision, and the Commission did not justify, on the ground of subsidiarity, the shift from Member States rules to the EU level.

Thirdly, the failure of the legislation proposed by the Commission was also due to the strong opposition of the non-official actors – the groups of interest. The groups of interest, instead of working in favour of the proposal, and agree on the justification on the shift from Member States rules to the EU level, created a real obstacle to the adoption of a European liability regime.[119]

---

117. 'The idea of subsidiarity' was introduced into Community law on environmental matters by the 1987 Single European Act although the express term 'principle of subsidiarity' did not find its way into the Treaty text until the adoption of the 1993 Maastricht Treaty. This does not mean however, that the subsidiarity requirement did not exist before this. See for that point, Olsen B.E., and Sørensen K.E., '*Regulation in the EU*', 2006, Thomson Sweet & Maxwell, page 40.
118. Article 130 R (4) of the EEC Treaty. Single European Act, OJ 1987 L 169/1.
119. In other words, the interpretation of what 'subsidiarity' actually meant was very broad and controversial, because the term, which is also a flexible and dynamic concept, was susceptible to be interpreted in different ways both from the national level (inclusive of the groups of interest) and the EU level (inclusive of the EC Institutions, such as the Commission). The interpretation was instrumental in the sense that was directed to take advantage from the parties in order to reach their profits. Generally, when new legislation was proposed by the Commission, it was not unusual for the non-official actors, especially, for the sector of the industry, to dispute the application of the concept of subsidiarity. The non-official actors (or 'non-official business or industrial actors' as they will be defined in section 4.1.4 of Chapter 4) were looking to take profit economically and satisfy their interests. Applied more specifically to environmental liability issues, a 'wrong' interpretation of the concept of subsidiarity, at that time period, and in that specific circumstance, made that the groups of interest 'used' instrumentally the concept of subsidiarity and to reverse the argument of the necessity of a shift of environmental liability rules on the waste sector from the national level

Hence, faced to the failure of the last 1991 Second Proposal and all the previous proposals,[120] the Commission decided to abandon the original idea of creating a harmonised civil liability regime for environmental damage in the waste sector. However, the Commission, at the same time, kept 'alive' this idea by 'reforming' the idea, toward a more general and gradual approach in creating a harmonised environmental civil liability regime, under the same mechanism of multilevel interplay, as it will be shown in the sub-sequent sections.

3.1.3   The 1993 Lugano Convention

In Oslo, in the 1986, the Ministers of Justice of the Council of Europe's Member States appointed a Committee of Experts, for the drafting of an instrument of environmental treaty law on civil liability for environmental damage from hazardous activities, the so-called 'Lugano Convention of the Liability for Environmental Damage from Hazardous Activities'.[121] The final text of the Convention was approved by the Committee of Ministers on 8 March 1993, and signed by eight countries on the 21–22 of June 1993.

During this lapse of time, from 1986 until 1993, when in the Lugano *fora* crucial solutions for the future of the environmental regime, were being negotiated, other events influenced the Lugano negotiators. From the EC level, the debate on the 1989 First Proposal from the Commission for a Council Directive Proposal on Civil Liability caused by Waste. Later on, the 1993 Green Paper on the Compensation of the Environmental Damage. From the non-EC level, the US Congress enacted an important body of legislation in 1990, the so-called CERCLA, which introduced into the US an innovative specific regime for damage to natural resources by implementing a compensation fund. From the domestic level, the adoption of the German Law in 1990 on Civil Liability for Environmental Damage, and the Environmental Protection Act in England in 1990.

The aim of the Lugano Convention is 'ensuring adequate compensation for damage resulting from activities dangerous to the environment' (Article 1) and to

---

to the EU level (in the latter case, being 'reversed subsidiarity' understood as the shift of environmental regulation from the EU level towards Member States' level).

120. The proposals were only formally withdrawn in 2004, which is also the date that corresponds to the certainty that 'finally' the adoption of a Directive designing a civil liability regime for environmental damage (the 'ELD') was not a fiction but become a reality.

121. See Explanatory Report, ETS No. 150, on the Convention on Civil Liability for Damage Resulting from Activities Dangerous to the Environment – General introduction, point 2 – Council of Europe's document. For the overall draft of the report which was used as a preliminary draft basis for the drafting of the Lugano Convention, see also the document 'Second Interim Report' prepared by the Directorate of Legal Affairs of the Council of Europe, in particular by the Committee of Experts on Compensation for Environmental Damage Caused to the Environment (CJ-EN) at its 6th Meeting (5–8 September 1989) of the CJEN with reference ACDCJ 8960, Strasbourg, 8 September 1998/Restricted CD CJ(89) 60.

acknowledge the same principles of the Green Paper[122] with the same objective of 'assuring proper repair for the damages resulting from hazardous activities'.

Even thought the Convention is based on tort law,[123] it was a very innovative and advanced piece of legal text for that time. Especially, as, in order to achieve the chief aim of the Convention, the drafters presented, in its first article, civil liability as an expression of the linkage between strict liability and the Polluter-pays principle, and since the text of the Convention was elaborated 'having regard to the desirability of providing for strict liability in this field taking into account the principle (who pollutes pays)'.[124]

The objectives are: to provide an adequate compensation in trans-boundary damage; achieve an environmental liability regime in favour of the victims[125] and the environment through the application of liability rules for a broad range of dangerous activities; to deal with grave and imminent threats of damage from dangerous activities; and to provide for strict liability.[126]

The regime of the Convention is for future damages; however, it could be applied also partly retroactively as there is a specific regime for waste disposal sites with retroactive effects.[127]

Specifically, if the operator is in control of the dangerous activity when the damage appears after entry into force of the Convention he cannot discharge himself from having caused (part of) it. In this situation, it would be the last operator that will be held liable for the whole damage, unless it is proved by him or the victim that the incident causing all or part of the damage occurred before he became operator. Additionally, the operator cannot discharge himself from having caused (part of) the damage in case of illegal closure before entry into force.[128]

---

122. The Green Paper is an important policy paper of the EU which is part of the background of the Environmental Liability Directive and which will be treated in sub-section 3.1.6.1 of the present chapter.
123. Larsson, M.L., '*The Law of Environmental Damage: Liability and Reparation*', 1999, Kluwer Law International-The Hague, page 222.
124. See the Preamble of the Lugano Convention.
125. Facilitating the burden of proof for the victims of pollution.
126. See Explanatory Report, in the General Introduction as approved on the 8 March 1993, Document ETS No. 150, and also Larsson, M.L., '*The Law of Environmental Damage: Liability and Reparation*', 1999, Kluwer Law International – The Hague, page 222.
127. See Art. 7, from paras 1 to 4 – Liability in respect of sites for the permanent deposit of waste -, of the Lugano Convention.
128. In line with European traditions, the liability is non-retroactive. But this does not hold in cases of long distance pollution where the manifestation of the environmental damage occurs a lot of time after the verification of the damaging event or accident. It is the case for example if the dangerous activity in the installation has ceased and the damages become known after the closure, the last operator will be held liable for the whole damage, unless it is proved by him or the victim that the incident causing all or part of the damage occurs before he became the operator. In that sense, the Convention is to be considered very advanced and novel for that time. For the same point, see also Larsson, M.L., '*The law of the Environmental Damage: Liability and Reparation*', 1999, Kluwer Law International-The Hague, page 226.

In light of that context, one method of understanding the way through which the Lugano drafters were attempting to design a model of effective environmental protection legislation, is based on the identification of the existence of zones of overlapping between the EU sources of law and policy (EU legal proposals, directives and policy papers) and the Lugano text (legal provisions).

Since the development phase of the environmental liability regime at the EC level, in what can be called 'the gestation process of the Environmental Liability Directive', there has been evidence of the existence of overlap between the EC and Lugano levels of legislation in regard to particular focal points, as noticed in the issues regulated by the 1984 EC directive on the Transfrontier Shipment of Hazardous Waste, the so-called 1989 First Proposal, and the 1991 Second Proposal. These examples of EC legislations and proposed legislations do have in common, with the Lugano Convention, the same crucial tasks which consist of regulating the treatment of contaminated waste sites, and industrial pollution. The two levels are comparable and interconnected, even if Thieffry has the opinion that the Lugano regime permits a more advanced environmental protection compared to the 1989 First Proposal.[129] The text of the Lugano Convention is considered a simultaneous and dynamic convergent point of interactions amongst different legal cultures. In the middle of the Lugano and the EC simultaneous interplay, the intermediation of the EU Commission played a key role with the 1976 original idea launched by the EC level. This idea was carried by the 1984 EC directive of the Shipment of Hazardous Waste and the EC 1989 First Proposal and was setting up a sectorial (waste) environmental civil liability.[130]

The same idea became general[131] at the EC level with the 1993 Green Paper, and also at the Lugano level, as it is this same 'reformed idea' that the Lugano drafters were attempting, ambitiously, to materialise in the 1993, in parallel with the Green Paper's works.

In the formation and design of the regime of the Convention, there are several areas where most sensitive focal points regulating issues of the environmental liability regime, debated at the table of decision-making, in the Lugano *fora*, are intersecting and overlapping with the corresponding reciprocal focal points of the EU level-debate. In a more concrete and precise way, there are six areas of overlap and interactions between the EC and Lugano level-spaces of legislation, such as: the definition of the environmental damage, the scope of application, the

---

129. Thieffry, P., '*Environmental Liability in Europe: The European's Union Projects, and the Convention of the Council of Europe*', 1994, in Int. Lawyers, page 1083.
130. See previous sub-section 3.1.2 of the present chapter.
131. As explained in sub-section 3.1.2, more specifically on the last page of this section of the present chapter, after the failure of 1991 Second Proposal of the Commission for the Council Directive on Civil Liability for Damage caused by Waste, and all the previous proposals, the Commission decided to abandon the original idea of creating a harmonised civil liability regime for environmental damage in the waste sector. However, the Commission, at the same time, kept 'alive' this idea by 'reforming the idea', toward a more general and gradual approach in creating a harmonised environmental civil liability regime, under the same mechanism of multilevel interplay.

problem of who is entitled to claim for environmental damage and have access to information, the choice of the type of liability, compensation, and the insurance mechanism.

3.1.3.1   Definition of Environmental Damage

With the Lugano Convention, for the very first time, there is an international instrument providing a definition of the environment, which should be not only inclusive of abiotic natural resources (such as water, air, soil) and the biotic ones (flora and fauna), but also the interactions between these same natural resources.[132] In that sense, the Convention was, at that time, more advanced when compared to the EC legislation and proposed legislation on the focal issue of the definition of the environment. The Lugano conception of environmental damage is comprehensive not only of the damage directly caused to the natural resources *per se*, but also to individual persons, health, property and environment, in the same line of conception of the notion of environmental damage formulated and launched by the drafters of the Explanatory Memorandum of the 1989 First Proposal for a directive on Civil Liability for Damage caused by Waste.[133] Hence, the term 'environment' has been defined, by the Lugano Convention, in an extensive and advanced manner, compared to the same concept treated at EC level, as the Lugano Convention, integrates the EC definition by accentuating that the term has different meanings.[134]

3.1.3.2   Scope of Application

With regards to the scope of application of the rules, the Convention selects all the hazardous activities, and also activities conducted professionally, which determine a hazard to man, the environment and the property.[135] The category of the

---

132.   Between the abiotic and biotic natural resources.
133.   See previous sub-section 3.1.2 of the present chapter.
134.   The Lugano conception of the definition of the environment, and the environmental damage, has different meanings as it is comprehensive not only of 1) the interactions between the abiotic natural resources (air, water, soil) plus the biotic one (flora and fauna); and 2) the three levels conception of the environmental damage: (i) damage to individuals (also health), (ii) goods (also property), and (iii) environment *per se*); but also of 3) the damage to landscape and the historic-artistic aspects of the environment.
135.   In the preamble of the Convention, it is stated that 'Realising that man, the environment and property are exposed to specific dangers caused by certain activities'; and also under the definition of dangerous activity, in Art. 2, letter b) 'the production, culturing, handling, storage, use, destruction, disposal, release or any other operation dealing with one or more: – genetically modified organisms which as a result of the proprieties of the organism, the genetic modification and the conditions under which the operation is exercised, pose significant risk to man, the environment or property; micro-organisms which as a result of their proprieties and the conditions under which the operation is exercised pose a significant risk for man, the environment or the property, such as those micro-organisms which are pathogenic or which produce toxins; and finally, also in Art. 2, para. 2, letter a), it is found, always under the definition of dangerous substance: 'substances or preparations which have properties which constitute a significant risk for man, the environment or property'.

list[136] of the hazardous activities of paragraph 1) is taken from the Annexes to EC directives.[137]

The Lugano Convention and the EC legislation, treats the same activities with the difference that the Lugano Convention's approach is broader, as it is trying to materialise the shift from a sectorial (waste) approach to a general gradual approach in regulating environmental civil liability, launched by the EC level. The design of the Lugano Convention, in the 'zone area' of the scope of application, is clearly elaborated under the influence of the EC law and has been complemented by it. Both the Lugano and the EC legislations are treating the same activities with the difference that the EC level is launching the general approach regulating environmental liability not only restricted to the waste sector. The text of the Lugano Convention is trying to materialise this shift from the sectorial (waste) approach to a more general gradual approach in regulating environmental civil liability. The Lugano Convention is 'elaborating' under the clear influence of the EC law the design of its legal document by using directives that complements its own provisions without which, the Lugano Convention would have remained vague and incomplete in that aspect.

3.1.3.3 Problem of Who Is Entitled to Claim for Environmental Damage

The issue of access to environmental information is treated in chapter III of the Lugano Convention and consists in reinforcing the prevention of the environmental damage by the establishing (1) the right of everyone, without to demonstrate a specific interest, to have access to information held by the Public administrations or (2) by organisations having the public authority in the environmental sector.

This issue overlap with the EC provision dedicated to the same problem as it was noticed in the 1991 Second Proposal for a Directive of Civil Liability caused

---

136. The list of the definitions of dangerous activities is very detailed (but not exhaustive) and is comprehensive of the so-called dangerous substances (inflammable, explosive, cancerous, etc.), dealing with the management of waste and final disposal into the environment, the activities related to the dealing with the management of microorganism and those genetically altered, and the activities which produce ionizing radiation. See for that point, Art. 2, from paras 1–4 of the Lugano Convention. The guiding criteria that determine if a substance is dangerous or not is based, once again, on the statement that it is found in the preamble of the Convention which is reproduced in the previous footnote ('Realizing that man, the environment and property are exposed to specific dangers caused by certain activities.'). The same statement guides also Art. 2, para. 2, letter a) is that these substances (the dangerous) have concretely 'proprieties which constitute a significant risk to men, the environment or property'.

137. The list of hazardous substances, are always updated by technical expertise on the basis of a general criterion that these substances have 'proprieties which constitutes a significant risk to man, the environment or property.' See Directive 67/584/EEC of 27 June 1967 (OJEC No. 196/1), Directive 88/379/EEC of 7 June 1988 (OJEC No. L187/14) and Directive 90/492/EEC of 5 October 1990 (OJEC No. L275/35), that are also mentioned in the Annex I, letter A of the Lugano Convention.

by Waste.[138] Both the provisions are aimed to facilitate causation. The EC legislation has influenced the Lugano legal text, in this area of access to information, if it is thought that the duty of public authorities is tailored on a special EC Directive[139] on the freedom of access to information and environment, and the corresponding duty of the operators has a counterpart in the German Environmental Liability Act. In addition, under the Lugano Convention, there is also the possibility and as launched initially at the EC level, to bring collective actions.[140]

3.1.3.4 Compensation for Environmental Damage

As to the type of compensation, it is noticed the different options exposed in Article 4 of the 1989 EC First Proposal[141] which includes, the prohibition of the act causing the damage; the reimbursement of expenditures arising from measures to prevent the damage; or to compensate for damage and the restoration of the environment to its state immediately prior to the occurrence of injury (*status quo ante*).

This is the same approach of the Lugano Convention with the difference that the Lugano text, integrates and advances the pre-existing EC regulation and proposed regulation in this sensitive zone-issue of compensation, by specifying, that, where *restitutio in integrum*[142] is technically impossible, it is possible to compel the damaging party by introducing into the environment equivalent resources for those that have been destroyed.[143] In case of *restitutio in integrum* is no longer possible because the damage made an animal or plant species extinct there will not be a pecuniary compensation.[144] The Lugano Convention overlaps and is strongly innovative as to the notion of restoration of the environmental damage that was launched at the EC level, initially with the 1989 EC First Proposal. The most innovative part of the Convention is in the notion of environmental damage, strictly related to the issue of compensation, that has been defined by the Convention as

---

138. See previous sub-section, 3.1.2 of the present chapter.
139. Directive 90/313, OJ L 158/56, 7/6/90. See also, for the same point, Larsson M.L., '*The Law of the Environmental Damage: Liability and Reparation*', 1999, Kluwer Law International-The Hague, pp. 228–229, footnote n. 174.
140. See the 1989 First Proposal in the previous sub-section 3.1.2 of the present chapter.
141. See previous sub-section, 3.1.2 of the present chapter.
142. *Restitutio in integrum* is a measure of restoration which concerns the establishment of the environment of an environmental situation identical to the one which existed before the damage or to compensate and to re-establish the 'previous situation' (litt. *restitutio in integrum*). See for that point, also Larsson, M.L., '*The law of the Environmental Damage*', in the section '*Terminology*', 1999, The Hague, pp. 19–20.
143. See the Explanatory Report to the Convention on Civil liability for Damage Resulting from Activities Dangerous to the Environment, Council of Europe's document ETS No. 150, point n. 40.
144. What it is stated about these kinds of damage (to animals or plant species), in the Explanatory Report to the Convention on Civil liability for Damage Resulting from Activities Dangerous to the Environment at the point n. 40, about the damage to the environment is: 'such damage cannot be evaluated financially'.

'impairment of the environment, insofar as it is not considered damage to goods or people, if and as this impairment causes a loss of profit'.[145] The damage to the environment consists in the cost of preventive measures and reinstatement adopted to restrain, minimise or reinstate the situation to what it was before the illegal act.

3.1.3.5   Choice of the Type of Liability

On the object of the criterion of charges for civil liability, or in other words, 'who is liable for the environmental damage', the Convention establishes, in line with the EU legislation, that the responsible party is the 'operator' and establishes strict liability for the person with the actual control of hazardous activities. Therefore, it is not necessary to prove *culpa*, for the victims in order to get compensated, but only the existence of the causality link between the activity and the damaging event. In that sense, the Convention is in favour of the victims. The draft of the Convention proposed by the Council of Europe, had an interesting reverberation on the 1991 Second draft Proposal of the directive and its amendments on one issue of regulation of the civil liability regime: the concept of operator of the Lugano Convention coincides with the added concept of eliminator[146] in the second version of the 1991 Proposal Directive.[147] The EC legislator has first, launched the initiative of the 'canalisation of the responsibility' on the producer of waste. The same responsibility on the producer of waste was completed by the Lugano Convention by shifting the same liability as a consequence of the environmental damage from the 'producer' to the 'eliminator' of waste.

In that sense, the Lugano text goes further, and even more, because integrates in this aspect, the EC law, by providing also for joint and several liabilities[148] and by encouraging for a division of liability or for sharing the liability: the operator can free himself (partially) by proving he did not cause the (whole) damage.[149]

3.1.3.6   Insurance Mechanism

Another important point of overlapping between the Lugano Convention and the EC level is the choice of introducing a compulsory insurance and the introduction, in the 1991 Second Proposal for a directive, of a compulsory insurance or other

---

145. See Art. 2, para. 7, letter c) of the Lugano Convention.
146. 'Eliminator', here, is the 'eliminator of waste' even if the little word 'waste' has not been written. See Amended Proposal for the Commission Proposal to the Council for a Directive on Civil Liability for Damage caused by Waste, COM(92) 219 final – SYN 217, Art. 2, letter (f).
147. See Amended Proposal for the Commission Proposal to the Council for a Directive on Civil Liability for Damage caused by Waste, COM(92) 219 final – SYN 217, Art. 2, letter (f) where it is written: 'eliminator' means a person who carries out any of the operations listed in Annex II A or Annex II B to Council Directive 75/442/EEC and Koppen I.J., Maugeri R.M., Pestillini, F., *'Environmental Liability in a European Perspective'*, EUI, Working Paper No. 91/12.
148. Which was launched with the first Original 1976 EC Proposal, see previous sub-section 3.1.2 of the present chapter.
149. Articles 6 and 11 of the Lugano Convention.

financial security, in its Article 11,[150] as only briefly and weakly suggested by the Lugano text.[151]

In which sense, the Second Proposal for a directive is more advanced than the Lugano provisions, as it proposes the establishment of a European Fund for Compensation for Damages and Impairment of the Environment caused by Waste.[152]

The Convention does not provide for any insurance mechanism or compensation found or for the determination of a limit for liability *per* typology of damage.[153]

After a brief examination carried out on the main crucial focal points of intersection between the EC and the Lugano level-spaces and issues of regulations, it appears, that, on several sensitive focal points, such as the scope of application, the concept of compensation, the access to information, and the insurance mechanism, the EC initiatives were very important. In some crucial issues, the EC sources of law were more than a *stimulus*, for the future legal environmental liability's template, as they were strongly leading the environmental regime. In a first moment, the EC initiatives often launched *in primis* the 'legal imprinting' and the preliminary design through which the focal point needed to be regulated. In a second moment, vice versa, it was the Lugano approach which completed and integrated the EC sources of law when treating the equivalent focal points.

For that reason, the Lugano Convention was highly novel, if it is thought, for example of the two sensitive focal points, such as, the definition of environmental damage, and the new method for compensation of the environmental damage elaborated by the drafters of the Convention.

Hence, there are several motives advocating the usefulness in analysing the Lugano level with the EC level in a two-way, reciprocally biunique direction, and within a frame individualising the zones of overlapping between the two level-spaces of legislation.

---

150. See previous sub-section 3.1.2 of the present chapter.
151. Financial security to be established by the Parties 'where appropriate', can be developed gradually, see Art. 12 of the Lugano Convention.
152. See previous section 3.1.2 of the present chapter, and also the Amended Proposal for the Commission Proposal to the Council for a Directive on Civil Liability for Damage caused by Waste, COM(92) 219 final — SYN 217, Art. 11, para. 2, determine that 'The Council, acting on a proposal from the Commission shall determine by 31 December 1992 common rules governing the situation arising: (i) where the person liable is incapable of providing full compensation for the damage and/or impairment of the environment caused; or (ii) the person liable under this Directive cannot be identified. In this regards the Commission shall study the feasibility of the establishment of a European fund for Compensation for Damage and Impairment of the Environment caused by Waste.
153. These tasks are remitted to the national legislations of the Member States that will ratify the Convention. In other words, the absence of a clear determination of a limit for liability per typology of damage make difficult to set up clear parameters between what is permitted or not, or what is considered be legal and illegal pollution. Such a gap of clarity render difficult, for a liability scheme, to be made operational and for the Member States that are those which have to support such a liability scheme.

The first motive is the individualisation of the zones of overlapping which in turn individualises, and verify, the existence of simultaneous synergistic interactions in several sensitive focal points in a bi-uniquely reciprocal direction whereby the EC law integrates and complement international environmental law on the environmental damage and vice versa. Hence, it is ascertained a situation of coexistence and complementarities between the different sources of law in several zone of overlapping. In a more detailed and concreted way, the nature of the overlap is such that in the zones of intersection between the issues of regulation and the different sources of law where the protection of the environment offered at the Lugano Convention is uncompleted, such as for example, in the choice of the scope of application, and in the case of the choice to set up a compulsory insurance mechanism, the adoptions of EC initiatives could play a key role in determining the right *stimulus* in strengthening the environmental liability regime.

The second motive is a better understanding of the existence of reciprocal influences existing between the international law (in the case under examination which is the Lugano Level) and the EU law. From that perspective, the EC law is a strong point of force for the improvement of environmental protection.

In fact, after having individualised and compared the six main important zones of overlapping between the Lugano and EC level, it was shown that the EC level has been able to stimulate, launch and improve, environmental protection against damages emerged at international level, by using the mechanism of the simultaneous interactions in a situation where the EC level is the leading level.[154] The analysis of the Lugano Convention also signifies to take into account the politico-legal circumstances under which the draft text of the Convention was adopted.[155] Overall, the Lugano Convention detailed all of the instruments necessary for a highly effective and advanced law in the environmental field. However, it is a matter of fact that the Convention is still not in force as presently, three ratifications are absent.[156] Nevertheless, even though the Convention was and is still not in force, it was and still is, an important tool for evaluation of the environmental law in terms of environmental goal achievements, especially in the case of the EU law.

---

154. It should be remembered also, as mentioned in the introduction of this chapter, in the subsection 3.1.2 of the present chapter, that the international level (the Lugano Convention) is used as a tool because it is the mirror where the current European level situation is reflected. Therefore, the use of the Lugano Convention as a tool, is part of the strategy to explain how the Environmental Liability Directive has developed, and most important, as a tool to evaluate the result of harmonisation of the environmental liability in Europe. The Lugano Convention is not in force, therefore the EU level is the 'only effective level in town' given that is the only regime that is in force. All this entails, that, in the 'real practical word,' the European Court of Justice would never refers to the Lugano Convention (and to the Basel Protocol) to decide or conclude a judgment in a given case law given that, the provisions of the Lugano Convention, are not in force.

155. As introduced in the previous sub-section 3.1.2 of the present chapter, the circumstances under the mechanism of multilevel interplay where the Lugano *fora* was involved with the EC Level.

156. For an immediate check of the status of ratifications, see the website of the Council of Europe www.conventions.coe.int/Treaty/Commun.

3.1.4   THE 1999 BASEL PROTOCOL

The Basel Convention on the Control of Transboundary Movements of Hazardous Wastes and their Disposal is adopted in 1989 and entered in force in May 1992. The aim of this Convention is to control, or limit and prohibit the illegal traffic of hazardous wastes by providing very strict regulations on the trans-boundary movements[157] of wastes. While providing a list of hazardous waste movements[158] which States Parties must prohibit, the text was weak as a consequence of the total absence of a precise rule on liability and compensation for damage. Even though a suggestion had been envisaged to fill this gap by a certain number of countries during the negotiation of the Convention, the question of the elaboration of rules on liability and compensation was postponed as no agreements among the State Parties could be reached at that time.

The compromise was the approval of an article (Article 12 of the Convention) stating which the parties shall cooperate with the view of to adopt as soon as possible, a protocol establishing such rules.[159]

The weakness of the rules under the Convention caused reservations on the part of some African States, especially for those to which waste was exported.

In the 1980s, the traffic of hazardous wastes caused terrible human and environmental disasters in the African countries.[160] The African States strongly suggested in the negotiating phase the absolute prohibition of trans-boundary movements of hazardous waste, as well a stringent provisions regarding State Responsibility. There was an urgent need for a provision on civil liability for environmental damage in the treaty.[161]

Ten years later, after a long period of gestation and difficult diplomatic negotiations, a protocol for the Convention was adopted, namely, the Basel Protocol of 1999 on Liability and Compensation for Damage resulting from Transboundary Movements of Hazardous Wastes and their Disposal.[162]

---

157. Both on sea and land.
158. The list is non-exhaustive and it is appended to the Basel Convention.
159. Article 12 of the Basel Convention only provided an enabling clause stating that 'The Parties shall cooperate with the view to adopting, as soon as practicable a protocol establishing appropriate rules and procedures in the field of liability and compensation for damage resulting from trans-boundary movements and disposal of hazardous wastes and other wastes'.
160. In 1987 a terrible accident took place in Koko (Nigeria) where two Italian ships released into the sea 4.000 tonnes of hazardous waste.
161. The Basel Convention reflects the peculiar situation where State Liability is left as a residual measure to be invoked in the event that liability of the private actor cannot be enforced, for example when the latter cannot be identified. The Basel case reflects the situation where one legal international instrument deals with two different situations, State Responsibility and civil liability for individuals under a single environmental treaty. See, for that point Articles 8 and 9 of the Basel Convention.
162. The Protocol for the Basel Convention contains several vague and ambiguous provisions that are the result of different and controversial interests, and negotiated provisions of the State Parties which were part of an *Ad Hoc* Working Group which lead to the adoption in 1993 of the Protocol. This *Ad Hoc* Working Group was appointed by the Executive Director of the UNDP,

Once again, the second version of the regime initiated by the Protocol demonstrates a liability regime designed on liability of subjects of domestic law and not only for States since 'civil liability appeared to be the most efficient way to enhance the ability of the State to control the individuals and firms responsible for these movements'.[163]

The ambition of the Convention is to end to the phenomenon of the transfer of hazardous waste from developed countries to poor countries, or to abolish the so-called 'environmental colonialism'. The aim of the Protocol is to provide a comprehensive regime of adequate compensation in cases of damage resulting from the movements of hazardous waste. In order to achieve such an aim, the Convention provides for a complex system of prior consensual notification and informed consent of the importing country prior to all of the hazardous waste being transferred to that country.[164] The *ratio* of this provision is to render traceable the movements of waste, especially in relation to movement between developed and developing countries. The Convention attempts to define hazardous waste in a specific annex, or refers to the national legislations of the State of import/ export, or transfer.

There are four main zones of overlap between the EC Level and the Basel Convention and Protocol, where issues of regulation of environmental liability are parallel and overlap, such as, the definition of environmental damage, the scope of application, the choice of the type of liability, and the insurance mechanism.

3.1.4.1   Definition of Environmental Damage

Similarly to the definition of environmental damage launched and proposed by the Explanatory Memorandum of the 1989 First Proposal for a Directive on Civil Liability for Environmental Damage caused by Waste,[165] the Protocol considered not only the environmental damage to natural resources but also the damage to

---

and the main task of this *Ad Hoc* Working Group was, to prepare a legal text (which is the Protocol of the Basel Convention) to be regularly submitted to the approval of the State Parties under regular Council Meetings. It took practically ten years to negotiate the text of the Protocol because of the divergent positions of the State Parties. One of the main crucial focal point which was really felt as a sensitive issue of controversy in order to reach *consensus*, was, precisely, the insurance mechanism. In fact, some State Parties, such as Columbia, South Africa, Peru, and Morocco, asked for a compulsory financial mechanism. See for this point, the Meetings Reports – *Meeting documents – First to tenth Sessions of the Ad Hoc Working Group (Protocol on Liability and Compensation) 13/10/1993 – 03/10/1999 – Reports of the Council Meetings*. French original language used for the reading of these Reports.

163. Silva Soares, G.F., Vieira Vargas, E., '*The Basel Liability Protocol on Liability and Compensation for Damage resulting from Transboundary movement of Hazardous Wastes and their Disposal*', 2001, in YIEL, page 70.

164. The Parties of the Protocol which are subject to procedural obligations are: the Exporter State, the Importer State and the Transit State where the movement of hazardous wastes occurs. The obligations are: duty to notify the movement of wastes for the Exporter State, the confirmation of acceptance of the Importer State. If these procedural obligations are not respected, the Exporter State must re-import the waste back in its territory.

165. See previous sub-section 3.1.2 of the present chapter.

health, property, and loss of income.[166] The Protocol contains a broad definition of environmental damage for which compensation may be sought.[167] Under the Basel regime, the environmental damage includes, the damage to persons and property and loss of income deriving from an economic interest in the environment, costs of measures of reinstating the impaired environment, and preventive measures.[168]

3.1.4.2   Scope of Application

With regards to the scope of application of the rules, the Basel Convention applies to trans-boundary movements of wastes between the State Parties[169] based on the prior notification and informative consent of the importing country before a waste transfer to that country.[170] The Basel Convention and the EC legislation treated similar areas of activity. The scope of application of the Basel Convention is wider as it focus on the movement of wastes between the State Parties signatory of the Convention[171] and materialise the concept of 'cradle-to-crave' launched from the EC level by the 1984 Directive on Transfrontier Shipment of Hazardous Waste.[172] The EC level was, once again, crucial as launched the legal imprinting for the Convention which was materialised through the concept of 'cradle-to-crave' registration of hazardous waste on the basis of which hazardous waste can be traced back to their source. The scope of application of the Protocol, applies 'to damage due to an incident occurring during a trans-boundary movement of hazardous wastes and other wastes and their disposals, including illegal traffic, from the point where the wastes are loaded on the means of transport in an area under the national jurisdiction of a State of export.'[173] Only damage suffered in a State Party to the Protocol falls within its scope,[174] even though certain exceptions are provided for in the Protocol.[175]

3.1.4.3   Choice of the Type of Liability

In the Basel Convention, the criterion of charge for civil liability is wider compared to the EC legislation. The EC legislation and proposed legislation established that the responsible party was the operator and established strict liability for the person with the actual control of hazardous waste. The Basel Convention and Protocol applied to the movements of trans-boundary waste. Therefore, several and

---

166. 'Loss of income' is the formulation used by the Basel Protocol, in Art. 2., letter iii).
167. Article 2, letter c); (i); (ii); (iii); (iv); (v) of the Basel Protocol.
168. Article 6 of the Basel Protocol.
169. The State Parties of the Convention.
170. Louka E., *'International Environmental Law – Fairness, Effectiveness, and World Order'*, 2006, Cambridge University Press, page 461.
171. Article 6 of the Basel Convention.
172. See previous sub-section 3.1.2 of the present chapter.
173. Article 3 para. 1, first sentence.
174. Article 3 para. 3, letter (a).
175. Article 3 para. 3, second sentence.

different subjects are involved in liability issues.[176] Liability is therefore not considered only canalised for a single subject but several. In order to individualise the different subjects that can be liable, the Protocol uses the same terminology and mechanism employed by the Convention consisting in setting up a detailed procedure that the State Party must follow if decide to moves its waste.[177] The Protocol provides for strict liability. Depending on when the damage occurs, strict liability is channelled to a different person: during the initial phase, the person who is notifying the transport in accordance with the Convention (the exporter) is liable for damage. This responsibility lasts until the disposer has taken possession of hazardous wastes. Thereafter, the disposer is responsible for any damage which may occur.[178] Also fault liability is established for any person who causes, or contributes to, damage by his/her lack of compliance with the provisions of the Basel Convention, or by his/her wrongful intentional, reckless, or negligent acts, or omissions.[179]

Similar to the EC proposed legislation, and the Lugano Convention, the Basel Protocol also provides for those treating hazardous wastes a joint and several liabilities.[180] When strict liability applies is limited[181] but when it is fault liability which applies there are no limits.[182]

3.1.4.4 Insurance Mechanism

The Basel Convention set up the so-called Basel Convention Trust Fund which should have ensured the functioning of the Convention. The initiative was clearly in line with the desire expressed in the 1991 Second Proposal for the Council Directive on Civil Liability for Damage caused by Waste to set up a European Fund of Compensation for Damage and Impairment of the Environment caused by Waste.[183] Also in the Basel Protocol, as in the EC proposed legislation, and in the Lugano Convention, the implementation of an international compensation fund was strongly recommended in order to compensate victims from hazardous wastes and to convince, in such a way, the developing countries to adopt such a regime.[184] The Protocol establish, in its Article 15, that, where the insurance do not cover the costs of possible accidental events as result of hazardous waste, 'some additional and supplementary measures' should be undertaken with the purpose to ensure fast and adequate compensation by using the 'existing mechanisms'.

---

176. See Art. 1 of the Basel Convention.
177. See Art. 6, para. 1 of the Basel Convention.
178. Article 4 para. 1 of the Basel Convention.
179. Article 5 of the Basel Convention.
180. Article 4 of the Basel Convention.
181. Article 12 of the Basel Protocol.
182. Article 12 of the Basel Protocol.
183. See previous sub-section 3.1.2 of the present chapter.
184. Lawrence P., '*Negotiations of a Protocol on Liability and Compensation for Damage resulting from Transboundary movements of Hazardous Waste and their Disposal*', page 251.

One of these mechanisms should therefore be the pre-existing Basel Convention Trust Fund.[185] In addition, it is stated in the second paragraph of the same Article 15 that 'the Meeting of the Parties, shall keep under review, the need for a possibility of improving existing mechanisms or establishing new mechanisms' which is a quite soft and vague provisions.

Overall, the regime initiated by the Protocol is much criticised, even though it can be considered as advancement for international environmental law. Several States criticise the vagueness of some crucial focal points, for the high level of limits of liability, and the obligation of persons who could be liable under the Protocol to maintain insurance, or other financial guarantee.[186] In reality, the regime of Basel does not protect the State of transit and the victims of the damage.[187]

There is overlap between EC level, Lugano level and the Basel level in several focal points, such as, the definition of the environmental damage, the scope of application, or the criterion of charge for liability, and insurance mechanism as treated and designed in the Basel case.

The 1984 EC directive on the Transfrontier Shipment of Hazardous Waste, and the 1989 First Proposal for a Directive on Civil Liability for Damage caused by Waste,[188] coincide and overlap with the *ratio* of the Basel Convention and Protocol to render traceable the movements of hazardous waste, in line with the concept from 'cradle-to-crave'. Furthermore, also the necessity to set up a compensation fund was a common trait between the Basel and the Lugano levels, and the EC level, which all together, with the Traceability principle, paved the way for identification of more overlaps with the Basel level, after the period of 1999–2000.[189]

Similarly to what has been experiencing by the Lugano Convention, the Basel Protocol is still not yet in force as it needs (as with the Lugano case) further ratifications.[190] Only 13 (of up to 20) countries have ratified the treaty, of which only Denmark, France, Finland, Sweden and Switzerland are considered significant hazardous waste producers. The EU and the United States have not signed the Protocol yet since the prohibition to export recyclable hazardous wastes would have jeopardised commercial exchanges with the developing countries.

---

185. Which is the same Fund that was set up by the Basel Convention and that should have been employed for the functioning of the Convention.
186. Annex B, the Art. 4 of the Basel Protocol, and Art. 14 of the Basel Protocol.
187. Bernasconi, C., '*Civil Liability resulting from Transfrontier Environmental Damage: a case for the Hague Conference?*', Note drawn by Christophe Bernasconi, Secretary at the Permanent Bureau, pp. 10–12.
188. See previous sub-section 3.1.2 of the present chapter.
189. As it will be examined in Chapter 4.
190. For an immediate check of the status of ratifications, see the website www.basel.int/ratif/protocol.

3.1.5   THE US EXAMPLE AS A HISTORICAL-COMPARATIVE MODEL

Not all countries legally protect natural resources in the same way. The historical legal comparative analysis demonstrates the different choices adopted from the modern legislator of the Common Law and Civil Law countries in protecting the environment. Specifically, there are three main models: (1) the German, (2) the US and (3) the Portuguese.[191] The present section will treat the US Model only, as the other choices, in protecting the natural resources of Germany and Italy (the latter is similar to the US Model) will be treated briefly further on.[192] The Portuguese model will not be treated as a selected model in this section because represents a peculiar case in protecting natural resources.[193]

In contrast to the German model, which protects natural resources in connection to individual traditional private rights such as the right of health and the right of property, in the US model, the legislator chooses to protect natural resources independently from the breach of the individual rights protected traditionally.

In particular, the US Model explains how to protect the environment directly, and is concerned with the environmental damage in *sensu strictu* and not in connection with other individual traditional injuries such as the damage to health or property. By choosing this way to protect the environment, the American choice had to face the difficult task to define the environment as a good to be protected, and the problem of who can claim rights as to this good. The object of protection of the environment has been defined, in the American model by typifying the harmful behaviour.[194] Therefore, on one hand, the countries which decide to adopt a model of environmental protection based on the German Model deals with environmental damage caused by pollution. On the other hand, the countries which adhere to US Model deals with environmental damage 'tout-court'. The Portuguese Model represents a novel choice of the legislator which protects the environment directly avoiding defining the object of protection by typifying the harmful behaviour.[195] With regards to the difference between the German Model and the US model, even thought this difference could seem of minor importance, it is, in reality, crucial.

In fact this difference entails for the laws of the countries, a different approach in the way to tackle with the focal points debated and designed by environmental civil liability regimes, such as, for example, the way to perceive the definition of

---

191. Pozzo, B., '*Danno ambientale ed imputazione della responsabilità – esperienze giuridiche a confronto*', 1996, Milano, Giuffré Editore, chapter II, pp. 113–184.
192. The German and Italian examples, will be the object, in the penultimate sub-section of the present chapter (3.1.6.4) of legal and comparative analysis, and are selected samples of model of legislations in protecting natural resources which have been chosen because explaining the two main different approaches or model in protecting the environment that were present in Europe before the introduction of the ELD.
193. The Portuguese model is only followed by Portugal. Therefore, it is not a very representative Model because too peculiar as a pattern for a study of environmental liability in Europe.
194. Pozzo, B, '*Danno ambientale ed imputazione della responsabilità – esperienze giuridiche a confronto*', 1996, Milano, Giuffré Editore, page 142.
195. See the Portuguese Law promulgated in Portugal on the 7 April 1987.

the environmental damage, the criterion of charge of civil liability, compensation, quantification of the environmental damage, the problem of the choice of type of liability, and causation.

The American choice, protecting natural resources 'directly', presents two types of different problems: on one hand, the difficulty to formulate a definition of the concept of the environment, taken as a protected good, and, therefore, the possible identification of environmental damage as a 'legal value'. On the other hand, the problem of rights, with regards to this good. Despite these difficulties, the US Model has been the object of scrutiny and analysis by the European law makers since protecting natural resources 'directly' (and not indirectly such as in the German case) offers the advantage of being able to internalise the external costs in protecting natural resources independently from the injury of individual private rights.[196]

Therefore, in cases of damage to the environment, or to natural resources, the enterprises, or the production-consumption activity, have to bear the costs. The enterprises have to internalise the external costs in such a way that it is not the society which bears the costs, but solely the polluter who is forced, through the mechanism of civil liability, to pay. This is a reasoning originating from the economic theories advocating that efficiency in achieving the goal of environmental protection is achieved when all the external costs are taken into account.[197]

A significant example of the US Model and of internalisation of the external costs is the already mentioned -in the previous sections- American law called 'CERCLA'.

In the 1980s, CERCLA gained recognition for having created the 'Superfund', providing the US government with the possibility to clean-up abandoned and uncontrolled hazardous waste sites.[198] The law is broader as it deals with hazardous substances release and not just hazardous waste disposals.[199] CERCLA provides for compensation, in case of damage to natural resources, independently from injuries of other individual traditional rights, such as the rights of property, or the right of health. The law is concerned with the decontamination of the sites subject to environmental risk and charges the liable parties with the reimbursement of the clean-up costs by creating a public fund (the so-called Superfund).[200]

---

196. Calabresi, G., *'The Costs of Accidents. A legal and economic analysis'*, 1970, New Haven, Yale University Press.
197. The concept of externalities relates to the activity of the potential polluter. The polluter is in this way (through the use of the instrument of civil liability) forced to also include in its costs for production the costs which could emerge from environmental damage through a mechanism called 'internalisation'. Therefore, internalisation is the mechanism remedying the externalities which have to be understood as 'external effects' of the production-consumption activity of individuals, in Cropper M.L., – Oates, W.E., *'Environmental Economics: A Survey'*, 1992, Journal of Economic Literature, 30, page 678.
198. www.epa.gov/Superfund/action/law/cercla.htm.
199. CERCLA, para. 102, 42, USCA S 9602.
200. Miller, P., Schzoeder Leape, *'Environmental regulation'*, 1996, Law, Science and Policy, Second Edition, Little, Brown and Company, pp. 279–399; Findley, R.W., and Faber, D.A., *'Environmental Law'*, 1991, West Publishing Company, Minesota, pp. 240–266.

A feature of this fund is that it is financed by potential polluter contributors, the so-called 'Potential Responsible Parties' (PRPs) with funding from national revenue taxes on petrol and chemical products. In addition, the US government initiated a special authority the 'Environmental Protection Agency' (EPA) which detains the powers to sue the PRPs in order to oblige them for 'response cost action' as a consequence of damage to natural resources. The fund compensates the environmental damage caused by unidentified sources.

The original ambition of CERCLA was to provide for the formulation and promulgation of criteria aimed to quantify the damage caused to natural resources and from hazardous activities. Among those responsible, not only the past and present owners, operators, but also those who are more exposed to risk activities and involved in the transportation of hazardous substances.[201]

The crucial focal points that the US model had to face when designing an environmental liability scheme, such as the CERCLA, can be identified and summarised as follow below, from sections 3.1.5.1 to 3.1.5.4.

3.1.5.1 Definition of Environmental Damage

The law offers a definition of environment, and the natural resources are defined by CERCLA as the ensemble of 'land, fish, wildlife, biota, air, water, drinking water supplies, and other such resources belonging to, managed by, held in trust by, appertaining to, or otherwise controlled by the United States . . . , any State or local government, or any foreign government.'[202] Thus, the notion of environmental damage, in the US Model encapsulates the whole biodiversity and any kinds of interactions between the different *media*.

Even though natural resources are 'free goods' as they do not belong to anyone, or public goods, in the American perspective, there is no reason why they should not be considered as 'economic goods' susceptible to be evaluated economically. The fact to consider the environment as an economic good is important as otherwise it would not be possible to quantify the restoration or compensation in cases of environmental damage and the mechanism of civil liability could not be put into functioning. Considering natural resources as an ordinary good permit the users and/or polluters to consider the price of this good by internalising the costs of externalities created from enterprises. In the CERCLA perspective, the fact to consider the environment as a public good, explains the reason why this law do not provide for any compensation mechanisms, in cases of environmental damage to private individual subjects.

---

201. Mukakis, W.A., '*Hazardous Waste Regulations – Enforcement and Liabilities*', 1999, Executives Entreprises Publications Co., Inc., pp. 75–113.
202. CERCLA, S 101 (8), 42 USCA S 6901 (8).

3.1.5.2   Problem of Who Is Entitled to Claim for Environmental Damage

The central problem of considering the environment as a public good in the US Model, and the fact that natural resources are not 'appropriable entities' (as they are free goods which do not belong to anyone) has opened the problem of who owns natural resources, who is entitled to act for the legal protection, and which type of appropriateness and ownership to establish.[203]

CERCLA establishes that it is the State, and its representatives, such as local, or territorial entities, which are entitled to ask directly for compensation, or *restitutio in integrum* (the bringing about of the material restoration of natural resources to the situation prior to the wrong -baseline condition- or damage compensation).[204] In addition, also the environmental associations played a specific role in the American legislation. In the 1970s, the US Congress started to insert into federal laws clauses permitting that environmental associations are granted *locus standi*. The Congress wanted to involve more the citizens in the formation of environmental policies. Typical of the US Model is also the use of class actions acting in the environmental field attempting to protect legal situations related to a certain number of subjects through representations.[205] The use of class actions, are to be connected with one of the motives for having this law. In fact, one of the reasons for having CERCLA in the US was the failure of the class actions in the achievement of improved environmental protection.

The identification of who is entitled to claim for damage to natural resources has been possible, in the US, thanks to the architecture of the Trusteeship principle determining the powers and duties of the federal and state governments as natural resources trustees.

In this architecture, the owners of the legal right to ask for damage compensation to natural resources are: the federal State (or US Government), the federal States (or state governments) and other entities (such as agencies and Indian reservations specifically mentioned by the law).[206]

---

203. Brighton, W.D., and Askman, D.F., '*The Role of Government Trustee in Recovering Compensation for Injury to Natural Resources*', in Wettersteins '*Harm to the Environment – the Right to Compensation and the Assessment of Damages*', 1997, Clarendon Press, Oxford, pp. 177–206.
204. Schoenbaum, Thomas, J., '*Environmental Damages: The Emerging Law in the United States*' in Wettersteins, P., '*Harm to the Environment – the Right to Compensation and the Assessment of Damages*', 1997, Clarendon Press, Oxford, pp. 159–174.
205. Pozzo, B., '*Danno ambientale ed imputazione della responsabilità – esperienze giuridiche a confronto*', 1996, Milano, page 123.
206. The typical scheme of the Trust's foundation demonstrates that for the same good (natural resources are the object of property in trust), it is possible to have two separate rights. On one hand, the right of Trustee which offer the entitlement of the administration and the disposal of the good, and on the other hand, the right of Trustees which is the right of being beneficiary of the trust. Who benefit from such a scheme are the trustees who are citizens. The Trustee is the Federal State, the federal States and other entities. See for that point Brighton, W.D., and Askman, D.F., '*The Role of Government Trustee in Recovering Compensation for Injury to*

3.1.5.3   Choice of the Type of Liability

With regards, to the type of liability chosen, CERCLA choose strict liability with regards to all PRPs. According to CERCLA, the Environmental Protection Agency (EPA) can claim on all the PRPs in order to obtain the compensation for the expenditure which the federal entities had to face for the clean-up of the polluted dumps and for the environmental damage. Therefore, CERCLA's liability does not require to demonstrate fault, is jointly and several given that all of the persons who contributed to a contaminated site are jointly and severally liable for the clean-up costs and the damages, and is retroactive.

3.1.5.4   Causality Link

Given that CERCLA cover unidentified sources of damage, as mentioned previously, there is no need under this law to demonstrate the causality link between the event and the author of the damage. The promulgation of CERCLA by the American Congress stems from the fact that the traditional remedies offered by the Common Law were too complicated and provided for restricted and limited protection, especially in cases of damage caused to natural resources, where no owner was identified and no property rights over natural resources were identified.[207]

In which sense, CERCLA coexists with the pre-existing Common Law treating environmental damage as an individual right or a Common Law based on 'environmental liability for bodily injury' (the so-called toxic torts) and a Common Law for property rights (land or water contamination). The US law became the motive of inspiration for the European legislator because of the way to perceive and treat the definition of environmental damage which interprets the environment and/or the natural resources as an ordinary good for the use of which the entrepreneur pay a corresponding price. This is the main originality of the US Model. In fact the EU legislator started to be inspired from the US Model especially since the 1990s. In more specific and concrete terms, the 1991 Second Proposal on liability connected to waste[208] was trying to address how the sites would be cleaned up and who would pay for this.

This Second Proposal of this directive was strongly influenced by CERCLA, as when the EC drafters were in the process of formulating the proposal for this legal act, 'they had hopes in exploiting the best elements of CERCLA, without falling into the litigation morass which had shaped CERCLA's developments over the past years'.[209] The strong synergistic influence of CERCLA on the legal design

---

Natural Resources', in Wettersteins '*Harm to the Environment – the Right to Compensation and the Assessment of Damages*', 1997, Clarendon Press, Oxford, pp. 177–206.
207. Jones, B., '*Deterring, Compensation, and Remedying Environmental Damage: The Contribution of Tort Liability*' in Wetterstein, '*Harm to the Environment – the Right to Compensation and the Assessment of Damages*', 1997, Calderon Press, Oxford, pp. 11–27.
208. See sub-section, 3.1.2 of the present chapter.
209. Tester, P., and Whitehead M., '*The EC Directive on Civil Liability for Damage Caused by Waste: Lessons from the 'Superfund Law*', 1992, EELR, Vol. 1, No. 1 June, pp. 26–27.

of the EC proposed legislation is also visible in the reading of the preamble of the above mentioned 1991 Second Proposal, which states that 'the liability of the producer and eliminator of waste must be covered by insurance or other financial security.'

In which sense, Article 11 of this Second Proposal states that:

the Council shall determine by December 1992 (1) the liability under this directive of the producer who is in the course of a commercial or industrial activity produces waste, and of the eliminator shall be covered by insurance, or any other financial security (2) common rule governing the situation (i) where the person liable is incapable of providing full compensation for the damage, and/or impairment of the environment caused, or (ii) the person liable under this Directive cannot be identified. In this regard, the Commission shall study the feasibility of the establishment a European Fund for Compensation for Damage and Impairment of the Environment Caused by Waste.[210]

Hence, from the lessons learned from the US as an historical-comparative Model together which justifies the motives that pushed the EU legislator to consider the US Model in the phase of the law-making process of the Environmental Liability Directive, two suggestions can be taken into consideration.

Firstly, the US Model is an inspiring pattern for the 'perception' of the definition of the environment as a 'protected good' and for the internalisation of external environmental costs. Secondly, the US Model can help to adapt a type of policy insurance which could better get close to the needs of enterprises presenting high environmental risk and treating or producing hazardous substances.

3.1.6   BACKGROUND OF THE LIABILITY DIRECTIVE

The analysis on the origins of the ELD explained why there was a need for an environmental liability Directive in Europe.[211] In particular, the gestation process of the law formation process of the development phase of the Environmental

---

210. See Amended Proposal for the Commission Proposal to the Council for a Directive on Civil liability for a Damage caused by Waste, COM(91) 219 final – SYN 217, Art. 11, para. 2. For the same point, see also sub-section 3.1.2 and sub-section 3.1.3 of the present chapter. In particular, in this latter section, it is shown that also the Lugano Convention influenced this same focal point of the 1991 Second Proposal for a directive. This, let us understands, that, both the Lugano Level and the US model, synergistically interacted and influenced on the design of the EC legal proposal.

211. In particular, in order to understand why there was a need for a Directive harmonising environmental liability rules, a special attention should be dedicated to a precise exam of the legal acts, such as the proposed EC legislation and legislations characterising the origins of the law formation process of the development process of the Environmental Liability Directive, as examined in the sub-section 3.1.2 of the present chapter; and to the policy papers, such as for example, the 1993 Green Paper, and the 2000 White Paper, which will be treated the first, in the next sub-section 3.1.6.1 of the present chapter, and the second, in the sub-section 3.1.6.2, and also the 2002 Proposal for a Directive on Environmental liability with Regard the

Liability Directive,[212] occurred under a political-legal mechanism of simultaneous interactions between multilevel *arena* which made interacts precise sources of EU law and policy of the development phase of the Environmental Liability Directive.

Generally, the formation of the European Community law was created also against different traditions and legal systems.[213] In particular, when issues of liability are involved in the EU law formation process, those differences emerged very clearly. Those differences emerged very clearly also in the decision-making of the development phase of the Environmental Liability Directive which is where it is found the answer as to why there was a need for a directive.

The gestation process of the Environmental Liability Directive showed us that there were divergences in the legal systems of Member States not only in the way to conceive regulation on environmental protection but also due to the existence of conflicts and controversies.[214] Some Member States felt that there was no need for harmonisation and that the shift from the Member States to the EU level of environmental liability rules was not justified on the grounds of the concept of subsidiarity.

Despite the pre-existence of different national legal designs on environmental liability rules and the existence of controversy in creating common environmental liability rules, harmonisation was desired especially from an economical perspective.

The reason why harmonisation was desired was mainly to eliminate distortion on competition for enterprises and to ensure the free movements of goods in a way so as to avoid differences in the level of protection of health, property and environment.

Thus, once the reason to have a harmonised liability regime in Europe was identified, the problem which remained to be solved was how the EC could achieve this harmonisation, and how far the EC could go in creating a European environmental liability regime.

For the latter purpose, a theoretical framework of law and economics was developed in order to explain the 'know-how' or the 'how to achieve harmonisation' and it was mainly based on an economical analysis of tort law, represented by the thinking which goes back to Calabresi[215] and other scholars.[216]

Prevention and Restoration of the Environmental Damage which will be treated in next section 3.1.6.5 of the present chapter.

212. The gestation process of the Environmental Liability Directive has been explained in the previous sub-section 3.1.2 of the present chapter.

213. The different traditions against which the background of the European Community Law was created are referred for example to the Civil Law and Common Law systems.

214. See previous sub-section 3.1.2 of the present chapter titled '*The Original Idea of Harmonising Environmental Damage*'.

215. Calabresi G., '*The Costs of accidents. A legal and Economical Analysis*', 1970, New Haven, Yale University Press.

216. Shavell S., '*Economic Analysis of Accidents Law*', 1987, Cambridge, Harvard University Press, or Posner R., '*Economic Analysis of law*', 1998, Aspen Law and Business.

This theoretical framework employed by the EC legal drafters to design an environmental liability scheme in Europe was mostly based in showing evidence that strict liability was better than fault liability, and on determining the optimal level of harmonisation for environmental liability rules. The study included both fault-based and strict liability. However, the choice of strict liability was found to be preferred over a fault based regime, because it applies best in cases where subject x damages subject y without the subjective element of guilt, or without fault behaviour, or in absence of negligence.[217] This is the case, when, for example, an industrial activity conducted by an enterprise damages in absence of fault and where there is only the obligation to demonstrate the causality link.

The analysis of Shavell started to advance the notion that it was the enterprise which profits from environmental risk, and consequently, for that reason the same enterprise should bear the costs associated with such a risk.[218] In addition, a firm notion explaining that strict liability was better than fault liability,[219] and that those who should bear the costs of environmental risk were supposed to be the industrial enterprises, started to be advocated by lawyers and economist involved in finding a method to design an environmental civil liability scheme.

Part of the framework was trying to examine not only the *pros* but also the *cons* of using a strict liability regime.[220]

The optimal level of harmonisation for environmental liability rules was examined from two different perspectives in a law and economic approach which consisted of a public interest approach and a private interest approach.[221]

The aim of the this framework was dual: firstly, to explain whether the regime of environmental liability rules existing at that historical time period was effective, and how to make harmonisation possible which was answered partly by the economical analysis of tort law described above,[222] and secondly, to explain also why there was a need for a European environmental liability regime. This second question was partly addressed by the arguments of the Commission. Additionally,

---

217. As explained in previous section 3.1.1 of the present chapter, it is discussed how the 'shift' or 'passage' from fault liability into strict liability that took place in both Common Law and Civil Law countries occurred and why. In that context, the analysis of Shavell of the criteria for assigning civil liability clearly demonstrated that a fault based regime present certain limitations and gaps, as it is no longer functioning in certain cases and in certain types of activity.
218. Shavell, S., '*Economic Analysis of Accidents Law*', 1987, Cambridge, Harvard University Press.
219. Also because a strict liability regime would 1) provide optimal incentives for individuals to take precautions for preventing environmental harm and 2) does not provide such high costs as a negligence rule 3) from a compensation point of view, can ensure full compensation of the damage which would not be the case for a negligence rule.
220. One element of *cons* of using strict liability in the framework of the Environmental Liability Directive was for example, the risk of insolvency which could distort the deterrence and compensation or restorative function of strict liability.
221. De Smedt, K., '*Is Harmonization Always Effective'? The Implementation of the Environmental Liability Directive*', 2009, European Energy and Environmental Law Review, page 3.
222. The economical analysis that was used as basis for designing the framework of the scheme of Environmental Liability Directive was based on the studies of Calabresi, Shavell, and Posner.

the concept of subsidiary was involved in this framework, as the EC must find justifications, on the grounds of subsidiary, in justifying and motivating the necessity to have a shift from Member States' rules to the EU level.[223] The assumption, at that historical time, was, that, there was no justification on the grounds of subsidiary which was also one of the reasons why it has not been possible to reach an agreement in designing an environmental liability in the waste sector, and therefore, explain also partly, the failure of the 1991 Second Proposal to the Council for a Directive on Civil Liability for damage Caused by Waste.[224]

Even though this framework was, in other words, attempting to design a strategy in order to find the optimal level of harmonisation at the EU level, and was solidly set up, the examination of the reasons why the Community felt the need to harmonise environmental liability rules did not came to an end.

In fact, the Community was still in the process of understanding why harmonisation was needed, and the question of why there was the necessity of the shift of environmental liability rules, arose once again at the surface in the year 1993 with the 1993 Green Paper in a subsequent phase of the decision-making process of the law formation process of the ELD, in between the years 2000–02, especially with the 2000 White Paper; and with the 2002 Proposal for a Directive.[225]

Once again, in the study of the Green Paper, the White Paper, (as well as in the 2002 Proposal for a Directive, as it will be observed in the next following chapters), the solutions offered by the Lugano Convention and the US approach, where again carefully taken into consideration by the drafter of these documents.[226] Nevertheless, what will be pending to be understood is, if the EU law-maker when involved in the phase of drafting of the legal text of the Environmental Liability Directive has really chosen to be inspired and drawn benefits from the potentials offered by the synergies and interactions of a multilevel context.

This holistic vision of a transnational multidimensional dimension, certainly let presume, that, the framework which was attempting to elaborate the strategy of the 'know-how or the 'how to harmonise' and the 'why' to harmonise, should have included the respect of the chain of the logical sequential order of the focal point and the context of the multilevel dimension where the Environmental Liability Directive grown up.

In fact, as it has been demonstrated from all that proceed in the previous sections of this historical-comparative analysis dedicated to the contextualisation of the development phase of the Environmental Liability Directive, the 'how to solve the focal points' and the 'what is the optimal level of harmonisation of environmental liability rules' is certainly not only an EU problem.

---

223. The Commission was in a process to find a justification and studying the arguments supporting the shift from Member States rule to the EU rules regulating the environmental liability regime.
224. See previous sub-section 3.1.2, of the present chapter.
225. In particular these two documents of the Environmental Liability Directive decision-making process explains the reasons for the shift from Member State rules to the EU level.
226. As it will be shown in the next following two sub-sections.

3.1.6.1 The Green Paper

At the beginning of the 1990s, at the EU level, the policy on environmental matters aim at a higher level of protection, and it is based on the Principle of precaution, prevention and on the Polluter-pays principle.[227] At international level, the negotiations of the Lugano Convention were still in the process to be debated. At the domestic level, the design of civil liability as a consequence of environmental damage was different in the systems where the law is codified[228] compared to those where the law is not codified.[229]

The motive for having a Green Paper was that some Member States had different designs of civil liability for environmental harm, and this could cause obstacles to the functioning of the EU internal market.

For which reason, the Commission decided to publish, on the 17 March 1993, a paper titled with the ambitious terms summarising the essence of its significance, which is the 'Green Paper on Compensation for Environmental Harm'.[230]

The study-approach of the Green Paper[231] was therefore aimed to propose a system of civil liability founded on the fault based liability regime, while for hazardous activities it was based on a system of strict liability. The system as proposed is, therefore, defined as 'integrative', as it integrates fault and strict liability together. The Green Paper also proposed the implementation of a public collective fund of compensation[232] for damages occurring when the responsible party is not identifiable. The fund should have been financed by the interested economic subjects.

---

227. As was outlined by Kramer in 1992, at the EU level, environmental protection is based on Art. 174 (ex Art. 130 R) of the EC Treaty. See Kramer, L., '*EEC Treaty and Environmental Protection*', 1992, London.
228. Such as Italy, Germany or France.
229. Such as the UK.
230. The Green Paper on Compensation for environmental damage was presented as a Communication of the Commission to the Council, the Parliament and the Economic and Social Committee of the EU in May 1993. See document of the Commission of the European communities, COM(93) 47, Brussels, 14 May 1993, in OJ no. C/149 of the 29 May 1993 See also the Information Memo issued by the spokesman service (Dienst Van de Woordvoerder) of the Commission titled 'The Commission Adopts a Communication on Repairing Damage to the Environment' on the 17 March 1993.
231. Both the Green Papers and the White Papers do not have a binding force, but they do have a strong political role in the law formation process. In general, the Green Papers are studies taking into account a given problem in an issue-area, in order to verify if it is necessary or not to introduce a new law. The Commission has defined 'White Papers' as follows: 'White Papers are documents containing proposals for community action in a specific area. They often follow a Green Paper published to launch a consultation process at EU level. While Green Papers set out a range of ideas presented for public discussions and debates, White Papers contains an official set of proposals in specific policy areas and are used as a vehicle for their development'. See Berkamp, L., '*The Proposed Environmental Liability Directive*', Nov. 2002, Environmental Law Review, page 1., footnote n. 6.
232. Green Paper, para. 7.

The Green Paper, even if dated from the 1993, is substantially trying to solve the same problem opened up three years before, with the 1989 First Proposal for a Directive on Civil Liability for Damage caused by Waste.[233]

What immediately draws the attention is the direct link and overlap with the Green Paper and the Lugano Convention. The paper is interconnected with the Lugano Convention because is trying to transplant the Lugano Convention, though, almost in a mechanic way, such as willing to overlap and juxtapose the Lugano provisions into the EC policy strategy. In the Green Paper, the Convention of the Council of Europe is practically 'reproduced' or 'uploaded'.[234]

The civil liability of the Green Paper embodies the Polluter-pays principle, the Principle of prevention and the necessity to avoid distortions of the market in a way which it is the polluter and not the State who should support the charges of the expenses to face environmental degradation. The study, provided by the Green Paper, considered the advantages and disadvantages of fault, or strict based liability and in which sectors to apply them, also taking into account the American experience.

The paper highlights the instrumental use of civil liability that should be understood both as an instrument that oblige those who pollutes to pay and also as a tool to achieve the smooth functioning of the EU internal market and harmonise, in this way, the different pre-existing environmental liability regimes. In that sense, the fact that there were various regimes of civil liability, concerning the accusation in charge in the different EC countries, jeopardise not only the environment but also free competition which led the Commission to search for a lowest common denominator amongst the Member States and analyse the *pro* and *cons* of the different criteria for imputability.[235]

The Green Paper suggested the duty for Member States to guarantee, in accordance with the domestic laws, minimum threshold for environmental quality (and provides for a list of directives in this field) in order to establish the obligation for Member States to repair the damage and define a threshold for environmental damage and a typology of reparation.

In the Green Paper, the Commission redefined and re-discussed all the focal points already acknowledged at international and national level. In two focal points only the Commission took a firm and strongest position: (1) the role of environmental associations and their entitlement to claim for environmental damage, and (2) the necessity to initiate a mandatory financial guarantee and insurance system for the environmental damage.[236] The linkage between a mandatory insurance

---

233. See previous sub-section 3.1.2 of the present chapter.
234. Specifically, what it is found, in the document, is a long list of doubts, regarding the way to tackle the focal points of the environmental liability regime. The only possible solution, to these focal points, seems to be found in the Lugano Convention. For that point, see for example, in the document, from paras 3.0 to 4.2, pp. 20–28 of the Green Paper COM(93) 47.
235. Pozzo, B., '*Towards Civil Liability for Environmental Damage in Europe: the White Paper of the Commission of the European Communities*', 2001, Global Jurist, Vol. 1, Issue 2, page 18.
236. Which was basically what was not proposed by the Lugano Convention: a mandatory insurance system for hazardous activities and hazardous waste. See for that point, also the previous sub-section 3.1.3, of the present chapter.

system and hazardous wastes was a way to create a direct connection with the waste sector and putting into practice what was already proposed with the 1991 Second draft Proposal of the Commission for a Council Directive on Civil Liability caused by Waste.[237] In that sense, the Commission was attempting to reinforce its role in rendering the environmental liability regime, at EU level, stricter in terms of environmental protection.

The intention of the Green Paper was to use the Lugano Convention as a tool for harmonise in a uniform way the different environmental liability regimes in force at Member State level and try to implement the Convention (within the establishment of the EU Single Market) for all the cases where the EC norm refers to the domestic laws. In which sense, the Lugano Convention was much more advanced and the Green Paper appeared quite outdated compared to the Lugano solutions.

The Lugano Convention considered damages to all dangerous activities with high risk and also to traditional damage which was not the case of the Green Paper.[238]

In substance, the Green Paper has a valuable force of policy in the environmental liability regime. In the spirit of this strong policy, the Commission started to show signals of strongest and more innovative positions in the way to tackle some of the most sensitive crucial focal points of the environmental liability regime, such as the question of who can claim for environmental damage and the issue to set up mandatory insurance mechanisms, as pointed out before. However, the Green Paper left unresolved three of these crucial focal points.[239]

The first is the definition of the environment which is not considered as a real good as there is a total absence of definition of the environment as a 'good'. The second is the notion of environmental damage, which is not conceived in a unitary approach.[240] The third is the solution for a collective public fund of compensation as suggested from the title – compensation of environmental damage – given that this piece of EC policy paper which was not binding was aimed, theoretically, at using civil liability for costs relative to environmental restoration.

Even thought the Green Paper left unsolved problems in relation to some crucial focal points, as explained above, the whole idea behind the Green Paper to generate further debate and reinforce the interests in strengthening the environmental liability regime was achieved.

In fact, one year after the issuance of the Green Paper, the Commission started an orientation debate for the follow up of the Green Paper to propose a Directive

---

237. See previous sub-section 3.1.2, of the present chapter.
238. In addition, the list of hazardous activities in the Green Paper was not exhaustive and discriminating, compared to other activities, which were hazardous but not include in the list.
239. See the Opinion of the 23 February 1994 of the Economic and Social Committee (ESC) on the Communication from the Commission to the Council and Parliament and the Economic and Social Committee: Green Paper on Remedying Environmental Damage COM(93) 47 final.
240. 'Unitary approach' means to unify and include in the notion of environmental damage, also the traditional damage, and not only the damage to natural resources.

related to regulation of civil liability as a consequence of environmental damage.[241] The suggested Directive was targeted to regulate environmental liability in general and not only the waste sector. The Directive was designed in a 'broad approach' on the basis of Article 174 and 175 (ex. Article 130 R and 130 S) of the EC Treaty[242] corresponding to the current Articles 192 and 193 of the TFEU.

The 'broad approach', as opposed to a 'focused approach', means that the definition of environmental damage is perceived with a 'unitary approach' as it is inclusive also of the traditional damage (including individual damages, such as health and property) while the focused approach is not covering such a damage, but only ecological damage and contaminated site clean-up.[243]

The Member State's reactions to the Green Paper and to the environmental liability EC initiatives were not positive for all. Some Member States such as Denmark, Luxembourg, Spain, Germany, Belgium, Portugal and Italy were in favour of the EU initiatives.

While other Member States such as Germany, Ireland and the Netherlands were not enthusiastic and the UK was even critical.[244] On January 1997, the Economic and Social Council (ESC) had to respond to the Resolution of the European Parliament on the 1994 Proposition for a Council Directive on environmental liability, and decided to prepare a 'White Paper on Liability for Environmental Damage'. In April 1997, a document was produced which was the 'Outline for the White Paper on Environmental Liability'[245], and in 1998, a 'Draft White Paper on Environmental Liability' appeared.[246]

3.1.6.2   The White Paper

In the year 2000, with the White Paper of the EU Community,[247] the European environmental liability regime started a new shift in its stance on the way of conceiving the focal points.[248] The White Paper reshapes the design of the

---

241. See the 'Communication of Mrs Bjerregaard to the Commission on Community Action as Regards Environmental Liability – Paper to Prepare an orientation Debate', and the Resolution of the 20 of April 1994, in OJ, 1994.

242. And not on the basis of Article 95 (ex Article 100 A of the EC Treaty) as it was the case for the 1989 First Proposal for a Directive on Civili Liability for Damage caused by Waste. See for that point, the previous sub-section 3.1.2 of the present chapter.

243. In *'Communication of Mrs Bjerregaard to the Commission on Community Action as Regards Environmental Liability – Paper to Prepare an orientation Debate'*.

244. Bryce, *'Civil Liability for Environmental Damage and the UK government's response to the Green Paper'*, in Gazette du Palais, 5 mai 1994. See also Poli, S., *'Shaping the EC Regime on Liability for Environmental Damage: Progress or Disillusionment?'* 1999, European Environmental Law Review.

245. See *'Outline for White Paper on Environmental Liability'*, PG 65/97 of the 14.04.97.

246. See *'Draft White Paper on Environmental Liability'*, (reference of the document /d.d 29.5.98).

247. The White Paper on Liability for Environmental Damage, COM(2000) 66 final.

248. The focal points of an environmental liability regime laid down in Chapter 2 and that all the environmental legislators, at all the levels, have to face.

EU liability rules as traced from its inception[249] into a new half-consolidated regime, much more defined in terms of environmental protection.

In fact, with the White Paper, the EU regime on environmental liability concentrates more on the importance of the focal points turning the environmental liability regime into a more effective law for two main reasons. The first is that the White Paper aims at introducing a general clause considering the environment at the same level as a normal good and the environmental damage in a novel unitary approach.[250] The second is that this policy paper finally faces the problem of who shall pay for the costs of environmental reinstatement and who shall compensate for environmental damage.

The first step toward a novel unitary approach of the concept of environment damage is materialised with the definition of environmental damage into two meanings: damage to the biodiversity and damage under the form of contamination of sites. The damage to the biodiversity is covered as protected in Natura 2000,[251] according to the 'Wild Birds directive' and the 'Habitat directive'.[252]

The White Paper draws the attention toward important focal points such as the compensation of environmental damage and the problem of risk assessment and quantification of environmental damage, highlighting the role of environmental insurability.

The Paper noted that if reinstatement of environmental damage is technically impossible, then the solution has to be searched into the Lugano Convention, which states that quantification of environmental damages shall be done taking into account the costs of alternative solutions, aimed at introducing into the environment equivalent resources, compared to those which have been destroyed.[253]

The White Paper contains the four different options which the EU Commission had to study in order to design the European environmental policy. The first option presented was the EC adhesion to the Lugano Convention, the second, an environmental liability regime restricted to the trans-boundary damages, the third, the adoption of an EU recommendation, and fourth, the adoption of a directive regulating environmental liability in general.[254]

The choice for the fourth option permitted the EU to use the context where the law on environmental liability was embedded. Hence, once again, the confrontation and use, in the White Paper of different experiences, international, US Model and national levels, permitted the adoption of environmental laws on

---

249. See the previous sub-section 3.1.2 of the present chapter.
250. Which the Green Paper did not. See for that point, and also for an explanation of the meaning of the 'unitary approach' the previous sub-section 3.1.6.1 of the present chapter.
251. Natura 2000 is a Community network of nature protection areas established under the EU Habitats Directive and includes areas designated under the EU Wild Birds Directive. The aim of the network is to assure the long-term survival of Europe's most valuable and threatened species and habitats.
252. White Paper 4.5.1. The two directives will be treated further on, in Chapter 5, section 5.18.
253. See previous sub-section 3.1.3 treating the Lugano Convention, of the present Chapter.
254. The different possibilities formulated by the Commission presented advantages and disadvantages.

environmental protection, approaching further to an optimal level of harmonisation of legislation in term of environmental protection.

The significance of the White Paper as a strong impulse of the shift of the EU liability policy culminating in the birth of the ELD, can be fully grasped through the comparison between the Green and White Paper. For that purpose, in the next section, a comparison between the Green Paper and White Paper will be shown, with the aim of understanding how the improvements in the White Paper can be considered as being first steps of advancement for the EU environmental liability policy, in terms of environmental protection goal achievements.

3.1.6.3   A Comparison between the Papers

The reason for comparing the Green Paper with the White Paper by observing the focal points in both the legal policy papers is to understand whether and how the environmental liability regime at the EU level advances in term of effectiveness in reaching environmental protection goal achievements.

The object of comparison is aimed on ascertaining what are the similarities and differences between the two EU policy papers with regard to their approach in treating the focal points existing at international and national levels of sources of law.

The comparison of these two policy papers shows that the most important innovations of the EU liability policy in term of results of environmental protection goal achievements results by the act of confrontation between the sources of law of the EU, international and domestic level.

The multilevel level comparison is, in a way, reorganised, reintroduced and applied into the EU law *via* policy papers.

3.1.6.3.1   *Definition of Environmental Damage*

As to the definition of environmental damage, differently to the Green Paper, the environmental damage of the White Paper is conceived in a broad approach which includes not only the damage to the biodiversity, but also the damage from polluting activities to goods and people. Therefore, by covering also the traditional damage, in the White Paper the EU legislator also considered the way of conceiving the environmental damage in the different domestic levels and especially the German and Italian approaches,[255] and the broad approach of environmental damage of the Lugano Convention.

The reason is also due to the willingness of the EU legislator to avoid the persistence of unequal situations (Member States which are including in the environmental damage traditional damage and those which are not), and the need to

---

255. That have already been introduced in the previous sub-section 3.1.5, and that will be further analysed in the penultimate sub-section 3.1.6.4 of the present chapter.

preserve human health.[256] For the first time, and differently to the Green Paper, the environmental liability of the EU regime of the White Paper tries to define environmental damage in a unitary approach and in a non-sectorial fashion.[257]

3.1.6.3.2 Scope of Application

With regard to the scope of application, it is worth noticing that civil liability as a consequence of environmental damage is, in the White Paper not sectorial restricted only to the waste sector, but general. Differently to the Green Paper, and in line with the German Law and the Lugano Convention, the White Paper considers, also, exceptions for environmental liability in cases of Act of God, or circumstances beyond ones control, or in cases of contributory negligence on behalf of the damaged party.[258] The exemption is also valuable in case the damage occurred after authorisation of activity by a public authority, or in case it was not possible to be aware of the hazardous effects at the same moment when the damage occurred.

3.1.6.3.3 Problem of Who Is Entitled to Claim
for Environmental Damage

Another important difference between the Papers is on the topic of access to justice and the problem of who is entitled to claim for environmental damage. The improvement in terms of effectiveness provided by the White Paper consists of the guarantee of wide access to justice to citizens and groups of interest acting in the defence of public interest. On the sensitive focal point of who can claim for environmental damage, the White Paper offered an approach, confronting and considering the international and national level.

Internationally, the White Paper took into account, in the shaping of the focal point of who can claim for environmental damage, the Aarhus Convention and the Lugano Convention.[259] From the national level, it is maintained that Member States have the power-duty to guarantee environmental compensation, and at the domestic level, only in a subsidiary way and if the state does not intervene,

---

256. In accordance to the objective stated in Art. 174 (1) of the EC Treaty, current Art. 192 of the TFEU.
257. Unitary approach, because includes in the definition of the damage not only damage to the biodiversity but also damage to goods and people, and non-sectorial approach, because it includes not only damages to the waste sector but environmental damages in general.
258. Pozzo, B., '*Toward Civil Liability For Environmental Damage in Europe: the White Paper of the Commission of the European Communities*', 2001, Global Jurist Topics, Vol 1, Issue 2, page 28.
259. It is possible to connect, on that point, with the Aarhus Convention (Aarhus Convention on access to information, public participation in decision-making and access to justice in environmental matters of June 1998); and the Art. 18 of the Lugano Convention stating the 'rights of the organisations which according to its statutes aims at the protection of the environment'.

the environmental associations, satisfying prerequisites required by national law, do have the faculty to act.[260]

3.1.6.3.4   Compensation for Environmental Damage

The White Paper indicates who must pay for the environmental damage which the Green Paper did not clarify: all of the operators exercising control of the activity which is under the jurisdiction of application of the new regime for liability for environmental damage as defined at the EU level. The financial lenders who do not exercise an operational control should not be considered liable. These exclusions are made in order to avoid the new community regime of liability for environmental damage causing the same problems which occurred in the US in the interpretation of cases-law for the term 'operator'. In fact, as already exposed in section 3.1.5 of this chapter, CERCLA introduced a regime of strict liability, retroactive, and joint and several for damage to natural resources.

This could certainly be positive in terms of 'environmental damage sharing' between several people, however, not as an incentive to prevent environmental harm. The US considered, therefore, a broad approach of environmental liability, especially in cases where the available funds of the companies liable for the damage were not sufficient for the decontamination required by the law. CERCLA was excessively broadened, especially for the banks which started a vicious circle. The result was over deterrence which did not encourage the lenders to make stricter checks, but to withhold credit to whole industrial sectors considered 'a high environmental risk'. Therefore, in order to avoid this situation of over deterrence, the Commission wanted to avoid this result and learn from the negative aspects of the US experience.[261]

3.1.6.3.5   Choice of the Type of Liability

With regards to the *unique* similarity, which is the choice of the type of liability regime, similarly to the Green Paper, the White Paper, maintains strict liability for the damage caused by dangerous activities[262] (including hazardous waste in the list of dangerous activities) and fault liability for the damage caused to biodiversity by non-dangerous activities.

In that sense, in the White Paper, the Commission took into account in the elaboration of the regime, the Lugano Convention[263] together with the pre-existing

---

260. See for that point, the White Paper, point 4.7.1.
261. Pozzo, B., '*Toward Civil Liability for Environmental Damage in Europe: the White Paper of the Commission of the European Communities*', Global Jurist Topics, Vol. 1, 2001, page 30.
262. The 'dangerous activities' of the White Paper still continues to be the same as those previously regulated by the EC legislation of environmental protection, such as that concerning dangerous substances and chemicals, the one for controlling and preventing risk of significant accident, the one of the production, handling, processing, recovery, recycling and transportation -even trans-boundary- of dangerous waste.
263. See sub-section 3.1.3 on the Lugano Convention.

differences at the domestic level, in the design of the environmental liability regime.

3.1.6.3.6   *Insurance Mechanism*

With regard to insurability, the White Paper considered very seriously the problem of environmental insurance,[264] and the importance of the management of risk and its preventive function. The White Paper advanced a step further, in terms of environmental protection goal achievements compared to the Green Paper, by fully connecting the insurance sector with civil liability and the concept of sustainable development.

The insurance sector is also strictly connected with the role of the non-official actors (interplay between public authorities/enterprises and individual subjects) as it plays a central role in the process of implementation at the domestic level for the elaboration of environmental policies based on the risk management.

In conclusion, with regards to the similarities and differences of the focal points contained in the policy papers, the finding of the present comparison shows that there is only one similarity, which is the choice of the type of liability, being instead all the rest of the result of this comparison, prominently highlighting significant differences between the papers. In fact with regards to precise focal points, such as, for example, the definition of the environmental damage, the scope of application, who can claim for environmental damage, compensation and who must pay for the environmental damage, and the insurance mechanism, it appears that there are differences in the way they are approached by the two policy papers. The White Paper acknowledges, therefore, the relevance of the relationship between civil liability and insurance, trying to elaborate, on the international level and on the US Model, the EU law into a more effective law in term of environmental protection goal achievement.[265]

In addition, an important innovation offered by the White Paper is in terms of unitary holistic perception, or integrative perception of the EU environmental liability regulations. In fact, the document integrates the EU norm with other sectorial directives, such as the previously mentioned 'Wild Bird', 'Habitat' directives.[266] Therefore, the White Paper makes a connection with sectorial norms already

---

264. See White Paper, point 4.9.
265. At international level, a relevant connection inspiring the White Paper is the 1995 Statement of Environmental Commitment by Insurance Industry by the United Nation Environmental Programme (UNEP), available in the link www.unepfi.org, in which it is found the relationship between sustainable development, risk management, ecological risk, the role of stakeholders and the diffusion of Public Awareness and Communications. In addition, a source of inspiration for the White Paper, certainly was the failure of the insurance market system in the US, which has been substantially taken into account by the Commission in the elaboration of this policy paper. See for that point, Monti A., '*L'assicurabilità del rischio ambientale in prospettiva europea*', pp. 207–235 in '*La nuova responsabilità civile per danno all'ambiente*', 2002, a cura di Barbara Pozzo, Quaderni della rivista giuridica dell'ambiente, n. 12, Giuffré Editore.
266. See previous sub-section 3.1.6.2, of the present chapter.

pre-existing, trying to give in this way a unitary holistic vision of the concept of civil liability for environmental damage.

The White Paper provides a new view in the perception of the environmental damage in term of unitary approach. This new perception is visible in the definition of the environmental damage provided by the paper and as noticed in the section concerning the definition of the environmental damage of this chapter.[267] However, the progress toward this new perception was slowly. This reminds that it shall not be forgotten that the definition of environmental damage, at EU level was still *in fieri* and not yet close to an optimal level of harmonisation of legislation in terms of environmental protection and environmental goal achievements. This allows it to be understood that, on one hand, as it stands from the White Paper, the EU environmental liability regime was still in the process of being shaped and the concept of environmental damage was still not conceived in a complete unitary broad approach.

On the other hand, the White Paper does have the merit of having unified the different types of environmental liability from different sectors, in order to attempt to reach a certain type of 'uniformity' and an integrative perception of the concept of civil liability, as explained in the previous paragraph. In which sense, the novelty of the White Paper is to have tried to elaborate a concept of environmental damage,[268] based on the three levels -EU, international and national-, and perceive it in a 'multidimensional holistic vision'.

3.1.6.4 Different Pre-existing Types of Environmental Liability in the EU Member States

The concept of environmental civil liability at EU level, assembles all the focal points which the domestic legal systems had to tackle. These focal points were, therefore, in existence before and during the long process of the adoption of a Directive regulating the European liability regime.

At the domestic level, the main pre-existing concerns can be individualised and summarised in two key problems which distinguish environmental damage to subjects and to natural resources:

(1) How to compensate for environmental damage, in case an enterprise damages some subjects which are all entitled to compensation.
(2) How to obtain compensation in case an enterprise damages natural resources which do not have owners.

According to some economical theories, the damage to subjects, in the first case, should be internalised by enterprises in a way which the costs of environmental

---

267. See sub-section 3.1.6.1 of the present chapter.
268. Given that the definition of the concept of environmental damage in a multilevel approach (taking into account the international and national level in defining the environmental damage) and in a integrative approach (integrating EU environmental liability regulations with other pre-existing directives, as explained in the section dedicated to the White Paper) was non-existent before the White Paper.

damages result as internal costs. This phenomenon is known as internalisation of internal costs.

When environmental damage occurs to natural resources, which is the second case, enterprises should bear the costs in what is already mentioned as being defined as internalisation of the external costs. The issue was mainly due to the idea of impeding the society from bearing the costs.

At the EU level, in the formation of the environmental liability regime the main concern was to avoid that some Member States started to make enterprises to bear the costs of environmental damage and others not. By implication, the concern was to avoid distortions of internal market, unequal conditions and unfair competition. Given the existence of undeniable differences in the pre-existing domestic regimes of environmental liability, when the EC legislators started to consider civil liability as a consequence of environmental damage for the very first time, it was mainly to guarantee the quality of the environment, as well as to avoid the existence of obstacles in the different environmental regimes.

Thus, the red line of the creation of the EU Environmental liability regime was pre-eminently based on the maintenance of the smooth functioning of the internal market.[269]

Initially, environmental protection at the domestic level was almost non-existent. At the beginning of the 1980s, some Member States, such as Germany and Italy, tried to develop the concept of civil liability both with general and sectorial norms. As mentioned in the introduction of this chapter,[270] it would not be possible to describe, in this book, the legislation of civil liability as a consequence of environmental damage for all the individual Member States.[271] Rather, in order to demonstrate how difficult it was for the EC level to harmonise environmental liability in Europe, a brief description will be provided and limited to the two examples of Germany and Italy. These two examples are significant for understanding the pre-existing type of domestic regime and understand, partly, the reasons for having a Directive regulating environmental liability for environmental harm. These countries are considered significant and as good samples, as they are ideal for grasping the basic differences in the shaping of the European liability legislation at the domestic level. Also, the cases under comparative examination, refers back to the different existing models of environmental legislation protecting natural resources (the German, the US and the Portuguese model), where the Italian Model is very similar to the US Model, as explained in section 3.1.5 of Chapter 3.

---

269. As observed in the previous sub-sections 3.1.2 of the present chapter. In fact, from the First Waste Proposal (1976) ahead, in all the subsequent pieces of EU legislation and legal proposals, the red line was always to avoid obstacles in the functioning of the internal market.
270. See the first section 3.1, of the present chapter.
271. Given that this is not the purpose of this study which is rather to approach the problem with an holistic vision, even if it would be certainly very interesting from a legal and political perspective to have a wide overview of all the legislations regulating environmental liability as a consequence of environmental damage.

3.1.6.5 A Comparison between the German and Italian Example

Both Germany and Italy, initially, developed a system of civil liability as a consequence of environmental damage which attempted to solve the focal points involving all of the EU legal systems.

In fact, for all the related problems of the focal points, for example on: the definition of the environmental damage, choice of liability, causation or quantification etc., the two countries offered completely different solutions (also the legislations of other Member States). The different approaches in protecting natural resources could have created dysfunctions in the smooth functioning of the internal market.

3.1.6.5.1 *The German Example*

With regards to Germany, for example, in 1991 this Member State introduced the *Umwelthaftungsgsetz* which is the Law on Civil Liability for Environmental damage.[272] In the 1970s, the German legislators started to introduce sectorial laws introducing strict liability without having specific norms in the German civil codes concerning hazardous activities. The German legal system introduced strict liability for all damages caused to health and integrity both to people and goods which are consequences of an emission harmful to the environment.

Thus, the German law exemplifies the first Model[273] which deals with the protection of natural resources indirectly and in connection with other individual traditional injuries such as the rights of health or property.[274]

In which way, the German law avoided facing the delicate problem of defining environmental damage[275] and by merely considering the damage to people and goods caused by dangerous emissions to the environment, protected the environment indirectly. With such a law, it certainly cannot be avoid of wondering where does the German law really protect the environment and outline also that there are no cases in law, up to the present, which apply this law. The German law has never been applied even not once. Hence, by adopting this solution, the German legislator took an opposite direction compared to the Italian one.

---

272. See Pozzo, B., '*La responsabilità per danni all'ambiente in Germania*' 1991, in Riv. dir. Civ.
273. This model called 'German Model' as opposed to the 'American Model' and 'Portuguese Model' is described in the previous sub-section 3.1.5 of the present chapter.
274. Pozzo, B., '*Towards Civil Liability for Environmental Damage in Europe: the White Paper of the Commission of the European Communities*', 2001, Vol. 1, Issue 2, Global Jurist, page 4.
275. And by consequence also other issues such as the *quantification* of ecological damages, which they probably wanted to avoid as pointed out by Pozzo, in Pozzo, B.,'*Towards Civil Liability for Environmental Damage in Europe: the White Paper of the Commission of the European Communities*', 2001, Vol. 1, Issue 2, Global Jurist, page 4.

3.1.6.5.2   The Italian Example

Regarding the *Italian legislation*, it is worth remembering the notorious Italian law no. 349 of 1986 which has also been defined as a 'futurist law' as it seems really aimed at protecting the environment.

The law introduced for the very first time in Italy a Ministry of the Environment which was non-existent before, and the Article 18 implemented a discipline in the field of civil liability as a consequence of environmental damage. In fact, Article 1 of the law states that:

> it is the duty of the Ministry to ensure . . . the promotion, conservation and recovery of the environmental conditions, in accordance with the fundamental interests of the general public and with the quality of life, as well as the conservation and the enhancement of the national natural patrimony of the defence of the national resources from pollution.

In this way, the Italian law seems to be a good example of the second legislative Model[276] protecting natural resources directly in contrast to the German case.

The Italian legislator adopts a broad and unitary notion of the environment, not only as a whole notion including in the biodiversity, environmental property, but also as in conceiving the environment an essential element for the well being of general public. Article 18 provides for 'compensation for environmental damage which can be requested by the State from whom, through negligence or fault, violated the provisions of the law or measures adopted based on the law by jeopardising the environment, damaging, altering, deteriorating or destroying it entirely or in part.'

According to the Italian law, anyone who damages by fault, or negligence, must repair the environmental damage to the State which becomes the subject entitled to act and to claim (and not other entities such as regions or provinces). Article 18 provides also for several specific norms involved with the problem of the quantification of the environmental damage such, as for example that if *'restitutio in integrum'* is possible then this should be the preferred solution. In addition, Article 2058 states that *restitutio in integrum* can be accorded only if not excessively costly.

On which point, the Italian law goes further, by providing that if *restitutio in integrum* cannot apply because too much dangerous and too expensive or difficult to put into practice,[277] then the judge must find a solution according to equity by taking into account three criteria: (1) cost of reinstatement, (2) profits achieved by the wrongdoer and (3) fault of the wrongdoer. By consequence, the three criteria are useful for the quantification of the damage.

---

276. The second legislative Model in protecting national resources is the US Model.
277. For example, there are cases when enterprises damage so seriously the land, or the sediments located in the ground, that the ground it-self should be removed. Often the removal of these sediments is not possible to materialise which makes the calculation in monetary terms of the environmental damage very difficult.

The German and Italian cases are extremely exemplificative of the different type of solutions addressing the focal points pre-existent at the domestic level, particularly concerning the definition of the damage, the choice of liability, causation and quantification. Therefore, different solutions have been taken into account at the EU level such as fault-based v. strict liability in the elaboration of the European environmental liability regime, especially the Italian case.

3.1.6.5.3   *Definition of Environmental Damage*

In general, German environmental law is characterised by a public administrative character with both civil and penal components. The German legislator chose to protect the environment not with a general environmentally protective broad attitude, like the Italian or the US Models but rather opted to decompose the environmental protection in accordance with the different sectorial *media* (water, soil, air, etc.,).[278] Therefore, in the German law, different sectorial rules apply and there is an absence of the term 'environment' and 'environmental damage', in contrast to the Italian example where there can be found a precise notion of the term 'environmental damage'.

Thus, the German law protecting the environment,[279] if compared with the Italian law, does not contain a 'broad general norm' for environmental damage similar to the previously mentioned Italian law no. 349 of 1986.[280] However, this does not entail that the German example leaves without sanctioning the environmental damage, in Germany. Differently to the Italian environmental protection example, the German example treats in a sectorial manner different hypothesis of environmental damage in relation to separate single *media* to be protected alternatively, sometimes by administrative laws, or civil and penal laws, or sometimes all together without alternance.

The notion of environmental damage in the German law differs when compared to the Italian, as the German law contains two typologies of environmental damage. The first, is the damage to individual goods and the manifestation of such kinds of damages occur through interactions with other environmentally damaging agents such as those caused by nuclear or radioactive contamination. The second type of environmental damage, contemplates what is called the 'Ökoschäden' which is the so-called ecological damage.[281] However, German rules do not contemplate the direct protection of the environment as in the Italian example. This is because the German law, protect *in primis* individual rights such as health, property and economic loss. The environment and the environmental damage are thus only secondary and taken into consideration only if associated with individual rights.

---

278. The German civil laws treating 'environmental damage' are contained in the German Civil Code, which is the 'Bürgerliches Gesetzbuch' (BGB) but also in other more sectorial laws.
279. The German law on Civil Liability for Environmental Damages as referred in the previous sub-section 3.1.6.4.1 of the present chapter, which is the 'Umwelthaftungsgesetz'.
280. See the analysis of Art. 18 of the Italian law no. 349 of 1986 in the previous sub-section 3.1.6.5.2.
281. The Ökoschäden' is also called the 'Ökologischer Schaden'.

3.1.6.5.4   Compensation

Differently to the Italian legislation, in the German environmental legislations, compensation for environmental damage does not represent a sanctioning but only a restoration to the environmental damage. Therefore, the amount of money for environmental damage is clearly low compared to the jurisprudential praxis in Italy and in the US. In addition, in contrast to the Italian example, the German laws protecting the environment do not protect the environment directly but only when related to individual goods or to the landscape[282] and compensation for liability as a consequence of environmental damage is limited by a maximum threshold of compensation of 85.000 Euro.[283]

3.1.6.5.5   Choice of the Type of Liability

The Umwelthaftungsgesetz set up a type of liability as a consequence of environmental damage for the administrator of a plant listed by the same law which is mainly strict based. This German law sets a liability as a consequence of environmental damage caused to the natural patrimony by plants conducting dangerous activities and damaging agents through air, water, land, natural and legal persons or their related goods. Differently to the Italian law no. 349 of 1986, the Umwelthaftungsgesetz establishes a type of civil liability as a consequence of environmental damage for all those damages caused to health and integrity both to individuals and goods and provides that in cases of emissions into the environment from a plant, causing death and injury, the owner of the plant, as indicated in the Appendix 1 of the Umwelthaftungsgesetz, is liable according to strict liability which is called in the German law 'Gefährdungshaftung'. The owners of such a plant have therefore the obligation to compensate.[284] The liability as a consequence of environmental damage caused to individual persons as well as to goods, is subject to a certain limitations, as mentioned in the previous sub-section.[285]

In the GMOs German law,[286] the German legislator introduced a system of strict liability for the administrator of the GMOs plant. The damage to the landscape or natural resources is protected only in cases of damage to individual goods and in cases that this damage is reflected into nature or to the landscape which means that also in cases of damage to GMOs there is no recognition of the existence of environmental damage 'as such'. Differently to the Italian example, civil German laws do not contain the possibility to protect the environment as such and therefore cannot compensate for environmental damage. Hence, in Germany, environmental protection as such, relies on rules of administrative law.

---

282. Paragraph 16 of the 'Umwelthaftungsgesetz'.
283. See para. 15 of the 'Umwelthaftungsgesetz'.
284. See Pozzo, B., *'Toward Civil Liability for Environmental Damage in Europe'*: The White Paper of the Commission of European Communities', 2001, Vol.1, Issue 2, Article 2, Global Jurist Topics, page 4.
285. See sub-section 3.1.6.5.4 of the present chapter.
286. The GMOs German law is called the 'Gentechnikgesetz'.

3.1.6.5.6   Causality Link

The Italian law no. 349 of 1986 set up a system of liability as a consequence of environmental damage with Article 18.[287] In the Italian law, the whole system of liability lies in a much broader provision of the Italian civil code which is Article 2043 based on a link between the damaging action committed by fault or negligence by a subject to another to which corresponds to an obligation of this subject to compensate for environmental damage. In the Italian law, Article 2043 is what it is called the system of 'Responsabilità aquiliana' which is also applicable to other specific cases of environmental damage.

Similarly, in the Umwelthaftungsgesetz, it is found the same similar type of Italian 'aquilian liability'. The difference between the German and Italian laws as to the causality link is that in the Italian law, the range of goods which are supposed to be protected by environmental protection laws, is narrow compared to the German solution contained in para. 823 of the BGB, and the Umwelthaftungsgesetz offers some advantages favouring the victims of the environmental damage.[288] This is because the German law set up a system of liability which is strict based and contains a 'presumption of causality link' in cases where, according to concrete circumstances, a plant should be considered as such as susceptible of having caused the manifested damage.[289] This 'presumption of causality link' is not applicable in cases where the owner of the plant is able to demonstrate that the plant's activity has been carried out in full respect of the law, provision the latter which explains why, up till now, the Umwelthaftungsgesetz has never been applied.

3.1.6.6   The 2002 Liability Proposal

After the publication of the EU Commission's White Paper [290] which outlined a clear progress in the environmental civil liability regime, the Commission enacted the 2002 Proposal for a Directive of the European Parliament and of the Council on Environmental Liability with regards to the prevention and remedying of environmental damage (thereafter the 2002 Proposal).[291]

Apparently, the objective of the 2002 Proposal was to frame a future legal framework for an environmental civil liability regime which would take into

---

287.   Article 18 of the Italian law no. 348 of 1986 states that: 'Any act committed with fault or negligence, in violation of provisions of law or provisions adopted by law which compromises the environment, causing damage to it, changing it, deteriorating it or destroying it, totally or partially, obliges the responsible party to compensate for it in front of the State'.
288.   See Pozzo, B., '*Toward Civil Liability for Environmental Damage in Europe'*: The White Paper of the Commission of European Communities', 2001, Vol.1, Issue 2, Article 2, Global Jurist Topics, page 10.
289.   Paragraph 6 (1) and 6(2) of the Umwelthaftungsgesetz.
290.   See sub-section 3.1.6.2 of the present chapter.
291.   See the Proposal for a Directive of the European Parliament and the Council on Environmental Liability with regards to the prevention and remedying of environmental damage, COM(2002) 17 final, 2002/0021 (COD), Brussels, 23.01.2002 which is also inclusive of: 1) an 'Explanatory Memorandum' from pp. 2–31; 2) a text proposal for a directive, including three annexes,

account the international level, the US Model and the different pre-existing types of environmental liability in the EU Member States.[292]

Additionally, the 2002 Proposal stresses the need to fully implement the Polluter-pays principle and the role of the competent authorities in relation to the 'orphan damages' (i.e., when the polluter cannot pay for repairing damage).

This section analyses the focal points of the 2002 Proposal, using the framework of analysis drawn up in Chapter 2. The 2002 Proposal's focal points are compared with those characterising the White Paper, as shown in sections 3.1.6.6.1 to 3.1.6.6.7, with the purpose of ascertaining whether the environmental civil liability of the 2002 Proposal regime is still effective, in terms of environmental protection goal achievements, as was the White Paper.

3.1.6.6.1   *Definition of Environmental Damage*

The notion of environmental damage of the 2002 Proposal does not encompass a broad definition of 'environmental damage', such as the one typified in the White Paper,[293] rather only the damage which is considered as being 'significant'. This is the environmental damage as a consequence of (potential) activities considered as dangerous, and which have already been disciplined by EC law previously.

In that sense, Article 2, paragraph 1, point 18, includes into the notion of environmental damage, the damage to biodiversity, waters, soil, subsoil, and, in some cases also, damage to human health.[294]

The White Paper outlined some of the key elements of an effective and practicable EU wide environmental liability regime, including damage to persons, goods and soil pollution, as well as damage to nature. However, regrettably, the 2002 Proposal does not include traditional damages in contrast to the White Paper.[295]

---

pp. 32–54 (the 'Proposed Directive') and 3) an Impact Assessment Form, from pp. 55–65 (the 'Impact Assessment') which duplicate much of the content of the Explanatory Memorandum.

292. See Bergkamp L., '*The Proposed Environmental Liability Directive*', November 2002, European Environmental Law Review, pp. 294–214; Pozzo, B., '*La nuova direttiva sulla prevenzione e il risarcimento del danno all'ambiente*, 2002, Quaderni della Rivista Giuridica dell'Ambiente, Giuffré Editore, pp. 273–292; Hartkampt, A., *et al*, '*Toward a Civil Code*', 2004, Kluwer Law International, page 679 and Clarke, C., '*The proposed EC Liability Directive Half-Way Through Co-decision*, 2003, RECIEL, pp. 254–268.

293. See sub-section 3.1.6.3.1 on the problem of 'Definition of Environmental Damage' treating the definition of environmental damage under the White Paper, compared to the same definition under the Green Paper.

294. The definition of environmental damage of the 2002 Proposal is contained in Article 2 of the 2002 Proposal and is explicitly referred to a) biodiversity damage, which is any damage that has serious adverse effects on the conservation status of biodiversity; b) water damage, which is any damage that adversely affects the ecological status, ecological and/or chemical status of the water concerned to such an extent that this status will or is likely to deteriorate from one of the categories defined in Directive 2000/60/EC with the exception of adverse effects where Article 4(7) of Directive 2000/60/EC applies; c) land damage, which is any damage that creates serious potential or actual harm to public health as a result of soil and subsoil contamination.

295. See White Paper point 4.2.

3.1.6.6.2   Scope of Application

The 2002 Proposal is directed to subjects exercising occupational activities determining a risk (potential or real) to human health and to the environment (the environment and the notion of environmental damage considered here, is the one defined in the aforementioned sub-section, whereby it is worth noting that the scope of application is strictly connected to that which it has been decided to include or not in the notion of environmental damage).[296] The dangerous activities of the 2002 Proposal are still those referred to in Annex I, as well as including other activities determining an identical risk to biodiversity as those referred to in Annex I.[297] The activities under the 2002 Proposal are those which are defined as 'occupational activities' and according to Article 2, paragraph 15, of the same Proposal, the expression 'occupational activities' includes also 'non-profit making activities and the rendering of services to the public' determining a risk to human health and the environment. This new terminology has been used with the specific purpose of substituting the previous legal wording adopted by the White Paper which only used the expression 'commercial and professional activities'. The purpose in fusing this terminology was to also include all kinds of activity, including non-profit activities, such as, all of the activities conducted by the State or other public entities which even though they are not considered as 'commercial and professional' in *strictu sensu*, do represent a threat to the environment.[298]

In cases of environmental damage to biodiversity, liability is extended to any kinds of occupational activities[299] provided that it is demonstrated that the operator is at fault or has been negligent.[300]

3.1.6.6.3   Problem of Who Is entitled to Claim for
*   Environmental Damage*

The initiative for claiming for environmental damage has been attributed, under the 2002 Proposal, to the competent authorities. The competent authorities are defined

---

296. On the interlacement between the two focal points: the notion of environmental damage, and the problem of the scope of application, see Chapter 2, sections 2.1.1 to 2.1.2.
297. The Annex I of the 2002 Proposal contains always the same list of dangerous activities launched originally by the EU level (updated regularly by technical expertise). The title of the Annex I is 'Activities referred to in Article 3(1)', pp. 48–50.
298. See Pozzo, B., '*La nuova responsabilità civile per danno all'ambientale*', 2002, Giuffré Editore, page 276.
299. 'Any kinds of activities' means here also those which are not listed in the Annex I of the 2002 Proposal. In fact it is written in Art. 3, second paragraph of the 2002 Proposal 'This Directive shall apply to significant biodiversity damage caused by the operator of any occupational activities listed in Annex I, and to any kind of imminent threat of such damage occurring by reason of any of those activities'.
300. Article 8 of the 2002 Proposal states 'where biodiversity damage has been caused by an operator in the course of another occupational activity than one of those identified by this proposal as posing an actual or potential risk for man or the environment, that the operator should not be financially responsible if he was not at fault or negligent.

as those designated by Member States, as Article 13 of the Proposal states that 'Member States shall designate a competent authority or competent authorities responsible for fulfilling the duties provided for in this Directive.'

Hence, in the 2002 Proposal, what is clearly excluded, and presents a sign of regression in terms of effectiveness of environmental protection goal achievements compared to the White Paper, is any role whatsoever for civil liability as a tool of private enforcement by private actors against polluters or as a mechanism to overcome barriers hindering access to justice.[301]

The complete exclusion of civil claims by private parties also impeded the Commission in maintaining promises to the European Parliament that the liability regime would also cover damage caused by genetically modified organisms (GMOs).[302] In addition, also the non-official actors such as the groups of interest and the environmental associations have been excluded from the possibility to exercise the *locus standi* in case of *inertia* of the competent authorities when faced to serious threats of environmental damage. Thus, these exclusions are certainly not compatible with the Aarhus Convention, to which the EU is signatory,[303] according to which member of the public should have the possibility to challenge acts or omissions by private persons and public authorities which are believed of breaching environmental national law.[304]

3.1.6.6.4   *Compensation for Environmental Damage*

In line with Article 174 of the EC Treaty (which is the current Article 191 of the TFEU) and with the Polluter-pays principle, the 2002 Proposal requires that it is the potential wrongdoer who shall pay for the costs of restoration as a consequence of environmental damage.

In cases of damage caused to biodiversity, the competent authority of each Member States requests that the wrongdoer who is identified as the operator[305] is to proceed with *restitutio ad integrum* only if acting at fault. In cases where *restitutio ad integrum* would not have been possible, the competent authorities should evaluate different options and, in particular, the possibility of introducing equivalent resources into the environment.

This solution has been inspired by the Lugano Convention,[306] although it is not certain that all of the potential of this solution has been extracted in the correct way, as this solution is only taken as an option which the competent authorities

---

301. See sub-section 3.1.6.3.3 of the present chapter.
302. See Hartkampt, A., *et al 'Toward a European Civil Code'*, 2004, Kluwer Law International, page 679.
303. See Hartkampt, A., *et al 'Towards a European Civil Code'*, 2004, Kluwer Law International, page 679.
304. See Art. 9.3 of the Aarhus Convention.
305. The operator is defined in Art. 2, para. 9 of the 2002 Proposal as 'any person who directs the operation of an activity covered by this Directive including the holder of a permit or authorisation for such an activity and/or the person registering or notifying such an activity'.
306. See sub-section 3.1.3.4 of the present chapter.

might take into consideration. Also, similarly to the White Paper, the 2002 Proposal leaves intact any rights of recourse or contribution by operators against other polluters in situations of multi-party causation.[307]

This means that in cases where the damage would be a consequence of more than one responsible, the Proposal provides that the competent authorities can consider all of the responsible parties solitarily liable or establish, according to equity and with reasonableness, the amount for each responsible. This solution is inspired by the US Model designed under CERCLA according to which the responsible parties have to be joint and severally liable.[308]

In addition, in order to reach a high standard of environmental protection, the proposal designates a series of cases where Member States guarantee the adoption of environmental preventative and remedying measures when, for example, it is not possible to identify the operator or even if identifiable he is not able to pay for the costs caused by environmental damage. The latter hypothesis includes, for example, cases where the operator cannot be considered liable as were not at fault or acting negligently. Whereby it is possible to ascertain that the 2002 Proposal reflects a 'two level approach' which was already pre-existing in the White Paper according to which Member States should have *in primis* (first level) guaranteed restoration of environmental damage to biodiversity and decontamination of sites, by utilising the amount of money paid by the wrongdoer.[309] The second level, being the initiative of the competent authorities being considered as subsidiary in case Member States would have not guaranteed restoration as a consequence of environmental damage.

3.1.6.6.5   *Choice of the Type of Liability Regime*

In cases of dangerous activities listed in Annex I of the 2002 Proposal, the choice of the type of liability is strict based, whilst in cases of activities determining immediate environmental threat or damage to biodiversity, the potential wrongdoer is considered liable only if at fault or negligent in behaviour.

However, the perceived use of civil liability fault and strict based as an instrument in solving legal problems and as a tool for implementing the Polluter-pays principle in the 2002 Proposal, was in fact strongly weakened as a result of the introduction, in the legal act, of certain exclusions from liability. These are the so-called exemptions from liability for the wrongdoer according to which the Proposal does not cover environmental damage as a consequence of 'certain events beyond their control or of specific emissions or events which are allowed by the applicable

---

307. Article 11 of the 2002 Proposal states 'Subject to paragraph 2, where the competent authority is able to establish with a sufficient degree of plausibility and probability that the same instance of damage has been caused by the actions or omissions or by several operators, Member States may provide either that the relevant operators shall be held jointly and severally liable for that damage or that the competent authorities is to apportion the share of costs to be borne by each operator on a fair and reasonable basis'.
308. See sub-section 3.1.5 of the present chapter.
309. See sub-section 3.1.6.3.3 of the present chapter.

laws and regulations or have been authorised by a permit'.[310] In that sense, the 2002 Proposal takes another direction, radically far away from the White Paper, making the law regressive in terms of effectiveness in reaching environmental protection goal achievements.

3.1.6.6.6   Causality Link

With regards to the damage caused to biodiversity, the 2002 Proposal, as remarked in section 3.1.6.5.2, does not consider any kind of limitations in terms of 'occupational activities'. This point might seem of minor importance, however, it has an important implication for causation. This is because if there are no limits in the meaning of 'occupational activities' and these activities are taken in a broad sense, the consequence of this will be that the system of liability will not be a 'real system combining fault and strict liability' (according to which in cases of strict liability the victim must demonstrate causation in order to get compensation) but rather a system without choice and automatically based on the existence of the proof of culpability or negligence between the event and the author of the damage. This was certainly not the perceived perspective of the White Paper.

This means that there are no choices and the system will turn automatically into a *culpa* based system where it will be very difficult for the victim of the environmental damage to establish the proof of guilt,[311] and by consequence the wrongdoer will remain unpunished. In that sense the 2002 Proposal is quite paradoxical.

3.1.6.6.7   Insurance Mechanism

The 2002 Proposal provides that insurance mechanisms or other kinds of financial guarantee are encouraged.[312] In doing this, it is not possible to avoid remarking that the whole system of the insurance mechanism implemented by the Proposal is inspired by US studies associated to environmental damage caused to natural resources and their insurability according to the US experience.[313] The insurance mechanism was a very hot focal point which the drafters of CERCLA had to face. However, the EU legislator did not take into account, from the US Model, the retroactivity of liability in case of environmental damage.[314] This is because, in the US Model, retroactivity in the environmental liability regime caused several

---

310. See 2002 Proposal, Art. 9.
311. It is worth remembering, here, what has been outlined in sub-section 3.1.1.3 of the present chapter, according to which in a fault based regime, there is a need to demonstrate fault which is an obstacle to the victims of the damages as they must prove *culpa* of the potential wrongdoer (if *culpa* is not proved, the Polluter-pays principle is not applied).
312. See Art. 16 of the 2002 Proposal.
313. See for example, the Explanatory Memorandum of the 2002 Proposal from pp. 8–15.
314. In the US Model, the choice of liability, in CERCLA, is retroactive. See sub-section 3.1.5.3 of the present chapter.

problems for the insurance mechanism[315] and the EU legislator was, therefore, afraid to replicate the same failures.

3.2   CONCLUSION

A number of several conclusions can be drawn from the historical-legal comparative approach focusing on the development in context of the law formation process of the Environmental Liability Directive. Starting from the EU level, progressing to the international level, and reaching the domestic dimension of the law, it is found that the concept of liability is used differently according to the levels:

3.2.1   EU LEVEL

A consistent part of the problems related to the focal points arising from the EU level are the same as those characterising the international level which becomes the mirror of the EU level. In which sense, the international level can be used as preventive tool by the EU level and the two regimes cannot be considered in an isolated way from each other. Their interdependency is also explained by the fact that some reverberations of the focal points, such as, the vagueness in the definition of the environmental damage, the difficult choice of liability, the absence of com-pensation funds and the lack of insurance mechanisms, and so forth, are the same focal points than those existing at both the levels.

At the EU level, there is no uniformity in the concept of environmental civil liability. The structure of the European environmental liability regime is based on the Polluter-pays principle, which can hardly perform its function since, at the EU level, it is only required to bear the costs for risks for hazardous activities. In which way, liability is only representing *ex post*, the price which the polluter pays in order to continue its activity.

The meaning of liability at EU level changed into a more public and admin-istrative concept and adapted its features to the context where it finds itself embed-ded, especially with the phenomenon of globalisation and the role of the official and non-official actors in order to secure trade.

At EU level, civil liability moved from a sectorial concept to a general concept as the first initiatives were, initially, focused on the damage caused by waste. Since 1976, it has been observed that there were several political obstacles not only for the different and opposing interests of Member States, but also for the weakness of certain official actors, such as the uncertainty of the Commission in adopting firm positions, and the weakness of the non-official actors. Despite these difficulties in the development of the EU environmental liability regime, it is possible to trace the

---

315.   Monti, A., '*Le responsabilità delle imprese in campo ambientale*', 1998, a cura di A. Gambaro, Milano.

red line which accompanied the birth, the development of the law formation's process of this regime which is to secure the functioning of the internal market together with a high level of environmental protection.

Kept together with this red line, the synergies and interdependencies between levels determined some signals of improvements in the law, such as the extension of liability to the eliminator of waste, and the *locus standi* for the groups of interest. However, the cooperation and the interactions between the EU level, and international level, are not linked enough and the linkage is not sufficiently strong, as there is still a lack of a unitary concept of environmental liability.

This is also due to the fact that the focal points that the environmental law makers have to face are still pending to be solved, especially when what is taken into consideration is the crucial focal point of the definition of the environmental damage.

The difficulty in defining the environmental harm is also depending on another problem, which is the definition of the environment. From the solution of this *dilemma* which is 'how to define the environment' depends not only the definition of the environmental damage but also the functioning of the other focal points placed into a chain of logic sequence of the law (scope of application, problem of who is entitled to claim for environmental damage, compensation, choice of liability, causality link, insurance mechanism). Therefore, these are factors determining the variation of the concept of environmental civil liability, its functioning in the environmental field and its degree of compactness.

Despite the complexity of these problems, the EU environmental liability regime undertook an important change with the White Paper. For the first time, there is an important step toward the creation of a uniform concept of liability, with the attempt to define environmental damage as a unitary concept. In the White Paper, it is finally found an attempt to consider the definition of environmental damage in a three dimensional level system. In considering environmental damage in a holistic way, the EU level tries to shape its law according to the context and the system where the law operates.

For example, it has been observed how the international level and particularly the content of the Lugano Convention can help the EU environmental liability regime, and also how the US experience, in the good or in the bad, can be 'used', in order to increase the effectiveness of the regime in term of environmental protection goal achievements. Which is why CERCLA was always on the table of discussion during the law formation's process of the EU environmental liability regime.

Nevertheless, even though the White Paper directed its attention and efforts on the design of the focal points which make an effective and practicable EU environmental liability regime in terms of environmental protection goal achievements, this was not reflected in the 2002 Proposal.

Compared to the Lugano Convention, the US Model, and the White Paper, the 2002 Proposal manifested a clear step back and a certain regression for the environmental liability regime. Hence, the 2002 Proposal represented more an attempt to find political solutions on the way to negotiate the focal points of the regime in order to find common solutions attracting the *consensus* of all Member States rather than the willingness to design an effective environmental liability regime.

The problem is that the finding of *consensus* among Member States does not always correspond to the searching of effectiveness in terms of environmental protection goal achievements.

Even though the 2002 proposal took into consideration the interactions among the different levels as sources of inspiration for its legal drafting, it does not seem to have reflected on it, and extracted, the good potentials and possibilities deriving from the three levels and the US Model.

3.2.2   INTERNATIONAL LEVEL

At international level, in international treaty law, the types of civil liability – fault based liability; strict liability; and absolute liability -, vary according to the treaties. Strict liability is often preferred.

In the two cases taken under examination, the Lugano Convention and Basel Protocol, there is still a lack of rules concerning responsibility and compensation for environmental harm, a lack of compensation funds, and the absence of insurance mechanisms. This is also because liability for costs cleaning is highly expensive.

Without rules concerning compensation and insurance mechanisms, the Polluter-pays principle is hardly applicable, especially in cases of diffuse pollution or remoteness of the damage. Often, the rules contained in the Lugano Convention and the Basel Protocol, are characterised by the vagueness of definitions such as, for example, the definition of the environmental damage, and the definition of hazardous wastes. In addition, the parameters between legal/illegal pollution are often uncertain.

In this context it is hard to consider the existence of a certain uniformity in the concept of environmental civil liability, also because both the Lugano Convention and the Basel Protocol are not ratified, and not in force. This certainly represents a huge legal and political responsibility for the EU level, which is the only existing level in force, as well as an opportunity for the EU, in 'taking over' the situation in the issue-area of environmental liability.

3.2.3   NATIONAL LEVEL

At national level, the concept of liability is very different according to the legal traditions of the Member States and there are different types of legal approaches in the Common Law and Civil Law countries, where there is often a different way to conceive what liability is in their own sources of laws.

These complexities are further complicated by the focal points facing environmental law in general. The domestic level is, without any doubt, sensible to the reverberations and synergies coming from the 'upper levels'. Members States have to implement international laws and EU laws in a vertical implementation and when there are problems from the 'up' this will be as a consequence reflected 'down' in the implementation phase of the law, impeding the law from being an effective law, able to achieve the initial environmental protection goals.

Globally, the lesson learned from the historical-legal multilevel comparative perspective of the law-formation process of the Environmental Liability Directive, highlights the use of the three level triangular structure -EU, international and national- in helping the law of the European environmental liability regime to take into account the context where it operates and ensure the law approaches closer to an optimal level of harmonisation for environmental legislation.

In addition, from the analysis of the development phase of the ELD since its inception conducted in a multilevel context, it is interesting to note that there is no legal framework for hazardous substances at EU, international and national level which leaves open a further serious legal and political debate in the future of the environmental liability in the hazardous waste sector, and perhaps, pave the way for a new area to research in the future.

Nevertheless, all three levels seem to be involved with common concerns which are to secure trade, implement the Polluter-pays principle and unify the concept of environmental liability. What remains to be observed in the following chapter is, whether in the EU liability regime, the EU legislator has been able to use the mechanism of the multilevel interplay 'strategically' by using the institutional interactions existing among the levels.

Chapter 4

Institutional Interactions in the EU Environmental Liability Regime-Formation

4.1   INTRODUCTION: LINKING INTERNATIONAL RELATIONS WITH THE EFFECTIVENESS OF THE ENVIRONMENTAL LIABILITY REGIME

In the previous chapter, the leading role of the EU in the parallel environmental civil liability regimes has been analysed, and both the influence of the systems that have influenced the EU environmental liability regime, and the influence of the EU environmental law on the international environmental law proven. However, it has also been demonstrated that, despite the leading role of the EU, the EU environmental liability regime is not exempted from certain existing *lacuna* which emerged during the regime formation-process, and which are protracted under the current ELD's legal architecture.[316] These *lacuna* in the European environmental liability regime-formation process are also referred to in terms of effectiveness, compliance and implementation.[317] The non-uniformity of the concept of environmental liability, problems in negotiation and formulation on punctual focal points, difficulties in implementing the Polluter-pays principle, weakness in the role of the non-official actors during the regime-formation process, all characterise weaknesses in the *sagoma* either of the three-levels (EU, international and national) or the US Model.

---

316. The analytical design of current legal architecture of the ELD will be the object of legal analysis in the forthcoming chapter.
317. See Chapter 3 for the existing *lacuna* in terms of effectiveness, but also chapters 5 and 6, especially for the protraction of these existing *lacuna* in the ELD in terms of compliance and implementation.

Drawing on the past in such a manner, and following the path of the theoretical-methodological, politico-legal thinking of the previous chapters, the contribution of the present chapter is to add humbly a further piece into the difficult puzzle unveiling of how to increase the effectiveness in the EU environmental liability regime. Additionally, improving the effectiveness is an important and delicate step towards reaching an optimal level of harmonisation. Thus, it is important, as a starting point, and even prior to evaluating the quality of harmonisation, to perceive the law-formation process of the Environmental Liability Directive also in terms of 'regime', especially in a way that political scientists would understand it, and with an international relation's eye-perception.

The motive for ineffectiveness of the regime under examination, is not only due to the imprecise linguistic formulation determining a low legal quality of regime-rules; difficulties in the negotiation on the formulation of the focal points;[318] or the fact of not having considered such focal points in a chain of logical sequence, as explained in Chapter 2; or a weak or 'cons' role of the non-official actors in its law formation-process.[319]

There is also an existing *lacuna* in the design of the mechanisms of the legal provisions organising the legal participation of the EU in international mixed agreements, as it is in the case of the environmental agreements[320] which *ceteris paribus* cause ineffectiveness of the EU environmental liability regime, and a low level of compliance reflected both in the quality of the harmonisation process and in the implementation phase.

This *lacuna* is also related to the role which the EU plays as an external 'actor'[321] in the middle of the interplay between the international and domestic levels. By consequence, the environmental regime's ineffectiveness is connected with problems of an international relation's nature,[322] and this same connection, also applies *mutatis mutandi* to the case of the environmental liability regime designed under the ELD law's formation process. Frequently, the EU is a cumbersome and inflexible international actor with difficulties in negotiating international environmental agreements and very slow to ratify environmental agreements. Thus, it is mooted, in that sense, as to whether the EU can be regarded as an effective actor in its own right, especially when involved in negotiations on environmental liability conventions and agreements.

The present chapter first, identifies and analyses factors affecting the effectiveness of the EU environmental liability regime and the significance of the institutional design of the configuration of the system where the EU operates as an external actor in the environmental *arena*. Subsequently, it discusses the

---

318. As it will be shown in sections 5.12.1 and 5.12.2 of Chapter 5.
319. The role of the non-official actors during the law formation process of the Environmental Liability Directive will be examined in the section 4.1.4.
320. The environmental agreements falls under the category of 'mixed agreements'.
321. The role of the EU as an external actor is also concerned with the problem of how to conceive 'actorness' or what is an actor in international relations. See also Vogler, J., '*The EU as an Actor in International Environmental Politics*', 1999, Environmental Politics, pp. 24–48.
322. See Vogler, J., Imber, M., '*The Environment & International Relations*', 1996, Routledge.

elements of the mechanism which have been identified in the previous chapter, as potential contributors to effectiveness or causes of ineffectiveness.

Nevertheless, before to suggesting how the environmental liability regime can be more effective, one must be aware of what 'effectiveness' actually means. For that reason, the first sub-section of this section (4.1.1) defines what is meant by 'effectiveness' and most importantly, how effectiveness can be improved. Section 4.1.2 explains that ambiguity in the EU internal rules and procedural provisions contributes to determining ineffectiveness in the EU environmental liability regime, also affecting its compliance and implementation.

The legal participation of the EU in mixed environmental agreements is not legally or clearly organised. In particular, these factors of ineffectiveness are analysed in sections 4.1.2.1, 4.1.2.2 and 4.1.2.3. Therefore, more clarity in the rules of the game together with a good EU law-maker's use of the mechanism for assuring the use of the benefits from the influx of constructive (rather than disruptive) interactions occurring in the EU environmental liability regime formation-process, should also be considered as part of the puzzle enhancing the effectiveness of environmental rules, such as environmental directives.

This is precisely demonstrated empirically in the following sub-sections of the present chapter which explains the case of negotiations of the EC with the Lugano and Basel Convention occurring under the mechanism of multilevel interplay occurring during a spatial-temporal law formation process in the development phase of the Environmental Liability Directive, selected *ad hoc*, namely the cases of: 'worst case scenarios', and a 'best case scenario' for effectiveness. In particular, on one hand, the worst case scenarios shows how the Commission, as an official actor, had in fact a weak role in calibrating Member State's interests and non-official actors' interests in the European environmental liability regime's formation process. On the other hand, the best case scenario photographs and demonstrates the existing issue-linkages between international relations and effectiveness in the environmental liability regime, and the crucial roles not only of the non-official actors, but also of the official actors, such as the Commission. In particular, sections 4.1.2.4.1 and 4.1.2.4.2 cave-in on the thesis advocating that interactions and synergies among levels should be used by the EU law-maker in a constructive and not disruptive fashion as representing a strong potential in the hands of the EU law-maker to be used for the benefits of the quality of the environmental norms of the regime, since the use of such good practice can determine progress in the provisions of the environmental liability regime, as will be shown in the following chapter.

The next sub-section is aimed at identifying and explicating the interactions of the development phase of the Environmental Liability Directive with the Lugano and Basel Conventions (section 4.1.3) and their impact in the effectiveness of the environmental liability regime rules.

Finally, the penultimate section 4.1.4 identifies that the role of the non-official actors 'matters' not only in the regime formation of the Environmental Liability Directive, but also for their contributory role in adding a further piece in terms of environmental effectiveness.

Section 4.2 concludes with modest suggestions on how best to improve the EU environmental liability regime. The same suggestions will then be concretely applied in the next chapter, and culminates in final recommendations for the EU legislator as to how best the optimal level of harmonisation in terms of environmental protection goal achievements can be reached.

4.1.1   How Can an Environmental Liability Regime Be 'Effective'?

In general, the manner in which legal science and political science treats effectiveness conceptually is not the same. However, since the environmental liability regime is not a unique causal phenomenon but a multi-causal one, and that it is concerned both with political and legal problems which need to be treated in a combined and integrated manner, there is a need for a multidisciplinary notion of effectiveness.

Obviously, this certainly does not entail an amalgamation or a prevarication of one discipline over the other, when one is involved in the difficult task of defining what effectiveness is, as a certain balance between law and policy is necessary. Hence, the notion of effectiveness should be an interdisciplinary and equitable one. Nevertheless, the task of defining effectiveness is very complex, as it is a multifaceted phenomenon and difficult to be measured and quantified. However, the act of explanation is in it-self an act of measurement and quantification.

The *fulcrum* of the enigma to the concept of effectiveness referred to in the environmental liability regime, resides in the selection of 'a definition' selected out of the *panacea* of different types of possible definitions for effectiveness.

The present section commences by selecting from the possible definitions offered by both disciplines, the contours of one legal definition, and one political science definition of effectiveness. Once the selection from both fields is achieved, this section continues by combing the two selected definitions as a starting point in order to reach a wholly integrated definition with the purpose of suggesting how an environmental liability regime can be effective in a multidisciplinary manner. The following sub-sections explain the steps to be undertaken and the factors playing a key role in the multidisciplinary concept of effectiveness.

From a legal science point of view, environmental rules presenting a strong degree of enforcement which are clear, precise and unconditional are effective.

The rules of the environmental regimes should also be well formulated, and the objectives and achievements of the regime must also be clearly elaborated and formulated.[323]

Furthermore, effective environmental rules should comprehend a space dedicated to an acceptable degree of justice which entails the participations of citizens

---

323. See the interesting definition of *'The Legal Approach of Effectiveness in International Regimes'* described by Young, O., *'The Effectiveness of International Environmental Regimes – Causal Connections and Behavioral Mechanisms'*, 1999, Cambridge, Massachusetts, page 4.

and other institutions, representing individual or collective groups, participating in the regulation for environmental protection rules such as in the present case under examination, namely the environmental liability regime.[324] The objectives and achievements of the regime should also include the capacity to apply guiding principles and values, such as the Polluter-pays principle and the concept of sustainable development which shall clearly be contained in the formulation of the linguistic wording of the provisions.[325]

The more the environmental liability regime is well formulated linguistically and presents a high degree of enforcement, the more it will be beneficial to the level of compliance.

A high degree of enforcement and compliance will consequentially also be beneficial toward implementation.[326] In substance, the idea of effectiveness for legal science embraces the urgent need to make the law effective and to put the law into a condition to work and have an immediate effect since if the law does not work well or is ineffective, what will suffer will automatically be the policy,[327] which is, in the factual situation, the environmental policy.

Nevertheless the definition of effectiveness furnished by legal science is weak in dedicating certain relevance to the context where the law operates, and to institutionalise strongly the role of the non-official actors and decision-making rules as key element to building a qualitative, updated and progressively effective environmental law. The improvement of effectiveness in the legal sense is crucial as a starting point upon which follows the political science definition of environmental effectiveness. Normally, in environmental law, policy always come first and previously, and what it is interesting, here, is to 'turn it around' and 'correct' ineffective environmental policy by correcting first, the legal definition of environmental effectiveness, which will thus, have a reverberating impact on environmental policy. Therefore, environmental policy relies firstly on the effectiveness of the environmental law, which is why environmental law and policy should be combined and integrated harmoniously.

Political scientists have tendency of defining effectiveness in behavioural terms which means that effective international institutions alter the behaviour of

---

324. See Ulfstein, G., *'Effectiveness of International Environmental Law. Regulations, decision-making, participation and enforcement'* in *'Environmental Law – From International Law too national law'*, 1999, Edited by Basse, E.M., pp. 345–363; De Burca, Graig, P., *'EU Law – Text, Cases and Materials'*, Third Edition, 2008, Oxford., Chapter 6, treating the notion of effectiveness as developed by the ECJ; Snyder, F., *'The Effectiveness of European Community Law: Institutions, Processes, Tools and Techniques'*, 1993, The Modern Law Review, Vol. 56, No. 1. pp. 19–54; Louka *'Fairness, Effectiveness and Word Order'*, 2006, pp. 70–75.

325. See also the criteria for evaluating the effectiveness of existing agreements or instruments in *'The Effectiveness of International Environmental Agreements'*, The United Nation Conference on Environment and Development (UNCED) edited by Sand, P., 1992, Cambridge Grotious Publications Limited, 1992, pp. 4–15.

326. Treves, T., Pineschi L., Tanzi A., Pitea C., Ragni, C., and Jacur, F. R., *'Non-Compliance Procedures and Mechanism and the Effectiveness of International Environmental Agreements'*, 2009, T.M.C, Asser Press.

327. See De Burca, Graig, P., *'EU Law – Text, Cases and Materials'*, 2008, Third Edition, Oxford.

political actors in accordance with institutional objectives. There are several ways of defining effectiveness in international environmental institutions.[328] The choice of utilising the political science definition as the means of defining environmental effectiveness in this section, is justified as integrates and is compatible with the definition of effectiveness in the legal sense presented previously. This is especially with regard to the integrated role of the political science definition of effectiveness in counteracting the weakness of the legal definition of effectiveness, in respect of the roles of the non-official and official actors in terms of behaviour and preferences, and synergistic interactions. The synergistic linkages and reverberations occurring under the mechanism of multilevel interplay are essential for updating the law since a 'law in progress' cannot avoid considering the mechanism of these interactions among different level of sources of law and policy as without these synergistic conditions, there would certainly be the risk to keep an 'outdated law' or a 'law out of the context'.

In the same line of conception, an interesting and inspiring definition of environmental effectiveness is the classical definition of Krasner, according to which and international regime is a set of 'principles, norms, rules and decision-making procedures around which actors' expectations converge in a given issue-area'.[329]

This distinguishes it from an international organisation, and also from international conventions or structures that apply across a wide range of issues areas and it encompasses both informal and rules politically agreed.[330]

The definition of environmental effectiveness operating in a framework of an international organisation is also concerned with the legal procedures involved in the organisation of the legal participation of the same international organisation as an actor acting 'externally' within other international organisations or environmental agreements.[331] Often, the organisation in a given international organisation of such a legal participation, is not clearly formulated and does not reflect, in its legal procedures, the multi-layered context under which the organisation is operating which gives a non-integrative view of the concept of environmental effectiveness. In that sense, the regime should be perceived as an international social institution interacting within a given configuration of a system which is characterised by different levels.

In the view of the author of this book, in the present section, the legal and political science definition of environmental effectiveness are integrated and coexists as a means of suggesting a coherent 'common sense' definition between law and political science.

---

328. See Levy, A., *'Political Science and the Question of Effectiveness of International Environmental Institutions'*, 1993, International Challenges, Vol. 13, No. 2, pp. 17–35.
329. Krasner, S., *'Structural Causes and Regimes Consequences: Regimes and Intervening Variable'*, 1983, International Regimes, London: Cornell U. P, pp. 1–21.
330. Greene, O., *'Environmental Regimes – Effectiveness and Implementation Review'* in *'The Environment & International Relations'*, 1996 edited by Vogler, J., and Imber F., 1996, Routledge, pp. 114–196.
331. In the case under examination, the EU, and its legal participation in other International Organisations or agreements.

This common sense definition considers a different combination of factors operating under a mechanism of interactions where the synergistic linkages; the role of the non-official actors; the capacity of an actor to use strategically synergistic linkages in a constructive way in order to design the focal points; are also all important factors in reaching a certain degree of effectiveness in terms of environmental protection goal achievements. Additionally, the role of the main negotiator as an external actor exercising leadership is significant for a regime in order to be effective. The main negotiator is able to draw attention towards important focal points which are the objects of negotiation and can be utilised to contribute to the success of the regime in terms of effectiveness.

There are three different types of leadership: intellectual, entrepreneurial and structural, that can influence a regime formation process in that sense and draw attention towards these important focal points. Oran Young has analysed this power of influence in regime formation, especially in the case of the EU.[332]

In addition, an environmental liability regime is effective when able to adapt to external changes and present the capacity to be guided by designing principles and concepts such as the Polluter-pays principle and the concept of sustainable development. The notion of environmental effectiveness conceived according to the preceding, is also beneficial for the quality of harmonisation.

In substance, in order to design an effective environmental law and reach optimal harmonisation in environmental regime-rules, it is relevant to find a point of contact between the law and policy and drawn a common definition of effectiveness. Under the conditions of absence of 'such a common definition of effectiveness' between law and policy, the same quality of the harmonisation process is jeopardised. By consequence, the EU environmental liability law will be far from reaching a high degree of optimisation.

---

332. As regarding to the three typologies of leadership conceptualized by Young, intellectual leadership consist of the ability of the negotiator to provide an input of new ideas which draw new policy streams. This type of leadership requires a lot of technical expertise which the Commission is certainly able to provide, and also makes it possible for an actor to manipulate information and ideas. Young also stress a certain attention to this kind of leadership without neglecting, at the same time, the other two kinds of leaderships, entrepreneurial and structural leadership. Entrepreneurial leadership occurs when an actor is able to dominate and steer the activities. In the sense that their behaviour shapes initiatives and manages the mandate by creating opportunity for issue-linkage, like those referring in order to maintain a regional balance between Member States. The entrepreneurial leadership enhances an actor's power of initiative, being their ability to change and decide which items to put, or even to avoid being put, on the domestic agenda (agenda-setting). Structural leadership is characterized by the use of economic and political power in order to reach a result. A typical example of this strategy is the Commission's option to offer side-payments, or promising rewards, to others in exchange for support. The use of side-payments has been applied through issue-linkage, the capacity of an actor to link different issues in a package deal. See Young, O., '*Political Leadership and Regime Formation: on The Development of Institutions in International Society*', 1991, International Organisation 45, 3, Summer, pp. 282–308.

4.1.2   THE ROLE OF THE EU AS AN ACTOR IN ENVIRONMENTAL
                MIXED AGREEMENTS

Effectiveness is also related to the legal provisions organising the legal participation of the EU in environmental agreements. The existing ambiguity is not only impeding the EU from playing an adequate leadership role in the international environmental *arena* but also partly causing the existing *status* of ineffectiveness of the EU environmental liability regime. Such ambiguity has a disturbing impact on the good practices that the EU law-maker could make of being inspired by potentials and opportunities deriving from the interactions and synergies of the intersecting levels of decision-making.

As practical examples of this phenomenon, it is worth noticing the spatial-temporal empirical examples of the cases of the negotiations between the EC with the Lugano and Basel Conventions occurring simultaneously during the development phase of the law-formation process of the Environmental Liability Directive.

These occurred simultaneously and the EU legislator could make a beneficial use of these interactions, especially with regards to the potential solutions offered by the different levels of sources of law which could represent a real source of inspiration for updating the law.

In particular, there are three main factors of ineffectiveness in the environmental liability regime of the Environmental Liability Directive's law-formation process.

The three factors manifested at the time of the negotiations between the EU and the Lugano and Basel Conventions, and are still persisting presently, even after the enforcement of the Treaty of Lisbon, and consist of: the legal basis to conclude environmental agreements; the internal voting procedure in case of mixed environmental agreements, and the question of legal competence of the EU and the level of harmonisation.

4.1.2.1   Legal Basis to Conclude Environmental Agreements

The legal basis to conclude environmental agreements cannot be understood without first having fully understood the way in which the competence[333] in the field of environmental protection is organised by the EU in the treaty provisions, especially after the enforcement of the Lisbon Treaty.

Originally, even before the entry into force of the Single European Act (SEA), and the conferral of explicit external competence in what was Article 174 paragraph 4, of the TEC ('the predecessor' of what has become the current Article 191, paragraphs 1 and 4 of the TFEU), the EC had concluded environmental agreements with third countries and International Organisations and such a competence was called implicit. The current Article 191, paragraphs 1 and 4 of the TFEU hold that the same competence, is now explicit. The Member States'

---

333. The term 'competences' should be understood, here, as 'the powers' of the EU in the field of environmental protection policy.

competence for negotiating and concluding environmental agreements is limited and depends on the division of powers and competencies established by the EU.

Only environmental agreements falling under Article 192 paragraph 4, falls under the scope of application of the regime of rules and Article 218 of TFEU (the 'old' Article 300 of the TEC on the 'shared mixed competence') regulate (environmental) agreements between the EU and third party states and International Organisations.[334]

The competence of the EU for negotiating environmental agreements[335] can be both exclusively or non-exclusively attributed. The difference between exclusively and non-exclusively attributed competencies is reflected in the way the EU negotiates. In policy areas where the EU has exclusive competence (i.e., trade or Common Agricultural Policy – CAP) Member States are no longer allowed to act, as the EU exercise its exclusive competence autonomously. In policy areas where the EU has shared competence between Member States and the EU (i.e., environment) both Member States and the EU are allowed to act.[336]

This means that in cases of exclusive competence in concluding international agreements having as its object an issue of exclusive competence, it is the EU (the Commission) which negotiates with third party countries or international organisations. In cases of shared competence, in what are called 'shared agreements' or 'mixed agreements', which has as its object an issue related to shared competence the negotiator is not exclusively the EU represented by the Commission, but also Member States, and denotes what has been defined as 'mixity' where the Commission and Member States acts jointly.

Thus, the conclusion of mixed agreements is not legally regulated in the EU, particularly in the field of environmental policy.[337] The choice of the legal basis is a crucial and delicate issue, since even if environmental agreements are by definition always called 'mixed', or 'environmental mixed agreements', it is precisely not always 'automatic' that these types of environmental agreements fall under Article 192 of the 'shared mixed competence'.

---

334. This provision establishes a parallelism between the voting procedure within the Council for conclusion of external environmental agreements and the voting procedure for the conclusion of internal corresponding rules. This means that according to Art. 218 para. 8, if the agreement is concerned with issues requiring unanimity voting procedure for the adoption of internal rules, the Council votes through unanimity. In other cases, the Council votes through qualified majority voting and the choice of the voting procedure can be object of conflicts. See for that point Eeckhout P., *'External Relations of the European Union, Legal and Constitutional Foundations'* 2009, Oxford EC Law Library, page 190; and De Sadeleer, N., *'Environment et marché intérieur'*, 2010, Edition de l'Université de Bruxelles, page 67.
335. When treating the competence to negotiate of the EU, it is worth remembering the importance of the Judgment of the European Court of Justice in the AETR Case, Case 22/70 of the 31 March 1971.
336. Eeckhout, P., *'External Relations of the European Union, Legal and Constitutional Foundations'* 2009, Oxford EC Law, and Vervey, D., *'The European Community, The European Union and the International Law of Treaties'*, 2004, T.M.C Asser Press, The Hague.
337. Fajardo del Castillo, T., *'La política exterior de la Unión Europea en materia de medio ambiente'*, Sectión IV *'los acuerdos mixtos'*, 2005, Editorial Tecnos, Madrid, pp. 76–82.

The difficulty lies in understanding and deciding on how to perceive such agreements and if these agreements are 'environmental agreements' in a strict sense. As to the matter, is seems that it is more a matter of 'belief'. The legal basis is decided on the basis of what is the primary aim of a legal document.

For example, some environmental agreements are concerned with biodiversity but yet are concluded under the CAP, and, therefore, do not fall under Article 192 paragraph 4, rather under Article 207 of the TFEU (which was the 'old' Article 133 of the TEU). This mechanism put into functioning by the EU legislator and consisting of attempting to categorise agreements which are concerned with both environmental protection and trade, results in being quite perilous for the legal certainty, the means of regulating effectively these types of mixed environmental problems, and the effectiveness of the environmental regime's rules.[338]

For example, it could raise problems for those environmental agreements having environmental protection, as objective, yet being at the same time, concerned with waste. The demarcation line for what constitutes 'a waste' and 'a product' is very difficult to delimit, as it is quite difficult to establish when it is that a waste ceases to be a waste and becomes a product, or can even be 'reconverted' into something else, such as, a for example, a commodity trade.[339]

In the latter situation, it is easy to understand that the object of such kinds of agreement would not fall under the regime of mixity and under Article 192 paragraph 4 of the TFEU, but rather under Article 207 of the TFEU.[340]

Thus, this situation of ambiguity may incite either the EU or the Member States into making an instrumental use of 'mixity' and solve the ambiguity on the question of division of shares/exclusive competencies as well, since the use of mixity is a *de facto* option that the EU may or may not use.[341]

---

338. In addition, the division of competence is a constantly *de facto* and evolving matter, for instance because the EU internal environmental legislation and also the fast evolution of processing technologies of production, if it is considered, for example, the handling, recycling, reconversion, re-use of waste which sometimes become also a commodity. In that sense there is a risk of establishing a huge gap on environmental legislation due to political problem of allocation of competence at the source.

339. See for example the new Directive 2008/98/EC of the European Parliament and the Council of the 19 November 2008 on waste and repealing certain Directives. In this directive, which has the 'end-of-waste' criteria, it is still difficult establishing the 'end-of-waste' and it is still difficult to trace the line of demarcation which render understandable and fully grasp when is that the agreement is about 'waste' or when is that the agreement is on 'trade' in waste.

340. In substance, in international agreements' negotiations within the EU, it is often very difficult to draw a demarcation line between issues falling under the EU competence and issues remaining under the competence of Member States. See for that point Bretherton C. & Vogler, J., '*The European Union as Global Actor*', 2003, Routledge.

341. The instrumental use of mixity in international environmental agreements can be observed from an EU advantage perspective in having such a mixity, or a Member States perspective advantage in having the same mixity. On one hand, from and EU advantage perspective, environmental mixed agreements offer the EU the possibility of acquiring, controlling and maintaining competence on a given environmental issue area, especially when there is uncertainty in establishing if an issue is under the EU *dominion* or should rather be left under the Member State *dominion* (see, in the text of the previous page, the example on waste).

Hence, despite the ambiguity in regulating international environmental agreements within the EU and the fact that it is often very difficult to draw a demarcation between issues falling under the EU competence and issues falling under the Member States competencies, mixed environmental agreements still continue to be stipulated and are still an integral part of the EU sources of law.

Mixed environmental agreements are imposed and have a productive effect on Member State's legislations, provided that their provisions are elaborated effectively which means that they are clear, unconditional and precise.[342] By consequence, the choice of the legal basis, or the choice of having 'mixity or not having mixity' is not absolute. The EU may wish to conclude environmental agreements besides the Member States, since it wants to avoid international laws violating EU law and Member States implementing international regulations differently.

Since it turns out to be very difficult to establish exclusivity or mixity on environmental matters, both the EU institutions and the Member States have to cooperate,[343] especially in order to adopt what is called 'EU common position'.

On that point, it is wondered as to what this common position is, and why the EU common position is so important in international mixed agreements. The EU effects international outcomes by concentrating the weight of its 27 Member States on a single substantive position called 'the common position', and rendering that position critical to any internationally negotiated agreement.

Critical, but also called pivotal, are those positions that when they defect from a coalition, cause that coalition to become loosing.[344] Analysing the ways in which EU rules shape the content of the common positions and the ways in which common positions, with the weight of the Member States, differently shapes bargaining outcomes of environmental mixed agreements, offers a way to measure the EU effectiveness on international outcomes and explains the level of effectiveness of the provisions shaping an international environmental agreement, or the reason for the inefficiency of regulations on environmental protection.

On the other hand, from an EU advantageous perspective, this mixity, is a way of perceiving the possibility of continuing to regulate a given issue-area, and a joint participation (EU and Member States) permits Member States to control and shape not only regulations, but also their interests through the agreement on international obligations, and shape the development of international environmental legislation during the development formation process of the law and even after the conclusion of the agreement. Also, through mixity, Member States are able to struggle and to push the environmental protective values of the most advanced countries in terms of environmental protection goal achievements and, in such a way, avoid the interference of the EU on sensitive focal points of the regime permitting the acceptance in the negotiating phase of the law, of the levels of environmental protection of the most advanced countries.

342. In that respect, if the EU is a signatory to an agreement on environmental issues, this agreement may have direct effect in the Member States if the provisions are clear, unconditional and precise. See the Case C-213/03 *'L'Étang de Bierre'*, 2004, ECR I-7357.
343. See Art. 4 para. 3 of the TUE.
344. Jupille J., *'The European Union and International Outcomes'*, International Organisation 53, 2, Spring 1999, page 410.

In view of adopting such a common position, the EU institutions, and Member States and Member States' local authorities often meet prior to participating in the conference of the parties. In cases where the competencies are exclusive, the common position is reached in a conference of parties chaired by the Commission. On the contrary, if the competencies are mixed or exclusive Member States' competencies, the common position is reached within working groups (i.e., biodiversity, climate change, or environment protection) chaired by the Council presidency.

The EU negotiator who negotiates together with the Member States within the framework of a given intergovernmental organisation in charge of administrating these mixed environmental agreements could be the Council presidency or the Commission. In general it is the Commission which is the negotiator and represents the EU in external environmental agreements.[345] However, and in practice, or in daily international bargaining within intergovernmental organisations in charge of administrating environmental mixed agreements, even though the Commission legally has the exclusive right of initiative under Article 218 of the TFEU, it is not a unitary actor, especially when it acts in the field of external environmental competence.[346] For example, the EU is a signatory to the multilateral environmental agreements of the Montreal Protocol for Protection of the Ozone Layer,[347] where the EC delegation acted wickedly and passively because the Commission, even if had the initiating role, was dominated by the non-official business (or industrial) actors and the Member State's interests and was therefore unable to dominate in 'block' during the negotiating process as a unitary actor and was therefore condemned to immobility.

Hence, the reason for the difficulty for the EU to act as a unitary actor has to be found in looking at what is that 'especially' when it is about 'environmental agreements'. Environmental agreements and environmental policy differs from the generality of EU external relations, because the EU participation in environmental agreements is strongly influenced by international diplomacy and States' interactions and most importantly, by the power of the non-official actors.[348]

Lobbying of non-official actors, namely the groups of interest, and Member State's preferences, may influence the Commission to make (or not to make or make in an ineffective way) any proposal of legal acts, as has been the case for the proposals of the legal acts in the development phase of the Environmental Liability Directive,[349] and also in the shaping of the 2002 Liability Directive Proposal, contributing to the ineffectiveness of environmental rules (i.e., directives), as it

---

345. Article 218 of the TFEU (corresponding to the 'old' Article 300 of the TEC) regulates representation of the EU during international negotiations and specifies that the Council authorizes the Commission to negotiate on behalf of EU and that the Council has the last word as it has to ratify the international agreement negotiated by the Commission.
346. Bretherton C. & Vogler J., *'The European Union as a Global Actor'*, 1999, Routledge.
347. Protocol on Substances that Deplete the Ozone Layer (Montreal, Canada, 16 September 1987, ILM 26 (1987) 1541, in force 22 September 1989, amended 1990.
348. See Bretherton C. & Vogler, J., *'The European Union as a Global Actor'*, 1999, Routledge.
349. See Chapter 3.

will be demonstrated in section 4.1.4 of the present chapter. Finally, it is worth remarking that in cases where mixed agreements take place, either the Commission or the Council negotiates with an authorisation which is mandatory whilst a mandate for negotiation is optional in the sense that it is not mandatory to have a mandate.

The reason why the mandate is optional and remains a 'top secret' issue and therefore not and never published in the Official Journal, and that it is not always really clear if there is a mandate or not, is made on purpose because the issue of the mandate is kept confidential as it is not strategically appropriate to publish the boundaries of the bargaining space for the Commission as it would weaken its position as an actor internationally. In substance, it could be noted that the option to negotiate with a mandate presents both an advantage and a disadvantage. The advantage is that a negotiator operates with a certain degree of flexibility. The disadvantage is that is not clear which party of the agreement they can call to account for performance of the obligations under the environmental agreement or convention, as it has been the case for the Basel Convention.[350]

4.1.2.2   Voting Procedures to Conclude Mixed Environmental Agreements

In cases of negotiations of the EU in environmental mixed agreements, there is a problem with regards to the voting rules. This is another crucial crux, if it is considered that international outcome strongly depends on the EU international bargaining and the EU voting system. In that sense, the EU affects international outcomes by concentrating the weight of 27 Member States on a single substantive position which has been defined in the previous section as the 'EU common position', and rendering the position crucial to all international agreements by avoiding for example defection, enhancing ratification or an instrumental use of the formation of possible coalitions between Member States during the law formation's process.

Thus, when Member States are represented within an international organisation which is in charge of administrating an international environmental agreement together with the EU, this double representation can pose some problems, for example, since Member States and the EU cannot simultaneously exercise their right to vote. It is either the EU or the Member States which can exercise their right to vote.

A clear distinction should be drawn, here, between the competence to negotiate which may be the Commission, and the right of vote in the external *arenas*, during official meetings taking place under and within the normal administration of international agreements under the *umbrella* of other international organisations

---

350. See for that point Jans, J.H., *'European Environmental Law'*, 2008, European Law Publishing, page 65; and for the mixed agreements in general, see the same author and the same book from pp. 65–66.

and where the EU participate with the right of vote.[351] The international agreement will have to allow the EU to be a signatory Part. Even if the EU is a signatory Part by it-self, each Member State will also have to sign but not all international agreements open-up for the EU as a participating Party formally.

However, it is not clear, who decides and who has the right to vote, whether it is the Commission or the Member States and where are the provisions regulating their voting procedures. In other words, in general it is not clear how the EU internal decision-making process with regards to external policy is organised and regulated especially in the case of the environmental policy.

4.1.2.3   The Question of Legal Competence and the Level of Harmonisation

The question of legal competence is primary to the question of harmonisation, since there is no harmonisation if there is no legal competence. The division of competence, in the field of environment, states clearly that the EU has the power to enter into international agreements on environmental matters but its competence is not in principle exclusive.[352] Thus, it is open to the EU and the Member States to participate together or separately in international environmental agreements. In case the EU has adopted common rules internally to regulate a given environmental issue, the EU is alone competent to enter into international agreements affecting such rules and their scope.[353] In such cases, the EU has an exclusive competence. In cases where that international rules adopted by the EU are in the nature of 'minimum requirements', Article 193 of the TFEU (previous Article 176 of the EC Treaty or the 'old' Article 130t) maintains the effect that it is up to the Member States to participate in mixed environmental agreements relating to the matter covering such rules.

In cases of minimum harmonisation, Member States have a lot of room for manoeuvre and can take stringent measures in terms of environmental protection whilst in cases of total or absolute harmonisation, Member States and the EU shall act jointly and then, Member States are not so free.

This signifies that cases of environmental mixed agreements should be concluded by the EU, being based on Article 192 of the TFEU, Member States can always take action subsequently, and under Article 193 of the TFEU, such agreement, do not infringe the EU international standing and the 'Union' as such.[354] However, there is a serious ambiguity in the linkage between the question of competence of EU and the level of harmonisation. This ambiguity is reflected

---

351. In that sense, the EU competence to negotiate which may be the Commission has to be distinguished from the EU participation with the right of vote, as the existence of such a competence to negotiate does not entail automatically the right of vote.
352. Eeckhout, P., '*External Relation of the European Union – Legal and Constitutional Foundations*', 2009, Oxford EC Law Library, page 201.
353. See the AETR Case 22/70, 131 March 1971.
354. Thieme D., '*European Community External Relations in the Field of the Environment*', 2001, August-September, European Environmental Law Review, page 252.

either on the effectiveness of environmental rules or on the quality of the process harmonisation.

The dysfunctional linkage between the question of competence of the EU and minimum and maximum harmonisation is mirrored in the danger appearing when much needed rules of environmental protection are interlaced with other categories of rules, and interacts, for example, with consumer health or labour protection, and when it is necessary to make a compromise between Article 192 of the TFEU (previous Article 175 of the TEU), and Article 114 of the TFEU (previous Article 95 of the TEU), or in what are called 'environmental protection measures related to internal market effects'.

At least, a solution to this difficulty is to make a compromise between protection of the environment and internal market and grasp the possibility that directives may have a double legal basis, both on Article 192 and 114 of the TFEU.

4.1.2.4   The EC Negotiations on the Lugano and the Basel Conventions

The motive for considering also the EC negotiations and not only the EU legislative instruments separately, is because of the necessity for understanding the causes of the malfunction within the design of the EU environmental liability regime and the level of quality of harmonisation, as well through the external EC relations and representations. Environmental liability regulations can have an important preventive and 'effective-effect', if there is integration of the actors' behaviours into the EU decision-making process occurring simultaneously and synergistically during external environmental negotiations (in the case under examination, the Lugano and Basel negotiations).

In the design of the EU environmental liability regime, legal effectiveness is entrenched and depends on the way the focal points of the environmental liability regime are negotiated. Those negotiations are often focusing on strongly politicised issues of discussions involving both official and non-official actors; the different views of Member States, NGOs or groups of interest which are all influenced by the emotional flow of a political and media attention often pumped up after sudden large environmental polluting accidents.

In addition, those negotiations on focal points are conducted by actors. In that sense, it is worth remembering that each time that an actor behaves in a certain manner in the law formation process, this will have repercussions on the quality, effectiveness, and efficiency of the regime rules and on the level of harmonisation.

In other words, considering EU negotiations in connection with regime rules is useful in order to show how internal EU environmental law and policy can play a crucial role in shaping external international environmental law and policy, and affects the level of harmonisation.

The Lugano negotiations brought the Council of Europe, together with the EU Member States, the European Free Trade Associations (EFTA) and countries of Central and Eastern Europe. The Council of Europe's project was developed under a working group chaired by the Dutch government. The Commission was playing only a minor role in these negotiations even though largely observing the Council of Europe's debate. Additionally, EC environmental legislations have being modelled on previously negotiated Council of Europe initiatives, but also the EC law consistently influenced the formulation of the Lugano Convention. Originally, during the development phase of the environmental liability directive, the EU Member States which were favouring an EC directive were also supporters of the Lugano Convention which became, at the very beginning of the negotiation stages, a key model for a possible directive despite doubts among EU Member States and legal experts as to its coherence as a legal text, and its strategy of using civil law rules to deal with environmental damage.

As outlined in Chapter 3, the Lugano Convention was only signed by nine countries, however none ratified it. Several discussions were concerned with the focal points, such as the vagueness of the definition of environmental damage, the wideness of the scope of application, and the development around the elaboration of an EU environmental liability regime, as these made its enforcement unlikely. Thus, the Lugano Convention initially served as a 'model' for a community regime and was for sometime even considered as an alternative for developing a community specific instrument.

The EC participated in the negotiations of the Lugano Convention under the *formula* of 'mixed environmental agreements' where Member States and the Commission both participated in the negotiations, and where Member State's influence did not play a crucial role in vertical interactions as it was mostly the Commission which was playing a prominent role which, however, determined *de facto* the demise of the Lugano Convention.

Despite these circumstances, in the EU environmental law and decision-making process, the EU had a leading role and influenced international environmental law even though it has not been possible to obtain the ratification of the Lugano Convention.[355]

The Community law did have, at that time, 'integrated' into its body of legislations the Lugano Convention which was, and still is, part of the *aquis communautaire*. Negotiations and debates occurred simultaneously (EU law formation of sources of law and policy coincided with the Lugano Convention and also with the Basel Convention).[356]

The Lugano Convention coincided with the adoption of the Commission's Green Paper.[357] Discussions were focusing mainly on how to design the focal points.

During the course of the decision-making process corresponding to the EU/ Lugano/Basel negotiations, it has been possible to observe the changing attitudes of actors, and outline their interactions, as well as the 'nature of interactions' between the parallel different regimes and institutional actors.[358]

---

355. See Chapter 3, section 3.1.3.
356. See Chapter 3.
357. See Chapter 3.
358. The nature of interactions will be examined in the present chapter in the forthcoming subsection 4.1.3.

Nevertheless, doubts persisted as to, whether or not, the Lugano Convention could have been used as a source of inspiration, as the Commission did not use the potential of the interactions on crucial focal points between the different sources of law strategically, and also because there were no real legal proposals or at least a legal draft of proposed legislation on the table of negotiations, at that exact time, where interactions and behavioural preferences could have been reflected into it concretely.[359]

The Basel Convention was signed by thirty-five Member States under the *consensus* rule as a preferred voting-system for decision-making. Nevertheless, if *consensus* failed, parties could make decisions by two-thirds vote of those present and voting, following the concept of one party one vote. Similarly to the Lugano Convention, the Basel negotiations also took place under the *formula* of mixed environmental agreements.

The constant discussion of the Basel' negotiation debate was centred on the necessity of improving regime-rules on waste liability with particular emphasis on the necessity for having a stricter and severer regime of control of waste shipments. This delicate question exacerbated the opposition between North-South countries and developed-developing countries. On one hand, the Less Developed Countries (LDCs) sought for a total ban on hazardous waste shipments from the Organisation for Economic Cooperation and Development (OECD) countries, and non-OECD countries. On the other hand, developed countries were supportive of a restriction of shipments of waste for final disposal, but allowing shipments of waste for recycling and reuse. This latter trend was later confirmed by the EU Common Position which reached a political agreement on legislation implementing the Basel Convention in October 1992, and finalised it by enacting the waste shipment regulation in February 1993.[360] Even though the latter regulation forbade exports to poorer countries of waste for disposal, it allowed, minimally, the transportation of such a waste destined for recycling and reuse to poor countries.[361]

The Basel Convention negotiations can be split into two rounds of negotiations: the first is called 'First Conference of the Parties' (COP-1), held in Uruguay in 1992; and the second, called 'Second Conference of the Parties' (COP-2), held in Geneva in 1994.

4.1.2.4.1   *Worst Case Scenarios for Environmental Effectiveness*

With regards to the EC negotiations with the Lugano Convention, the aftermath of the 2000 White Paper marked the beginning of the period of the final break with the

---

359. Lefevre J., *'Interactions of the EU Environmental Liability Regime'*, 2002, FIELD.
360. The Waste Shipment Regulation implements the Basel Convention.
361. It is worth noting that transportation and movements of waste destined for recycling and reuse to poor countries was (and still is) going on, even after the ban amendments to the Basel Convention in 1995, according to which the practice of exporting waste, including e-waste, was banned. According the United Nation Development Programme (UNEP), at this moment, the exports of hazardous waste continues.

Lugano Convention which increased with the 2002 Liability Directive Proposal, which was no longer covering civil aspects, but also public liability regulatory aspects. At that point the name 'liability' became misleading because it is not longer covering private aspects.

The period of negotiations on the Lugano Convention, was also characterised by strong disagreements by Member States at the EU level, which were attempting to negotiate the focal points in order to come up with a legal design and compromising wording, and balancing their different legal and political views and perspectives on these focal points.

In the middle of the decision-making process interacting in parallel with the external *fora* dimension (Lugano *arena*) of the EU, where Member States and the Commission were the 'core' parties, the Commission did not really play a strong role in calibrating Member State's interests.

The Commission had, actually, a weak role as it was not able to act in 'bloc' which caused the Lugano Convention to be rejected. Also, among the causes of rejection of this Convention, the fact that the EU was starting to build up its own 'alternative liability regime', was, partly, a cause of defection from the Lugano Convention from the EU Member States, together with the fact that, as mentioned previously, there were no legal drafts or proposed legislation on the table of negotiations at that specific time.

In that sense, questions of ineffectiveness on the quality of the law are intertwined with the question of the external representation of the EU not coordinating its position externally. The failure of the Lugano Convention can be attributed to the weakness of the Commission in coordinating its position on focal points especially in finding a balance on the design of these focal points, in finding a common position of Member States and a uniform voting bloc. Perhaps, in order to avoid such a situation, more clarity in the question of competencies should have been provided previously.

With regards to the negotiations between the EC and the Basel Convention, in the COP-1, the Commission sent only two officials without a negotiating mandate to the meeting. This negotiating strategy was thought to be as a consequence of the COP-1 being negotiated under the *formula* of mixed environmental agreements, and because the EU regulation implementing the Basel Convention had not entered into force yet. In a way, the COP-1 was characterised by a weak representation of the EU.

One of the reasons of this weakness in the EU external representation was due to the fact that the Commission had a weak role in arguing the necessity for a total ban on the shipment of waste for recycling and reuse and nothing was written into the mandate as to the issue. Also, because the EU was not competent on the latter issue, Member States acted as free agents without cooperation and coherency, or without a unitary position.

By consequence, due to the weak diplomatic *savoir fair* of the Commission as a negotiator, Member States fell into the temptation of not respecting the duty of 'external unity and loyalty to Community power', as established in what was at that time, Article 5 of the Treaty of Rome. Member States were not cooperating in order to adopt an EU common position and were divided into the 'proponents' and the 'opponents'. The proponents were Member States advocating the total ban on the shipment of waste for recycling and reuse, amongst which the prominent role was represented by Denmark and the Nordic Countries. The opponents for a total ban, were a group of industrialised countries still part of the EU Common Positions such as, the UK, Germany; but also countries which were not part of the EU Common Position, such as the US, Canada and Japan.[362]

It is worth noting that Denmark, which was the most supportive country in advocating a severe waste liability regime,[363] was not able to push for a total ban, not only because of the weak leadership capacity of the Commission and the absence of a mandate, but also for the *consensus* rules operating in the decision-making mechanism. Additionally, the ban issue was also linked to the question of ratification of the Convention.

The 'ban proponents' were afraid that the 'ban opponents' (including or excluding Member States part of the EU common position) would have not ratified the Convention. The Commission did not take a firm position as a unitary actor and operated only as a mediator between EU Member States and non-EU countries (including the Less Developed Countries, the LDCs) which was probably not enough, as such a role left the victory to the more industrialised countries.

EU Member States were unable to shape the legal text of the Convention because they were acting as free-agents. The Commission shaped the international environmental legal and political outcome, undermining the effectiveness of the environmental liability regime on waste shipment by permitting less and effective strict regime rules.

4.1.2.4.2   *Best Case Scenario for Environmental Effectiveness*

The way the negotiations between the EC and the Basel Convention of the second phase called COP-2 were conducted, was definitely in a manner which made progress and advance the effectiveness of European environmental regime rules, especially as it is confronted and compared with the strategy of the two case scenarios analysed in the previous section, the Basel Convention of the phase called COP-1, and the Lugano case scenario.[364]

The propitious best case scenario characterising the COP-2 favouring environmental effectiveness was prominently ensured by (1) the strong leadership role of the Commission as a negotiator, acting, this time, more than an as a simple 'mediator' between the EC and the external environmental negotiating *fora*; (2) the active role of the non-official actors; and (3) the shift of voting rule in the decision-making process at the EU level. In the COP-2, the first step of a 'strong' position of the Commission was undertaken with the drafting enhancing an EU Common Position on recyclable waste exports to non-OECD countries.

---

362. Jupille, J., '*The European Union and the International Outcomes*', 1999, International Organisation, pp. 408–425.
363. Denmark strongly supported a total ban, and for this, made use of a Swiss text calling for a total ban.
364. See the previous sub-section.

The Commission's leading role pushed toward the non-shipment of recyclable waste exports unless the potential recipient country registered it-self on a special list and indicated its willingness to receive the waste onto its territory.

In the middle of the mechanism of simultaneous and overlapping interplay of negotiations occurring both at EU level and at international level, the Commission was able to calibrate and act more than as a simple mediator 'internally', which means between the Member State's positions at the EU level decision-making (where the Commission was trying to find an agreement among Member States in the decision-making at the EU level), and 'externally' between the EC and also the Parties to the Basel Convention in the second phase COP-2 held in Geneva (trying to find an agreement amongst the EU Member States and the other Parties of the Basel Convention).

Internally, at the EU decision-making level, the Commission had to find a way to group the Member States positions into an EU Common Position. Denmark was able to work in favour of a severe regime.

Also the non-official actors, such as Greenpeace, and lobbyist groups started to lobby together with the Less Developed Countries (LDCs) and with the help of other countries supportive of the EU common position: Greece, Ireland, Italy, Luxembourg Portugal and Spain. The Commission facilitated in finding a compromise on the ban issue both internally and externally because of the EU shift in the voting-system from *consensus* to qualify majority voting (QMV), a shift which made it possible for Denmark to 'isolate' the opponents to a total ban, such as the UK and Germany, and made it possible for the proponents to set a 'revisionist position export waste prohibiting one' getting off, finally, from the political *impasse* on the legal negotiating issue.

The strong role of the EU made possible that the UK and Germany could not maintain the *status quo ante* of an 'export waste allowing position'. This meant that the EU voting rule at EU level, contributed to altering international environmental law and policy on waste negotiations, if Member States could have worked under a QMV system. The EU QMV system could have leaded the more revisionist EU Common Position with an outcome revisionist of the *status quo ante*. The passage from the voting system of *consensus* to QMV system in the environmental liability regime of the waste rules, determined advancement instead of regression in terms of effectiveness of the EU environmental liability regime. This is also the reason why this scenario has been defined in this sub-section, as the 'best case scenario' for environmental effectiveness in contrast to the two 'worst cases scenario' described in the previous sub-section.

4.1.3   INTERACTIONS IN THE DEVELOPMENT PHASE OF THE LIABILITY
          DIRECTIVE WITH THE LUGANO AND BASEL CONVENTIONS

The EU decision-making process of the law formation can occurs simultaneously and in parallel with other *arenas* and therefore overlap with other decision-making processes taking place within the frameworks of other international organisations (i.e., the WTO; the Council of Europe; the OECD; or the UNEP, etc.). In the case of the law-making process of the Environmental Liability Directive, the EU decision-making process was entrenched with the EU external treaty making capacity involved in simultaneous overlapping negotiations with the Lugano Convention (the latter, within the framework of the Council of Europe decision-making) and the Basel Convention (the latter, within the framework of the UNEP).

This interplay between the two levels of decision-making process EU/Lugano and Basel (EU level and international level) in characterised by the influence of one game to the other, and both games (EU and international) exercised a certain pressure from 'game' to 'game'. This overlap, is characterised by a phenomenon of 'reverberation' occurring when the EU level exercise 'pressure' on the Lugano and Basel decision-levels and vice versa which determine interactions and synergistic linkages between levels of sources of law and policy that made the EU legal acts or legal drafts (depending on what is on the table of the negotiation debate) to be influenced by international law and vice versa.[365]

Under these conditions, the role of the EU Commission mattered both in the 'internal EU decision-making' (between EU Member States and other EU official and non-official actors) and in the 'external decision-making process' (between EU Member States, other EU official and non-official actors, and the frameworks of other International Organisations, characterised by other institutions and players and other Parties such as, non-EU Member States). The two internal and external decision-makings are entrenched and interconnected by interactions and synergistic linkages between the levels.

Interactions manifested not only a different typology but also a different nature which open the path for their possible systematic categorisation.[366]

Their different natures, visibilities, intensities, and effects, are dependent on the role of actors, especially the main negotiators in external relations which is, in the case of the development phase of the Environmental Liability Directive entrenched with the Lugano and Basel Convention, the Commission.

In fact, the Commission has in its hands a power-capacity for acting more than as simple 'mediator', by catalysing and increasing interactions and acting as sort of 'bridge-force' amongst the different level of sources of law and policy.

This is in order to take the maximum profit from its 'go-in between force' between synergies in connecting the different levels.[367] At that stage it could be

---

365. See Chapter 3.
366. There are no studies, up to the present time, focusing on the categorisation of interactions occurring during the development phase of the law formation process of the Liability Directive.
367. The Commission has also an important 'potential power' in its hands which linked to its intellectual leadership role in drawing the attention, during negotiation phases, on important focal points by using important principles (i.e., the Polluter-pays principle) and concept-values (i.e., the concept of sustainable development) in order to 'convince ideologically' the EU Member States and Parties of Environmental Conventions in finding a compromise when re-designing more effectively important focal points of the EU environmental regime. In that sense the Commission has the potential power to act as a bridge force among the different levels and contribute to the uniformity of the concept of environmental liability as a consequence of environmental damage.

mooted as to why it is so important to cave-in on the interactions of the different sources of law[368] and policy[369] during the law formation process of a legal act. The answer is because the variation and intensity of the synergistic interactions amongst the different levels of sources of law and policy have an impact on the effectiveness of the environmental liability regime-rules and are able to determine either the advancement or regression of the legal acts in terms of environmental protection goal achievement.[370]

Interactions can be more intense or less intense, visible or not visible or transparent, more synergistic or less synergistic.

Interactions occurring in the case of the development phase of the ELD, both internally and externally are different.

Interactions occurring 'internally' are those which take place during the EU decision-making of the law-making of the Environmental Liability Directive. Interactions occurring 'externally' are those which take place as a consequence of the external role of the EU in environmental agreements (Lugano and Basel Conventions) and which occurs during the mechanism of multilevel interplay in different *fora* (Council of Europe and UNEP) where the law formation of parallel environmental liability regime is taking place on issues which overlap in both levels (EU and international).

The latter case is typical for example in situations when the interactions take place at a negotiating time during which there is no specific legal drafts or legal texts on the negotiating table and it is not so evident (and therefore falls into the category of 'non-visible interactions') the way in which they shape a given legal act even though it is sure that they do shape it.

Not only the Commission, the main negotiator of the external representation of the EU in mixed agreements, but other different actors, such as the non-official actors, can be involved in the environmental liability regime interactions of regime-rules. The Commission often interacts with the industry sectors, NGOs, environmental groups, stakeholders, and Member States, all participating in the formation of the development of legal acts influencing the shape of environmental liability regime-rules.

Interactions have been quite visible in the 2002 Liability Directive Proposal and less evident during the EC negotiations between the EC and the Basel Convention,[371] even though interactions undeniably exist, in the latter case, as it has been explained in the previous section.

---

368. Sources of law such as provisions of proposal of legal acts or legal acts.
369. Sources of policy such as the Green and the White Papers which are policy papers and not pieces of legislation.
370. The period which led to the drafting of the White Paper was characterised by strong interactions occurring at different levels which made the law advancing in terms of effectiveness, if compared with other phases.
371. Interactions have been less visible in the case of the EC negotiations between the EC and the Basel Convention because there were no legal drafts or proposed legislation on the table of the negotiation debate. In that sense, the EU law-maker should have been aware of both the existence and the importance of the synergistic interactions.

Interactions can also have different effects which could be synergistic or less synergistic. The different degrees in the synergistic force, according to what has been explained in the previous sections[372] depends also on the role of actors, and on how these different official actors interact and cooperate amongst themselves, such as, the Commission interacting with the Council or the Parliament, the Member States, and the non-official actors.[373]

The effects of the different synergistic interactions amongst levels can be either proactive or disruptive. The effects of synergistic interactions are proactive when the Commission, in quality of the main negotiator, internally, acts in cooperation with other actors and is able to draw attention onto the focal points of the environmental liability regime, and to cooperate in symbiosis with Member States and the non-official actors in order to improve the provisions determining a severe, effective and updated environmental liability regime.

Contrarily, the effects of synergistic interactions are instead disruptive when the Commission acts alone and is weak in avoiding important elements which are crucial in the design of the focal points from being excluded from their[374] legal wording formulation and allowing the prevarication of political interests to take over on important legal elements belonging to the formulation of the focal points, or in introducing elements determining regression of the environmental liability regime.

Thus, the role of the Commission as a 'key player' is important in the mechanism of the synergistic interactions of the development phase of the environmental liability regime, not only in the 'internal horizontal dimension' but also in the 'external vertical dimension'.

On one hand, analysing the role of the Commission 'horizontally' means explicating the interactions 'internally' or at the EU level of the horizontal dimension between the Commission, Member States, and both official actors (i.e., the Council, or the Parliament) and non-official actors (i.e., NGOs, lobbies, etc.,) in their capacity to shape environmental regime-rules and policy.

On the other hand, explicating the role of the Commission 'externally' entails delving into the role of the EU main negotiator as an 'actor' acting in the middle of the international and domestic level dimensions in what is the real 'essence' of its role in external representation of mixed agreements.[375] Additionally, during the

---

372. See the previous section, and also Chapter 3.
373. The way the Commission interacts with the non-official actors, will be object of analysis in the next sub-section.
374. 'Their' is referred, here, to the focal points.
375. The real 'essence' of the role of the EU as an external actor in mixed agreements unveils the real nature of the EU which is a *unique* nature compared to other International Organisations. The EU is an International Organisation *sui generis*. The question of the role of the EU as an actor in mixed agreements certainly has a more general theoretical significance as point out the problem of defining the legal nature of the EU in international law. In that sense, it is not surprising that the allocation of external powers in the process of European integration does not follow the lines of any other contemporary legal experience. The fact is that to give a positive definition of the legal nature of the EU, and explaining the uniqueness of its feature in the framework of the existing conceptual categories of international law, constitute formidable challenges for legal research and could lead to a renewal of the traditional conceptions of the

negotiating process of a legal act or proposed legislations, both horizontal and vertical interactions can occur simultaneously, in a cumulative (both horizontal and vertical ways) or non-cumulative fashion (only horizontal or only vertical way), phenomena the latter of which is susceptible to determining variation in terms of advancement or regression of the law and on the level of harmonisation.

For example, in the negotiating phase in the lapse of time previously to the adoption leading to the 2002 Liability Directive Proposal, which is to say, the period 1994–2000 which led to the drafting of the White Paper, it can be observed that this phase was characterised by more cooperation and interaction occurring between the Commission and the Council. The presence of strong synergistic interactions determined a certain impacts of the quality and effectiveness of the law and harmonisation.

However, several beneficial and proactive interactions with the international environmental instruments were dropped in the legislative process which led to the 2002 Liability Directive Proposal in a way that rendered this proposal to become more the fruits of political debate and conflicts between Member States interests and their difficulty in finding a compromise rather than maintaining or enhancing the interactions.

Political barriers meant that focal points were negotiated in what could be defined more as a 'business of the law' or 'legal bargaining' or a use of the law (the provisions of the legal acts or proposed legislation) as if it was 'currency of exchange', rather than crucial elements to be designed for reaching high objectives for creating an effective and advanced valuable piece of environmental legislation. Member States were more concerned in bargaining the formulation of the focal points to protect their own interests rather than effectively protect the environment.

Trade offs in this phase meant that focal points and elements were eliminated or reinserted, as was the case for example deriving from the lobbies' pressure which, in the 2002 Liability Directive Proposal, won on several points such as, the issue of the 'exemptions'.[376]

Nevertheless, if it is taken into consideration the subsequent period where more collaboration is found between the Commission and Parliament, and when the Environmental Committee adopted an opinion in January 2003, containing 85 amendments to the 2002 Liability Directive Proposal, it is found that there is advancement in terms of effectiveness and environmental goal achievements. Another fruit of the interactions between the Commission and the Parliament at this time occurred on 14 May 2003, with the Parliament's resolution of 14 May 2003, including 76 amendments, which were good amendments in terms of

---

hierarchy of the sources of law and statehood and sovereignty. See Canizzaro, E., *'The European Union as an Actor in International Relations'*, 2002, Kluwer Law International-The Hague.

376. The 'exemptions' are a sort of 'derogations' from liability as a consequence of environmental damage and they means that in certain cases, the liable parties are not liable for the consequences of environmental damage and shall not pay. The issue of the extensions will be treated in the next chapter.

environmental protection goal achievements being reached. However, subsequently, with the new presidency, the text was changed again at the Environmental Council Meeting of 13 June 2003, when only few of the effective amendments were retained.

Another document, the Council Minister text of 20 June 2003, showed a more public law oriented environmental liability regime, where several interactions from the international instruments were dropped and the new text looked very different from that which was envisaged in the White Paper,[377] or the Lugano Convention,[378] or even in what was proposed in the 1991 Second Proposal of the Commission for the Council Directive on Civil liability for Damage caused by waste retaining all the interactions with the Basel Convention, but which died in 1991.[379]

The last version of the Council Meeting of 20 June 2003, which was also the last legal version before the adoption of ELD, left unsolved several ambiguous issues on focal points, dropping the proactive interactions and left too, discretion in the hands of Member States detaching the environmental liability regime from the holistic vision taking into account synergistic interactions with international instruments and policy.

Nevertheless, since interactions are also driven at the external vertical dimension and that the role of the Commission is involved in eternal representation, the Commission can also play an important role at the external, vertical dimension in representing the EU at the external negotiations influencing international negotiations on important focal points, as it has been the case in the Lugano and Basel Conventions. In that sense, both horizontal and vertical interactions are relevant for the effectiveness of the environmental liability regime as the international outcome depends on the internal EU decision-making[380] and both of the dimensions are intertwined and merged when explicating how environmental effectiveness can be improved and how the optimal level of harmonisation can be reached.

By consequence, the EU environmental legislations should have also been perceived in light of international instruments and the way in which they fit into the configuration of the EU legislation as a whole.

At the present time, in the final text of the ELD, there are still several problems in the way in which the focal points have been formulated as a consequence of the weak role of the Commission, as will be explained in the next chapter.

In the period elapsed from the year 2000–2004, which is also the period previous to the enactment of the final act of the ELD, the Commission should have played a stronger role as a driving force amongst the different levels of sources of law and policy.

A strong role as a 'calibrator' between Member States and non-official actor's interests in striking a balance between law and policy would have permitted using 'strategically' the mechanism of the synergistic interactions proper of the

---

377. See Chapter 3, section 3.1.6.2.
378. See Chapter 3, section 3.
379. See Chapter 3.
380. In particular, as it has been shown in the previous sub-section of the present chapter.

multilevel interplay. In substance, the strategic use of the mechanism of synergistic interactions is important as determine advancement in the regime rule of environmental liability, because it improves both effectiveness and the optimisation of the level of harmonisation as it will be demonstrated in the next chapter.

4.1.4   THE ROLE OF THE NON-OFFICIAL ACTORS IN THE INTERACTIONS
               OF THE 2002 LIABILITY PROPOSAL

The present sub-section aims at individualising categories of the non-official actors[381] operating in environmental protection issues, and at explaining that the role of these non-official actors 'matters' in building a progressive environmental protection law in terms of 'quality'.

In general, the influence on the shaping of EU environmental law by non-official actors is relevant, even though it is very difficult to prove during the development of the law formation process, especially in the shaping of the proposed legislation or legal acts.[382]

In the environmental realm, the non-official actors are divided in two typologies: the non-official business (or industrial) actors, and the non-official environmental actors. The first type of group, is composed of professional organisations (i.e., economic operators operating in the common market which are usually active in the business sector); and the second type of group, of environmental organisations or 'associations' and environmental NGOs (which are active in the field of environmental protection).

The latter type of non-official actors, are in general financially too weak to defend environmental interests effectively, and there is a lack of common strategy enabling those environmental associations to speak with a single voice during the environmental law-making process.

In the case of the development phase of the EU environmental liability regime, as has been observed in the previous chapter, beyond the governmental actors (Member States), and the EU official actors (Commission, European Parliament or the ECJ), the non-official actors, have influenced the law-making process of the development phase of the ELD. At EU level, the role of the non-official actors 'matters' in contributing to designing an environmental law which is updated and effective in terms of environmental protection goal achievements.

Additionally, they are able to influence the decision-making process as they can contribute to a regression of the law by creating a deadlock situation pushing towards a failure of the proposed EU environmental legislation or formation of

---

381. The 'non-official actors' of the EU need to be differentiated from the 'official actors' of the EU. The non-official actors will be defined in the next paragraphs of this chapter. The 'official actors' are the main institutional actors of the EU decision-making framework (i.e., the Commission, the Council of the EU, the Parliament etc.).

382. Kramer, L., '*EC Environmental Law*', 5th edition, page 46; Peterson, J. '*Decision-Making in the European Union: Towards a Framework for Analysis*', Journal of European Public Policy, 1995, Vol. 2, pp. 69–93.

legal acts, or *vice versa*, they can contribute to the advancement of the law, as it has been demonstrated in the analysis of the 1991 Second Proposal of the Commission for the Council Directive on Civil Liability for Damage caused by Waste.[383]

Since the first stages of the development phase of the Environmental Liability Directive, the non-official actors playing a role in the formation of the environmental liability regime, have never been homogeneous.

Thus, heterogeneity was characterising the nature of their typology since they were pursuing different objectives and had different interests and preferences.

The non-official actors were not acting with a common strategy as they were divided into those which were against such an effective EU environmental liability regime preferring a less rigorous environmental liability regime or not have it at all, and those which were in favour of the formation of a strong and effective EU environmental liability regime.

The first type of non-official actors, the non-official business (or industrial) actors which were against an effective EU environmental liability regime, were a grouping of industries, lobbyists, which had as their objective the pursuance of economic profit.[384] The second type of non-official actors, the non-official environmental actors, was having as objective, the protection of the nature *versus* economic profit and was grouping, for example, environmental associations, NGOs, and non-profit organisations.[385]

Nevertheless, after a deep analysis of the 2002 Liability Directive Proposal, and despite the individualisation of the non-official actors, as explained in the preceding paragraphs, it was still not clear at that time, exactly what the identity of these non-official actors acting at EU level was.

However, it was clear that their role was relevant for the creation of an effective EU environmental liability regime and that they were not only operating at EU level, but also at the international and domestic levels.

In addition, it is not only surprising but also worth noting that, the insurers, are also included in the list of 'non-official actors', and have to be considered as such, given that the 2002 Proposal included them in the list of 'European Industrial and Professional Federations and Associations': the 'Comité Européen des Assurances' (CEO) which is actually mentioned by the 2002 Liability Directive Proposal, as

---

383. See section 3.1.2, Chapter 3 on the 'Original Idea of Harmonising Environmental Liability'.
384. The non-official actors which were against the formation of an EU environmental liability regime, are individualized in the present sub-section, as the 'first type of non-official actors', the non-official business (or industrial) actors, and are composed by European Industrial and Professional Federations and Associations, such as, the Union of Industries and Employee's Confederations of Europe (UIECE), the European Chemical Industry Council (ECIC), the Union Européenne de l'Artisanat et des Petites et Moyennes Entreprises (UEAPME), and the Comité Européen des Assurances (CEO).
385. The non-official actors which were in favor for the formation of an EU environmental liability regime, are individualized in the present sub-section, as the 'second type of non-official actors' (the non-official environmental actors) and are composed by representatives of International Organisations (such as EFTA), International Environmental Organisations or Associations, and Environmental NGOs (such as UNEP; European Environmental Bureau, EEB; World Wildlife Fund, WWF; WorldLife Fund; Green Peace; BirdLife, and other Environmental NGOs).

being part (also according to the categorisation drawn in the present sub-section) of the first category of non-official business (or industrial) actors.[386] Thus, the insurance sector contributed in the shaping of the environmental liability regime.

In substance, in the case of the development phase of the law-making process of the Environmental Liability Directive, both types of non-official actors, have an influence during the 'conceptualisation' of the development phase of the law-formation process of the Environmental Liability Directive, from the origins of the regime formation's process, and thus contributed to shape the development of the European environmental liability regime and policy.

However, had the second type of non-official actors, the non-official environmental actors, been given a stronger role, the environmental liability regime of the EU level could have been more effective in terms of environmental protection goal achievements.

The difficulty in that sense has not only to be attributed to the weak role of the latter groups of interest, but also to the weak role of the Commission, especially with regards to the difficulty that this official actor had in calibrating the cleavages between the divergence of interests of these groups of interest within the win-set[387] of the decision-making process of the development phase of the Environmental Liability Directive. In that sense the Commission lacked a leadership role.

The Commission had difficulties in operating in 'symbiosis' with these non-official actors, and the Council was obliged to make concessions to the first group, the non-official business (or industrial) actors which forced the environmental liability regime to shift to being a far more protective regime in terms of environmental protection goal achievements, because permitting 'negotiations' to take place.[388] This means that the non-official business (or industrial) actors did not contribute to elaborate an effective EU environmental liability regime.

The result of this is a negotiation or trade-offs on the focal points of the legal acts and in precise provisions of the legal acts. One example of this negotiation is, in the

---

386. See the 2002 Liability Directive Proposal.
387. In technical political science terminology, especially when referring to international bargaining situations, the notion of 'win-set' created in a given level, is the space of a range created by a certain number of governments (i.e., EU Member States in the case of the EU) of a number of possible x agreements that can possibly and potentially gain a majority domestically. This bargaining space can facilitate the acceptance (or not) of agreements. It is also the connecting link between the levels through synergistic linkages and reverberations. The contour of a win-set exists at all the levels: the contour of a win-set created at a lower level, the domestic level where the groups of interest interacts with other national constituencies; the one situated at a upper level (EU Level); and at international level. It is therefore assumed that a win-set can be created both a lower level (domestic), and intermediate or higher level (EU and international level) of negotiations.
388. See also all the 'Positions Papers' on the 2002 Liability Directive Proposal of the non-official actors appearing in the web-site www.euroactiv.com/en/climate-environment; and also the document drafted by a team-work between BirdLife International, the European Environmental Bureau, EEB, Friends of Earth Europe, Greenpeace and WWF titled '*The European Directive on Environmental Liability – Polluter-pays: from principle to practice? An Environmental NGO commentary on the Environmental Liability Directive: its adoption at EU level and what it means for the future*', July 2004, pp.1–58.

2002 Liability Directive Proposal, the fact of allowing concessions to the non-official business (or industrial) actors of 'defences and exemptions' from the liability regime which were clearly inserted as a business exchange practice. Another example, of such trade-offs occurring in the decision-making process of the Environmental Liability Directive, can be found in the debate on the shaping of the focal point of 'the scope of application'. During the debate of the 2002 Liability Directive Proposal, on 4 March, Member States were in favour of a clearer definition of the scope of application of the directive and its expansion to include issues such as genetically modified organisms (GMOs) and injury to persons.

However, clear indicators would have had to be developed to measure environmental damage. The outcome of the debate in the Council endorsed some of the European Environmental Bureau (EEB)'s concern, (i.e., regarding the inclusion of GMOs and the insurance mechanism).

Hence, the case for negotiation in the shaping of the latter focal point was just an example to show how the focal points, in general, have been negotiated under the influence of the non-official actors.

The synoptical table, see Table 4.1, individualises and explains, in a more specific way, the preferences of the non-official actors in the shaping of the negotiations of the focal points of the EU environmental liability regime and the divergences of interests in the decision-making process of the 2002 Liability Directive Proposal between the non-official actors and the Member States.[389]

Table 4.1   Preferences of the Non-official Actors in the Shaping of Negotiations of the Environmental Liability Regime

Focal Points	*Non-Official Business (or Industrial) Actors*	*Non-Official Environmental Actors*	*Member States*
1. Definition of Environmental Damage	Prefer traditional damage left out	Prefer traditional damage left in	Some prefer traditional damage left out, some prefer left in: divergence of preferences

---

389. The synoptical table, on the next page, has been elaborated using the data and information contained in the 2002 Liability Directive Proposal; the 'Position Paper' on the 2002 Liability Directive Proposal appearing in the web-site www.euroactiv.com/en/climate-environment; and also in the document drafted by a team-work between BirdLife International, the European Environmental Bureau (EEB), Friends of Earth Europe, Greenpeace and WWF titled *'The European Directive on Environmental Liability – Polluter-pays: from principle to practice? An Environmental NGO commentary on the Environmental Liability Directive: its adoption at EU level and what it means for the future'*, July 2004, pp.1–58.

Table 4.1 (cont'd)

Focal Points	Non-Official Business (or Industrial) Actors	Non-Official Environmental Actors	Member States
2. Scope of Application	Not in favour of expanding it (especially to GMOs/all potential dangerous activities)	In favour of expanding it (especially to GMOs/all potential dangerous activities)	Divergence of preferences
3. Problem of Who is entitled to Claim for Environmental Damage	Oppose *Locus Standi* to NGOs	Advocate *Locus Standi* also for citizens	Divergence of preferences
4. Compensation for the Environmental Damage	Are worried about the evaluation techniques for the quantification of the damage	Are in favour of strengthening the evaluation techniques for the quantification of the damage	Doubts expressed with regards to the inclusions of *interim loss*
5. Choice of the Type of Liability	Suggests exemptions and are not in favour of retroactivity	Oppose exemptions and are in favour of retroactivity	Divergence of preferences
6. Causality Link	Oppose joint and several liability and the shift of the burden of proof	In favour of joint and several liability and the shift of the burden of proof	Divergence of preferences
7. Insurance Mechanism	Oppose a mandatory insurance mechanism	In favour of a mandatory insurance mechanism	Divergence of preferences

In the case of the development phase of the Environmental Liability Directive, it is interesting to note how both types of non-official actors utilised the Principle of subsidiary, as an argument for behavioural action. For example, the first type of non-official actors, the group defined as non-official business (or industrial) actors, was also the group which strongly disputed the application of the Principle of subsidiary as what this group of non-official actors was looking for was more for economic profit and to satisfy their interests.

This group of non-official actors was therefore more in favour of 'manipulating' the Principle of subsidiarity by reversing the subsidiarity argument, justifying the necessity for a shift of environmental liability rules on the waste sector from the national level to the EU level. This group was therefore arguing the 'reverse argument of subsidiary' which means that there was no need to shift environmental liability rules from the national level to the EU level, but that there was instead, the need to keep the rules at national level on the basis of subsidiarity.

On the contrary, the second group of non-official actors, the non-official environmental actors, were in favour of the subsidiarity argument, justifying the necessity for a shift from the domestic level to the EU level. This group of non-official actors was acting in favour of implementing a serious EU environmental liability regime and making the law of the legal acts advance in terms of environmental protection goal achievements.

Also, the fact that this group of non-official actors was given a strong role in environmental protection by the EU legislator with provisions ensuring its *locus standi*, determined advancement in the quality of the legal proposal.[390]

4.2   CONCLUSION

In the law-formation process of the Environmental Liability Directive, the point of convergence in the theoretical dialogue between environmental law and policy lies in the concept of effectiveness. The point of intersection between law and policy proves that in order to be effective, the environmental liability regime must rely on a multidisciplinary concept of effectiveness. In that sense, the concept of effectiveness must encapsulate a legal and political definition to be integrated, and coexist in a way of suggesting a 'common sense definition'.

This common sense definition comprehends different factors under a same mechanism of interactions and synergistic linkages among different levels (EU, international and national) of sources of law and policy. Amongst the factors, the role of non-official actors, the capacity of an actor to use, strategically, synergistic linkages in a constructive rather than disruptive way when designing focal points of the regime, are relevant for reaching environmental protection goal achievements, and optimisation of the level of harmonisation.

Nevertheless, some doubts still persist on the full capacity of the EU in exploiting the multilevel system 'strategically' in order to improve the law, doubts which will be concretely verified in 'the field' through the legal analysis into the

---

390. See also section 3.1.5 of Chapter 3.

outcome of the long gestation process of the Environmental Liability Directive: the final draft of the Directive, called from Chapter 5 headed with the abbreviation 'ELD'.

There is an important relationship between the concept of effectiveness and the role of the EU as an external actor in mixed environmental agreements which are reflected also in the quality of the law and in the optimisation of harmonisation or the capacity of the EU to guarantee a good level of harmonisation. The challenge of optimisation of the level of harmonisation through the use of synergistic linkages and interactions deriving from the mechanism of multilevel interplay is to render concrete the benefits deriving from these interactions in a way that the interactions are visible in the output (the law) as an effective product of the decision-making process. This can also be achieved thanks to the power of influence of official and non-official actors in shaping the legal acts under bargaining. The role of the Commission has been crucial in that sense. However, according to the analysis of the institutional interactions in the development phase of the European environmental liability regime, it seems that overall, interactions have been more rhetorical than concrete and effective. This suspicion has to be ascertained and verified deeply in the legal analysis of the final draft of the ELD which will be conducted in the next chapter.

According to the findings emerging from the linkage of international relations with the effectiveness of the environmental liability regime, it has been proven that there is a necessity to have some clarity in the legal procedural rules, especially in the external representation of the EU in mixed environmental agreements.

Approaching this latter delicate aspect means also touching the heart of the question of legal competence of the EU. However, once that competence of the EU is accepted, it is not totally certain that other States or International Organisations will accept it as a fully fledged participant, with the consequence that some of the sources of law will be shared and coexist.

Chapter 5

The ELD on the Prevention and Remedying of Environmental Damage

5.1   INTRODUCTION: APPLYING THE
                   FRAMEWORK OF ANALYSIS

The principal task of the present chapter is to conduct a legal analysis of the ELD through the framework of analysis which has been laid down in Chapter 2 and which is based on the focal points of intersection between the legal and political context of the multilevel dimension.[391] In the present chapter, the goals and ambitions of the ELD are revisited and evaluated not only in compliance with the Polluter-pays principle and the Subsidiarity principle, but also within the context of where the ELD found it-self embedded.[392] The same context is transfused and incorporated into the present legal text of the ELD.

The framework of analysis is based on the use of the focal points and respects their sequential order of analysis, as exposed in Chapter 2 with the specific purpose of sustaining and reinforcing the message that the definition of environmental damage is the capital problem.[393]

Also, the adjustment of the legal wording of its stylistic formulation, in case there should be a redrafting of its definition, would have reverberating effects on the other focal points and render the ELD better in terms of environmental protection goal achievements.

By 30 April 2014, the ELD will be the object of a procedure of revision for possible amendments and a redrafting of its provisions, in accordance with

---

391. The focal points existing at the EU, international, and national levels, as identified in section 2.1, Chapter 2.
392. See Chapter 3.
393. The framework of analysis is based on the focal points and retains the same sequential order which place them in a 'chain of legal logical sequence.' See Chapter 2.

Article 18, stipulating: 'Member States shall report to the Commission on the experience gained in the application of this Directive by 30 April 2013 at the latest. The reports shall include the information and data set out in Annex VI. 2. On that basis the Commission shall submit a Report to the European Parliament and to the Council before 30 April 2014, which shall include any proposals for amendments'. The thesis advocating the necessity to redefine the notion of environmental damage is further sustained in the penultimate sub-section of this chapter, where the interactions between the ELD and other parts of EU law, such as the Habitat Directive, the Wild Birds Directive and the Water Framework Directive, show that if the definition of environmental damage is maintained as such, it will scarcely lead toward a real protection in terms of environmental goal achievements. Finally, some general conclusions are drawn in the last sub-section.

5.2   GOALS, AMBITIONS AND CHALLENGES

On 21 April 2007, the European Parliament and the Council of the EU finally succeeded in adopting an Environmental Liability Directive.[394] As can be seen in Chapter 3, the long gestation phase of the ELD was characterised by a proposal for a directive on Civil Liability for Environmental Damage caused by Waste which was never adopted,[395] and by both Green and White Papers[396] as valuable policy papers reinforcing the environmental liability regime.

The ELD is concerned with the prevention of, and remedying of, environmental damage, and the overall ambitious objective of the ELD is to establish a common European framework of environmental liability for environmental damage to air, water, land, protected species and natural resources. The threefold goals of the ELD, within this framework are as follows:

(1) to harmonise environmental liability by establishing common criteria to which national legislators will have to conform when setting up an environmental liability regime;

(2) to ensure the application of the Polluter-pays principle;[397]

(3) to eliminate situations of internal market distortions and secure trade.

The ELD can be considered as a novel and ambitious instrument realising the prevention and remedying of environmental damage by using environmental international law as a source of inspiration. In order to evaluate harmonisation, in this study, international law is used as a tool, especially the Lugano approach.

---

394. Directive 2004/35/EC of the European Parliament and of the Council of the 21 of April 2004 on Environmental Liability with regard to the Prevention and Remedying of Environmental Damage, OJ 30.04.2004 L 143/56.

395. This is the last 1991 Second Proposal of the Commission for the Council Directive on Civil Liability for Damage caused by Waste. See sub-section 3.1.2, Chapter 3.

396. See sections 3.1.6.1 and 3.1.6.2, Chapter 3.

397. And to ensure also the application of the other two principles: the Principle of prevention and the Principle of precaution.

Although the Lugano Convention is not in force, it has some potential and possibilities that the EU legislator seems to rely upon.

Nevertheless, at the EU level, the legal effect deriving from the interconnections and interactions between these different sources of law, do not have a full impact in terms of improvement in the ELD. This is because the EU legislator should adopt and be inspired by provisions similar to those of the Lugano Convention and the US Model as this would determine advancement in terms of effectiveness and a new way in which to optimise harmonisation in terms of environmental protection goal achievements.

Thus, such a method by which to optimise harmonisation would also ensure that the ELD progresses and facilitate implementation, as it will be shown from section 5.5 and onwards.

In that sense, the EU liability regime should be able to be inspired by the mechanism of multilevel interplay between the different sources of laws (international, domestic and US the Model) 'strategically', by utilising the potential deriving from the interactions of the different levels of sources of law in a manner in which to update and advance effectively the ELD.

The optimality, in term of level of harmonisation, would be determined in a situation where the sources of law coexist without primacy of one source of law over the other. Which means that the special international law (the Lugano Convention and the Basel Convention and protocol) do not prevail over the EU treaty law, also because the Lugano Convention is not in force.

There is no primacy between sources of law, and the sources of law, are not in contrast, which entails that the negative sides of the phenomenon of fragmentation of the law are minimised in the sense that there is no conflict between these different sources of law. Within this system of legal overlap, international environmental law and EU law coexist and complement each other in an integrative way without conflicts and divergences. The sources of law deriving from the different levels are laying in a common system of legal space where the EU is attempting to take benefit from the overlap of the different sources of law in a manner by which to optimise the harmony of the laws. The space of overlap of the different sources of law manifests into a legal space which evolve and opens the path toward a new system of simultaneous interactions and synergies between sources of law eliminating derogations, limits, and conflicts between the legal sources.

Within this same systemic legal context but from a political science perspective, the ELD still partly retains the same ambitions existing in the pre-works of its development phase.[398]

Among the ambitions of the ELD, the Commission still advocate and promote the willingness to face effectively the problems arising from environmental damage to biodiversity and damage under the form of contamination of sites (where waste is deposited) and the phenomenon of loss of biodiversity.[399]

---

398. See Chapter 3.
399. The ambitions of the ELD were already pre-existing in the pre-works of the ELD especially as exposed in the White Paper. See section 3.1.6.2, Chapter 3.

Hence, what makes the difference between the past, compared to the present situation, is that now amongst the ambitions of the ELD, there is not only the goal to harmonise internal markets and achieve environmental protection but also to underline the role of the EU as an external actor with a willingness to be part of the global economy by also promoting environmental protection goals at the external level.

Fundamentally, there is an implicit goal in the ELD linked to the external dimension as the EU through the ELD is attempting to indirectly 'export ideological values' to be protected and promoted politically and legally.

One of these values is 'the concept of sustainability'.

In the ELD, the concept of sustainability becomes a value, at the same level as the concept of 'equality' or 'freedom', and is the carrier of an objective of universal environmental global change, which is to consider economical growth, social rights, and environmental protection, in simultaneous combination and both unified under an environmental pattern of human environmental responsibility. Additionally, the EU combination-economical growth, social rights and environmental protection-, unified under an European environmental liability system, will necessarily have an effect at international level, if it is considered that the EU is a partner, in international external trade relations, of other non-EU States and trading blocs playing within and under different frameworks.

In that respect, the message launched by the EU law makers is to follow the value of sustainability contained in the principles of the ELD, ensure their applicability and launch a new pattern of environmental protection sustaining an economic growth based on the necessity to follow a new model of qualitative rather than quantitative environmental production. In that respect, the ELD become an instrument applying a sustainable developed environmental production by preventing environmental damage trough the Polluter-pays principle.

Additionally, for the first time, in a directive, the EU legislator links the Polluter-pays principle to the concept of sustainable development, both unified under a *unique* umbrella of a 'European model of environmental responsibility'.

In that sense, it is interesting noting, the stylistic and strategic manner through which the EU legislator introduces the concept of sustainable development within the legal architecture of the ELD. This implies that the EU legislator could not avoid connecting the repercussions of the ELD with environmentally damaging events, not only on biodiversity, but also on the economic and social dimensions. This means that the EU legislator has therefore considered the impact of the environmental liability regime on the internal market. As a consequence, the ELD marks the beginning of the period when there is a general awareness of a necessity to recognise 'the value environment' at the same level as the 'the value of sustainable development' in a binomial relationship setting the foundations for the birth of a fundamental principle of environmental protection as a prerogative for a model of eco-responsible economic growth and 'repressive at the source' of environmental damaging activities.

À première vue, the implication of this reasoning might seem banal. However, this latter observation is definitely not true, if it is considered that the legal order of the EU was originally thought of in terms of economic integration ignoring the fact that natural resources were not unlimited or that they were *res communes*, or *res nullius*, left as an inheritance to future generations.[400]

By implication, the unavoidable confrontation between ecologic imperatives (of which the ELD is a carrier) and economic integration, justifies a deep analysis of the compatibility of the kind of regime of environmental protection proposed by the ELD with the last provisions of the TFEU on free movement of goods, services and free competition rules.

In which sense, the ELD gives added valued to the concept of sustainable development since it manifests a large notion of the term 'environment' strictly connected to internal markets. This large notion of the term 'environment', seen in a sustainable perspective, is a carrier of an expanded notion of the term environment based on three strategic pillars: (1) the pillar of the biodiversity dimension (struggle against pollution and protection of biodiversity); (2) the pillar of the economic dimension (notion of consumer to be protected against environmental pollution and (3) the pillar of the social dimension (workers protection against environmental pollution).

In substance, the ELD is therefore a crucial directive for the concretisation of the concept of sustainable development which becomes a plus-value in the ELD. In this way, the ELD becomes the legal act carrier of a new economical-socio-political environmental liability model operating in a top down/bottom-up approach playing a pivotal role between Europeanisation and European Integration.

Of course, the EU environmental law-makers have to be ready and elaborate a legal framework able to design a type of effective environmental law updated to this new multidimensional and 'three-pillar' European model of environmental protection.

In the ELD, the EU manifests a proactive attitude rather than a reactive by promoting that environmental protection has to be combined with the economical growth and internal market. This latter combination clarifies and reinforces the law which in turn ensures that goods circulate freely at EU level, and consequently also improve environmental protection in a global dimension.

In that sense, the ELD is highly ambitious as, through the Polluter-pays principle, its legal text universally advocates harmonising trade and competition whilst taking into account the global context. Nevertheless, this does not mean that these goals and ambitions are really achieved and that the EU environmental normative protection is effective in the case of the ELD.

The ELD is very often unclear,[401] as there are several problems[402] for example, in conceiving and finding a solution for a better legal formulation and

---

400. De Sadeleer, N., '*Environment et marché interieur*', Commentaire J. Mégret, 3e édition entièrement refondue et mise à jour, 2010, Éditions de l'Université de Bruxelles.
401. As it will be shown in the next following sub-sections of the present chapter.
402. The problems were already pre-existing in the development phase of the Environmental Liability Directive. See Chapter 4.

bargaining solutions to the focal points; problems of disagreements among Member States; a weakness in implementation; and in sanctioning.

The EU legislator in the ELD is trying to be inspired by the provisions of the Lugano and the Basel Conventions[403] in order to attempt to clarify the law and improve harmonisation. Thus, clarity in the text of the ELD will certainly have a beneficial effective effect at the domestic level especially when the Member States will be confronted with the implementation. The judges will be facilitated by the improvement of the ELD's provisions especially when they will have to interpret and apply them.

Clarity in the formulation of the ELD is, on one hand, beneficial for the internal market as it will enhance EU competition, and on the other hand, also for the international market outside the EU and for international trade law, as a clear and advanced EU environmental liability regime helps to avoid, for example, the formation of the phenomenon of the so-called 'pollution heavens'.[404]

By consequence, the effect of 'an improved ELD' is to enhance an environmental pattern towards more environmental friendly clean technologies, which entails the establishment of a three level virtual triangle operating in a circle for environmental protection, and, simultaneously, the enhancement of international market competition, and a progress of international commercial law, especially in the field of newly clean and eco-friendly technologies.

Nevertheless, and in practice, even though the EU attempted, through the ELD, to 'do better' than the other legislative levels such as the international and the domestic level of legislation, it is not totally certain whether or not the EU has actually 'amplified' the potential but also the problems of the international level,[405] especially those related to the focal points, and then reversing them at the domestic level of legislation. In that respect, for example, it is not clear if the international level, and the US Model, which often, as it will be shown in the following sub-sections, could offer solutions on how to overcome the ELD's shortcomings, are taken as sources of inspiration by the EU law-maker. The use by the EU law-maker of the possibilities offered by the international level and the US Model (or vice versa the 'non-use' or 'non-optimal use' of the possibilities of the international level and the US Model) would in turn be re-mirrored at the domestic level of EU Member States implementation's process.

From the domestic level, they[406] would be re-incorporated at the international level once again, in 'a sort of boomerang' within a three-level virtual triangle

---

403. The EU legislator re-employs and interconnects the provisions of the ELD with the provisions of the Lugano and Basel Convention. See section 3.2.1, Chapter 3.
404. The phenomenon of 'pollution heavens' exists when, for example, industrial activities also in term of 'waste deposit' are moved in other non-EU countries in order to circumvent the costs of waste-disposals.
405. The international level of the Lugano Convention and the Basel Convention and Protocol.
406. 'They' is referred to the potential and possibilities offered by the international level and the US Model to fill the gap of the ELD's shortcomings. The potential and possibilities could be used or not used by the EU legislator in the drafting of the legal text. In that sense, the EU legislator

operating within a circle, starting from the EU to the international and national level, and reverberating on the other way round, from national to the EU and international level.

Even though the international level is not in force, the use or non-use of its provisions, taken as a source of inspiration by the EU law-maker, would have an effect both on the quality of the ELD's provisions and on the implementation phase. This is mainly due to, as it will be shown in the next sections, the non-use of the potential offered by the international level, or the US Model, leading to a non-optimal level of harmonisation as a result of an inappropriate formulation of the ELD and as a consequence also to a non-adequate implementation. Hence, an appropriate use of the interactions is beneficial for harmonisation.

This latter aspect is very important, as if the EU gives a negative example of harmonisation to the external word, no positive pattern will be launched externally, especially in the fields of international commercial law and in new technologies, which would in turn undermine the unification of the concept of environmental liability. That is why it is so important for the ELD to preserve the 'multilevel thinking' which characterises so much of the context in which it has found it-self embedded since its inception, and also to maintain its proactive role of launching values, such as the concept of sustainability.

5.3   INNOVATIONS AND DIFFERENT DIRECTIONS

The ELD contains a very important 'innovation' which is carrier of a strong message for which it is the operator[407] which has *in primis* the obligation to act, protect and maintain the environment. On that point, it is therefore important to understand that when the text of the ELD highlight that it is the 'operator' which has the primary responsibility and obligations, a relationship must be established between the operator and the fulfilment of the goals of the ELD[408] amongst which, as has been previously discussed,[409] is making sure that the Polluter-pays principle is respected. The choice of the operator as the potential responsible party who must pay if pollutes strengthen the effectiveness of the Polluter-pays principle. The respect of the Polluter-pays principle ensures that enterprises of the Member States understand that there is a necessity to protect trade and to implement the ELD in a straightforward way. As a consequence, if the Polluter-pays principle is not respected and applied because it is not clear who the responsible party is who

---

   has the option of the use or non-use of the potential and possibilities offered by the multilevel context.
407. The concept of 'operator' is contained in Art. 2.6 of the ELD where it is defined as 'any natural or legal, private or public person who operates or controls the occupational activity or where this is provided for in a national legislation, to whom decisive economic power over technical functioning of such an activity has been delegated, including the holder of a permit or author-isation or the person registering or notifying such an activity'.
408. In line with Art. 191 (1) TFEU, previous Art. 174 (1) of the EU Treaty.
409. See the previous section 5.2, second paragraph, point 2.

has to act (for example, if there are several possible definitions of the term 'operator') then this confusion in terms may become an obstacle and jeopardise the process of implementation of the ELD.[410]

Also the competent authorities play an important role in the functioning of the ELD, because they ensure the questions of enforcement of the EU law at national level, whereby it is the operator which has to pay and undertake the necessary measures for repairing the environmental harm.

Even though the ELD is aimed at establishing the foundations for an environmental liability regime on the prevention and remedying for environmental damage in the EU, and has been entitled as the Environmental 'Civil Liability' Directive, the title of the ELD is misleading. The ELD does not offer a real civil liability regime but rather a public law regime to be enforced by administrative authorities.[411]

The ELD combines a public law regime with private aspects, as fault liability and strict liability. The ELD does not offer a 'real civil liability regime' since it does not consider the important shift through which the ELD underwent in the final stages of its development phase.[412] The environmental liability regime has changed from a civil law to a public law compensation scheme. An important shift occurred between the 1989 First Proposal[413] to Directive 2004/35/EC: the 1989 First Proposal was aimed at establishing the foundations for an environmental civil liability regime applicable to damage in the waste sector.

Whilst the ELD essentially provides more for a system reinforcing the police and administrative powers ensuring that the polluters restore the environmental damage, rather than a real environmental liability regime.

Hence, there is the feeling that the ELD is more concerned with developing the procedure of the public authorities in a public perspective by indicating the fundamental principles according to which these procedures should be based upon.

The result of this structure is the set up of a 'European administrative environmental protection legal model' rather than an environmental liability regime. Particularly, the ELD contains the principle of the giving the reason of an administrative act, the principle of transparency and the principle of public participation to administrative procedures.

One of the difficulties of the ELD lies in the problem of competencies of the competent authorities which are supposed to fulfil the obligations set up by the ELD. The competent authorities of the Member States will have certain difficulties

---

410. The problem of the formulation of the term 'operator' will be treated and discussed, further on, in sub-section 5.8.1 of the present chapter.
411. De Smedt, K., '*Is Harmonization Always Effective? The Implementation of the Environmental Liability Directive*', 2009, European Energy Environmental Law Review, p. 1; and Winter G., Jans J.H., Macrory, R., and Krämer L., '*Weighing up the EC Environmental Liability Directive*,' 2008, Journal of Environmental Law, page 2.
412. Winter G., Jan H. Jans, Macrory, R., and Krämer L., '*Weighing up the EC Environmental Liability Directive*', 2008, Journal of Environmental Law, page 2.
413. The 1989 First Proposal for a Directive on Civil Liability for Damage caused by Waste. See section 3.1.2, Chapter 3.

when confronted with this mixture of administrative duties and civil law issues[414] which could differs significantly according to the legal traditions in which the ELD will have to be implemented.[415]

Another difficulty is that Member States dispose of the choice and the form when implementing the ELD. Given that the ELD contains several ambiguous and vague provisions,[416] it is clear that Member State regimes will differ not only because of the varying legal traditions but also due to economic difficulties.

In addition, this type of directive is a 'minimum harmonisation directive,'[417] and the legal foundation of the ELD is based on Article 192 of the TFEU (previous Article 175 of the EU Treaty). Article 192 of the TFEU allow Member States to adopt national laws that go beyond what is permitted at the EU level. Another provision which stress more straightness on Member States force to have more room to manoeuvre, is Article 193 of the TFEU (previous Article 176 of the EC Treaty) which provides that Member States (and by consequence their competent authorities) have the choice and the power to adopt environmental rules to protect the environment which are more strict when compared to European legislation or, in our case, when compared to the ELD. Nevertheless, it should also be remembered that these stricter rules always have to comply with EU law and the EU Treaties, and that Article 193 of the TFEU is not directed toward Member States directly but allows and 'empowers' them to adopt stricter environmental legislations, leaving to them a free way to grasp an open option.

Thus, Article 193 of the TFEU adds even more emphasis on the Member States' freedom of action provided by the above mentioned Article 192 of the TFEU. Article 193 of the TFEU (previous Article 176 of the EU Treaty) acknowledges that because the environment differs in Europe, different solutions are required in the Member States.

In that sense, the whole system within the EU environmental policies is therefore based on the assumption that Member States would make use of Article 193 of the TFEU.[418] The assumption behind this article is therefore that Member States would use the power to adopt stricter rules and standards conferred by Article 192 of the TFEU in order to reach environmental protection goal achievements. The main interest should be to protect the environment rather than the economic

---

414. As it has been outlined in the previous chapters, the Environmental Liability Directive, combined a public law regime with private aspects as fault and strict liability
415. As widely explained in Chapter 3, section 3.1.6.4 dedicated to 'The Different Pre-existing Types of Environmental Liability'.
416. Also because directives are by definition vague.
417. This is refereed as 'level playing field' (as opposed to 'gold—playing field'). The expression of this phenomenon can be found in Art. 16 of the Directive, where it is written that Member States are allowed to 'maintain or adopt more stringent provisions in relation to the prevention and remedying of environmental damage' which means that Member States are free to maintain or not maintain stricter rules for environmental protection or even exacerbate legislations in case of environmental damage.
418. See Jans, J.H, Squitani L., Aragao, A., Macrory R., Wegener, B.W., *'Gold plating of European Environmental Measures?'*, 2009, Journal for European Environmental Planning Law, page 417.

profit of enterprises or let the industrial sector a free way to produce by combining simultaneously economical growth with environmental protection. The idea behind Article 193 of the TFEU is therefore to make industrial development eco-compatible.

Regarding environmental directives in general, some authors have outlined their opinion that, in reality, Member States are not making use of this power to maintain or lay down more stringent standards.[419]

An explanation for this non-usage of the aforementioned articles to implement EU law is that non-official business (or industrial) actors pressure Member States to protect their interests rather than protect the environment.[420]

The consequence is a decreasing use of Article 192 (as a legal basis), and of Article 193 of the TFEU (as derogation clause as regards harmonisation) leads to the jeopardising of the functioning of the system of the minimum harmonisation technique. In addition, in case that those more stringent protective measures are established by the Member States, Article 193 of the TFEU does not anywhere indicate that Member States are allowed to act in contravention of the fundaments of the free movement of goods, or in breach of Articles 34 and 36 of the TFEU (previous Articles 28 and 30 of the EC Treaty), or in contravention to human health or life of humans.

Despite the latter observation, there are still no indications, in Article 193 of the TFEU, to include human health in its formulation. Although there is a reference to health in Article 191 of the TFEU, Article 193 of the TFEU does not include human health in its formulation even though it does refer to or take into consideration Article 191 of the TFEU which sets the overall goals.

In the specific case of the ELD, the impact on harmonisation is partly a consequence of all that proceeded previously. This means, as it will be explained in the following sections, that the ELD is providing, in reality, more for a minimum of harmonisation for 'administrative regulations', reinforcing administrative bureaucratic mechanisms in the hands of the competent authorities 'aiming' at ensuring that the polluter pays, rather than a real minimum harmonisation of 'environmental liability rules' as planned initially amongst the goals of the ELD.

5.4   RELEVANT PRINCIPLES INVOLVED

The Polluter-pays Principle and the Subsidiarity Principle.

The ELD is based on the Polluter-pays principle and must respect, at the same time, the Subsidiarity principle.

---

419. See Jans, J.H, Squitani L., Aragao, A., Macrory R., Wegener, B.W., '*Gold plating of European Environmental Measures?*', 2009, Journal for European Environmental Planning Law, pp. 417–435.
420. The pressure exercised by the non-official business (or industrial) actors has been shown in section 4.1.4 of Chapter 4.

5.4.1   THE POLLUTER-PAYS PRINCIPLE

The important question is whether the ELD is impeding or facilitating the application of the Polluter-pays principle in the *formula* designed by its framework. The ELD frames an environmental liability regime aimed at establishing the Polluter-pays principle.[421] In that respect, civil liability should[422] represents an instrument of application of the Polluter-pays principle. In the preamble to the ELD there is another reference to the principle with an explicit link of the principle to the operator in the sense that it is the operator who must pay in cases of pollution.[423]

The ELD provides for the prevention and remedying of environmental damage and the Polluter-pays principle is also supported by two other principles which are the Principle of prevention, and the Principle of precaution of environmental damage.[424]

The reparative function of the ELD entails that the environmental damage of enterprises caused to the environment must be internalised in the costs of production and that the operators must bear the costs of this prevention.[425]

The preventative function entails also that the costs deriving from an accident are borne by the operator.[426] The ELD traces and establishes a clear general relationship between civil liability and the Polluter-pays principle in a line of thinking based on the obligation of the polluter to pay for restoration carried out by public authorities and ensuring that victims can obtain compensation from the polluter.[427]

---

421.   What it is written in Art. 1 of the ELD is: 'The purpose of this Directive is to establish a framework of environmental liability based on the "polluter-pays" principle, to prevent and remedy environmental damage'.

422.   The term 'should' in that sentence stress the statement followed by the argumentation exposed in the section 5.3 of this chapter that the ELD did not turn up to be a truly 'civil liability regime' as originally envisaged.

423.   In the preamble of the ELD, whereas n. 2.

424.   The effect and interaction between the Polluter-pays principle coupled with the two other Principles involved in the ELD (Principle of prevention and Principle of precaution) renders the Polluter-pays principle it-self stronger in terms of environmental protection goal achievements since it gives more emphasis to what the 'pivotal role' of the Polluter-pays principle is in protecting natural resources. The Polluter-pays principle operates in the middle of 'past situations' and 'future situations' of possible environmental damage's commitments. In substance, the Polluter-pays principle, if coupled with the Principle of prevention and the Principle of precaution, gains more importance in the 'go-in-between function' between a 'past-restorative phase' of environmental protection or '*ex-post* damage situation' (only when the damage is there, or only once and after the environmental damage occurred) and 'future-preventing phase' of environmental protection or '*ex-ante* damage situation' (before the environmental damage occurs) by producing, in the latter case, an incentive effect on the operators to take preventative measures as they will otherwise have to pay if the damage occurs.

425.   In the preamble of the ELD, whereas n. 21.

426.   In the preamble of the ELD whereas n. 18 – the operator must also recover the costs incurred as a consequence of environmental damage which are sustained by the public authorities.

427.   De Sadeleer, N., '*Polluter-Pays, Precautionary Principle and Liability*' in Betlem G., Brans, E., '*Environmental Liability. The 2004 Directive compared with US and Member State Law*', Cameron, 2006, pp. 89–101.

Nevertheless, there are other more specific relationships between the Polluter-pays principle and important focal points of the environmental liability regime which are still unclear and under researched, as they have also not as yet been related to cases brought before the ECJ.

The existence of ambiguity in these relationships allows doubts to emerge as to whether the legal architecture built up by the EU legal drafter of the ELD is really facilitating the application of this principle.[428]

With regards to the relationship between the definition of environmental damage and the Polluter-pays principle, a first obstacle of the ELD, in the effective application of the Polluter-pays principle, is linked to one of the prerequisites for environmental damage. According to one of these prerequisites, there is environmental damage only if the subject of the environmental damage is identifiable. This means that if there is environmental damage and the polluter is not identifiable, then the Polluter-pays principle cannot be applied.[429]

As to the relationship between the Polluter-pays principle and the choice of liability, it could be posited as to why the choice of liability in the ELD (whether it is fault based or strict based liability) should be important in relation to the Polluter-pays principle. The ELD provides for a dual system of liability: strict liability[430] and fault based liability.[431]

The choice of one system rather than the other can facilitate or impede the application of the principle which will in turn reflect on the facilitation or in creating obstacles to the implementation of the ELD.

As already discussed in section 3.1.1 of Chapter 3, in cases of a fault based liability regime, the need to demonstrate fault is considered as an obstacle to the victim of the environmental damage, since it must prove *culpa* of the potential wrongdoer. In that sense, if *culpa* is not proved, then the Polluter-pays principle cannot be applied; this results in an obstacle to the implementation of the ELD.

Another important relationship is between the Polluter-pays principle and the choice of the legal basis for the ELD. The Commission chose Article 192 of the TFEU (previous Article 175 of the EC Treaty) in contrast to the 1991 Second Proposal of the Commission for the Council Directive on Civil Liability for

---

428. Reflections from the oral presentation by the author of this book on the topical discussion *'Environmental Liability and the Polluter-pays principle'*, NELN, December 2007, Aarhus.
429. The Polluter-pays principle will remain merely 'a principle in the air' and will not be applied in an effective manner at the domestic level by the courts of the Member States, if the definition of environmental damage, as it stands within the current legal architecture of the ELD, still persists in maintaining the same drafting characteristics which are now present.
430. Strict liability for environmental damage caused by any of the occupational activities listed in Annex III (which means that there is environmental damage even in absence of fault or negligence).
431. Fault based with regards to all the other remaining activities not included in Annex III. Therefore liability is fault based (there is damage in cases of damage committed by an operator through fault or negligence) and the regime of fault based liability applies in cases of environmental damage to protected species/natural resources. Liability is in those cases fault based, since this damage could derive from activities not included in Annex III (in that case *culpa* must be proved).

Damage caused by Waste which choose Article 114 of the TFEU (at that time period it was the 'predecessor' Article 100 A and Article 95 of the EC Treaty).[432] The use of Article 114 of the TFEU (previous Article 95 of the EC Treaty) instead of Article 192 of the TFEU (previous Article 175 of the EC Treaty) would have entailed that the traditional harm (to property and health) should have been included in the notion of environmental damage.[433]

The objective of the ELD seems, on that point, quite limited because it applies only in cases of damage of 'public nature' in the sense of something which does not belong to anyone or is not the object of ownership because it cannot 'be owned' but rather belongs to the collectivity excluding pollution that causes personal or private property damage.

Actually, there are numerous situations where the public sphere overlaps with the private sphere. In that sense, environmental damage does not involve only the public sphere but also individual rights and the private sphere where very often the natural resources are present in the private sphere, it would be quite difficult to keep these two sphere separated. For example: any privately owned lake or marsh is part of the integrated ecosystem which sustains fish or birds. The two spheres are strictly interconnected and they cannot be considered as separated.

Restoration should therefore be inclusive of both spheres and should be based on ecological concepts.

Thus, especially in these latter cases where private and public spheres overlap, the Polluter-pays principle will remain in vain, due to the choice of the legal basis of the particular legal act.[434]

Another obstacle in the terms of application of this principle is based on the relationship between the Polluter-pays principle and the issue of retroactivity.

The ELD is non-retrospective,[435] since it does not apply to damage caused by events which took place before 30 April 2007; or damage caused by events which occurred after 30 April 2007 if deriving from an activity set up and ended-up before 30 April 2007; or damage for which 30 years has elapsed since the event which determined it occurred.[436] The ELD does not have retroactive effects in cases of historical contamination. However, this is diametrically opposed to the Polluter-pays principle. The non-retroactivity of the ELD reflects the approach adopted by the majority of Member States[437] even though the majority of the contaminated

---

432. See section 3.1.2, Chapter 3.
433. The ELD does not cover these types of damage and does not apply in cases of personal injury or damage to private property or to economic loss, and does not affect any rights regarding these kinds of damage, as mentioned in the whereas of the ELD's point n. 14.
434. The choice to use Art. 114 of the EU Treaty instead of using Art. 192 of the EU Treaty and *vice-versa* affects the enforcement's force of the general environmental principles of law such as the Polluter-pays principle.
435. Differently to the Lugano Convention and CERCLA, see section 3.1.3, Chapter 3 on the Lugano Convention, and section 3.1.5, Chapter 3 on the US approach.
436. See Art. 17 of the ELD.
437. In most part of the Member States legislations, the regulations covering contaminated sites and the obligations to restore them, fixes liability rules only after the dates of enforcement of these environmental liability rules.

sites, in Europe, are those affected by the historical contamination which is not covered by the ELD.

Finally, the obstacles to the application of the Polluter-pays principle are certainly more visible in the relationship between the Polluter-pays principle and the problem of the quantification of the environmental damage when comes time to repair the environmental damage. The obstacles to the application of this principle are more visible in Annex II of the ELD,[438] which will be the focus of section 5.8.

The Polluter-pays principle and the obstacles to its application are related to the problem of the quantification of the environmental damage because there is a direct link between civil liability and the quantification of the environmental damage.

In fact, the criteria for quantification have a direct incidence on the preventive function of liability, and the prevention of the quantification is important for the risk assessment and for the insurers. The insurers have to take into account the quantification of the damage if they have to draw up insurance policies.

5.4.2   THE SUBSIDIARITY PRINCIPLE

An important question is whether the ELD respects the subsidiarity criteria established by the Subsidiarity principle enshrined in Article 5(1) of the TEU. As previously discussed in Chapter 3 of this book, the 1987 Single European Act had with Article 130 R (4), already introduced into Community law, the idea of fulfilling the requirements of the concept of subsidiarity solely with regards to environmental policy.[439]

The Subsidiarity principle was, subsequently generalised for the EC policies (and not restricted solely to environmental policy) with the former Article 5 of the EC Treaty. Following the Lisbon Treaty, the current paragraph 3 of Article 5 of the TEU states that in areas which do not fall within the Union exclusive competencies, such as the environmental one, the Union shall take action, in accordance with the Subsidiarity principle 'only if and in so far as the objectives of the proposed action cannot be sufficiently achieved by the Member States and can therefore, by reason of the scale or effects of the proposed action, be better achieved at Union level.'

Hence, the Subsidiarity principle has a multidisciplinary 'double soul', because it represents a parameter of review or standard of review, not only from a legal dimension (to check the right sharing of allocation of competencies between the EU level and the Member States level and what the EU should regulate or remains in Member States' regulatory competencies), but also from a political dimension (to check if 'by reason of the scale or effects of the proposed action, its objectives can be better achieved at EU level'). From a legal dimension, the first

---

438. Titled 'Remedying of Environmental Damage' and dealing with the measures aimed at repairing environmental damage.
439. See section 3.1.2, Chapter 3.

step is to ascertain whether the EU has competencies to act. This corresponds to the first test which is the 'legal basis test' which addressed the question of whether the legal act is within the material scope of powers conferred on the EU. The second political dimension is the 'subsidiary test'.[440] Thus, the double soul of the Subsidiarity principle exists because on one hand, the principle outlines the need to regulate the exercise of powers, and on the other hand, to justify their existence. This latter point reflects the political significance of this principle and gives to the principle it-self, a strong political significance.

The Subsidiarity principle from a legal dimension is similar to a 'legal test', checking as to whether the allocation of competencies in terms of regulations between the EU level and the Member State level is 'justified'. By implication, the Subsidiarity principle is similar to a rule of allocation of competencies between the EU level and the Member States level, the breach of which could be sanctioned.[441]

However, it was only after the Amsterdam Treaty that the Subsidiarity principle begun to gain a real 'legal recognition' and only after it was incorporated into the Subsidiarity Protocol of the EC Treaty text did it become 'legally binding.' In that sense, the breach of the Subsidiarity principle should be understood as a lack of justification in explaining the shift from Member States' rules to the EU level, with the consequence of a possible sanction imposed on it.[442]

The principle has considerably influenced the substance of environmental policies. In fact, following its enshrinement in the Article 5 of the Treaty, the Commission has the obligation (when adopting a given legal acts and/or a proposition of legal acts) to lay down clearly what the motivations are or what the legal foundations justifying the necessity to adopt the given legal acts and/or a proposal of legal acts are, and therefore, to evaluate their conformity[443] with the Subsidiarity principle. Thus, what should be noticed immediately is that there is a link between the Subsidiarity principle and the question of the legal basis justifying (the necessity of) an action at the EU level.[444]

The second point of Article 5 of the TEU points out the existence of two criteria which could justify the necessity of an action at the EU level: (1) when the objectives of the proposed action cannot be sufficiently achieved by the

---

440. See also Olsen, E.B. & Sørensen, K.E., (eds), '*Regulation in the EU*', 2006, Thomson A/S, pp. 38–39.
441. De Sadeleer, N., '*Environnement et marché intérieur*', Commentaire Maigret J., 2009, Éditions de l'Université de Bruxelles, Institut d'études Européennes.
442. The 'test' of allocation of competences is aimed at understanding whether there is a motive justifying the shift from Member States rules to the EU rules for regulating a given issue-area (i.e., the issue-area of environmental liability as a consequence of environmental damage) and also at understanding the reason why there is a need to have a given area regulated at the EU level rather than simply leaving it at the domestic level. See also, for a deep insight of the Subsidiarity principle, Olsen E.B. & Sørensen Engsig K., '*Regulation in the EU*', 2006, Thomson Sweet & Maxwell, Chapter 2, pp. 35–81.
443. The conformity of the legal acts and/or the proposal of legal acts with the Subsidiarity principle.
444. As discussed in sub-section 3.1.2, Chapter 3.

Member States; and (2) that this action, would be better achieved at the EU level compared to the Member States level.

Therefore, the justification for the necessity to shift the environmental liability rules as a consequence of environmental damage from the Member States level to the EU level seems to be inadequate, as what it is demanded by the EU legislator, is 'not only to do, but to do better.'

In the text of the ELD, the justification for the necessity for action at the EU level can be found in its preamble.[445]

Further justification, with regards to the ELD, for the shift from the Member State level to the EU level of environmental liability rules is the existence of a considerable number of pre-existing EC regulatory instruments.[446] This means that the EU legislators are not operating in a new sector rather they have considerable experience in that field, in contrast to that at the Member State level.

The issue of conformity of the ELD to the Subsidiarity principle has opened an academic debate among legal academics.

One author[447] outlined the argument that an important aspect justifying the necessity for a Community action is the trans-boundary nature of the environmental damage which means that ecological damage with trans-boundary nature only, justifies an EU intervention.

According to this line of reasoning, the EU intervention would be justified only in cases of damage regulated by the EU Habitat Directive,[448] the Wild Birds Directive,[449] and the Water Framework Directive[450] with the exclusion, for

---

445. What is written in the ELD's whereas of the point n. 3 is: 'Since the objective of this Directive, namely to establish a common framework for the prevention and remedying of environmental damage at a reasonable cost to society, cannot be sufficiently achieved by the Member States and can therefore be better achieved at Community level by reason of scale of this Directive and its implications in respect of other Community legislation, namely Council Directive 79/ 409/EEC of 2 April 1979 on the conservation of wild birds (4), Council Directive 92/43/EEC of 21 May 1992 on the conservation of natural habitats and of wild fauna and flora (5), and Directive 2000/60/EC of European Parliament and of the Council of 23 October 2000 establishing a framework for Community action in the field of water policy (6)'.

446. As the Wild Birds Directive (Council Directive 79/409/EEC on the Conservation of Wild Birds, OJ 1979 L103/I as amended by Directive 2006/105, OJ 2006 L 363/368) the Habitat Directive (Council Directive 92/43/EEC of 21 of May 1992 on the Conservation of Natural Habitat and Protected Species, OJ 1992 L 206/7) and the Water Framework Directive (Directive 2000/60/EEC of the European Parliament and the Council of the 23 October 2000 establishing a Framework for Community Action in the Field of Water Policy) and all the instruments targeted to protect water and the biodiversity. See, for that point, de Sadeleer N., and Born, C.H., '*Droit international et communautaire de la biodiversité*', 2004 Paris, Dalloz, pp. 470–472.

447. Berkamp, L., '*Implementation of the Environmental Liability Directive in the EU Member State*' 2005, ERA.

448. The Habitat Directive 92/43 on the Conservation of Natural Habitats and Wild Fauna and Flora of 21 May 1992, OJ 1992 L 206/7.

449. The Wild Birds Directive 79/409 on the Conservation of Wild Birds, OJ 1979 L 103/I as amended by Directive 2006/105, OJ 2006 L 363/368.

450. The Water Framework Directive 2000/60 of the European Parliament and the Council of the 23 October 2000 establishing a Framework for a Community Action in the Field of Water Policy.

example, of cases where there is no element of trans-boundary nature, such as soil pollution.[451]

Other authors do not share this line of reasoning, as they advocate that the Subsidiarity principle is not impeding the EU legislators from also adopting environmental regulations for ecological damage in cases where the trans-boundary element is not so important.[452]

The European Commission stated that the ELD has among its main goals, to confront in an efficient way the problems of environmental damage through contamination of sites and the loss of biodiversity.[453]

Given that the ELD treats the prevention and remediation of environmental damage to waters and biodiversity, which are issues under the domain and overlap with the three directives so far mentioned,[454] the ELD can be maintained to be in conformity with the Subsidiarity principle in those fields (water and biodiversity) which opens some doubts as to the conformity of the principle in cases of environmental damage to soil.[455] In that sense, soil protection does not present a clear environmental liability regime, except for the existence of some directives on the waste sector.[456]

However, this latter matter is still pending evaluation as, for the time being, there is a draft soil directive which has been recently issued which is the draft on a new Framework Directive on the Protection of Soil. The Council failed to reach political agreement on this Directive in December 2007.

The final compromise, which provided for a larger degree of flexibility for Member States and reduced costs for implementation was not acceptable for a blocking minority for reasons related to subsidiarity and proportionality. Discussions at a technical level continued in 2008.[457]

In the following sub-sections, further clarity will be forthcoming on the *formula* which should make it possible for the ELD to apply the Polluter-pays

451. This is taken into consideration by the ELD in Art. 2, para. 1, letter C).
452. De Sadeleer, N., and Born, C.H., *'Droit International et Communautaire de la biodiversité'*, 2004, Paris, Dalloz.
453. COM(2002) 17, page 4.
454. The Habitat Directive 92/43 on the Conservation of Natural Habitat and Wild Fauna and Flora; the Wild Birds Directive 79/409 on the Conservation of Wild Birds; and the Water Framework Directive 2000/60/EC establishing a Framework for Community action in the field of Water Policy.
455. De Sadeleer, N., *'Les Responsabilités environnementales dans l'espace européen'*, 2006, Brulant page 738.
456. For example, one of those directives, is Directive 86/278/EC.
457. See COM(2009) 504 final – Report from the Commission on Subsidiarity and Proportionality, 16th Report on Better Lawmaking covering the year 2008, page 7; and also COM(2010) 547 final – Report from the Commission on Subsidiarity and Proporionality, 16th Report on Better Lawmaking covering the year 2009, page 8 on the Commission's proposal that was supported by the European Parliament, but stopped in the Council by a blocking minority of delegations, some of which opposed the proposal on the grounds of subsidiarity, and others because of expected costs and administrative burdens. The file was a priority of the Spanish presidency in the first half of 2010, but a *consensus* has still not been reached.

principle and respect the Subsidiarity principle at the same time, with regard to a number of focal points. In which respect, it is posited, as to whether the result in terms of environmental goal achievements for the ELD will be successful, as the way in which the focal points are designed is often a compromise.

The focal points which will be treated in the section following the present chapter such as: the definition of environmental damage; the problem of who is entitled to claim for environmental damage; the choice of liability and the cases of exemptions from liability; the causality link; compensation as a consequence of the environmental damage and the measures of reparation; and finally the insurance mechanism are, as already introduced in an anticipatory way in the introduction to Chapter 3,[458] the result of obvious tradeoffs. These tradeoffs are clearly mirroring political compromises issued through clear negotiations.

5.5   DEFINITION OF ENVIRONMENTAL DAMAGE

Environmental damage in the ELD is a notion which includes three types of specific natural resources: (a) damage to protected species and habitats;[459] (b) damage to water;[460] (c) damage to land.

The notion of damage to protected species and habitats is quite narrow since the damage must be damage to one of the species of birds included in the list in the Wild Birds Directive and their habitats, and damages to species listed in the Habitat Directive and any other species or habitats determined in the same way by the Member States.[461]

The damage to water is solely the damage falling into the scope of the Water Framework Directive.

The damage to land (soil) is solely the damage as a consequence of land contamination, which determines a significant risk to human health[462] or if the negative pollutants which are present in the ground adversely affect the human health, in contrast to the damage to water, where the human health criteria does not apply.

---

458. See the section 3.1, Chapter 3 titled 'Introduction: the Context of the ELD. The Structure of the Historical Comparative chapter'.
459. As covered by Council Directive 92/43/EEC of 21 May 1992 on the conservation of natural habitats and the protection of natural habitats and of wild flora and fauna, OJ L 206 of 22.07.1992 and Council Directive 79/409 EEC of the 2 April 1979 on the conservation of the Wild Birds, OJ L 103 of 25.04. 1979.
460. As covered and defined by the commonly known Water Framework Directive, which is Directive 2000/60/EC of the European Parliament and the Council of the 23 October 2000.
461. Article 2, para. 3 of the ELD which means that Member States have the opportunity to enlarge the scope of the ELD and include species which are not contained in the list of the ELD but included in the lists at the national level and therefore covered by national law. This means that Member States are free and have room to manoeuvre in deciding whether to enlarge or not to enlarge the scope of application of the provisions of the ELD.
462. As stated in section 5.2 of the present chapter, Art. 193 of the TFEU does not include human heath.

The notion of damage to soil is therefore less restrictive when compared with damage to protected species and natural habitat, as it considers the human health component. Thus, the EU legislator took another direction when defining damage to soil as the definition did not only consider the damage to biodiversity or to natural resources[463] such as in the cases of the type of environmental damage mentioned in (a) and (b) above,[464] but also included damage to human health. The environmental damage to natural resources only (not inclusive also of the damage to human health) is the environmental damage which belongs to an 'ecological vision' of the protection of the environment. However, the environmental damage to soil 'enlarges' the notion of environmental damage to human health and belongs to an 'anthropocentric vision' in the way it encompasses the damage to human health where human beings are also considered to be included in the protection of the environment.

Hence, on that point, it is hard to understand why this anthropocentric vision should pertain to the notion of environmental damage to soil only, given that, in the case of environmental damage to water, there could also be several damaging situations reverberating from the ecosystem to the humans and damaging to human health as well.

In contrast to the White Paper,[465] the ELD does not include, in the definition of damage, the so called traditional damage which is damage to goods or individuals.[466] Private individuals do not have the rights to be compensated in cases of environmental damage or in cases of an imminent threat of damage.[467] These types of damages are difficult to regulate through the mechanism of civil liability.

The reason why these kind of damages are so difficult to be regulated through the mechanism of civil liability is because environmental damage caused to collective goods such as 'the environment' (where the human being is the vehicle of the damaging activity) does not present the characteristic of being an individual right or a personal right and does not belong to anyone[468] and for that reason does not allow for the existence of a right of compensation in cases of a breach of 'a right to enjoy a healthy and unpolluted environment.'[469] In addition, the distinct

---

463. The environmental damage to natural resources only (not inclusive also of the damage to human health) is the environmental damage which belongs to an 'ecological vision' of the protection of the environment.
464. See the first paragraph of this section.
465. See sub-section 3.1.6.3 titled 'Comparison between the Papers', Chapter 3, on the 'unitary approach of the notion of environmental damage'; and also sub-section 3.1.6.3.1, on the 'Definition of Environmental Damage', and the corresponding footnote of this section, last sentence.
466. In the whereas of the ELD, n. 14.
467. Article 3, para. 3 of the Directive states 'Without prejudice to relevant national legislation, this Directive shall not give private parties a right of compensation as a consequence of environmental damage or of an imminent threat of such damage'.
468. The air, the water, are *res communes*; the flora and fauna are *res nullius*.
469. De Sadeleer, N., '*Les Responsabilité environnementales dans l'espace européen*', 2007, Brulant, page 743.

interactions between the different environmental components such as the *flora* and *fauna* are not covered by the ELD.[470] Therefore, the scope of the ELD is rather restricted even though Member States have the opportunity to enlarge this scope. However, if Member States do not enlarge the scope of the ELD, the scope remains restricted.

5.5.1   COMPARISON WITH THE DEFINITION OF ENVIRONMENTAL
         DAMAGE AT THE INTERNATIONAL LEVEL

The definition of environmental damage in the ELD differs significantly from the more extensive definition of environmental damage in the Lugano Convention, as it has been described in section 3.1.3.1 of Chapter 3. In fact, according to this Convention, the environmental damages which have to be considered as 'relevant' should not only be those caused to the environment but also those which have an impact on human beings as a consequence of all environmentally damaging situations, as formulated in the Lugano Convention in its Chapter 1 of the 'General Provisions', point 7. The damages in the Lugano Convention are conceived of as: 'loss of life or personal injury; loss or damage to property other than to the installation itself or property held under the control of the operator, at the site of the dangerous activity.'[471]

In substance, the definition of environmental damages under the Lugano regime are those touching the 'private sphere' (death, personal injury or damages to goods), as well as damages to the landscape.

The Lugano Convention conceives of environmental damage 'in general' (all damages which could touch personal individual rights) and which are susceptible to being repaired according to civil law regulations. Whilst in the ELD, environmental damage is conceived of as damage to biodiversity, namely the protection of species, natural habitat, land and water.[472]

In the Basel Protocol,[473] environmental damage is the damage occurring during the trans-boundary movements of 'dangerous wastes' in the area under the jurisdictions of (one) of the Contracting Parties.[474] Similar to the Lugano Convention, in the Basel regime, the definition of environmental damage is the one stipulated in Article 2 of the Basel Protocol which is not inclusive of environmental damage 'purely' to biodiversity. Even though the ELD is not inclusive of traditional damages, in contrast to the Basel Protocol, the ELD partly overlaps with the definition of environmental damage of the Basel Protocol, as both (the ELD and the

---

470. In contrast to the Lugano Convention where they are: see sub-section 3.1.3 of the Lugano Convention of the Chapter 3.
471. This is the definition contained in point 7, of Art. II under the 'definitions' of the Lugano Convention.
472. See previous pages.
473. The text of the Basel Protocol is available on line at www.unep.ch.
474. See sub-section 3.1.4.1, Chapter 3 and also Art. 3, para. 1 of the Basel Protocol.

Protocol) considers as being 'environmental damage', the damage as a result of the transportation or movement of dangerous substances.[475]

The definition of environmental damage, stipulated under Article 2 of the Basel Protocol, is not inclusive of the pure damage to natural resources. In fact, it considers damages as being suitable for compensation only when there are damages involving loss of life and personal injury;[476] damages determining costs of measures of reinstatement of impaired environment;[477] and also 'loss of income' directly deriving from an economical interest in any use of the environment.[478] In contrast to the ELD, the definition of environmental damage, in the Basel Protocol, is restricted to waste. The notion of 'waste' under the Basel Convention regime was less restricted and treated more severely compared to the same definition under the Basel Protocol as the Convention was also inclusive of 'hazardous waste.'[479] Whilst the current Article 3, paragraph 6, letter b) of the Protocol restricts the scope of application of the Protocol to the case of 'hazardous waste' existing at the national level (domestic level of the Contracting Parities)[480] by the State of Import of waste solely, and the Protocol applies only if the damage occurs in the aforementioned Importer State.

In fact, with respect to the waste which has been classified as 'hazardous' by the State of Import but not by the State of Export, the importer shall be liable until the disposer has taken possession of the wastes. Thereafter, the disposer shall be liable for the waste.

However, despite the fact that the State of Import considers and defines as 'hazardous' the waste which the State of Export is to export within its territory, exports continue to take place. This means that neither the way in which the definition of waste as 'damaging the environment' has been negotiated and designed under the Protocol, nor the fact that the State of Import considers the waste 'dangerous', are strong enough argumentations to discourage waste exports.[481]

---

475. In the Annex III of the ELD, under the 'activities' referred to in Art. 3(1) in the second part of this article, it is written that environmental damage is the damage as a consequence of 'waste management operations, including the collection, transport, recovery and disposal of waste and hazardous waste, including the supervision of such operations and after care of disposal of sites, subject to permit or registration in pursuance of Council Directive 74/422/EEC of 15 July 1975 on Waste and Council Directive 91/689/EEC of 12 December 1991 on Hazardous Waste'.
476. See Art. 2, para. 2, letter C, point (i) and (ii) of the Basel Protocol.
477. See Art. 2, para. 2, letter C, point (iv).
478. See Art. 2, para. 2, letter C, point (iii).
479. See Art. 3, para. 1 of the Basel Convention. In fact, Art. 3, para. 2 of the Basel Convention take into consideration 'waste' defined as 'dangerous' from the national legislations of the Contracting Parties.
480. In addition, the Basel Convention was even more rigorous with regards to the definition of hazardous waste as imposed in its regime even if waste is defined as 'dangerous' from the national law of the Contracting Parties involved in the trans-boundary movement only (one Member State).
481. Fodella A., '*Il Protocollo di Basilea sulla responsabilità per i danni derivanti dal movimento tranfrontaliero di rifiuti pericolosi: il 'perfetto' è davvero 'nemico del buono'?*', a cura di Tullio Scovazzi, Osservatiorio Internazionale, 2000, Rivista Giuridica dell'Ambiente.

In any case, even though there are lists stating what is dangerous and what is not, neither at the time the Basel Protocol was drafted nor at the present time, is there a definition of 'dangerous waste' or 'hazardous waste', as pointed out in the conclusion to Chapter 3 of this book[482] and also by Fouad Bitar[483] when he highlights that 'il n'existe à ce jour aucune definition internationallement acceptée de la notion de déchets dangereux. Toutefois, il convient de rappeller la definition de déchets dangereux adoptée par l'Organisation mondiale de la santé'.[484]

Through the legal comparative analysis between the international level and the EU level, this section outlines the fact that the ELD presents signs of regression when compared to the solution offered by the international level.

The Lugano Convention and the Basel regime, point out a wide perception of the environmental damage with a wide and general notion of the damaging activities including the human dimension, and thus avoiding narrowing down the definition of environmental damage, such as the one negotiated in the ELD. Such a shortcoming, identified in the ELD through comparison with the international sources of law, should be filled out by using the potential and possibilities offered by the international level. The advancement of the ELD should be achieved in line with the solutions offered from the international level which would open the way for upgrading and updating the ELD.

5.5.2   Comparison with the Definition of Environmental Damage in the US Model

The definition of environmental damage in the CERCLA is not as restricted compared to the definition of environmental damage in the ELD. The CERCLA's conception of environmental damage is much broader[485] since the ELD conceives of environmental damage to soil only in cases of the existence of a negative risk to human health and excludes environmental damage to air except for airborne elements.[486]

The ELD conceives as damage only that which is caused to natural habitat and protected species (and water), whilst the US model, with CERCLA, includes within the notion of environmental damage the whole biodiversity (water, land, animals and plants) of any kind of environmental *media* or the interactions between abiotic and biotic natural resources.

---

482. See section 3.2, Chapter 3.
483. Consultant at the United Nations.
484. Bitard, F., '*Les mouvements transfrontaliers des déchets dangereux selon la Convention de Bale. Étude des regimes de responsabilité*', Section 4 entitled 'Le champ d'application', 1997, Paris, Ed. Pedone.
485. See the US definition of environmental damage in sub-section 3.1.5.1, Chapter 3.
486. See in the ELD, whereas n. 4.

CERCLA provides that the quantification of environmental damage has to be achieved by evaluating the damage to natural resources and also the value of the services of benefits which the same natural resources were offering before the environmental damage.[487] The ELD does not cover economic damage even though the ecosystem (water and land) offers economic and social advantages which are often very difficult to quantify (i.e., the landscape view). In CERCLA, this is not the case, since the federal American law has taken into account restoration of natural resources and also of the value of services or benefits from the services which the same natural resources were providing prior to the occurrence of the environmentally damaging event. As already introduced in section 3.1.5.1 of Chapter 3, CERCLA does not provide for any compensation in cases of environmental damage to private individuals as it conceives of the environment as a public issue or a public domain. Hence, both the US and the EU responded by creating liability schemes for damage to the environment some two decade ago. Although neither scheme provides for liability for personal injury or property values, leaving this to the 50 individual US States and EU Member States, respectively. Both the US Model and the EU do not seem to have found a solution for the potential conflicts between environmental protection rules containing human health protection and rules of environmental protection aimed to protect natural resources under an economic *formula* of environmental sustainability.

In conclusion, this section shows that the notion of environmental damage in the US Model is much wider compared to the same notion in the ELD. The latter is quite limited and presents several shortcomings. In this section, the purpose of the comparison between the ELD's notion of environmental damage with the US Model's definition of environmental damage, serves to show how it is possible to update the ELD formulation, by using some potential aspects of the US Model which could or better should represent a source of inspiration for the ELD, especially where:

- the ELD definition of environmental damage is only comprehensive of the human component in the damage to land which is, the latter notion of 'land' a very narrow notion compared to the US model where the term 'land', is perceived in much wider perspective;
- the ELD excluded the 'air' except for airborne elements whilst the US definition does not exclude the air;
- the ELD considers only the species and protected habitat where the US definition of *biota* is comprehensive of the whole biodiversity, and takes into account the interactions of different environmental *media*.

---

487. This entails that in CERCLA, the environmental damage is evaluated by comparing it with the *status quo ante*. In which sense, one should be aware and should dispose of data in relation to the pre-existing situation and must be aware of the situation before the damage occurs, in order to be able to compare the *status quo ante* with the *post*-damage situation, otherwise the comparison between the two phases would not be possible (and it would not be possible to quantify the environmental damage and by consequence to apply liability).

5.6 SCOPE OF APPLICATION

The scope of application of the activities determining environmental damage is rather narrow,[488] as in the case of the definition of environmental damage. In fact, the activities in the ELD selected by the EU legislator and determining environmental damage are only those which are mentioned in Annex III of the ELD[489] which determine a significant potential or real risk to health and environment.[490] By implication, the scope of application is therefore strictly 'enchained' and dependent upon what has been chosen by the legislator to be considered as damage or from what has been decided and negotiated as being part of the definition of environmental damage.

The ELD in Annex III lists what the conditions are in respect to carry on and maintains these activities (such as for example, authorisations, special conditions and registrations). However, in cases of damage to biodiversity, this method of choosing and individualising what the professional activities determining the environmental damage are does not really apply, as liability is extended to any kind of professional activities, even those not mentioned in the EU law provided that it is possible to demonstrate *culpa* or negligence of the potential wrongdoer.[491]

The scope of application is a focal point which is extremely dependent from the notion of environmental damage and belongs to the 'chain of logical sequence' of the focal points characterising the environmental liability regimes at different levels.[492] In general, it will be only those activities susceptible of determining 'the environmental damage' (and not 'other' environmental damages) defined by a legislator that will need to be protected by environmental regulations.

On that point, a question emerges as to why the EU legislator has decided to retain the same definition of activities[493] defined on the basis of the definition of environmental damage and also lists the conditions for carrying on these activities,[494] if, in the cases of damage to biodiversity, liability is extended to 'any kind of professional activities', even those which are not mentioned in the

---

488. The scope of application is also narrow as a consequence of the fact that the definition of environmental damage is narrow.
489. More specifically, the activities selected in Annex III, from paras 2–7 of the ELD are: 'waste management operations including collection, manufacture, transport, disposal of waste, hazardous waste, incinerations, discharge into waters, manufacture, use storage of dangerous activities, plant protection products, and transport of genetically modified organisms'.
490. Whereas of the ELD, n. 8.
491. Article 3, para. 1, letter b) of the ELD.
492. See section 2.1, Chapter 2 on 'The Chain of Logical Sequence of the Focal Points at EU, International and National Level'.
493. The activities which are included in Annex III of the ELD.
494. The conditions to carry on the professional activities are contained in Art. 3, letter b) which stipulate that the ELD shall apply 'to damage to protected species and natural habitats caused by any occupational activities other than those listed in Annex III, and to any imminent threat of such damage occurring by reason of any of those activities, whenever the operator has been at fault or negligent'.

Annex III of the ELD, but provided that (or with the only conditions that) it is possible to demonstrate *culpa* or negligent behaviour of the potential polluter.

Hence, being aware of this strict interconnection between the definition of environmental damage and the scope of application, the EU legislator has provided for a sort of artificial extension or enlargement of the scope of application by providing the option to Member States of considering activities other than those mentioned in Annex III, in cases of negligence of the operator.

The extension of the scope of application has been done *a posteriori*, without changing the notion of environmental damage first, probably as a way to avoid a 'renegotiations' among the Member States of the definition of environmental damage which would have been, in any case, difficult to reach.

Nevertheless, the negative effect of this voluntary extension will be that some Member States will enlarge the scope of application and others will not, which will increase disparities in the degree of liability for the operators. Additionally, some competent authorities will have to act more than others, which will certainly contribute to the increase of disharmonisation instead of harmonisation as the means of regulating the environmental harm in Europe. The reason why some competent authorities will have to act more than others is because they are responsible for the obligations set up by the ELD, amongst which, those related to the crucial task consisting in evaluating the seriousness of the environmental damage.[495]

5.7   PROBLEM OF WHO IS ENTITLED TO CLAIM FOR ENVIRONMENTAL DAMAGE

The ELD prescribes that both the competent authorities and the operator undertake all of the measures of prevention[496] and reparation[497] as a consequence of environmental harm. The prevention and reparation of the environmental damage is therefore the central issue of the ELD, together with the Annex III.[498]

In the prevention and reparation of environmental damage, it is important to identify and differentiate between those who are the 'active claimants' and those who are not the active claimants but rather the 'passive subjects.'

The active claimants are called, in this section, 'active' because they must 'act directly' to claim for environmental damage. The active subjects are in the ELD the so-called 'competent authorities' and play a key role in administrating and providing that reparation is concretely done, once that they[499] ascertain the existence of environmental damage.

---

495. See Art.11 of the ELD.
496. Article 5 of the ELD.
497. Article 6 of the ELD.
498. Articles 5, 6 and 7 of the ELD.
499. 'They' is referred to the competent authorities.

Conversely, the 'passive subjects' are those who must 'passively bear' the costs of reparation as a consequence of the environmental damage and are not raising any claims.

They are, in the case of the ELD, the 'operators' and that is why they will be treated in the next sub-section, 'as part' of the section 'measure of restoration,' given that, they are the central (passive) subjects who must 'passively' provide and bear the restoration as the consequence of environmental damage.

Both the active claimants (the competent authorities) and the passive subjects (the operators) have some obligations and responsibilities in the prevention and reparation of environmental damage.

It is worth noting that it is not because the competent authorities are called, in the present section, 'active claimants' that they play a major role as compared with the operators, which are called 'passive subjects.' On the contrary, the competent authorities have a secondary role as the primary role is attributed, in the ELD, to the operators. The operator is the primary responsible party in paying the costs of restoration as a consequence of environmental damage.

The distinction between the primary and secondary roles attributed to the operators and the competent authorities in the ELD, will be treated in further detail, in the sub-section below discussing how compensation as a consequence of environmental damage is structured – and how the measures of reparations, as a consequence of environmental harm, are organised in the EU.

The measures of reparation[500] will be examined in section 5.8 together with the costs of reparation[501] for the prevention and remedy of the environmental damage, and the obligations of the operator as a 'passive subject' who must pay for environmental damages.[502] Thus, the obligations of the operator will be treated, in section 5.8.1, and 'as part' of the measure of reparations since they deal with the 'passive role' of the operator in bearing the restoration.

In the following sub-section, more light is shed on the obligations of the competent authorities and the role they play as active claimants in claiming for environmental damage. The sub-section also provides for the identification of 'other active claimants' in claiming for environmental damage, who can be assimilated into the category of the 'active claimants,' and for that reason have been included in the section below.

5.7.1   OBLIGATIONS FOR THE COMPETENT AUTHORITIES AS 'ACTIVE CLAIMANTS' AND 'OTHER ACTIVE CLAIMANTS'

The subjects having the power to raise a claim for environmental damage are the competent authorities. They are 'active claimants' since they act to claim for the

---

500. Article 7 of the Directive.
501. Articles 8 and 9 of the ELD.
502. The operator is a 'passive subject', as explained in the previous paragraph, since must bear the costs of reparation as a consequence of environmental harm.

restoration of the environmental damage. Member States have to ensure the implementation of the ELD and the task of designating these competent authorities is remitted to the Member States themselves.

The competent authorities are provided with a number of responsibilities in order to fulfil the obligations prescribed by the ELD.[503] For example, the competent authority has the duty to (1) individualise the operator who committed the damage or the imminent threat of damage; (2) assess the significance of the damage; and (3) determine the measures of reparation.

The ELD establishes also that qualified natural or legal persons interested and involved on environmental issues,[504] who can submit observations to the competent authorities concerning environmental damage or an imminent threat of damage, can ask the competent authority to act under the ELD. It is always the Member States which determines the existence of sufficient elements of the legitimate interests to claim for the breach of a right. In that sense also the NGOs operating in environmental protection which are recognised under national laws, can submit observations and enquire on issues concerning environmental protection.

In line with international environmental law, specifically with the Aarhus Convention of 25 June 1998,[505] the ELD provides that the NGOs are entitled to claim for a right which could be breached in the meaning of Article 12, letter C) of that Convention.[506] However, NGOs, had more power in the pre-legal acts of the pre-works of the ELD, namely under the White Paper[507] when compared to the final text of the ELD. In the final version of the ELD, the NGOs no longer retain

---

503. Article 11, para. 1, states: 'Member States shall designate the competent authority(ies) responsible for fulfilling the duties provided for this Directive'.
504. The qualified natural and/or legal persons interested and involved in environmental issues could be various parties, such as the victims of environmental damage, or subjects having a special interest in the decision-making process concerning the environmental field, or could also be the claimants for the breach of a right.
505. The Aarhus Convention on Access to Information, Public Participation in the Decision-Making and Access to Justice in Environmental Matters, done in Aarhus, Denmark on the 25 June 1998.
506. Article 12 of the ELD treating the 'Request for action' state that: '1. Natural or legal persons: a) affected or likely to be affected by environmental damage or b) having a sufficient interest in environmental decision making relating to the damage or, alternatively, *c) alleging the impairment of a right, where administrative procedural law of a Member State requires this as a precondition, shall be entitled to submit to the competent authority any observations relating to instances of environmental damage or an imminent threat of such a damage of which they are aware and shall be entitled to request the competent authority to take action under this Directive. What constitute a 'sufficient interest' and 'impairment of right' shall be determined by Member States. To this end, the interest of any non-governmental organisation promoting environmental protection and meeting any requirements under national law shall be deemed sufficient for the purpose of subparagraph (b). Such organisations shall also be deemed to have rights capable of being impaired for the purpose of subparagraph (c)...'* (cursive emphasis added).
507. See the sub-section 3.1.6.3.3 of Chapter 3.

this power[508] to act directly for claiming an interest which means that they only have the entitlement or the option to ask an operator to take actions for preventative and remedial measures. Whether preventative and remedial measures are taken will depend solely on the competent authorities. The competent authorities will evaluate whether it is the case of submitting observations which should contain the evidence of the existence of environmental damage.[509]

Therefore, it is possible to deduce that in the final text of the ELD the NGOs do not retain the power of entitlement to claim for the same rights which means that they cannot participate in the effective implementation of the ELD and have a 'direct role' in environmental protection goal achievements as laid down in the preamble of the ELD.[510]

Additionally, citizens had the right to claim or at least had acquired rights for damage to health or property under the White Paper. Subsequently, the citizens have lost these rights, given that, in the final text of the ELD, the damage to health and property has been deemed as outside the scope of the ELD.

In reality, when identifying the subjects which are entitled to claim for environmental damage, both in the cases of the NGOs and the citizens claiming for a breach of rights, there has been an evident regression in their capacity to play a role in terms of environmental protection goal achievements. This regression which has been stipulated and translated in the final text of the ELD will certainly not be beneficial for an effective implementation of the ELD.

5.7.1.1 The Role of the Non-official Actors as 'The Other Active Claimants'

The role of the non-official actors identified as 'groups of interest' divided, on one hand, into non-official business (or industrial) actors, and, on the other hand, into non-official environmental actors,[511] was one of the main concerns of the drafters of the Green Paper. The focal point of 'who is entitled to claim for environmental damage' and, in particular, whether this focal point was to also include the non-official actors in the meaning of the definition as described above, was one of the live motifs of the political debate during the drafting of the Green Paper.[512]

Nevertheless, after having analysed the nature, behavioural preferences and positions of these non-official actors, especially during the law-making process of

---

508. The power is referred, here, as the claimants' power or option to claim (or to act directly for the claim of) a right, or to claim the costs of restoration as a consequence of an environmental damage.
509. The evidence of environmental damage are based, for example, on the existence of data, observations, or information submitted, for example, by the NGOs.
510. See the Preamble of the ELD, whereas n. 25.
511. See sub-section 4.1.4 of Chapter 4.
512. See sub-section 3.1.6.1 of Chapter 3 on the 'Green Paper'. In particular, the Commission decided to take a firm position in attributing a strongest role to environmental associations and NGOs and their entitlement to claim for environmental damage, together with the necessity to initiate a mandatory insurance system.

the 2002 Proposal, it appears that they are quite heterogeneous and fragmented.[513] Moreover, as previously explained,[514] it has been demonstrated also that these non-official actors, do not actually play a strong role in the legal architecture of the ELD.

This sub-section explains why in the ELD these non-official actors do not have the role of 'actors' similar to the one assigned to the Member State's competent authorities by the EU legislator. This is an important question to be elucidated, especially if it is considered that the role of environmental associations and NGOs is actually crucial in the correct implementation of the ELD. Very often, the role of environmental associations and NGOs is a role of *stimulus* for the adequate and correct implementation of the EU environmental law at the domestic level.

In that sense, it is not new that Member States frequently implement directives inadequately or do not transpose them at all, which gives rise to actions against those Member State brought by the Commission or other Member States according to the infringements procedure under Articles 258–260 of the TFEU (previous Articles 226–228 of the EU Treaty).[515]

In that respect it is worth noting the conspicuous number of judicial actions brought by these environmental associations at the EU level, which are also the object of a study commissioned by the EU to a group of researchers headed by Prof. Nicolas de Sadeleer who worked jointly with a group of experts of the Member States on the matter.[516]

In order to explain why the non-official actors are not acting as 'actors' in contradiction to that which was promised in the Green Paper and to that which was suggested by the legal architecture designed in the ELD, it is sufficient to examine, three provisions contained in the ELD in conjunction with each other, and in a sub-sequential order. The first, is the preamble of the ELD, in particular the whereas n. 25, and the other two provisions are Articles 12 and 13 of the ELD.

In that sense, even though, apparently, the ELD seems attributing a certain relevance to actions promoted by environmental associations and NGOs toward the 'prevention' and 'repression' of damaging conducts to the environment,[517] in reality the ELD is not really giving such a role to these non-official actors.

---

513. See sub-section 4.1.3 of Chapter 4 on the 'Role of the Non-Official Actors'.
514. See previous sub-section on the 'Obligations for the Competent Authorities as 'Active Claimants' and 'Other Active Claimants' where the 'Other Active Claimants' are precisely the 'Non-Official Actors' referred in this sub-section.
515. See De Búrca G., Craig P., '*EU law-Text, Cases and Materials*', 2008, Oxford, pp. 428–458. The infringement procedure will be treated in the next Chapter 6 of the present book.
516. See the document ENVA3/ETU/2002/2003.
517. The whereas n. 25 of the ELD states 'Persons adversely affected or likely to be adversely affected by environmental damage should be entitled to ask the competent authorities to take action. Environmental protection is, however, a diffuse interest on behalf of which individuals will not always act or will not be in a position to act. Non-governmental organisations promoting environmental protection should therefore also be given the opportunity to properly contribute to the effective implementation of this Directive'.

Delving more deeply into the legal research, the two aforementioned articles in the ELD, Articles 12 and 13, unveils a clear gap in that respect, as to the correct role which should have been attributed to these non-official actors.

Article 12 of the ELD, considers environmental associations and NGOs as entitled to be deemed of having a 'sufficient interest in environmental decision-making related to the damage'[518] and entitle them[519] to autonomously bring an action in law and to give them the opportunity to claim for a right which is breached in the meaning of issues related to environmentally damaging situations.

However, the way by which this provision entitles environmental associations and NGOs to act, is through making them first pass, through the competent authorities.[520] This means that environmental associations and NGOs cannot autonomously act or directly bring an action in law.

Prior to acting, environmental associations and NGOs must make their request to the competent authorities in the Member States and must accompany the request for action, with relevant data and information which demonstrates 'in a plausible manner that environmental damage exists'.[521]

This means that the competent authorities will only consider bringing an action for the damage if it is demonstrated in a 'plausible manner that environmental damage exists'. This is also a significant 'administrative power' conferred in the hands on the competent authorities and further complicates the administrative bureaucratic *iter* when claiming for environmental damage, because if the competent authorities do not reply formally to the environmental associations and NGOs that there is environmental damage, the environmental associations and NGOs will never be able to act 'before' the occurrence and the manifestation of the environmental damage which is in evident contradiction with that which has been promised in the ambitions and goals of the ELD and in the message contained in its whereas n. 25.

The EU legislator has therefore conferred on the competent authorities the opportunity to omit or the option of not considering a request for action presented

---

518. See Art. 12, letter b) of the ELD.
519. 'Them' here is referred to 'environmental associations and NGOs'.
520. Article 12 of the ELD titled 'Request for Action' states '1. Natural or legal persons: (a) affected or likely to be affected by environmental damage or (b) having a sufficient interest in environmental decision making relating to the damage or, alternatively, (c) alleging the impairment of a right, where administrative procedural law of a Member State requires this as a precondition, shall be entitled to submit to the competent authority any observations relating to instances of environmental damage or an imminent threat of such a damage of which they are aware and shall be entitled to request the competent authority to take action under this Directive'.
521. Article 12, paras 2 and 3 states '2. The request for action shall be accompanied by the relevant information and data supporting the observations submitted in relation to the environmental damage in question. 3. Where the request for action and the accompanying observations show in a plausible manner that environmental damage exists, the competent authority shall consider any such observations and requests for action. In such circumstances the competent authority shall give the relevant operator and opportunity to make his views known with respect to the request for action and the accompanying observations'.

by environmental associations or NGOs in cases of imminent threat of environmental damage.

Furthermore, the linguistic formulation of the legal wording chosen by the EU legislator in Article 13 of the ELD according to which environmental associations and NGOs have 'access to a court or other independent and impartial public body competent to review the procedural and substantive legality of the decisions, acts or failure to act of the competent authority under this Directive' does not correspond to the reality as there is in reality no such 'direct access', as explained previously in the analysis of Article 12, as environmental associations and NGOs have first to pass through the competent authorities, and therefore they cannot act directly.

Moreover, the competent authorities have the right to have access to a court which is competent to review the legality of acts or the legality of a failure to act, and the term 'acts' here, always refers to acts emanating from public authorities and not acts of private individuals.[522] This latter solution is, without any doubts, the result of an administrative compromise strongly pursued by lobbyists and industries,[523] and is to be considered as the obvious fruits of a political compromise which will have a negative reverberating effect at the domestic level.

The negative effect of this obvious trade-off will be mirrored at the domestic level in the correct implementation of the EU environmental law, given that those environmental associations and NGOs will in such a way be excluded from their role as active contributors[524] to the correct implementation of the EU environmental law at national level.

In conclusion, it is difficult to individualise who among the subjects is competent to claim for environmental damage at all levels, because the environment is comprehensive both of individual and collective situations where there is often an overlap between the private sphere and the public sphere. The fact of perceiving the environment as a diffuse interest does not mean that individuals should be excluded. Environmental associations and NGOs are representative of the interests of these individuals. When individuals are not able to act environmental associations and NGOs represent their 'voice' expressing the will to defend natural resources.

The interest in living in a healthy environment pertains not only to individuals (the citizen or the private interest), but is also linked to the interests of the groups (environmental associations, NGOs and professional organisations) and to the collectivity, in which sense, both groups form a whole and cannot be separated.[525]

---

522. See Art. 13 of the ELD titled 'Review Procedures'.
523. Lobbies and industries which are part of groups of interest of the professional organisations identified as the *cons* EU environmental regime formation in sub-section 4.1.2 of Chapter 4.
524. The role of active contributors of the non-official actors is found in the whereas n. 25 of the ELD.
525. For example the interest of enjoying a healthy air pertains not only to the individual but also to the collectivity. Both individual interests and collective interests are unified by the awareness that natural resources (such as for example the air) are not unlimited and must be used in a sustainable manner. An unhealthy environment is not only damaging the single individual but

The ELD do not take into account this environmental socio-economic reality, as environmental associations and NGOs do not have an active role in the ELD, but rather a passive role to be understood merely as 'spectators' rather than 'actors' as the title of this sub-section initially suggests.

The choice of the EU legislator in the design of the role on the non-official actors in the ELD, is therefore negative for two reasons: (1) for the effectiveness of the ELD in reaching environmental protection goal achievements, since the environment represents 'a diffuse interest on behalf of which individuals will not always act or will not be in a position to act'[526] and for that reason it should not be precluded that the environmental associations and NGOs contribute to protecting natural resources; and (2) for harmonisation, since each Member State will transpose the ELD by giving to these non-official actors sometimes a strong role and sometimes a weak role, depending on the administrative systems of the Member States and the different timing according to each Member States bureaucratic *apparatus'* capacity to work quickly.

Thus, the legal wording of the ELD in the provision dedicated to the role attributed to the non-official actors should change in such a way as to provide these non-official actors with the opportunity to play the stronger role which will make the ELD more effective in terms of environmental protection goal achievements.

5.8   COMPENSATION FOR ENVIRONMENTAL DAMAGE

The operator[527] has the duty, to adopt all of the measures for reparations[528] after the environmental damage has occurred. Member States may take preventative or remedial measures if the operator is not identified or is not required to bear the costs of the damage;[529] however, they are not obliged to do so. The goal of reparations for environmental harm is considerably compromised in cases where the Member States which should be responsible for the clean-up are not acting as a result of the existence of derogations from liability.[530] Furthermore, as a negative corollary compromising the rigour and the severity of the environmental protection goal achievements, this good option which was provided to Member States for repairing the damage, if and where the operator is not identified, and

---

also the group which risk to be decomposed and further fragmented, especially if each component of the group would start to move for a desperate search of an unpolluted environment or for a territory where the air is not polluted.
526. See whereas n. 25 of the ELD.
527. The concept of operator as already been introduced in section 5.3 of the present chapter containing also a reproduction of the article *per esteso* in a footnote.
528. Article 6, para. 1of the ELD.
529. Article 5 para. 4, and Art. 6 para. 3 of the ELD.
530. The cases when Member States have the option to derogate from liability will be analyzed in the sub-section 5.9.1 of the present chapter.

which was introduced in the 2002 Commission's Proposal;[531] was not retained in the final text of the ELD.[532]

These measures of reparations are the object of a separate Annex in the ELD which is Annex II. Annex II, titled 'Measures aimed at repairing environmental damage,' establishes, in general, all of the criteria which the operators, and the competent authorities, have to follow in order to repair the environmental damage.

Annex II proposes a general scheme of restorative measures in cases of damage to natural resources, and separates the remedial measures according to the various categories of remediation (Primary, Secondary and Compensatory Remediation), and the objectives to be achieved, according to the different types of remedies.

The ELD distinguishes between: (1) damage to protected species and natural habitat and water and (2) damage to land. Regarding the first kind of damage (damage to protected species and natural habitat and water), compensation consists of returning the natural resources to the baseline conditions (*restitutio in integrum*).

For the second type of damage (which is the environmental damage to the land), the ELD provides for the adoption of the minimum necessary measures to guarantee that the polluting substances are removed or controlled or decreased in a way in which the land does not present a significant risk for human health.[533]

The scheme clearly has a strong American inspiration, especially if what is taken into account is the US Model proposed by CERCLA.[534]

The scheme of restorative measures proposed by the EU legislator outlines the differences between Primary, Secondary and Compensatory Remediation, and is explained, in further details in Table 5.1.

Table 5.1   Scheme of Restorative Measures Proposed by the EU Legislator in the ELD

Category	Type	Objectives
Primary Remediation	Measures which return the damaged natural resources and/or impaired services to baseline conditions	To return the resources to the baseline conditions
Secondary Remediation	To compensate for the fact that primary remediation does not result in full restoration of the damage	To obtain a level of natural resources similar to the one which could have been obtained if the

531. See the 2002 Commission's Proposal, sub-section 3.1.6.5.4 of Chapter 3.
532. De Smedt K., '*Is harmonisation always effective? The Implementation of the Environmental Liability Directive*', 2009, European Energy Environmental Law Review.
533. In Annex II, 'Remediation of Land Damage' of the ELD.
534. See the sub-section 3.1.5 on 'The US as a Historical-Comparative Model', Chapter 3.

Table 5 (cont'd)

Category	Type	Objectives
	to natural resources of services	polluted area had been drained
Compensatory Remediation	Actions to compensate *interim* losses of natural resources until primary remediation is not fully financed	To compensate *interim* losses of natural resources

As can be noted in Table 5.1, in cases where it is not possible to return the damaged natural resources to the baseline conditions, then the measures undertaken will be based on the Secondary Remediation. The Compensatory Remediation has to be understood as a compensation for '*interim* losses' of natural resources which is just a temporary compensation.[535]

However, the scheme does not outline clearly when the environmental damage is 'compensable,'[536] and the EU legislator seems to have distinguished incorrectly what the 'Secondary Remediation' is which is aimed at compensating and what the 'Compensatory Remediation' is which actually does not compensate.[537] When determining the extent of the meaning between Secondary and Compensatory remediation, it is very often not clear what the instructions are which need to be followed in order to achieve environmental compensation. This is a difficulty linked to the problem of the methods of evaluation and quantification of the environmental damage.

What has been used as a method for quantification of the damage is the equivalency method: resource-to-resource, or service-to-service, which means that remedial actions should be able to render natural resources and/or services of the same kind (equivalent) both in terms of quality and quantity.[538] In cases where it is not possible to apply this method of equivalency, then the damage should be compensated by providing alternative natural resources and/or alternative services,[539] as suggested by the Lugano Convention.[540] The lack of clarity could also represent an obstacle to the application of the Polluter-pays principle and the probability of the ELD succeeding in its environmental goals.

Paradoxically, the ELD is based on making the polluters pay and on the Polluter-pays principle the payment is equivalent to what the costs are of bringing about the

---

535. See the third column, the third box, bottom-right of Table 5.1.
536. Pozzo, B. '*La Responsabilità ambientale*', 2005, Diritto ed Economica dell'Ambiente, Giuffré Editore.
537. De Sadeleer N., '*Les Responsabilités environnementales dans l'espace Européen. Point de vue franco-belge*', 2007, Brulant, page 764.
538. Pozzo, B., '*La Responsabilità ambientale*', 2005, Diritto ed Economica dell'Ambiente, Giuffré Editore.
539. Such as for example in case of reduction of the quality of the environment, to repair quality with quantity.
540. See sub-section 3.1.3, Chapter 3.

material restoration of natural resources to the baseline situation (the situation prior to the wrong or *status quo ante*) by the liable party. Furthermore, as has been observed, these payments are very often insufficient, and the reason for this is the absence of criteria targeted at quantifying the monetary equivalent of the damage or the absence of such methods. In addition, even if the methods for the quantification of the environmental damage exist, they can sometime be very difficult to apply.

This has led the EU legislator to design a European reparation scheme which is, in the case of the ELD, not truly aimed at restoring the damage to natural resources, but rather at furnishing equivalent resources (at minor costs).

All of this means that even though the US influence has certainly been beneficial, the *formula* by which the ELD applies the Polluter-pays principle is still unknown. Hence, this latter aspect could represents a further incentive for the EU legislator to seek American inspirations for tackling problems of restoration and remedying natural resources and the idea of establishing a Fund of Compensation which can be financed by the potential polluters. This solution provides the opportunity for combining the application of the Polluter-pays principle with imposing costs on the polluters and not on the collective.

A possible solution is therefore the one chosen by CERCLA dealing with the problems of decontamination of the sites subject to environmental risk which charges the liable parties with the reimbursement of the clean-up costs by creating a public fund, the so-called Superfund granted by taxes on the potential responsible parties, such as oil and petrol producers.[541]

5.8.1   OBLIGATIONS OF OPERATORS AS THE 'PASSIVE SUBJECTS'
          RESTORING ENVIRONMENTAL DAMAGE

In accordance with one of the main goals of the ELD, namely to ensure that the Polluter-pays principle is applied,[542] the ELD prescribes that it is those who are responsible, the polluters, who have to pay the costs of prevention and reparation for the damage. The potential responsible party or the potential polluter is the operator.[543] The competent authority has the power to ensure that the operator sustains the costs of prevention and reparation of the environmental harm.[544] The environmental liability regime established with the ELD highlights the crucial role of the operator which is considered to be the primary responsible party.

The legal architecture designed by the EU legislator in the ELD resembles a typical model based on a Trusteeship construction, similar to the one used by the US Model when legally protecting natural resources.[545]

---

541. See sub-section 3.1.5, Chapter 3.
542. As previously discussed in section 5.5 of the present chapter.
543. Article 8, para. 1 of the ELD states 'The operator shall bear the costs for the preventative and remedial actions taken pursuant to this Directive'.
544. One way in which to ensure that the polluter sustains the costs of prevention and reparation of environmental damage is, for example, to set up a system of financial insurance guarantees.
545. The Trusteeship construction used by the US model as a pattern to protect legally natural resources has been described and analysed in sub-section 3.1.5.2 of Chapter 3 dedicated to the

Actually, the EU legislator, in line with the lessons learned from the American method used to protect natural resources, applies the typical Trusteeship construction with a mutually shared approach: the primary responsibility to restore the damage being with the 'operators', and the subsidiary responsibility being placed on the competent authorities.

In such a Trusteeship construction, the operator has the 'primary responsibility' due to an obligation to act. The operator must take preventative and remedial measures irrespective of the type of liability (fault based or strict based), the importance of the damage, the technical difficulties encountered, and the costs for the operators. The competent authorities have a 'subsidiary responsibility' because if the operator fails to comply with the request or cannot be identified, or is not required to bear the costs, then the competent authorities may take subsidiary measures.[546]

Nevertheless, even though such a legal architecture confers the primary responsibility to the operator as the 'subject legally responsible or potentially responsible' for the environmental damage and seems to design a two-pronged and well organised approach between 'active claimants' and 'passive subjects' and between a primary and subsidiary construction, there are still two problems which are strictly intertwined with each other and which remain unsolved:

(1) The difficulty in identifying the operator.
(2) The difficulty in attributing liability in cases where the operator is more than one (i.e., the problem of multiple operators which could be assimilated to the problem of diffuse pollution or cumulative emissions, as explained in section 2.1.5 letter b) of Chapter 2).

With regards to the first problem above (1), even though the text of the ELD indicates that it is the operator who is the best placed to control an activity and, therefore, best placed to bear liability should environmental damage arise, it would be a disaster if the responsible party, which is the operator, could not be identified, and this is highly likely in the environmental field.[547]

US as a historical-comparative model. The section is titled 'The Problem of the Type of Ownership or the Problem of Who is Entitled to Claim for Environmental Damage'. See also Bringhton, W.D., and Askman, D.F., '*The Role of government Trustee in Recovering Compensation for Injury to Natural Resources*', in Wettersteins, '*Harm to the Environment – the Right Compensation for Injury to Natural Resources of Damages*', 1997, Calderon Press, Oxford, pp. 177–206.

546. What is important to grasp here in this Trusteeship construction is that whether the natural resources are owned or not owned, the competent authorities act as their 'Trusteeship.' The competent authorities have the right to require, at any time, and whatever the importance of the damage is the operators to take: a) preventative measures (see Art. 5 (1) of the ELD); and b) restorative measures (see Art. 6, para. 2 of the ELD). In case the operator fails to comply with the requests, the competent authorities, in a subsidiary way, may take measures, such as: a) preventative measures (see Art. 4, para. 4 of the ELD); b) restorative measures determined in accordance with Annex II (see Art. 6, para. 3 of the ELD); c) recover the costs from the operators (see Art. 8, para. 2 of the ELD).

547. As explained and outlined in Chapter 3.

The operator is potentially responsible because it has the technical knowledge of the activity and has the best knowledge to take preventative and restorative measures in case of environmental damage. Article 2, paragraph 2 of the ELD defines the operator as 'any natural or legal, private or public person who operates or controls the occupational activity or where this is provided for in by national legislation, to whom decisive economic power over the technical functioning of such an activity has been delegated, including the holder of a permit or authorisation for such an activity or the person registering or notifying an activity.'

The problem of the definition of the term 'operator' as drafted in Article 2, paragraph 6 previously described in the first problem above (1) is that it is too broad and much too vague.

It is not clear who the operator is and it is not easy to identify the operator because not only 'the holder of a permit or authorisation for such an activity' can be considered as the 'operator' but also others such as 'the persons registering or notifying an activity.' By implication, also those who are neither not holders of an activity nor not registering an activity, but simply running or controlling an economic activity can be considered as 'operators' and thus a potential responsible parties and liable for environmental damage. This definition can create doubts as to who the responsible parties are and who must pay for the costs of restorations as a consequence of environmental damage.

An example of the kind of confusion and difficulties deriving from the unclear definition of the term 'operator' and related to the difficulty of identifying the operator with the consequential uncertainty to attribute liability could be, for example, in case a multinational company that is producing and placing into the market a new phytopharmaceutical product for agricultural companies.

The assumption that the product is creating damage to the environment because it kills species of insects and plants which are important for the ecosystem. The pending question in such a case would be: who is liable and must repair the environmental damage? Is it the multinational or is the agricultural company? Who is, in such a case the one which has the 'economical power' and who has the 'technical functioning power'? Is it the multinational that has the economical power or is it the agricultural company? Moreover, once such a definition of the operator has been drafted, the EU legislator has also 'canalised'[548] this liability toward the operator, as outlined in problem (2). However, this is not going to work, as canalisation blocks liability as it ensures that the operators cannot share liability

---

548. As already employed in sub-section 3.1.1.4 (titled 'Environmental Liability and the Polluter-pays principle') of Chapter 3, the expression 'canalise' or 'canalisation' used on that point means to direct liability in one direction only or upon one natural or legal person. In other words, it means to 'channel' liability to the person (natural or legal) who is in control of the environmentally damaging activity instead of spreading liability and diluting liability toward a greater number of subjects. The advantage in canalising liability allows the retention of compactness and avoids dispersion of liability and facilitates, in that a way, the victim of the environmental damage who has to show the causality link between the potential wrongdoer and the environmental damage. In this sense, canalisation facilitates the application of the Polluter-pays principle.

in case there would be 'others' or 'other responsible parties' who contribute to the environmental damage.

As to the second problem (2), and strictly in connection with the first problematic (1), the reason why the aforementioned article 'defining' the operator (Article 2, paragraph 6 of the ELD) points out that the operator is the potential responsible party may be because the responsible party could be, precisely, more than one. There could be multiple potential responsible parties (not just one operator) which could create the risk that liability is diluted and compactness is lost.

The choice of the EU legislator in this article is to permit 'canalisation' of liability toward 'a potential responsible party.' By implication, the victim of the damage must prove causation. If causation is proved, then 'the potential responsible operator' becomes 'the responsible operator' *tout-court* (and such a responsible operator is not 'potential' anymore because it has been proven that he/it[549] committed the wrong or the environmental damage) and must bear the costs passively.

The latter problem also unveils another sub-problem (2a) which is the case of multiple parties or companies succeeding one another in the same location where the economic activity was carried on and the environmental damage was caused by previous companies or a combination of current and previous companies.

In this case, and in connection to the formulation of the term 'operator,' given that the activity is run by a new operator (a new enterprise), the past enterprise cannot be held liable solely because of not falling under the definition of the term 'operator' given that the 'operator', is the new company.[550]

In that sense, this entails that even if liability is shared, it would not be possible to make a distinction between past and present pollution or assess each firm's responsibility (and the percentages of the monetary costs of restoration as a consequence of liability shared among the multiple operators) particularly due to the difficulty in case of potential multiple operators, to establish causation on the basis of technical parameters, with the consequence that the Polluter-pays principle, even if liability is assigned, would remain in vain. By consequence, the definition of the term operator needs to be redrafted for the sake of the application of the Polluter-pays principle and harmonisation. In substance, the fundamental novel principle of the ELD should be that the operator is the primary responsible party and, in line with the Polluter-pays principle, must pay in cases of committing environmental damage.[551] This is supposed to incite the other operators to adopt measures and develop new practices aimed at reducing to a minimum the risks of environmental damage. Nevertheless, it would be difficult if the responsible party who is the operator, could not be identified, which is, highly likely in the environmental field.

---

549. With the term 'he' or 'it' here, it is referred to the natural or legal person of the operator.
550. This example illustrating the second problem (2a) is also a clear example on how and when the problematic (1) on the difficulty in identifying the operator, is intertwined with problem (2) on the difficulty in attributing liability in case the liable parties would be more than one.
551. See section 5.2 of the present chapter.

Moreover, even when the operator is identified, and liability canalised on his person, it would be difficult in concrete terms for the operator to share liability with several and joint responsible parties who could have contributed to the damage, which would in turn render problematic the homogeneous application of the Polluter-pays principle, and harmonisation. An emblematic example showing how and when the entrenchment of the two problems analysed occurs is contained in the Case C-378/08, and Joined Cases C-379/08 and C-380/08 Raffinerie Mediterranee.[552] In the latter judgments, the ECJ clarified in this case that the competent authorities do not have to provide absolute proof of responsibility for environmental damage before requiring an installation to clean-up a polluted area, but they must carry out an investigation first. The competent authorities must also make sure they can provide 'plausible evidence' such as the installation being close to the pollution and a correlation between the pollutants causing the damage and the plant's activities. The ruling, which deals with the formulation of the ELD, responds to one of three questions sent by the Sicilian Court to the ECJ in a case involving competent authorities and several firms operating near the Sicilian town of Augusta (Italy). The competent authorities made the companies bear responsibility for pollution in the area without making a distinction between past and present pollution or assessing each firm's responsibility.

However, according to the conclusions in the opinion of the ECJ's Advocate General, Kokott, presented on the 22 October 2009 in the Cases C-378/08, and C-379/08, in case it wouldn't be possible to identify the operator, it is possible to make other subjects pay the costs of restoration without interpreting such a possibility as being in contrast with the ELD. The issue still remains unclear, as the formulation of the ELD is unclear on that matter. The entrenchments of the two problems (1) and (2) in the formulation of the ELD is a reality and not a speculative issue, otherwise there wouldn't have been the need for interpretation from the ECJ in the application of the ELD in Italy, as the Raffinerie Mediterranee's Case unveils.

Finally, a solution aimed at facilitating the identification of the operator or to make the operator responsible is to transpose and integrate the concept of liability of the producer contained in the Directive of Industrial Emission or better known as the 'IE (IPPC) Directive'[553] of the IEP (Industrial Emission Production) into the

---

552. See Judgments in Case C-378/08 and Joined Cases C-379/08 and C-380/08 Raffinerie Mediterranee (ERG) SpA, Polimeri Europea SpA and Syndial SpA v Ministero dello Sviluppo economico and Others and ENI Spa v Minitero Ambiente e Tutela del Territorio e del Mare and Others, where the ECJ had to clarify the formulation of the ELD through the mechanism of reference for preliminary ruling from the Tribunale Amministrativo Regionale per la Sicilia (Italy).

553. Directive 2008/1/EC of the European Parliament and of the Council of 15 January 2008 entered into force on the 1st January 2011. This Directive reviewed and recasted the 'old' Directive 96/61/EC on the Integrated Pollution Prevention and Control (IPPC) Directive. The new IE (IPPC) Directive is not aiming at altering the main underlying principles of the IPPC Directive but to improving it and by complementing it by making a connection with other industrial emissions-related legislations. Today, the IE (IPPC) Directive has unified directives

ELD. The IE (IPPC) Directive is a harmonisation measure based on the EU power to approximate national laws and establish an internal market.

Thus, establishing a direct relation of the IE (IPPC) into the formulation of the ELD would reinforce the role of the operators in what would be their 'preventative function' in avoiding causing environmental damage as there would be an integration of this concept[554] into the text of the ELD.

In that sense, the ELD is sufficiently broad enough to contain the liability concept of the IE (IPPC) Directive and the issue of the operator for liability especially in reference and for the existence of Article 5, paragraph 3, letter c) of the ELD which is susceptible to be integrated by IE (IPPC) Directive. Article 5, paragraph 3, letter c) states: 'the competent authorities may, at any time: (a) give instructions to the operator to be followed on the necessary preventive measures to be taken'. Hence, in this article, there is room enough to establish a direct and specific connection with the producer liability as the link between the IE (IPPC) Directive and the ELD is possible because environmental damage can also be caused by products and by the producers of these products.

Therefore, there is also a responsibility for the producers, and in general for the economical actors which should bear the whole responsibility of products that they place on the market. The operators should therefore provide information on the environmental impact of their products. In that sense, the integration between the IE (IPPC) Directive and the ELD offers a possible application of the Polluter-pays principle in case of environmental damage caused by products, and in cases of environmental risks caused by these products because if the products cause harm, then the producers should pay.

The direct integration between the IE (IPPC) and the ELD would have an important role of reinforcing the preventative function of the operator as it would strengthen liability because 'inform' in a predictable way before the damage occurs whenever a production risks to injury health and the environment during the use cycle of a product. Hence, integrating the IE (IPPC) and the ELD together, in such a manner, would render the ELD more effective in its function of predictive liability legal tool.

5.8.2   THE CONCEPT OF OPERATOR AT THE INTERNATIONAL LEVEL

When protecting natural resources, the EU legislator attempts, in the ELD, to apply the typical Trusteeship construction used by the US Model. Nevertheless, the central problem in the ELD has been (and still is) to identify the liable party or

---

on waste surveillance and monitoring and elimination of pollution from the titanium dioxide industry, the 'Titanium Dioxide Production Directives', the 'Integrated Pollution Prevention and Control Directive' (IPPC), the 'Solvent Emission Directive' (SED); the 'Waste Incineration Directive' (WID), and the 'Large Combustion Plant Directive' (LCPD).

554. The concept-function of the operators in what is its 'preventative role' consisting in avoiding causing environmental damage.

the 'potential liable party' causing environmental harm.[555] The problem of inter-pretation of the notion of 'operator' in order to establish who the subject exercising control upon an activity dangerous to the environment is, it is a common problem at all the levels, as is the problem of how to define environmental damage, as pre-viously shown.

Thus, it has been outlined in section 5.8.1 of the present chapter how the formulation of the ELD with regard to the term 'operator' has left unsolved the problem of rendering liability in cases of multiple tortfeasors. It also remains impossible to make a distinction between past and present pollution or assessing, for example, each firm's liability.

In that sense, the Lugano Convention is extremely innovative because it links the obligations of the operators with past and present pollution and addresses the above problem and should, therefore, be incorporated into the formulation of the legal text of the ELD which would make progress the ELD. If the ELD is redrafted using the Lugano Convention's formulation of the term 'operator', the provisions of the ELD would be much clearer, and this clarity would lead to the success of environmental protection goal achievements. Such an improvement of the term 'operator' in the ELD formulation, would lead to a more homogeneous and optimal level of harmonisation, and also the Member State's implementations of the ELD in national legislations would benefit from a better definition of the term 'operator'.

In fact, going more deeply into the legal research of the international level of the sources of law, the interesting part of the Lugano Convention's formulation, with regards to the duties of the operator, is the shift of the burden of proof from the victim to the potential operator.

That means that the burden of proof is not placed on the victim but on the operator.[556] In fact, in cases of continuous occurrences or a series of occurrences of damaging events, joint and several liability applies, even in situations of successors which makes it possible to make a distinction between past and present pollution.[557]

This potential and possibilities of the Lugano Convention are applicable also in cases of 'gradual occurrence' or 'series of occurrences' which is equivalent to the problem of diffuse pollution or gradual pollution in cases where the manifes-tation of the damage emerges a considerable time after that the environmentally damaging events occurred.[558] This is because even though liability in the Lugano Convention is not retroactive, in reality, such type of liability cannot be conceived as 'totally' non-retroactive. In fact, even if there is a general rule of non-retroactivity, the Lugano Convention takes into consideration the following situ-ation: if a dangerous activity has ceased and the damage becomes known after the

---

555. See the previous sub-section 5.8.1 of the present chapter.
556. Larsson, M.L., *'The Law of Environmental Damage: Liability and Reparation'*, 1999, Kluwer Law International – The Hague, page 226.
557. See Art. 6. 2 and 3 of the Lugano Convention.
558. See sub-section 2.1.5, Chapter 2.

closure, the last operator will be held liable for the whole damage, unless it is proved by him or the victim that the incident causing all the damage or part of the damage occurred before he became operator. Thus, potentially, in that sense, the Lugano Convention could address the gap of civil liability used in the ELD as an instrument to make the polluter liable in case of diffuse pollution, multiple tortfeasors of environmental damage, including air pollution cases.

Perhaps this could open the path for some new liability legal solutions which would also include the damage as a consequence of climate change events due to CO2 emissions and damage caused by acid rain.

With regards to the Basel regime, the combination of the formulation of Articles 3 and 4 of the Basel Protocol assigns, in accordance with Article 6 of the Basel Convention,[559] to the subject notifying the trans-boundary movement, a kind of 'strict liability'[560] as a consequence of environmental damage[561] occurring during such a trans-boundary movement of hazardous waste.

These environmental damages are damages which occurred within the area of jurisdiction of one of the Contracting Parties within the lapse of time calculated from the moment the dangerous wastes are loaded onto the vehicle of transportation, until the disposer takes possession of the dangerous wastes: from that final moment, and until the operations of disposal are not concluded, the responsible party or the 'operator' will still be the disposer.[562]

At first glance, even though the choice of the Basel regime is to delegate to the 'notifier' the task of indicating the 'responsible party', which certainly facilitates the identification of the polluter, in the Basel Protocol, liability is assigned to the 'disposer' and not to the producer of waste or to 'generator' of waste. This choice to assign liability to the disposer does not facilitate the application of the Polluter-pays principle as, in order to facilitate the application of this principle, the normal reasoning would be to assign liability to the producer of the waste (or generator of the waste).[563] Due to the fact that the Protocol imposes strict liability upon the 'notifier' and on the 'disposer' and not on the producer of the waste, this allocation is contrary to the Polluter-pays principle. The result is that the Protocol is easy to

---

559. Article 6 of the Basel Convention stipulates 'the State of Export shall notify, or shall require the generator or exporter to notify, in writing, through the channel of the competent authority of the State of Export, the competent authority of the States concerned of any proposed trans-boundary movement of hazardous wastes or other wastes. Such notification shall contain the declarations and information specified in Annex V A, written in a language acceptable to the State of Import. Only one notification needs to be sent to each State concerned'.

560. Article 4, para. 1 of the Basel Protocol formulates a kind of 'strict liability' which is 'presumed' and not written in black and white (similarly to the ELD final draft text).

561. Environmental damage as defined in Art. 2 of the Basel Protocol. See for that point also the previous sub-section 3.1.4.1, Chapter 3, on the definition of the environmental damage under the Basel regime.

562. See the above mentioned combination of Arts 3 and 4 of the Basel Protocol, as mentioned in the first paragraph of the present section.

563. Fodella, A., '*Il Protocollo di Basilea sulla responsabilità per danni derivanti dal movimento transfrontaliero di rifiuti pericolosi: il perfetto è davvero nemico del buono?*', 2000, Rivista Giuridica dell'Ambiente, pp. 557–586.

evade[564] and encourages the export of dangerous wastes (in the same manner as those special provisions on wastes defined as 'hazardous' by national legislations do). The Basel regime concerns trans-boundary movements of waste. The ELD is concerned also with environmental damage as a consequence of transportation of waste. Nevertheless, the ELD is extremely weak in cases of trans-boundary environmental damages as the only article treating that issue is Article 15 of the ELD, and it is an extremely limited article.[565] A possible explanation of this weakness may lie in the awareness that the issue is also the object of waste regulations.

However, the text of the White Paper had a different formulation when compared to the way that same issue has been contextualised and negotiated in the final draft of the ELD. In that sense, at the general level and not only in relation to the waste sector, in the final draft of the ELD, Member States have been given a very weak role in case of restoration as a consequence of the environmental damage. This is reflected in their duties and options in case of damage as a consequence of trans-boundary damage also due to waste transportation. This means that damage as a consequence of waste transportation is very weakly regulated, because it has been negotiated. In the final draft of the ELD, this point has been literally 'expunged.' Not only has the latter point been taken away with a sponge, as a consequence of an obvious trade-off, but also the so-called 'two-level approach' which was introduced in the White Paper, and maintained later on also in the 2002 Proposal,[566] has been moved out of the final draft of the ELD. The two-level approach was the approach by which Member States should have had, *in primis*, (at the 'first level') the 'primary' responsibility of ensuring restoration as a consequence of environmental damage. Whilst the 'secondary' liability (at the 'second level'), was on the competent authority. The result of the opt-out of the latter two-level approach in the final text has been that in the text of ELD the EU legislator formulates the exact opposite: primary responsibility on the operator, and secondary (or subsidiary) responsibility on the competent authorities, as a consequence of the incorporation, in the ELD, of the so-called Trusteeship construction based on the US Model.[567] Through that legal strategic 'alibi', disguised by those willing to adopt the US legal architecture in protecting natural resources, the key

---

564. Under the Basel regime, the producer of the waste, who is normally responsible under domestic law, is incentivised to use a nominee as an intermediate or as a man of straw (a dummy figure) acting officially as a 'notifier' and thus escapes, in such a manner, from liability. The producer is also tempted to use an enterprise with a mere apparent role.

565. Article 15 of the ELD states: 'Where environmental damage affects or is likely to affect several Member States, those Member States shall cooperate, including through the appropriate exchange of information with a view to ensuring that preventive action and, where necessary, remedial action is taken in respect of any such environmental damage. Where environmental damage has occurred, the Member States in whose territory the damage originates shall provide sufficiently information to the potentially affected Member States'.

566. See sub-section 3.1.6.5.4 of Chapter 3.

567. The Trusteeship construction based on the US Model which has been 'adapted' in the ELD, is treated in sub-section 5.8.1 of the present chapter, and has been presented for the first time in sub-section 3.1.5.2, Chapter 3 as well as explained at the beginning of the present section.

argument of the waste issue has been literally negotiated, and gradually placed, automatically, in a secondary line of importance.

5.8.3   THE CONCEPT OF OPERATOR IN THE US MODEL

According to that which has been generally highlighted in the previous sections, when environmental legislators, at the EU and international levels, have to structure and design liability schemes, they are faced with the difficult task of individualising the subject responsible for the environmental damage and addressing the problem of interpretation of the notion of 'operator.' Normally, in a multi-level perspective, if one looks at the levels – international and national – and at the US Model, the concept of operator refers to the responsibility of the legal, natural person who has legal ownership of a given activity causing environmental damage even though the same damage is not caused by the administrators of the latter activity or by employees working in the same activity.

Thus, the concept of 'control' of a given activity turns out to be quite ambiguous, as it can be connected both to (1) the bodies supposed to verify the work of the administrator of a given activity;[568] and to (2) the subjects or bodies controlling and verifying the good respect of environmental norms.[569]

The *formula* of the concept of operator negotiated in the final text of the ELD 'seems' to attribute liability to the subject controlling, from an operational point of view, the activity which causes environmental damage.[570] Such a formulation in the ELD is, therefore, reincorporating and adapting into the EU law the notion of 'operator' elaborated by CERCLA, according to which, the notion of operator is referred to as the 'entrepreneur' who has the effective and not only the formal control of the risk of the activity causing environmental damage. It is, therefore, understandable and clearly specified, and not left open to question of interpretation, compared to the ELD's formulation of the concept of operator that of CERCLA's also includes into the notion of operator the 'shareholders' or the business partners of the activity, or the bodies having the task of verifying the activity.[571]

---

568. For example, the board of auditors of a joint stock company or a company limited by shares or a limited company.

569. For example, public subjects or public entities that are competent and entitled to issue environmental authorisation or environmental permits.

570. As it will be developed in details, further on, in sub-section 5.9.1 of the present chapter.

571. The CERCLA, in fact, holds liable, different kind of persons: 1) the owner and operator of a vessel (otherwise subject to the jurisdiction of the United States) or a facility; 2) any person who at the time of disposal of any hazardous substances owned or operated any facility at which such hazardous substances were disposed of; 3) any person who by contract, agreement, or otherwise arranged for disposal or treatment, or arranged with a transporter for transport for disposal or treatment, of hazardous substances owned or possessed by such person, by any other party or entity, at any facility owned or operated by other party or entity and containing such hazardous substances; and 4) any person who accepts or accepted any hazardous substances for transport to disposal or treatment facilities or sites selected by such a person.

The concept of operator in the US has generated a significant debate, especially with regards to the body or enterprise which was, as a major task, the one controlling the environmental activities.[572] The majority of the district courts in the US agreed that the notion of operator is comprehensive also of the bodies and subjects controlling environmental activities. The Supreme Court decided, in 1998, with the case United State *versus* Bestfood, 118 S.Ct, 1976, (1998) that the notion of operator has to be most restrictive in cases where the body or subject or the enterprise exercising a control over the dangerous activity causes environmental damage.

According to CERCLA, as has been highlighted in section 3.1.5 of Chapter 3, those that are considered liable, are included in the definition of operator, and this includes all the subjects who have a direct relationship with the contaminated sites.

This means that the notion of operator is inclusive of owners, controllers and enterprises, exercising, *in loco*, environmentally damaging activities. However, all of these 'potential responsible parties' can free themselves from liability if they indicate who the environmental wrongdoer is.[573]

Therefore, liability among the potential responsible parties can be joint and several. In the US *versus* A. & F. Materials Co., Inc.'s, the Court found that liability issues not resolved by the statute, including joint and several liability, should be governed by traditional and evolving principles of Common Law.

In substance, the concept of operator designed by the CERCLA's legislator is extended to individuals and corporations. A sole proprietor or partner in a business can be held liable for response costs under the act. Corporate officers can be held personally liable under the statute if they participated in the hazardous waste disposal decisions by using a broad definition of the term 'owner or operator.' In addition, lending institutions that foreclose a mortgage on a hazardous waste facility may be held liable as the owner of the property.[574] A lending institution that engages in management of a borrowers' business may also be held liable. Normally, a successor corporation is not charged with the former corporation's liabilities unless it expressly or implicitly assumes them.

However, if the transaction amounts to a *de facto* merger, the purchasing corporation is a continuation of the former corporation, or if the transaction is

---

See Miller, P., Schroeder Leape, '*Environmental Regulation*', Law, Science and Policy, 1996, Little Brown and Company, pp. 293–316.
572. See Anderson, R., '*Natural Resource Damages, Superfund and the Courts*', 16, Environmental Affairs, 1989, pp. 410–429; Kipnis, S.A., '*The conflict between CERCLA and FIRREA: Environmental Liability of the Resolution Trust Corporation*', 39, UCLA Law Review, 1996, pp. 439–456; Tauch, D.D., '*Getting Snagged in the Environmental Liability Web: The Trouble with CERCLA and Brownfields Act Provides only Modest Relief*', 35, Texas Tech Law Review, 2004, pp. 1325–1336.
573. Prebble, A.L., '*Corporate Law Confines to Parent Liability under CERCLA*', 67, University of Cincinnati Review, 1999, page 1357.
574. See the case US v. Maryland Bank & Trust Co., 632 F., Supp, pp. 573–579 (D. Md. 1986) and case United States v. Mirable, 15, Envtl. L. Rep. (Envt L. Inst.), 20, page 992 (E. D. Pa. 1985).

entered into to avoid liability, the successor will take on the obligation.[575] Lessees may also be held liable if they have control of the facility at the time of the disposal.[576]

The US concept of operator inspired the ELD. However, it has been used without utilising the right potential which could have been identified and picked up in CERCLA and used in a different way in order to suggest innovative changes into the ELD legal text. Such a different way to be inspired by extracting different potentials by the US Model would have rendered the EU concept of operator more precise and less vague.

In general, if the US formulation of the term operator had been inspiring the ELD, it would have certainly rendered the law better and more progressive, since the US Model acknowledges that liability issues include joint and several liabilities which should be also governed by a combination of traditional and non-traditional methods.

Going more deeply into the depth of the legal research of the US concept of the term operator, a better use of its potentials as source of inspiration for the ELD text, would have resolved the problem of ambiguity existing in the formulation of the EU concept of operator.

This problem of ambiguity in the formulation of the EU concept of operator has been widely explained in section 5.8.1, according to which it is not clear who the operator is at EU level, and neither is it easy to identify the operator since not only the holder of a permit or authorisation for such an activity can be considered as 'operator', but also others such as 'the person notifying or notifying an activity'. The ELD definition of the concept of operator creates doubts as to who has the economical power of the activity or the 'formal power' and who has the technical functioning power, or the 'effective' power, and by consequence this ambiguity in the ELD formulation creates doubts about who is liable and must pay for costs of restoration as a consequence of environmental harm.

More specifically, the US concept of operator can be assimilated to an 'entrepreneur' who has the effective power and not only the formal power to control the risk of an activity causing environmental harm. Moreover, the US concept of operator is more restrictive and specific when referring to the subjects controlling the activity.

The US formulation of the concept of operator is, therefore, more precise, and clearer, especially, on who is liable and the different types of persons who are liable. In that sense, the US formulation of the concept of operator, used as inspiring source, would have rendered the ELD more progressive, as it would have improved the environmental protection goal achievements and pushed toward an optimal level of harmonisation.

---

575. See the case Philadelphia Electric Co. v. Hercules, Inc., 762 F. 2d, pp. 303–308 (3rd Cir. 1985).
576. See the case US v. South Carolina, Recycling and disposal, Inc, 21, Env't Rep. Cas. (BNA), pp. 1577–1581 (D.S.C).

5.9   CHOICE OF THE TYPE OF LIABILITY

The ELD provides for a dual system of liability based on fault based liability and strict liability.[577] When liability is fault based, the victim, in order to receive restoration must prove *culpa* of the potential wrongdoer in order to receive compensation. When liability is strict, the victim must prove the existence of the causality link between the potential wrongdoer and the damaging event, and there is no need for the victim to demonstrate *culpa*.

At a general level, the choice of the type of liability made by the EU legislator in the ELD, in cases of environmental damage, has to be considered as strict liability as to the professional activities indicated in Annex III.[578]

The choice of liability is very important, in relation to the Polluter-pays principle as has been highlighted previously, and the relevance of strict liability as a more effective instrument in achieving the environmental aims of the ELD is not new, since it has already been debated both at international level,[579] and EU level.[580]

The system of the choice of liability, based on the typical scheme 'dangerous activities – strict liability', is not based on the shift of the burden of proof as it is always the victim of the environmental damage who must bring proof.

At a more specific level, with regards to damage to biodiversity, even if derived from activities which are not included in Annex III (but concerning damage to biodiversity), the ELD provides for fault based liability. In the latter case, this means that there is environmental liability for damage committed to protected species and natural resources by an operator through fault and negligent behaviour.

5.9.1   OPTIONAL EXEMPTIONS FROM LIABILITY

An important issue of the ELD is the opportunity given to Member States to allow operators to enjoy certain exemptions from liability as a consequence of environmental damage. Member States can decide to use them or not which entails that these exemptions are optional and 'not eternal', and differ, in their nature, when compared with other kinds of exemptions provided by the ELD which are not optional.[581]

---

577. In the ELD, whereas n. 9.
578. The activities contained in Annex III are mentioned in section 5.6 of the present chapter treating the second focal point ('The Scope of Application of the ELD').
579. See the sub-section 3.1.3, Chapter 3, on the Lugano Convention.
580. See the sub-section 3.1.6.2, Chapter 3, on the White Paper.
581. The ELD also provides for other kinds of exemptions which are not optional (and therefore differ in their nature when compared with the 'optional exemptions' treated in the present section) but merely mandatory and exempts from liability in case of: a) Act of God, armed conflict, civil war, natural phenomenon (Art. 4, para. 1, letter a); b) caused by third party, provided that the operator took appropriate preventative measures (Art. 8, para. 3, letter

The exemptions are in other words 'a sort of derogations from liability' meaning that in certain cases, the liable parties are not liable for the consequences of an environmental damage and shall not pay.

Originally, the White Paper did not contain these exemptions, and the Commission did not intend to allow the existence of these kinds of exemptions.[582]

But the final draft of the ELD contains a mechanism which confers to Member States the ability to derogate from liability. This occurs for subjects causing damage without being at fault or negligent in cases of damage caused by emissions or events expressly authorised by domestic laws in force in Member States;[583] or whose damaging nature was unknown at the moment of the manifestation of the environmental damage.[584] In this latter case, the possibility for the operator to be liable in cases where there is a risk that a given activity could be polluting or for which there is a risk that the polluting effects of this same activity are susceptible to an increase over time, is therefore excluded.

This type of liability could be explained as a sort of liability for 'potential risk of development'[585] and is found, for example, in German law, in its corresponding provision formulated as 'risk of development' under German law called 'Entwicklundgsrisiko.'[586]

With regards to the first kind of exemption described in letter a) of Article 8 of the ELD a representative example is when an operator of a waste treatment disposal is exercising its activity as a consequence of an express authorisation from a Member State's competent authority.

This kind of derogation also referred to by the ELD as 'a) permit-defence' means that the same above mentioned operator (or manager or administrator) can enjoy permission to avoid liability and defend himself from the accusation of having committed environmental damage (as the expression says 'permit-defence') if the damage was a consequence of an authorised activity.

---

a); c) resulted from compliance with a compulsory order or instruction emanating from public authority (Art. 8, para. 3, letter b). In addition, the ELD, in its Art. 4, provides also for other exemptions in cases of oil spills and nuclear disaster. However, these exemptions apply, provided that the international instruments listed in Annex II are in force in the Member States concerned. It is worth noticing that these international agreements are not a satisfactory alternative. The remedies provided by these agreements are much less refined with respect to: a) the nature and measures to be taken, 2) the problem of who bears the cost, and c) the level of remediation.

582. White Paper on Environmental Liability, COM(2000) 66, page 18.
583. See Art. 8.4 letter a) of the ELD.
584. See Art. 8.4 letter b) of the ELD.
585. Liability for 'potential risk of development' is the liability which the operator incurs when responsible for damage caused by substances the scientific and technical damaging effects of which, were not known at the moment of the manifestation of the environmental damage.
586. This is also the liability that includes the risk from development occurring when the damage derives from the use of certain substances which, through science and technology up to the time of occurrence of the damage, it was not possible to know their toxic and noxious characteristics. See Pozzo, B., *'Towards Civil Liability for Environmental Damage in Europe: the "White Paper" of the Commission of the European Communities'*, 2001, Global Jurist Topics, Vol. 1, Issue 2, page 11.

The hypothesis establishing this kind of exemption concerns an operator not liable if the environmental damage was caused by a product for which it was not proven, at the time of the manifestation of the damage, to have damaging effects.

This kind of derogation is defined in Article 8, letter b) in the ELD as 'b) state-of-the-art' and is related to 'an emission or activity or any manner of using a product in the course of an activity which the operator demonstrates was not considered likely to cause environmental damage according to the state of the scientific and technical knowledge.' An example of this second kind of 'state-of-the-art' derogation is in the case where an enterprise placed into the market genetically modified organisms (GMOs). Given that there are considerable divergent opinions on the risk of the polluting and damaging effects which GMOs could have on biodiversity, in a case in which there was a manifestation of environmental damage due to the GMOs, it is more than evident that these enterprises (operators) will have a certain facility to avoid liability (and escape liability) by using the following argument: such types of activity were not considered dangerous on the basis of the scientific and technical conditions which were existing at the time period when they were authorised.

It is worth noticing that the IE (IPPC) Directive would play an interesting integrative role in strengthen the ELD regime as the ELD is enforcing the obligations laid down in the IE (IPPC) Directive, the GMOs regulations and other waste directives. Under the IE (IPPC) Directive, a producer is liable for damage caused by a defect of activities and production process. The term 'product' is broadly defined including many products containing GMOs, including foodstuff. Article 2, paragraph 7 of the ELD states: 'occupational activity means any activity carried out in the course of an economic activity, a business or an undertaking, irrespective of its private or public, profit or non-profit character'.

In that sense, Article 2, paragraph 7 of the ELD is sufficiently broad to include also producer liability by the manufacturer.

The damages that are covered in the IE (IPPC) Directive contemplate damages caused by death and by personal injury, liability it is not absolute and certain limitation applies. However, it is the Member States that have the competence of regulating such kind of damages.

Nevertheless, the implementation of the ELD by Member States will not end anyway the debate about liability for damage caused by GMOs. As it has been already mentioned, the ELD covers only some damages that might hypothetically be caused by GMOs. Heath damage arising from GMOs is not covered by the ELD but it is covered by the IE (IPPC) Directive.

Thus, if there is integration between the ELD and the IE (IPPC) Directive, then GMOs-products that have been placed on the market and that does not meet reasonable safety expectations, will be deemed defective and the manufacturer will be liable for damage caused by this defection. The damages that are covered by the IE (IPPC) Directive will be extended to the ELD and would include 'damage caused by death or by personal injuries and damages to, or destruction of, any items of property other than the defective product itself.' In the substance, the integration between the IE (IPPC) Directive and the ELD, would contribute to render the environmental liability regime stricter, more severe and stronger as the optional character of the exemptions from liability in the ELD would be mitigated, especially as to the room for manoeuvre for Member States to apply them or not, freedom the latter which would be, in such a manner rescaled.

In reality, the two kinds of exemptions which have been discussed until now, the (a) permit-defence; and the (b) state-of-the-art are of the same (optional) nature and are derived from the same mechanism of derogations put into function by the ELD.

In some manner, their motive of existence seems *à première vue* a paradox if it is thought that they are placed in a norm which is actually attempting to make the polluter liable and to apply the Polluter-pays principle.

However, the fact that these derogations exists, and are differentiated from those which are not optional[587] must have a legal logical reason. In other words, there should be a positive side in their motive of existence in the ELD. Both the first and the second kinds of these derogations could be interpreted as derogations to the principle of restoration of the costs as a consequence of environmental damage or derogation to the fact that the polluter must pay *tout-court*. A possible justification of these derogations is to create a sort of 'balancing effect' or 'a counter balancing effect' on a discipline which would otherwise be too rigorous. Nevertheless, it is difficult to evaluate the necessity for having these kinds of exemptions.

If it is taken the first case of exemptions, which is the case of the 'authorised activities' (permit-defence): on the one hand, it would be unequal to oblige the operator to pay for damages as a consequence of an activity which was previously permitted by a competent authority; on the other hand, however, this derogation is likely to generate concerns as, authorised or not, these emissions are likely to constitute environmental damage, and, if permitted, they will still remain 'authorised' in the future.[588] Therefore, this exemption is dangerous and leaves too much freedom to Member State in deciding to use it or not. Each Member States could decide to make an instrumental use of this exemption and decide to use the exemption in order for the operators avoid paying the costs of restoration in case of pollution.

Also with regard to the second kind of exemptions (state-of-the-art), it is difficult to evaluate its *raison d'être*. It seems that the reason that the EU legislator has permitted this exemption is once again based on equity. In one respect, it would not be fair to oblige the operator to pay for damages as a consequence of its activity, if it was unknown, at that moment, that the activity was dangerous and potentially polluting. In another respect, if the activity continues and will not be stopped, there will be no incentives to stop potential polluting activities because there is no liability for 'the potential risk of development in potential polluting activities.'

The opportunity to include or not to include the 'permit-defence' and the 'state-of-the-art' was also one of the most sensitive issues debated at the Council

---

587. See footnote of the first paragraph of the present sub-section.
588. Which would be not only in contrast with the Polluter-pays principle but also with the Principle of prevention and the Principle of precaution.

of the EU and was a source of conflict between Member States during the law-formation process of the ELD.[589]

The insertion in the final text of these exemptions is the clear consequence of trade-offs and negotiations pushed through under the intense influencing activity of some non-official actors who worked to avoid liability in several situations.[590] As a consequence of an eternal *dilemma* opposing growth and economical interest *versus* the rigour of a severe environmental liability regime protecting and regulating natural resources, industry groups, lobbies, and enterprises pressed hard for obtaining concessions and 'won' a reward at the highest level of decision-making: the insertion of these broad defences against liability stipulated and negotiated in terms of regulatory compliance and state-of-the-art knowledge at the time of the causative events.

The existence of these exemptions from liability allow too great an opportunity of manoeuvre to Member States, which in turn jeopardises not only harmonisation but also the achievements of the goals of the ELD among which, is the application of the Polluter-pays principle. The arguments based on the positive aspects of maintaining these derogations and on the necessity to respect equity and balance the needs of the operator are too weak and lack coherency if it is considered the goals and ambitions of the ELD, since there is such an urgency to have a rigorous legal protection of natural resources.

The inclusion of these exemptions in the final text of the ELD is not only in diametric contrast with the Polluter-pays principle but also represents an obstacle to the implementation of the ELD, since when one is faced with environmental damage, no one should be exonerated from liability even in the absence of a subjective element such as fault or negligence, and the damage should always be recoverable.

Thus, the exemptions in the ELD should be updated because if they remain as there are like know, they are allowing too great opportunity for Member States which in turn jeopardise harmonisation and the achievement of the goals of the ELD among which is the application of the Polluter-pays principle. Also, the issue of environmental permit is quite complicated because they are strongly influenced by legal traditions. These environmental permits have actually old traditions for administrative control of hazardous and polluting activities.[591] The ELD has tried to unify the requirements for such permits but did not succeeded in it and their differences have little to do with black letter law.

Their differences are rather due to a systematic approach, such as, for example, if the permit is regarded as a right or as a duty for the applicant and what is the legal effect of a permit.

---

589. ENDS Europe Daily, www.endseuropedalily.com, 10 June 2003.
590. See www.europa.eu.int/comm/environmental liability.
591. Darpo, J. '*Komparation och Tradition*', Abstract, Report of the Workshop, Comparative Environmental Law and Policy case studies and methodological perspectives, 15–17 August 2007, Finnish Environmental Institute (SYKE), NELN (Nordic Environmental Law Network).

The legal effect can differ from 'country' to 'country' and other components are relevant and have to be found in organisational social and economical factors and not only in black letter law, or in the frame of the different perception of a private *versus* public approach.

In substance, the EU legislator, choose to attribute less importance on the *culpa* element as the existence of a causality *nexus* between the environmental damaging event and the activity of the agent (or 'potential wrongdoer') has been considered enough to assign liability. Nevertheless, the EU scheme of dangerous activity connected to strict liability is not based on the shift of the burden of proof.[592]

In such a case, it would not be the victim that has the burden to prove that there is causalisation, but rather the potential wrongdoer who must prove that did not commit the environmental damage.

The EU scheme is therefore constructed in a way that the absence of *culpa* is relevant in specific situations only. Such kind of set-up could be incompatible with Member State's legislations, especially if the latter are connected with administrative procedures of restoration of environmental damage. In some Member State's administrative law systems, even in case where the legal system is fault-based and presumed, the shift of the burden of proof is admitted. Hence, the ELD do not admit the shift of the burden of proof but admits only, as previously examined, exemptions to liability which could be optional or not. The fact that the EU legislator has based the choice of liability in a way that the *culpa* element can never stands alone, and that there is always the need of strict liability elements, is the proof that the EU environmental liability regime has chosen a strict liability system, even if this system is presumed and not written in black and white and contained clearly in an Article of the ELD, but instead only briefly 'suggested' in a whereas[593] of the ELD.

The consequence of the tactical introduction of the suggested element of strict liability in the non-binding areas of the ELD, is that Member States have too much freedom in interpreting which choice to apply, fault liability or strict liability. The effect of such an excessive freedom in the choice of liability leads Member States to use mostly of the time fault liability rather than strict liability, by consequence, they tend to act in the opposite way: instead of guaranteeing a system based more on strict liability, they end up using the fault based liability system more often, as, also, a strict liability system can be very costly. However, this represents a negative, harking back to the past, and means taking the ELD out of its historical context as it ignores the important shift from fault liability into strict liability which took place in both Common Law and Civil Law countries after the period of industrialisation.[594]

---

592. The shift of the burned of proof is also called 'rebuttable presumption'.
593. The 'whereas' of a directive is non-binding law contrary to the 'articles' of a directive.
594. See sub-section 3.1.1, Chapter 3.

Also the choice of the Green and the White papers was based on a strict liability regime. The Green paper opted for the preference of a strict liability system as a preventive tool for environmental damage.[595]

Also the White Paper was in favour of a strict liability regime in cases of damages caused by dangerous activities and a fault based liability regime, in case of damage to biodiversity caused by non-dangerous activities.[596]

5.9.2   CHOICE OF THE TYPE OF LIABILITY AT THE INTERNATIONAL LEVEL

In the Lugano Convention, the preference for a strict liability regime is contained in the preamble stipulating: 'Having regard to the desirability of providing for strict liability in this field taking into account the Polluter-pays principle.' The basic feature of the liability scheme in the Lugano Convention is that it is a strict, joint, several and unlimited liability imposed on the operator(s) of a dangerous activity. The Convention admits the shift of the burden of proof. In addition, as introduced in the section 5.8.2, the Lugano Convention has this interesting novel and potential aspect of retroactivity which can be used at the EU level.[597] On one hand, the Convention applies only in incidents occurring after the entry into force of the Treaty. The same rule applies for gradual pollution or series of gradual pollution.

However, if the damaging situation has ceased and becomes known only after closure of a site, the last operator will be held liable for those damages.[598] The Lugano Convention also, contains the exemptions from liability in the case of the state-of-the-art event, such as the ELD.

Liability under the Basel regime is strict but also limited, according to the same limitations set-up from national legislations (of the Contracting Parties) and which should not be below the minimal thresholds indicated in Annex B of the Basel Convention.

The subjects involved in the trans-boundary movement shall maintain within those limits an insurance coverage or other financial guarantees. The wish to apply strict liability attempt to reach a precise objective: the setting-up of a better protection both for the victims and the environment.

According to the Basel regime, the victims of the environmental damage caused from waste disposals have to demonstrate the existence of the environmental damage that they experienced, as well as causation and without proving *culpa* of the eliminator of wastes. According to the Polluter-pays principle, the damage of

---

595. See sub-section 3.1.6.1, Chapter 3.
596. See sub-sections 3.1.6.2 and 3.1.6.3, Chapter 3 and also on the point 4.3 of the White Paper, which is titled 'The Type of Liability, the Defenses to be Allowed and The Burden of Proof' – White Paper on Environmental Liability COM(2000) 66 final, 9 February 2000, page 18.
597. However, it is worth noting, here, that this important element of 'retroactivity' is also the main reason why the Lugano Convention has not been ratified and it is also an element which is very difficult to accept at EU level.
598. Larsson, M.L., *'The Law of Environmental Damage: Liability and Reparation'* Kluwer Law International, 1999, the Hague, page 226.

the eliminator of waste causing damage to persons and to the environment has to be restored. In that regard, the EU level influenced the Basel regime when the Commission presented in 1991, the so-called 1991 second Draft Proposal of the Commission for the Council Directive on Civil Liability for damage caused by waste.[599]According to Article 7 of this directive's proposal: 'No liability for damage or impairment of the environment caused by waste shall attach to the eliminator if he can prove that, in absence of fault on his part, the producer of the waste deceived him as to the true character of the consignment of waste which caused such damage or impairment; in such an eventuality, liability shall rest with the producer.'[600] Therefore, the important novelty of the proposal of this directive was that it was attempting to offer a strict liability regime which was trying to admit the shift of the burden of proof.

The Basel Convention is also based on fault-based liability as is the Basel Protocol. The Protocol includes not only fault-based liability but also strict liability in its Article 5. Liability under the Basel regime is, therefore, strict but subject to limitations as in the ELD. The question of these exemptions to different subjects is an example, and it serves to prove the enormous difficulties which occur whilst conducting the negotiations on the legal text between the Contracting Parties.[601]

In substance, the purpose of insight into the choice of liability at international level and the comparison between the Lugano Convention and the Basel regime with the ELD, is to use, as a source of inspiration, their structures and formulations and suggest the need to incorporate their relevant aspects into the text of the ELD, at the time when there will be a redrafting phase of the ELD. This way to be inspired by selected elements of the international environmental sources of law into the EU law will render the ELD more progressive, and more successful in environmental protection goal achievements.

5.9.3   CHOICE OF THE TYPE OF LIABILITY IN THE US MODEL

The comparison between the US Model and the ELD with regard to the important issue of the type of the choice of liability as a consequence of the environmental harm, and the possibility to utilise some aspects of the US Model shows some *pro* and *cons* for the ELD. The use or non-use of some elements of the US Model could determine signs of regression or progress in the ELD. In particular, the analysis of the US Model on the choice of the type of liability is able to unveil some elements

---

599. See sub-section 3.1.2, Chapter 3, in reference to the Commission proposal to the Council for a Directive on Civil Liability for Damage caused by Waste, COM(91) 219 final – SYN 217, OJ C 23.7.1991, 192/5.
600. See COM(91) 219 final – SYN 217, OJ, C 23.7.1, 1991, 192/5, page 12.
601. Regarding that point, see Art. 12 of the Basel Convention, and also sub-section 3.1.4, Chapter 3. The difficulty in reaching a compromise was mainly due to the divergent interests of the developing countries (with the pressure from some types of NGOs) which were strongly opposed to the weak limits of liability.

useful for the improvement of the ELD scheme, especially with regards to the structure of the ELD.

Additionally, the US Model, in particular the relevant provisions of CERCLA, is in line with the Lugano and Basel schemes, and suggests some guidelines, especially with regards to CERCLA's impositions of joint, several, and retroactive liability which could be incorporated into the text of the ELD.

Not only are the ELD and the International choice on the type of liability dual, but also the US legal Model is based on both fault-based liability and strict liability. The US authority for regulation and liability is divided between Federal and State Governments.

The US law establishes therefore strict liability for pollution of land and water[602] in sites qualified from National Priority List (NPL) designations, and also set up a Hazardous Response Trust Fund ('the Superfund') as explained in Chapter 3.

The CERCLA imposes joint, several and retroactive liability as explained in the section dedicated to the role of the operators under CERCLA, which means that if any polluter is unable to pay for the clean-up of a site, then, the burden of proof is imposed on the contributor who is requested to pay more than their fair share of the clean-up expenses. The liability for response costs associated with violations under section 104, 106 (a) and 107 (a) for actual or threatened releases, has been held to be strict liability. The potential responsible parties are liable for conduct which occurred before the enactment of CERCLA. However, a split of authority exists as to whether responses costs expended prior to enactment of CERCLA, are recoverable.[603]

There are not only positive elements which can be used by the EU legislator from the US Model, but also important negative elements which should be taken into account in the ELD in order for the EU legislator to avoid replicating the same negative American experiences. In fact, there is a negative aspect in the US Model which should be considered as a 'lesson' for the ELD.

This negative aspect is that, as pointed out by Ashford,[604] to date, billions of dollars have been spent and not all of the designated sites have been cleaned-up.[605]

---

602. Except for pesticides, applicators, petroleum and most nuclear material.
603. Mukakis, A.W., '*Hazardous Waste Regulations: Enforcement & Liability*', 1999, Executive Enterprises Publications, page 86.
604. Ashford, N.A., '*Reflections on the Environmental Liability Scheme in the US and the EU: limitations and prospects for improvements*', Paper Presented at the Conference on Environmental Liability, Pireaus Bar Association, Pireaus, Greece, 26–27 June 2009.
605. USDA, Hazardous Materials Management Programme Strategic Plan for 2003–07, February 2003, in www.usda.gov; Gao, '*Funding and Reported Costs of Enforcement and Administration Activities*', June 2008, United States Government Accountability Office, Washington DC, in www.gao.gov/new/hazardouswaste; Report Card for American Infrastructure, in www.infrastructureportal.org/fact sheet; US Environmental Protection Agency, '*Clean up the National Waste Sites*', 2004, in www.epa.gov/Superfund; '*Obama's 2010 Budget: Becker's Iowa Environmental update*' April 2009, published by Berlin Mc Cormick P.C., A., Professional Corporation.

Thus, also in the US Model, there are still, currently, a lot of problems, as the Superfund clean-up is currently funded through an ongoing non-appropriate fund, due to the lack of coordination through the clean-up under the EPA's control and restoration of environmental damage under the different Trustee's control. On one hand, the coordination between the EPA and the Trustees is difficult since they both have different interests. The EPA demands measures of restoration (aimed at achieving health protection). The Trustees demand the clean-up of soils. On the other hand, there is an evident overlap of the different Trustees which led to a multiplication of different forms of restoration as a consequence of environmental damage, which had led to increases in legal conflicts, costs, and timings of restoring environmental damage.

5.10   CAUSALITY LINK

The causality link is one of the most crucial focal points in the environmental liability regime at all the levels, as already individualised in section 2.1.5 of Chapter 2. The requirement of a causality link between the wrongdoer of the damage and the event is very important, as liability is precisely applied on the basis of the existence of this link. The relevance of the causality link can be explained by arguing that the victim of environmental damage must prove causation, and if causation is not proved, the operator will not pay for restoration as a consequence of the environmental damage. In the ELD, it is the operator which is obliged to take the necessary measures or remedial measures in cases of environmental damage and these measures require the existence of a causality link between the event (the environmental damage) and the operator.[606] As explained, in section 5.8.1 dedicated to the obligations of the operator, the ELD does not provide for joint and several liability, and does not require demonstration of a causality link between the damage and several operators.[607] This result is another practical challenge consisting of the difficulty of establishing the causality link between the event and the hypothesis that the operator is more than one.

The problem relates to the case of 'diffuse pollution' which has been carefully avoided in the ELD[608] and refers to the case of multiple tortfeasors as also explained in section 2.1.5 of Chapter 2, and in the case of 'cumulative emissions', where the legislator has difficulties in determining the percentage of liability for each polluter to the polluting activity due to the difficulty in establishing causation.

---

606. See Arts 5 and 6 of the ELD.
607. For that point see also, Art. 4 para 5 of the ELD.
608. See for that point the whereas n. 13 stating 'Not all forms of environmental damage can be remedied by means of the liability mechanism. For the latter to be effective, there need to be one or more identifiable polluters, the damage should be concrete and quantifiable, and a causality link should be established between the damage and the identified polluter(s). Liability is therefore not a suitable instrument for dealing with pollution of a widespread, diffuse character, where it is impossible to link the negative environmental effects with acts or failure to act of certain individual actors'.

The final text of the ELD remits the solution of this focal point to the Member States, as Article 9 of the ELD states that if more than one operator causes environmental damage, the damage is allocated among operators. This will certainly create an obstacle to the application of the Polluter-pays principle and cause implementation to differ as there will be some Member States providing for joint and several liability and others that will not.

Joint and several responsibility and retroactivity are two problems which are strictly interlinked. For example, it has been observed in section 5.8, the case of the multiple parties or companies succeeding one and another in the same location where the economic activity was carried on and where the environmental damage was caused by previous companies or a combination of current and previous companies.

One of the most difficult tasks in such cases is to determine, economically, how much should be paid in case of joint and several liabilities. With that respect, the ELD does not consider the phenomenon of multiple torfeasors and the long distance pollution. Perhaps a solution might be sought into a deep analysis of the American experiences and the possible American solutions offered in that sense which could address the difficulties of the ELD as to joint and several liability and retroactivity for example, in what is called the (1) 'alternative liability theory'; and (2) the so-called 'proportional responsibility' or 'market-share liability'.

In the case of the 'alternative liability theory', this theory explains that in case of wrong behaviour committed by two or more individuals, and in case it has been proved that the damage has been caused to the victims, even if only by one of these people, but there is uncertainty about who committed the wrong, each of the subject has the burden to prove that he did not commit the wrong. That is the case when the American courts established the possibility of reversing the burden of proof on the defendants by determining a joint responsibility.

This theory shows the evolution of the joint tortfeasor responsibility especially when it is possible for the plaintiff, to determine the *nexus* between on one hand the damage inflicted to himself and on the other hand, the interactions of several cumulative wrongful actions.

In the case of 'proportional responsibility' or the 'market share-liability', it is found, here, another solution offered by the legal science of the American Courts to address the problem of the identification of those potentially responsible which is based on the 'preponderance of evidence' which means that it is the plaintiff's obligation to provide for evidence and the probative material.

The solution of the 'market share-liability' which translated into environmental language, is 'pollution-share liability', it is the case when the victim should take into Court as many private networks as possible that were present in the area of contamination in a way to solve in the matter of substance share of the 'polluters-markets'. These polluters markets should then be considered as proportionally liable according to the 'pollution quota' provoked by them. However, this solution is not perfect and not ideal as even though it would be possible to take into the Court what can be conceived by the same Court as a 'substantial share' of the polluter's market, it appears that the existence of the risk, that among the defendants the real wrongdoer is not present or that not all the responsible parties should be considered liable for the environmental damage, turns to be quite high.

5.11   INSURANCE MECHANISM

One of the most controversial and crucial focal points in the development process of the ELD concerned on the necessity to have a mandatory insurance mechanism. The solutions offered by the ELD to the economic operators, on the problem of a financial insurance guarantee are ambiguous. One author has proposed that a strict liability regime should not be introduced without a mechanism of financial guarantee since if a strict liability regime were in place, there would be a high risk of insolvency.[609]

The discussion on this crucial focal point was based on whether to set up a mandatory insurance mechanism or not. A mandatory insurance mechanism is opposed by several Member States. In fact some Member States are *pro*-insurance mechanism,[610] whereas others are not.[611]

In particular, the discussion concerning the reluctance to introduce a mandatory system has been strongly debated among Member States during the development phase of the ELD[612] and this controversy has also been reflected in the final draft of the text of the ELD, in particular in Article 14 which states that: 'Member States shall take measures to encourage the development of financial security instruments and markets by the appropriate economic financial mechanisms in cases of insolvency, with the aim of enabling operators to use financial guarantees to cover their responsibility under the Directive.' Nevertheless, this Article 14 is quite weak on the issue of 'financial guarantees.' The article gives the impression that the arguments used to justify a mandatory insurance mechanism system are not sufficiently strong and that the EU legislator is 'caving in' on the intention to harmonise. There is a feeling that the EU is not really pushing to find a justification on the basis of the Subsidiary principle. As to the shift to a mandatory regulation for financial guarantees, it is more than evident that if it were not for the pressure at the EU level pushing for such a mandatory insurance system, it would certainly not be happening by any initiative of Member States.

For that reason, a Commission's report, which was due by April 2010, outlined a first evaluation in terms of effectiveness of the ELD, where the need for an obligatory financial security scheme for the activities mentioned in Annex III, was exposed.[613] This Commission's report could be followed by a Proposal of the Commission for a system of mandatory insurance mechanism in Europe.

---

609. Faure, M., '*Deterrence, Insurability, and Compensation in Environmental Liability*', 2003, Tort and Insurance Law, Wien/New York, page 39.
610. The UK, Italy, France, Ireland and the EU Commission it self.
611. Germany, Belgium and initially Denmark.
612. See the section on the origins of the ELD of Chapter 3.
613. The Commission's report must address the availability at reasonable costs and conditions of insurance and other types of financial security for the activities covered by the ELD. See the

Also the White Paper strongly argued in favour of a mandatory insurance mechanism.[614]

However, the Commission failed to provide a solid argument for the necessity of introducing such a mandatory system also in the White Paper. In reality this reluctance is due to the difficulty of insuring against environmental damage to biodiversity which is a problem common at the international level and in the US.[615] The reluctance to set up a mandatory mechanism is also related to the formulation of the definition of the term 'environmental damage' offered by the ELD and to the facilities or difficulties that this definition has in determining the possibility of rendering the damage 'insurable.' Additionally, other characteristics of the environmental damage are making the insertion of the insurance mechanism hard to establish. Difficulties range from the problem of gathering information, to drawing up insurance policies, to identifying environmental risks, and to quantifying environmental damage. The latter focal point is of great relevance as there are practically no methods of evaluation which are 'universally recognised.' Other difficulties are related to the problem of long distance pollution,[616] the non-retroactivity of the ELD (to make the ELD retroactive would render environmental liability extremely costly at the short-term), and to the fact that the ELD, does not provide for joint and several liability. From and insurance point of view, these latter aspects should be considered as a central problem for the creation of a true insurance mechanism.

In conclusion, according to all that proceeds, the ELD contains several articles which should be carefully re-examined and redrafted in order to combine them with an insurance mechanism being set up.

Some of these articles are, for example Article 4 dealing with the exemptions; Article 9 on the criteria of costs allocation in cases of multiple party causation which takes into consideration the possibility of also applying 'any provisions at national level'; and Article 17 dealing with the temporal applicability of the ELD which establishes the non-applicability of the ELD in cases of damage, if more than thirty years have passed since the emission, event or incident, resulting in the damage, occurred.

In addition, from an insurance point of view, the ELD is always problematic with regards to the damage to biodiversity, water and soil, as it provides the Member States with only general guidelines which should be implemented concretely by each Member State through the implementation of laws. At present, in all these cases, there are still no precise criteria for the quantification of the environmental damage to water and soil, for example. The absence of criteria for

---

Report Survey of Industrial Companies-Insurance and other Financial Security Instruments and Remediation of Environmental Damages under the EU Environmental Liability Directive, February 2010, Brussels, *Ad-Hoc* Industry-Natural Resource Damage Group.
614. See sub-section 3.1.6.2, Chapter 3.
615. See sub-section 2.1.6, Chapter 2, and sub-section 3.1.5, Chapter 3.
616. In case of long distance pollution, such kinds of damage could be difficult to insure because they manifest only after a long period or gradually over time during the time.

quantification impedes the possibility of setting insurance parameters for the drawing up of insurance policies, as there are no possibilities for evaluating the environmental risk which needs to be insured.

Overall, there is a necessity to find other financial mechanisms. This necessity to find other mechanism is actually what it is found in Article 14, paragraph 1 of the ELD, where in the substance the EU legislator recommend finding 'mechanism other than insurance mechanisms'.

This necessity and wish from the EU legislator is, of course, in the opinion of the author of this book, due to the difficulty for the victims in identifying the wrongdoers especially after long fugitive period which represent obviously and obstacle for receiving compensation. For that reason, there is an express requirement to develop alternative solutions in different legal systems at EU, International and domestic level.

In that sense, some inspirations can be found in four different kinds of possible alternatives to the insurance mechanisms which are, for example: (1) Direct Environmental Damage Insurance; (2) Compensation Funds; (3) General Compensation Systems; and (4) Direct Compensation from the State.

Direct Environmental Damage Insurance is the first possible option for the insurance mechanism based on civil liability and is the one deriving from the possibility offered to the victims, of getting insured directly against environmental damage.

Compensation Funds are alternatives which are representing a much more concrete ways of approaching the problem. Compensation Fund takes shape of a different typology and can interact in a vague way with the mechanism of civil liability. Compensation Insurance Guarantee Funds would intervene only if it has been possible to identify those responsible and in case the latter are insolvent or the insurance coverage are insufficient or the insurer is insolvent.

A typical example of such an alternative insurance compensation mechanism is given by the Oil Pollution Act (OPA) promulgated by the US in 1991; and the International Oil Pollution Compensation Fund (IOPCF) set up by the Convention of Brussels on Civil Liability for Environmental Damage caused by Hydrocarbon Pollution in 1969 which is financed by the contributions from the potential polluters.

The OPA is this important American law targeted at improving the rules of liability in case of oil spill and hazardous accident. In the OPA, the wrongdoer is identifiable as the owner or the ship's operator or the structure from which the oil is spilled. The liability is strict and joint and limited by a maximum threshold.

The 1969 Convention established a strict liability with regards to the ship owner of the ship for damages provoked against subjects/individuals and against the State due to the pouring (spill) into the sea of hydrocarbons (oil). At the same time, this Convention provides conditions according to which the polluter will be exempted from these responsibilities. Among these expectations, the most important is the one providing for a certain limitation of the maximum threshold of the damage's compensation, as in the OPA. From the accusation in charge point of view, there is a difference compared to the normal mechanism of civil liability because after fund intervention, the damage is borne by all the potential polluters, and not just by the specific polluters provoking the damage. In that case, the accusation in charge on the potential polluter is the best instrument of putting into operation the Polluter-pays principle.

These kinds of funds, such as the OPA, differ from the compensation autonomy funds that compensate damage caused by pollution when it has not been possible to identify the origin like in CERCLA's scheme.[617] The aim of these funds is to compensate from damage deriving from atmospheric pollution to the subjects or parties that cannot find any kind of solution from the civil liability mechanism. This is the case of the Dutch fund called the Netherlands Air Pollution Fund (NAPF)[618] set up in 1972 for the victims of the air pollution and, of course, the Superfund CERCLA.

With regards to the General Compensation Systems, it has been highlighted several times to also set up social security systems representing a valid alternative to the mechanism of civil liability and the insurance scheme.

Finally, the Direct Compensation from the State is mainly utilised for huge accidents, such as the Seveso case and the Amoco Cadiz in France, where it is the State that intervened directly through general public funds. At the international level, only the Convention of Brussels of 1963 Regarding Liability for Nuclear Enterprises considers that the State should take care and cover the damage caused by nuclear accidents, the damages exceeding the limits of the owner's enterprises.

5.12   LEGAL TERMINOLOGY USED AS A RESULT
              OF A COMPROMISE

The legal terminology employed by the ELD is the result of a compromise between Member States belonging to Common Law and Civil Law traditions.[619] Often, the

---

617. See Chapter 3, sub-section 3.1.5.
618. See OECD Report, OCDE/GD(92)18, OECD Environmental Monographs No. 42 Pollution Insurance, 1992.
619. The legal terminology in the ELD is a result of a compromise where different models for protecting natural resources, as introduced in sub-section 3.1.5, Chapter 3 of this book (such as, for instance, the German example, Italian example, and the American Model), played a role and influenced the law-formation process of the ELD. In fact, as introduced in the same chapter, not all the countries legally protect natural resources in the same manner. Indeed, it has not been so obvious for those 'players' belonging to different traditions (i.e., Germany, UK, Italy and other Member States) to reach agreements at the EU level, and achieve a common view or a common perception on the way to tackle these focal points regulating the protection of natural resources. Of course, the US is not an EU Member State, but it has been explained in sub-section 3.1.5 of Chapter 3, and also in section 5.8 and sub-section 5.8.1 of the present chapter, how and where the US Model was used by the EU as an important source of inspiration in the shaping of the ELD. By consequence, the US can be considered as an 'indirect player' in the law-formation process of the Liability Directive, as the American Model has been taken into account in the law-formation process of the ELD, and has considerably influenced and shaped the current legal architecture of the ELD.

choice and the clarity of the terminology used by Community drafters during the law formation process (especially in the drafting of the legal acts) did not always assist a clear development of the ELD.[620] The legal terminology employed by the ELD as a compromise is the result of discussions and debates between Member States in the decision-making law process which was necessary in order to 'finally' have a Directive.

Which legal terminology to use is not only a problem for the ELD, but a problem, in general, for EU secondary legislation and directives especially.[621]

EU directives are often aimed at harmonising certain specific aspects of private law and public law within the EU. Generally, directives contain detailed definitions of any kind of concept; except those which should designate legal concepts. The lack of definitions of legal concepts inside the directives leave room for interpreting them according to the national legal traditions of the different national systems in which they are introduced. The legal concepts are the result of the arrangement and classification of different meanings which have been developed by the various traditions over the course of time and may vary widely from legal system to legal system.[622]

The problem of which legal terminology to choose, is a hard task for the European Institutions not only in situations characterising the drafting of secondary legislation, but also the Treaty it-self, as well as in the decisions of the ECJ which have to be translated and interpreted. Therefore, the challenge that the EU legislator has to face in the drafting of the EU law is not only in the drafting phase but it is also a problem of the translating phase.

For example, in the translation phase of the law, an EU legal act drafted by a lawyer with a background in Civil Law tradition, employing civil law concepts, will hardly be understood by a translator-lawyer with a background in Common Law, and so forth.

Some efforts have been made by the Commission in order to cope with this problem of how to deal with those 23 official languages, and to address the need to improve the quality of the drafting process of the legal acts.[623] For example, in daily business, the Commission has adopted the practice of working with only three languages: English, French and German. Under this practice, the draft's legal proposals and the draft policy papers are written in one of these three working

---

620. Winter G., Jans H, Macrory R., and Krämer L., '*Weighing up the EC Environmental Liability Directive*', in section 2 titled: '*Terminological Disentanglement*', 2008, Journal of Environmental Law, Vol. 20., N. 2, page 2.
621. Pozzo, B., Jacometti, V., '*Multilingualism and the Harmonisation of European Law*', 2006, Kluwer Law International – The Hague, page 13.
622. Pozzo, B., '*Multilingualism, legal terminology and the problems of harmonising European private law*' 2006, in Multilingualism and Harmonisation of European Law, ed. Pozzo, B., and Jacometti, V.
623. Pozzo, B., and Jacometti, V., '*Multilingualism and the Harmonisation of European Law*', 2006, Kluwer Law International – The Hague, pp. 1–20.

languages whilst the texts are translated into the remaining official languages only in the final phase with the precise aim of trying to avoid problems in translation.[624]

Hence, the difficulty in drafting directives with the appropriate legal concepts and legal coherence is crucial for the two different phases of creation and application of the EU law and also for two categories of legal professionals: (a) those which have to translate the legal concepts contained in directives into other languages, and (b) those who have to transpose them into domestic legislation. A lack of coherence between phase (a) and (b) creates a perilous situation in the very harmonisation process which directives are aimed at achieving. In fact, if there is a problem in the drafting phase, or in the pre-works of a given legal act (i.e., a directive's proposal), and the text is not written in an appropriate way, choosing the adequate legal concepts, this will reverberates not only in the translation from the original linguistic version (which is as explained above, written in one of the three above mentioned languages) into the other official languages but also in the implementation phase of the law.

The effect of this convention is that the implementation phase will vary and the way the different legal systems will 'translate' and 'transpose' and understand the legal concepts contained in the directives will differ too much, and, as a result, what can be understood by a Member State belonging to a given legal tradition may not be understood in the same way by another Member State belonging to a different legal tradition.

Other similar problems, related to the difficulty in achieving a harmonised result, can be met in cases where directives present, not only the wrong formulation or the inappropriate choice of the legal terminology of legal concepts but also the wrong stylistic technique and a lack of coherence in the application of the terminology, again, in the draft of the same original version, or when translated from language to language. In a more concrete way, when the EU Law draftsman is involved and starts to draft a proposal of a directive, or a directive, he/she should keep in mind that what will be written in the original version of a project proposal of a directive or a directive will be translated into 22 other official languages by legal translators of other legal traditions. The draftsman should bear in mind the multilingual nature of EU Law before starting to create the law.[625]

For that reason, the draftsmen should take extreme care in the choice of the legal concepts and the way of formulating the (proposed) legal act. This should also include an understanding that legal concepts which run the risk of not being understood or of being difficult (or impossible) to translate, should be avoided *ex ante*

---

624. The version of the draft legal proposals or draft policy papers will be referred to as the 'original version' and will be quoted as such, on the right upper most part of the document of the EU proposed legislation, and has to be written in one of the three above mentioned languages. This system permits, in cases of misunderstanding or problems of interpretation, the going back-to the original version which is supposed to be the version of reference in case of linguistic doubts.

625. This is not a suggestion of the author of this book, but a precise reference highlighted in the 'Join Practical Guide of the European Parliament, the Council and the Commission' for persons involved in the drafting of legislation within the EU Institutions. See Chapter 5 of this Guide which can be downloaded in http://europa.eu.int/about/techleg/guide.

before starting the drafting of the original version, in order to avoid problems *ex post*, once the law is enacted, and has to be applied.[626] In summary, avoiding problems at the point of origin (pre-works of the law or the phase of proposed legislation) would avoid problems in the translation phase, in the point of arrival (the final drafts of the legal text) and also in the implementation phase.[627]

The use of a non-appropriate terminology, or the inappropriate stylistic technique, in the legal wording or the lack of coherence used in the formulation of directives may lead to a situation which can produce divergent results in the implementation at national level, causing difficulties for national judges when faced with applying such laws, and as a consequence, make them differ and jeopardise the process of harmonisation. The difficulty in the process of the creation of EU law is that, sometimes, a legal term or a legal concept employed or chosen for the drafting stage in the EU legal acts or EU proposed legislation does not have corresponding term in another official language.

Legal terms, when translated, have different meanings in the different domestic legal systems and even have different classifications from jurisdiction to jurisdiction. As pointed out by some authors, in the specific case of the ELD: '... it may be obvious to a lawyer from a Civil Law tradition that the concept of – civil liability – is confined to liability under private law, and to dealing with wrongs that are equivalent to torts in a Common Law jurisdiction'.[628] It is, therefore, not always possible, to exactly translate the same legal concept into another language, rather it is only possible to 'get closer' to a similar concept,[629] and this idea of having to 'get closer' sometimes causes problems to arise through causing differing implementations in the Member States, and is quite perilous for a Common Law lawyer and for harmonisation.

Hence, the problem of how to achieve a harmonised result is also strictly concerned with the development phase of the law formation process of the ELD. In fact, if the development phase of the Liability Directive is re-observed, at a particular historical time, it can be noticed, as pointed out in section 3.1.2 of Chapter 3, that, after the failure of the last 1991 Second Proposal which attempted to establish a strong environmental liability in the waste sector, there were no documents which could be drawn up.

---

626. In order to avoid problems in the legal drafting of legal acts and avoid problems 'at the source,' the 'ideal legal draftsmen of EU legislation' working in the phase of the pre-works of the law formation process of directives, should be a bilingual or trilingual speaker, with experience in legal professional translations, with mother tongue in one of the three above mentioned languages, and possibly a specialist in Comparative Law. This choice would avoid radically, from the start, problems present at the beginning of the process.

627. Because if there are problems in the formulation of the law, these problems are automatically and implicitly reflected in the implementation and in the application of the law.

628. Winter, G., Jans, Jan H., Macrory R., Krämer L., '*Weighing up the EC Environmental Liability Directive*' 2006, Vol. 20, n. 2, section 2 'Terminological Disentanglement', page 2.

629. Eco, U., '*Dire presque la même chose. Expérience de traduction*', 2003, Introduction, Milan, pp. 1–26.

This absence of documents, together with the presence of an unpublished document circulating at the beginning of 1992 which was written by North American Common Law lawyer with Common Law background, are examples of these difficulties. Hence, the problem consist in finding a compromise on focal points containing key terms such a 'damage', 'liability' or 'civil', the meanings of which differ significantly from the interpretation attributed to them by most of the Civil Law countries.

One author[630] highlights this difficulty of terminology in the context which followed the debate after the 1992 Second Proposal and the circulation of the above mentioned 1992 document and the follow up debate which occurred following these drafts: ' *. . . key terms such as, 'liability and 'civil' differed significantly from the interpretation attributed to them by many of the participants of the later debate.* '[631]

The legal and cultural cross-differences in the ways of perceiving and understanding key focal points has generated confusion and misunderstanding in the EU law making process of the ELD, and certainly this linguistic confusion and misunderstanding has been reflected in the pre-works of the ELD, and from the pre-works of the ELD into the legal translations. Therefore, there is an increasing return from the past to the present of the difficult questions which the EU legal draftsmen are faced with, which is to formulate a legislation able to mesh into different legal cultures, employing different languages, linguistic formulations and legal concepts. The successful overcoming of the latter linguistic challenge in the ELD should be considered as a priority, if the true and genuine objective of the ELD is to reach harmonisation.

5.12.1   LINGUISTIC COMPROMISE IN THE FORMULATION OF THE DEFINITION
            OF ENVIRONMENTAL DAMAGE

In the drafting of the final draft of the ELD, the problem of finding a compromise on the definition of environmental damage in relation to the difficulty in achieving a harmonised result has been met by the EU draftsmen through opting for a deliberately non-technical definition.[632]

In fact, the style chosen by the drafters in the ELD was based on the use of a non-legal technical definition of the environmental damage, i.e., a technical definition was used which can be understood by natural scientists but certainly not by lawyers.

---

630.   Clark, *'The Proposed EC Liability Directive: Half-Way Through Co-Decision'*, 2003, 12, (2), RECIEL, page 256.
631.   Clark, *'The Proposed EC Liability Directive: Half-Way Through Co-Decision'*, 2003, 12, (2), RECIEL, page 256, footnote n. 16.
632.   Pozzo, B., *'Multilingualism and the Harmonization of European Law'*, 2006, Kluwer Law International – The Hague, page 13.

In accordance with the definition of the term environmental damage, established under Article 2 of the ELD the term 'damage' means 'a measurable adverse change in a natural resource or measurable impairment of a natural resource service which may occur directly or indirectly.' The scientific language employed in this definition, and the failure to supply concrete and clear criteria, allows for the possibility of having different interpretations of the definition of the environmental damage in the various national domestic systems. The different interpretations of the definition of environmental damage in the various national domestic systems is also accentuated by the fact that what can be understood as being an 'environmental damage' from a Member State is not for another Member State.

By implication, there is a need for a definition of environmental damage that can fix a 'minimum common denominator.' However, this 'minimum common denominator' should not be a scientific minimum common denominator, but a legal one, because if it stands like that (as a scientific minimum common denominator), then the judges will have difficulties in understand it.

By implication, if such a definition of environmental damage is maintained in the ELD, the implementation in Member States will differ with the risk of undermining the process of harmonisation. Such a scientific definition of environmental damage provided by the ELD imposes much too high a threshold in order to consider 'damage' as environmental damage.[633]

The ELD imposes much too high a threshold which will not be exceeded in many instances of damage using scientific wording in the formulation without any 'common notion' in the definition of environmental damage which could be detected, understood and transposed by Member States.

On that point, it is therefore questioned, whether this means of harmonisation is the right means. Is it possible to delegate this hard task of harmonisation to the scientific community?

It seems very hard to delegate the formulation of provisions, legal concepts, and harmonisation to natural scientists, since even though this may be the apparent method by which to find an 'immediate solution' for harmonisation, it is a dangerous method for harmonisation.

Insofar as the problem of the definition of environmental damage, which was a pre-existing problem from its inception, during the drafts and prior to the law being applied and implemented, it has simply been deferred and postponed until a future date, in the application of the EU law at the domestic level. The problem of the lack of clarity in definition of environmental damage will be exactly the same at the implementation level, and will be reflected in the interpretation phase of the law at the domestic level, when the judges will be faced with this definition in the application of the law.

---

633. Van de Broek, G.M., *'Environmental liability and Nature Protection Areas. Will the EU Environmental Liability Directive actually Lead to the Restoration of Damaged Natural Resources?'*, 2009, Utrecht Law Review, Published by Igitur, pp. 117–131.

The definition of environmental damage should be a definition which is able to fix limits or the precise criteria able to make the mechanism of liability functioning. The delimitation or the boundaries for when it is considered to have environmental damage are too vague in this definition and the high threshold will not easily be exceeded which entails that in the practical application of the ELD the protection provided is minimal since this renders the mechanism of liability unable to function immediately. In addition, if the boundaries by which it is considered environmental damage to exist are not clear, this will create problems for the insurers and for the evaluation and quantification of environmental damage.

5.12.2   Linguistic Compromise in the Formulation
      of the Choice of the Type of Liability

The choice of the legal terminology as a compromise in the ELD is also related to a specific writing technique which consists of 'minimising' important and key aspects of the language especially in relation to crucial focal points by omitting the writing of important elements which are objects of legal discussion. Here, in the specific case of the ELD the omission was on the writing of the little word 'strict' before the word 'liability,' in the choice of the type of liability in the ELD.

In fact, even though the ELD establishes a dual system of liability[634] based on strict liability for environmental damage caused by any of the occupational activities listed in Annex III,[635] and fault based liability with regards to the remaining activities not included in Annex III,[636] it is worth noticing that in the whereas n. 9 of the ELD, the term 'strict' is absent. The term 'strict' has not been included because it was too difficult to use a (legal) word which could have aggravated the disagreement among Member States, and probably would have jeopardised and further delayed the final agreement on the final text of the ELD. Hence, the 'little' word 'strict' when referring to liability is presumed, and not written in black and white in the final text.

This was also the way which the EU drafters utilised legal language as a compromise, even though, to be more specific, in that case, it is rather the 'non-use' of legal terminology which has been applied as a stylistic technique of drafting in order to reach a compromise. A compromise has certainly been reached, since there exists both a final draft and a directive which is the ELD; however, the question remains: is this the best way to harmonise?

---

634. See the previous section 5.9 of the present chapter.
635. In the case of activities mentioned in Annex III, there is environmental damage even in absence of fault.
636. In the ELD, liability is fault based in case of damage to biodiversity.

5.13 INTERACTIONS BETWEEN THE ELD AND OTHER
PARTS OF EU LAW: THE HABITAT DIRECTIVE,
THE WILD BIRDS DIRECTIVE AND THE WATER
FRAMEWORK DIRECTIVE

5.13.1 INTRODUCTION

The existence of the phenomenon of loss of biodiversity is increasingly representing a serious threat to Europe and to the entire globe. The crisis of biodiversity is
mainly due to the human activities which make the degree of this *dilemma* touch
the highest level of planetary alarm. In the name of profit for the business world,
natural landscapes, forests, seas, and the air, are under serious threat as a result of
the exploitation and commercialisation of biodiversity.

There is a certain reluctance in understanding the proper significance of the
term 'biodiversity' which should be fully grasped by policy-makers and legal
experts, whose tasks are to build environmental policies and legally protect biodiversity. Biodiversity has to be conceived as an *ensemble* of different interactions
between different *media*[637] and components of natural resources, and as such, must
be governed and regulated in line with those interactions, and also in line with the
progress of modern industrialisation. Also, the term 'biodiversity' is a relatively
modern term which was not coined until the 1980s, when an eminent Harvard
biologist, Edward Osborne Wilson, elaborated a definition. According to Wilson's
definition, biodiversity entails at the macro-level eco-systemic diversity (ecosystem and landscapes), specific diversity (the species of plants, animals and micro-
organisms that surround us), and at the micro-level it includes genetic diversity.[638]
Wilson's definition of the term biodiversity has also been retaken and refined by
the drafters of the 1992 RIO Convention on Biological Diversity that defines
'biological diversity' as meaning 'the variability among living organisms from
all sources, *inter alia*, terrestrial, marine and other aquatic ecosystems and the
ecological complexes of which they are part' including diversity 'within species,
between species and of ecosystems' (Article 2).[639]

Within a global framework of political conservation of biodiversity, both at
EU level and internationally, the law plays a central role in achieving environmental protection goal achievements. Undoubtedly, the protection of biodiversity
has to be achieved by combining law and policy.

With the view of fostering conservation regimes for both eco-systemic and
systemic diversity, and reducing their degradation, the ELD is attempting to regulate the protection of the biodiversity along with other categories of rules protecting the same eco-systemic diversity and specific diversity.

---

637. The different *media* in environmental law language means: water, ground, habitat, and animal
species.
638. Edward, O.W., '*Biodiversity*', 1988, National Academic Press.
639. See Birnie, P., Boyle, A., Redgwell C., '*International Law & the Environment*', section 2(3)
'*The Concept of Biological Diversity*', 2009, Third Edition, Oxford, page 588.

One of the main challenges for environmental rules, at EU level (and also at international level) is to drawn up effective rules capable of functioning in the context of environmental globalisation.

Effective rules mean rules which are able to achieve their objectives and goals, and maintain the promises of their pre-determined environmental ambitions successfully.[640] Effective environmental rules are also rules which are applicable and which are able to take into account the existing interactions between the different *media*. Nevertheless, this effectiveness is always difficult to achieve due to a number of different hard obstacles, such as the degree of *consensus* and participation of (EU) Member States, cooperation, ratification, degree of weak sanctioning, the quality of environmental regulations and also the financial possibilities.

At EU level, biodiversity is protected by three groups of rules protecting the habitat, the birds and the water. However, the existence of legislation protecting biodiversity in the aforementioned three categories of rules, and the regime of the ELD, does not mean that the protection of biodiversity in Europe should be interpreted as successful. Moreover, the concrete interactions existing scientifically between the different *media* should be reflected also in the environmental regulations. This means that the EU legislator[641] must take into account and create an integrated environmental law mirroring the interactions occurring naturally in the real word of biodiversity. That is why there is a need to consider and strengthen the interactions between the different categories of rules, as only a holistic vision of these rules for protecting biodiversity, can lead to an understanding as to whether these rules are really effective and efficient in protecting natural recourses.

This section is aimed at specifying which interactions of the ELD, with other parts of directives regulate the damage to protected species and natural habitats, and attempts to evaluate whether the ELD is effective in terms of environmental protection goal achievements. The focus of this section is on the definition of the notion of environmental damage in the ELD, and attempts to understand why the EU legislator decided to refer to other directives when involved in the process of elaborating this notion, and how parts of the current ELD are interacting and 'complementing' the pre-existing EU legislation (the *pre*-ELD directives) regulating the damage to protected species and natural habitats.

Finally, the section deeps the validity of legal environmental protection provided by the ELD; in particular analysing whether this protection is really effective in restoring biodiversity once damaged, and, if not, why this is so.

5.13.2   GENERAL CONSIDERATIONS

The notion of environmental damage chosen by the EU legislator in the ELD is based on three prerequisites: (a) the peculiar notion of environmental damage as

---

640. See Chapter 4.
641. The EU legislator or an environmental legislator in general.

such (b) the identification of the natural resources which are included in the notion of environmental damage; and (c) the seriousness of the damage. The present sub-section focuses on prerequisite (b). This prerequisite corresponds and characterises the focal point of 'the scope of application' of the ELD.

In particular, this sub-section provides in-depth insight on this focal point, given that it is with respect to that particular focal point that the EU legislator has employed a specific particular technique which is to create a law by 'reference', using other types of secondary legislation (other pre-existing directives protecting natural resources) in order to design, in the ELD, the peculiar notion of environmental damage as such.

In the ELD, the natural resources which have been identified and chosen to be included in the definition of environmental damage are of three types,[642] specifically:

(1) Damage caused to habitat and protected species as regulated, respectively, by Directive 92/43/EEC[643] and Directive 79/409/EEC;[644]
(2) Damage caused to water which means any type of damage which affect in a significant way the water conditions as defined by the Directive 2000/60/EC known as 'The Water Framework Directive';[645]
(3) The damage to soil or 'land damage' which is 'any land contamination that creates a significant risk on human health being adversely affected as a result of the direct or indirect introduction, in, on or under the land, of substances, preparations, organisms or micro-organisms.'[646]

The reason why this sub-section is focusing on damage to natural resources and protected species only (and not on the soil damage), is because it is for this kinds of damage (together with damage to water, which will be discussed below) that it is possible to identify a complementary and integrative role of the ELD in designing the formulation of notion of environmental damage. It is, in fact, in those three cases: area of legal protection of natural habitat, protected species, and protection of waters, where it appears that the EU legislator is strongly engaged in the technique of legal drafting by reference and complementarity. As previously introduced in the analysis of the White Paper in Chapter 3,[647] the novel and unitary approach of the concept of environmental damage designed by the EU law-makers materialise in two meanings: (a) the damage to biodiversity; and (b) the damage in

---

642. This is different to what was established in the White Paper. The ELD does not take into account the so called 'traditional damage' or the damage to goods and persons but only the damage to natural resources.
643. Council Directive 92/43/EEC of 21 of May 1992 on the Conservation of Natural Habitats and Protected Species, OJ 1992 L 206/7.
644. Council Directive 79/409/EEC on the Conservation of Wild Birds, OJ 1979 L103/I as amended by Directive 2006/105, OJ 2006 L 363/368.
645. Directive 2000/60/EC of the European Parliament and the Council of the 23 October 2000 establishing a Framework for Community Action in the Field of Water Policy.
646. See ELD, Art. 2, letter c).
647. See sub-section 3.1.6.2, Chapter 3.

the form of contamination of sites. In addition, as it is also mentioned in the same Chapter 3, the damage to biodiversity is covered, as protected in the Natura 2000,[648] according to the Habitat Directive and the Wild Birds Directive.

By implication the notion of biodiversity is central in the ELD and has to be interpreted and understood as the whole of ecosystemic and systemic diversity that need to be protected in order to avoid deterioration.

In the attempt to avoid deterioration and halt the loss of biodiversity, the EU legislator is not operating in a new sector. On the contrary, the legislator draws on considerable experience in that field as compared to experience at the national and international level.[649] The ELD is operating in a sector which is not 'virgin' territory, as there were already pre-existing legislations in the field of conservation regimes for both ecosystemic and systemic diversity. For that reason, the ELD is 'integrating' other part of the pre-existing secondary EU sources of law (i.e. Habitat Directive, Wild Birds Directive, and the Water Framework Directive).

This phenomenon is the one which creates interactions and complementarities among the sources of law of the ELD pre-existing secondary legislation, the ELD it-self, and the national legislations,[650] and which the EU legislator is using to elaborate the definition of environmental damage. It is for that reason that the ELD has to be perceived as a corollary of an edifice, adding more pieces and bricks to the pre-existing legislation, in order to define more clearly and precisely what the notion is of environmental damage to habitat, protected species, water and soil.

The technique of legislation by reference helps, in that sense, to understand when it is that there is environmental damage to the different *media* by simply making reference to previous directives.

The technique of legislation by reference is to be understood also as a mixture and coexistence of different sources of laws, at the EU level[651] and at the national level[652] with no hierarchy of one source of law over the other. The motive for having delimited the contour of the definition of environmental damage caused to biodiversity by using the technique of integration or incorporation with other pieces of secondary sources of law and national legislation is to broaden the notion of environmental damage which is presently too narrow. Hence, with this technique of legislation based on integrative construction, according to the critical de Sadeleer's view, the notion of environmental damage starts to resemble more and more to a Russian Matrioska Doll.[653]

---

648. For a reminder of Natura 2000, see sub-section 3.1.6.2.
649. For example, if it is considered the recent regulation existing at the international level, such as the 1983 Convention on the Migratory Species. In '*Droit International et Communautaire de la Diversité*', 2004, De Sadeleer N., and Born, C.H., Dalloz.
650. The national legislations applies when the Member States decides to protect habitat and protected species which are not considered to be covered by the ELD (and which are not part of the EU law).
651. See Art. 2, para. 3 a) of the ELD.
652. See Art. 2, para. 3 a) of the ELD.
653. De Sadeleer N., '*Les responsabilités environnementales dans l'espace européen. Point de vue franco-belge*', 2006, Brulant, Bruxelles.

According to the author's view of the present book, this technique of reference based on integrative construction through the incorporation of different sources of law of secondary legislation between the EU level and the national level, can also be perceived in a less critical way and therefore be explained through the existence of the Principle of integration which is Treaty based. The Principle of integration is one of the most important principles of EU law for environmental protection, as stated in the current Article 117 of the TFEU (previous Article 6 of the EC Treaty, and Article 97 of the TEU), according to which 'environmental protection requirements must be integrated into the definition of implementation of the Union's policies and must guarantee in particular with a view to promoting sustainable development'.

Hence, with the Principle of integration, the EU legislator stresses the need not only for harmonising environmental protection with other policies, but also the need for setting up and using a 'system of integration' unifying and coordinating different sources of law which are sharing a common space of interactions and synergies.

5.13.3   DAMAGE TO HABITAT AND WILD BIRDS

An important question as to the damage to habitat and wild birds, when related to the ELD, is why is there a need to integrate these two directives covering these kinds of damages into the ELD. There is an evident zone of overlap between the ELD and the two directives: Habitat-Wild Birds, as the ELD is also dealing with the protection of natural resources, but first and foremost the emphasis is on halting the loss of biodiversity by making the regime 'better' by strengthening the environmental protection effectively as compared to those laws which were pre-existing.

The ELD is literally borrowing aspects of the definition of the environmental damage from the protected species and natural habitat directives. In the same line of scientific reasoning typical of the Natural Habitat and Wild Birds Directives, the EU legislator has incorporated in the ELD the same scientific concepts which have been used in the construction of those two directives. For example, Directive 92/43/EC on the Natural Habitat presents concepts such as 'conservation' or 'stability of population',[654] whilst Directive 79/408/EC of Wild Birds presents specific techniques such as, for example, that endangered species must be placed on a list. These scientific concepts and techniques have been integrated into the provisions of the ELD.

More specifically, the interactions between the ELD and the two above mentioned directives help with the construction of the formulation of environmental damage in the ELD: Article 2, paragraph 1, defines environmental damage as 'any

---

654. The scientific concepts help to understand when it is that it is possible to talk about environmental damage. For example, in that sense, there is environmental damage when there is a negative impact on conservation, stability of population, etc.

damage that has significant adverse effects on reaching or maintaining the favourable conservation *status* of such habitat or species.'

The scope of the ELD is broader still when compared to those negotiated in the two directives, as the ELD should not be interpreted or restricted to the Natura 2000 Network.[655]

The ELD does not limited itself to damage caused to species included in designated Special Protection Areas (SPAs) under the Wild Birds Directive or species designated in Special Areas of Conservation (SACs) under the Habitat Directive.

By implication, any damage caused to sites hosting a sufficiently important number of specimens of species protected under an Annex either to the Wild Birds Directive or Habitat Directive, falls within the ambit of the ELD, provided that the damage has a negative impact on the conservation *status* of protected species.

Regarding the definition of environmental damage, in the ELD, it is questioned as to whether in the previously mentioned definition of environmental damage stipulated in Article 2, paragraph 1, all environmental damages entail liability. The answer to this question is negative as according to Article 2, paragraph 2, of the ELD, the damages for which the mechanism of liability is put into play are only damages which entail:

(1) a measurable adverse change in a natural resource or measurable impairment of a natural recourses service in relation to the baseline conditions;
(2) which have significant adverse effects on reaching or maintaining the favourable status of conservation of such habitat or species.

Article 2, paragraph 1 of the ELD contains therefore a threshold criteria for negotiating the significance of 'adverse effects' on the favourable conservation *status* of habitat and species included in the ELD, and is to be assessed with reference to the 'baseline conditions.'

However, as already mentioned in the section dedicated to legal terminology used as a compromise in the formulation of the ELD on the intentional use by the EU legislator of a scientific terminology in the formulation of the definition of environmental damage[656] (formulation which has been clearly negotiated in order to achieve a political compromise), the protection of the ELD is minimal.

The protection is minimal since the (scientific) definition of the damage imposes much too high a threshold in order to consider 'damage' as environmental damage, because not all adverse effects on the conditions of habitat or species prior to the harmful incident are covered, but only those that determine 'significant adverse effects' on reaching or maintaining the favourable conservation *status* of the affected habitat or species.

---

655. Van den Broek, G.M., '*Environmental Liability and Nature Protection Areas. Will the EU Environmental Liability Directive actually Lead to the Restoration of Damaged Natural Resources?*' 2009, Utrecht Law Review, Vol. 5, Issue 1 (June).
656. See previous sub-section 5.12.1 of the present chapter.

Article 2, paragraph 2 of the ELD shows another important interaction between the ELD and the Habitat Directive in the definition of the '*status* of conservation.' In order to establish the existence of environmental damage under the ELD, Article 2 paragraph 4, in defining environmental damage, requires identifying the *status* of conservation.

The identification of the *status* of conservation requires scientific evidence and if there is no scientific support or data, then, there is no damage, and, by consequence, no liability for the potential tortfeasor.

Also, without accurate information on the conservation *status* prior to the harmful event, it will be difficult to prove that an adverse change has taken place.

With regards to the damage to protected species, only a specific number of species are protected, under either the Habitat Directive or the Wild Birds Directive. The Wild Birds Directive protects all species which the EU finds to be vulnerable, endangered or endemic.[657]

However, by virtue of Article 193 of the TFEU (the previous Article 176 of the EU Treaty)[658] Member States can broader the notion of damage to protected species by including also protected species which are not included in the Annexes to the Habitat and the Wild Birds Directives. In that sense, it is not totally certain that this freedom, left to Member States, will be used in the manner intended.

5.13.4   DAMAGE TO WATERS

Not only has the damage to habitat and protected species been used by the EU legislator in order to complement the notion of environmental damage in the ELD, but also damage to water. Therefore, in the case of environmental damage to water, the technique of legislation by reference also applies. Actually, the notion of environmental damage to water, in the ELD, has been built upon the already pre-existing notion of environmental damage to water contained in the Directive 2000/60/EC, better known as the 'Water Framework Directive.'[659]

The scope of application of Water Framework Directive is broad and it applies to good surface water, ground-water, coastal water, and transitional waters. In addition, if it is compared the scope of application of this directive with the scope of application of the ELD, it is possible to note that the scope of application in the ELD has been extensively enlarged, given that the ELD covers not only surface water, ground-water, coastal water, and transitional water, but also the continental shelf and the economic exclusive zone.[660] Also, the EU legislator maintains in the ELD the same terminology used in the Water Framework Directive.

---

657. See Article 1 of the Habitat Directive.
658. See section 5.2 of the present chapter.
659. Directive 2000/60/EC of the European Parliament and of the Council of the 23 October 2000 establishing a Framework for the Community Action in the Field of Water Policy.
660. De Sadeleer, N., '*Les responsabilités environnementales dans l'espace européen. Point de vue franco-belge*', 2006, Brulant-Bruxelles, page 755.

The ELD, like the Water Framework Directive, selects the same damages that entail liability: damage is considered only those events that affect the 'surface' water *status* which is the general expression of the *status* of a body of surface water, determined by the degradation of its ecological and chemical *status*.[661] The latter formulation is also in line with the stipulation of Article 2, paragraph 18 which states that, 'the good surface water *status* is affected when both its ecological *status* and its chemical *status*, are less good.' Hence, in the ELD, the notion of ecological damage *status*, chemical *status* and the measurement of the 'more or less good' chemical *status*, have been defined by references taken from the Water Framework Directive. In the ELD, the competent authorities have the duty to prove that the damage is affecting the water condition seriously and negatively. However, there are no precise indications in the ELD as to this matter, which leaves a lot of leeway to Member States when they are attempting to define the standards that should be employed in order to establish when it is that the damage is affecting the water negatively and seriously. The ELD does not really offer guidelines or any indications as to this problem.

5.14   CONCLUSION

The ELD contains several gaps which should force the EU legislator to fill by taking into account the historical comparative multilevel context in which the ELD found it-self embedded and developed.

This includes not only a traditional way of comparing the different sources of law, but also a non-traditional way of comparing the different sources of law (EU, international, national) and the US Model with the ELD provisions by selecting focal points of a multilevel system of intersection between law and policy.

The ELD needs to be re-evaluated through a framework of analysis which considers the real potentials and opportunities offered by the international sources of law and the US Model. This framework permit the ELD to advance and mitigate the points of regressions and the aforementioned gaps, amongst which are also the linguistic incoherencies and wording formulation which are sometime used in an Machiavellian manner and as a surrogate to a bargaining of results more politicised rather than legally effective in terms of environmental goal achievements.

One of the problems is the EU legislator's practice of continuously 'deferring' to the national disciplines of Member States which leave them free to adopt more stringent measures on crucial focal points such as the definition of environmental damage, and the scope of application, etc. The practice of 'deferring' determines the risk of creating diverse practical applications of the ELD which manifests them as being extremely damaging not only for the EU competition and internal market but also for interests of international trade. This latter reflection explains why the ELD has also an external implicit effect which may open the way to a new path of

---

661.   See Art. 2, para. 17 of Directive 2000/65/EC.

research according to which there is also trade to be treated as an important element of the three-levels of decision-making.

The latter idea suggests the existence of the possibility for trade to be added in the integrative framework of analysis which considers not only the three-levels, but also 'the international trading system dimension' as part of the international level of sources of law which could be used to evaluate the ELD further. The existence of the 'trade level dimension' is justified since other countries could also be indirectly affected by the EU environmental liability regime, such as the developing countries, especially if it is considered waste and recycling issues.[662]

The ELD adopts a too limited notion of environmental damage which excludes the damage to air and to climate. This political solution is more an expression of a bargaining practice embedded in a scientific knowledge on such a capital focal point of the EU environmental liability regime, rather than on a legal solution to a problem.

A *formula* such as this encourages the risk of falling into the temptation to pollute by encouraging the operators to pollute the air (because air pollution is permitted), rather than soils or waters, since those environmental *media*, as demonstrated in the previous sections, present several shortcomings.

In that sense, the definition of the environmental damage provided by the ELD is in contrast with the concept of Sustainable Development which is why there is an urgent need to find an economic-politico-legal balance and adjust the notion in a way that science and policy do not prevaricate on law.

Undoubtedly, in order to solve the ELD shortcomings, the EU legislator will have to consider the important evaluation of the reconstruction of the EU decision-making process, both in terms of legal issues of regulations and environmental policies. Such a multidisciplinary evaluation scheme cannot be constructed without considering the multilevel context of the ELD and the different solutions offered at all of the levels which can potentially cover these shortcomings.

The ELD has not yet achieved a unified solution in regulating the environmental liability regime. Moreover, an updated ELD will certainly not 'save the world'. However, the EU, through an 'updated ELD' offers, potentially, the opportunity to draw up a general and global evaluation scheme, estimating the optimal level of harmonisation which should take into account, when up-dating the law, the multilevel context.

Perhaps, for once, it will be the US system which will have to learn something from the EU system rather than the opposite, which has always been the case previously, according to the lessons learned from historical experiences.

---

662. See for example the problematique case of the DPGs system (Domestic Prohibited Goods) as regulated under the World Trade Organisation (WTO) regime. Crucial focal points of the DPGs system are overlapping with the EU law and several issues in the zone of overlap between the WTO regime and the EU law, were also the same motives of controversy opposing the EU and the US in the Basel Protocol's negotiations. These controversies lead the two latter players defecting from the signature of the Basel Protocol, as explained in Chapter 3. In that sense, the Basel Protocol was not signed by the EU and the US because of the fear that for example an effective system on the domestic hazardous waste with severe regulations, would have had in jeopardizing trade an commercial exchanges with developing countries.

Part III

Implementation of Law and Policy at the Domestic Level

Chapter 6

Implementation of the Environmental Liability Directive: The Italian Example

6.1   INTRODUCTORY *PANORAMA* ON THE PROBLEMS
                 OF TRANSPOSITION OF THE ENVIRONMENTAL
                 LIABILITY DIRECTIVE IN GENERAL

In the light of the framework and methodology outlined throughout this book, the present chapter aims both at portraying in an analytical and systematic fashion, the problems of transposition of the ELD in general, and subsequently, at focussing more specifically into the problems of transposition of the ELD in Italy. The difficulty for Member States in drawing up effective laws of implementation lies in the historical problems of the difficult negotiations occurring in the development of the law-making of the Environmental Liability Directive, which caused several problems that are mirrored not only in the current legal text of the ELD, as advocated in Chapter 5, but also in the process of implementation. The present chapter includes the reaction of the EU towards the inadequate implementation of the ELD carried out by Italy. The conduct of this Member State was such that it forced the Commission to commence proceedings against the Italian Government, under the infringement procedure, for 'inadequate implementation of a directive'.[663] The chapter contains also the response of Italy as to the Infringement Procedure started against its government. Finally, some conclusions are drawn

---

663. On the 31 January 2008, the Commission commenced the Infringement Procedure 2007/4679 against Italy 'Liability-Non Conformity with Directive 2004/35 of Part IV, Titolo V and Part VII of Decree 152 of 3 April 2006 Avis Motivé 226'. See Infringement Procedure n. 2007/4670. Application du droit communautaire – Infractions, page 10, in http://ec.europa.eu/eu_law/eulaw/decisions.

both on the implementation of the ELD in general, and on the Italian example more specifically.

6.2   THE CURRENT *STATUS* OF IMPLEMENTATION

At a general level, the process implementation of the ELD has been uneven, cumbersome and challenging in the majority of the Member States.[664] The ELD entered into force on 30 April 2004 and only four Member States[665] met the deadline for its transposition of the 30 April 2007. After five years that the ELD entered into force, there were still nine Member States[666] which did not provide adequate legislative instruments to face the EU duties required for the implementation.[667]

Partly for the difficult negotiations occurring in the development phase of the decision-making of the Environmental Liability Directive and the 'too much political character' of the final text of the ELD, the process of transposition of the ELD remained slow thereafter, so that the Commission had to start infringement procedures against twenty-three Member States.[668]

Of course, the reasons for the transposition delay, at the general level, are also due to the ELD's different types of pre-existing environmental liability legal frameworks within the Member States.[669] Frequently, the laws of implementation of the ELD enacted by each Member State presented legal frameworks quite heterogeneous and fragmented depending on the pre-existing legal frameworks on which the ELD had to adapt. For example, it has been noted previously in this book, that Italy and Germany in the situation pre-existing the ELD, already had some pre-existing laws on civil liability as a consequence of environmental damage.[670]

---

664. See Coroner F., *'Environmental Liability Directive: How well are Member States handling transpositions?'* 2006, Environmental Liability, pp. 226–229; Giampietro F., *'La Responsabilità per danno all'ambiente – l'attuazione della Direttiva 2004/35/CE'*, 2006, Giuffré Editore; Lopatta H., *'ELD Report – Presentation for the EEB'*, 24 September 2010, Square de Meeûs 18, 1040 Brussels; European Environmental Bureau (EEB) Seminar on the Transposition of the Environmental Liability Directive (2004/35/CE) – Critical aspects and opportunities to strengthen it – Brussels, 29 May 2006, Seminar Report pp. 1–32.
665. The Member States which met the transposition deadline of 30 April 2007 were Italy, Lithuania, Latvia, and Hungary.
666. The Member States which after the year 2009 did not provide for legislative instruments implementing the ELD were Austria, Belgium (only the Region of Bruxelles-Capitale), Greece, Finland, France, Ireland, Luxembourg, Slovenia and the UK.
667. See Lopatta, H., *'ELD Report – Presentation for the EEB'*, 11 February 2011, Boulevard de Waterloo 34, Brussels, Belgium, DG Environment, Unit A.1; and *'ELD Report – Presentation for EEB'*, 24 September 2010, Square de Meeûs 18, 1040 Brussels.
668. Report from the Commission to the Council, the European Parliament, the European Economic and Social Committee and the Committee of Regions – Under Article 14(2) of Directive 2004/35/EC on the environmental liability with regard to the prevention and remedying of environmental damage, OJ L 143, 30.4.2004, English version, page 3.
669. See Chapter 3, sub-section 3.1.6.4.
670. See Chapter 3, sub-sections 3.1.6.4.1 and 3.1.6.4.2.

Contrarily, this was not the case for other Member States such as, Spain, France, the UK and Greece.[671]

The reason for a slow transposition can also be found not only in the different legal frameworks (adaptation, restructuring works), but also in the existence of challenging technical requirements, such as, problems in evaluating economically the environmental damage, choice of the type of remedies to apply, as well as the 'framework character of the ELD' which leave too much discretion and many options for Member States leading to lengthy domestic debate and legislative process.[672]

6.2.1   IMPLEMENTATION OF THE ELD IN DIFFERENT NATIONAL CONTEXTS

With regards to the transposition process of the ELD in the above Member States (those referred in the previous sub-section) it is worth noting that, in Spain, the Spanish Law of implementation[673] goes further than the ELD in several aspects and denotes a highly ambitious project.[674] One example testifying to this ambition is the mandatory requirements of financial guarantee which have to face several barriers from enterprises.

However, there is some scepticism at the present time as to the factual concretisation of the ambitious Spanish project on mandatory system of financial guarantee.[675]

Germany transposed the ELD with the Law on Environmental Damage[676] which presented a tight structure which stands together with the previous Law on Environmental Damage of 1991.[677] The German law entails a minimum transposition of the ELD compared to other laws of implementation, such as the Spanish law of implementation. The German law does not contain rules on the quantification of the environmental damage, insurance mechanisms and other financial guarantees which the operator liable for the environmental damage can utilise.[678] 'Insurance, for the German Environmental Damage Act ('GEDA') is likely to cover only environmental damages which are caused by disruption of operations. As a consequence, environmental damage which is caused in the course of normal

---

671. Giampietro F., '*La responsabilità per danno all'ambiente – l'attuazione della direttiva 2004/ 35/CE*', 2006, Giuffré Editore.
672. Lopatta H., '*ELD Report – Presentation for the EEB*', 11 February 2011, Boulevard de Waterloo 34, Brussels, Belgium, DG Environment, Unit A.1.
673. See the '*Ley 26/2007 de 23 de octubre, de Responsabilidad Medioambiental*' (BOE núm. 255, Miércoles 24 de Octubre 2007, 43229).
674. See from Article 1 to Article 8 of the '*Ley 26/2007 de 23 de octubre, de Responsabilidad Medioambiental*' (BOE núm. 255, Miércoles 24 de Octubre 2007, 43229).
675. Alvarez L., '*La responsabilidad civil por daños al medio ambiente*' in '*Tratado de responsabilidad civil*', Fernando Reglero Campos, 2008, Vol. 3 (parte especial segunda).
676. See the '*Umweltschadensgesets*' published in November 2007 (B6B1, 2007 I, 2631).
677. See Chapter 3, sub-section 3.1.6.4.1.
678. Rehbinder E., '*Implementation of the Environmental Liability Directive in Germany*', 2007, Environmental Liability, Vol. 5.

and permitted operations of the plant is not covered under the insurance policy offered'.[679]

In France, the implementation of the ELD was achieved with the Law of the 22 July 2008,[680] which transpose in a very precise way the ELD's text, but with a minimum transposition by inserting in the 'Livre 1er' of the Environmental Code, a new Title VI which is 'Titre VI' titled 'Prévention et reparation de certains dommage causés à l'environnement'.

The transposition of the ELD through the French law has been judged by the EU as not sufficient to implement the ELD, since the French government was also recently involved in the infringement procedure due to non-implementation of the ELD and therefore committing a breach of EU law. Of course, being late does not automatically mean being wrong. The reason for being wrong is the huge difficulty for France to design an effective law of implementation.

With regards to the UK, in February 2009, the Law on Environmental Damage (on the Prevention and Remediation) came into force.[681] Nevertheless, 'Regulation 2009' omits to treat key issues, such as which rules to apply in multi-party cases, insurance mechanism and financial guarantee. [682]

Also in Greece, in September 2009, the law implementing the ELD came into force.[683] However, several aspects of the Greek law implementing the ELD have not been regulated, in the sense that the Greek implementation of the ELD failed to add definitions to some focal points and aspects related to these focal points (such as aspects of land protection).[684] Greek implementation of the ELD failed to add some definitions on focal points which lead to uncertainty that cannot be solved, neither by national legislations nor in cases law.

6.3   REASONS FOR MEMBER STATE'S DIFFICULTIES IN HANDLING TRANSPOSITION

The transposition of the ELD was finally accomplished on 1 July 2010 which is more than three years after the deadline for transposition expired and '*where the*

---

679. Clifford Change, '*Germany : update on the German Environmental Damages Act (Umweltschadensgesets) and its effects on insurance products*', 11 September 2008, Global Environmental Group.
680. See the 'Project de loi relatif à la responsabilité environnementale et à diverses dispositions d'adaptation au droit communautaire dans le domaine de l'environnement', Texte définitif adopté n. 175, 'Petite Loi', Assemblée Nationale, 22 juillet 2008.
681. See 'Regulation 2009 -The Environmental Damage (Prevention and Remediation)', No. 153.
682. See 'Regulation 2009 -The Environmental Damage (Prevention and Remediation)', No. 153 from pp. 1–25 where it is possible to observe the total lack of rules in multi-party cases, insurance mechanisms and financial guarantee.
683. See the '*Presidential Decree on Environmental Liability that implements the ELD*' of 21 September 2009', No. 148 of September 28th, Official Gazette on 29, 2009 (FEK A' 190/29.9.2009).
684. See Charalampidou, N., '*The Protection of Land in Greece – before and after the implementation of the Environmental Liability Directive*', August 2010, European Energy and Environmental Law Review, pp. 160–174.

directive gives Member States the flexibility to choose what action to take, we see a diverse picture across Europe' as expressed by Hans Lopatta, civil servant at the Commission's environment directorate.[685] The implementation of the ELD has been one of the most difficult that Member States have had to transpose, especially due to the difficulty in drawing-up effective laws of implementation even for most green Member States, such as Denmark, known the world over for its strong tradition in protecting the environment.

Denmark had to modify a considerable number of times the laws of implementation before being able to adapt the Danish laws of implementation to the ELD.[686] The result of this cumbersome implementation will be proven shortly, in the following sub-sections, by using Italy as an empirical example demonstrating this negative 're-mirroring' (sections 6.1.2 to 6.1.3).

In that sense, the problems of the past negotiations of the development phase of the Environmental Liability Directive on the focal points, are reflected in three sequential phases: from phase (1) which is the phase of different sequences of key past decision-making processes of the Environmental Liability Directive;[687] to phase (2) which is the phase of the final legal text of the ELD;[688] to be reflected into the third phase (3) which is the phase of the current transposition phase in each Member State. This signifies that problems that are not solved at the origin (in phase (1) the ELD decision-making processes of the law or 'phase of *input* of the law-formation') will still continue to go on into the phase of the legal outcome or 'legal *output*' (phase (2) of the legal text of the ELD), and subsequently the same problems on the formulation of the focal points during this phase, will be spilled over in a 'negative knock effect' at the level of the national legislative process on the phase of the application of the law (phase (3) of the uneven transposition of the ELD in general).

The reasons for the difficulties lies, in the character of 'political compromise' which strongly characterised the legal text of the ELD, which entailed, and still entails, that Member States are required to ascertain important solutions to 'solve' key problems on focal points of an whole framework on an entire regime which is the EU environmental liability regime existing from more than fifty years ago.

---

685. Newsletter '*Implementation of EU Green Liability Law – Uneven*', Thursday 5 February, 2009, ENDS Europe DAILY.

686. See 'Lov om undersøgelse, forebyggelse og afhjælpning af miljøskader' (miljøskadeloven), senere ændringer fra LBK nr. 978/af 26/09/2008, til LBK nr. 856 af 01/07/2010 (14 changes), in www. retsinformation.dk.

687. The key decision-making phases which are referred to here, consists of those having as object of negotiations the EU legal acts or proposed legal acts of secondary legislations characterizing the development phase of the ELD since its inception, *à savoir* from the very first initial 1976 'Directive Proposal on the Waste Sector for a Council Directive on Toxic and Dangerous Wastes', OJ 1976 to the 2002 'Proposal for a Directive of the European Parliament and of the Council on Environmental Liability with regards to the prevention and remedying of environmental damage' COM(2002) 17 final, 2002/0021 (COD), Brussels, 23 January 2002.

688. Directive 2004/35/EC of the European Parliament and the Council of the 21 April 2004, on Environmental Liability with regards to the Prevention and Remedying of Environmental Damage, OJ 30 April 2004, L 143/56.

In that sense, according to ELD's goals and ambitions that the ELD set out to deal with it is too much to demand that Member States solve problems that the EU law-maker of the Liability Directive it-self, during the development phase of its law-formation process, should have had solved *a priori*.

This could mean that now, it is too late, however it is never too late (as it will be shown in the last chapter) to solve the problems of ineffectiveness in 'the field' as what the Member States are currently facing, is no more than a 'negative spill over effect' *a posteriori* of what were the 'past politico-legal imbalances' and 'trade-offs' (the 'past' is the developing phase of the law-formation process of the Environmental Liability Directive) which are reflected into the present (the 'present' is the transposition process of the ELD). The EU current legal interpretation 'welcomes' the 'past' with numerous infringements procedures against Member States due to their inability to correctly implement the ELD as its legal text is too political and therefore leaves too great a lack of clarity and ambiguities, on several focal points.

This lack of clarity and ambiguity allows Member States to use too much flexibility for choosing as how to transpose the ELD, with the risk that the Member States could manipulate the misunderstandings deriving from the low level of quality in the formulation of the legal draft of ELD. Hence, in that sense, a doubt persists as to the fact that these ambiguities, in the legal wording used in the formulation of the ELD's provisions, have been left on purpose as a 'technique of camouflage', in order to cover-up political compromises on several focal points, and to protect certain Member State's interests on sensitive issues, especially on issues where it is difficult to find a balance between trade and environmental protection or where environmental protection is used as a 'tool' to protect other interests not necessarily related to environmental protection.

6.3.1   THE ITALIAN IMPLEMENTATION: *STATUS* OF LEGISLATION BEFORE
          AND AFTER THE ENFORCEMENT OF THE ENVIRONMENTAL
          LIABILITY DIRECTIVE

Before the implementation of the ELD, the Italian legislation on environmental liability was based on the Law 349/86.[689] Article 18 of this law denoted a system of civil liability according to which: 'any act committed with fault or negligence, in violation of provisions of law or provisions adopted by law which compromises the environment, causing damage to it, changing it, deteriorating it or destroying it, totally or partially, obliges the responsible party to compensate for it in front of the State'.[690] The article was based on a broader legislative framework of the Italian

---

689. Law of the President of the Republic No. 349 of 8 July 1986, establishing the Italian Ministry of Environment and including some provisions on environmental damage, published in Supplement to the Official Journal of the Italian Republic No. 59 of 15 July 1986.
690. Article 18 of the Law 349/86.

Civil Code, Article 2043, and according to which 'anyone causing damage by fault or negligence must provide reparation for the damage'.

Basically, Article 2043 entitled individuals to claim compensation for personal injury or property damage caused by an environmentally harmful act or omission when proving fault or negligence of the liable party. Therefore, the ELD organises a system much broader than the Law 349/86. The main differences between the ELD and the Law 349/86 were centred on issues related to the focal points: the definition of environmental damage, the scope of application, choice of the type of liability, and so forth.

In particular, with regards to the definition of environmental damage, the ELD prefers to link this definition to specific *media* situations such as biodiversity, soil, water with the exclusion of air pollution. In contrast, air pollution was included in the definition of environmental damage offered by the Law 349/86 aforementioned. As to the scope of application, the ELD subordinates the environmental liability regime to solely specific activities which are included in a specific technical Annex which the Italian legislator did not.

In addition, the ELD provides for a system of double based liability regime, fault and strict based whilst the Italian legislator before the enforcement of the ELD did not.

The Italian system was a fault-based liability regime even though the jurisprudence[691] interpreted this rule in the light of the Italian Civil Code's provisions (Articles 2050 and 2051) which also included situation giving rise to a strict based liability regime.[692] Another important provision existing before the ELD, in Italy, was the 1999 Ronchi Decree concerned with sites contamination.

Under Article 17 of the Ronchi Decree, anyone who, for whatever reason, was responsible for the contamination of soil or water beyond the prescribed safety limits, should pay the costs for clean-up and restoration of the polluted area. This provision introduced a strict liability regime for whenever certain limits were overstepped or there was significant health risk.

After the implementation of the ELD, in Italy, from the very beginning, once the Italian Law of the implementation of the ELD was enacted with the Law introduced by Part VI of Decree 152/2006, thereafter, called 'Italian law of implementation', the law was strongly criticised because of the confusing formulation of several of its provisions.

This led the Commission to start the infringement procedure against the Italian government.[693] One of the main criticisms of the EU debate against the Italian law

---

691. D'Orta C., *'Ambiente e danno ambientale: dalla giurisprudenza della Corte dei Conti alla legge sul Ministero dell'ambiente'*, 1987, Rivista Trimestrale di diritto pubblico, pp. 60–112.

692. In particular, Art. 2050 of the Italian Civil Code provides a specific system based on strict liability for dangerous activities applicable in cases of environmental damage. This article establishes that: *'whoever, in the course of a dangerous activity, causes harm to another person, shall provide compensation for the damage, if he is not able to prove that he/she has taken also the necessary measures to avoid the damage'*.

693. Infringement Procedure n. 2007/4679 against Italy (as previously introduced in the first section of the present chapter)

of implementation, was the existence of the fault based liability regime which was considered outdated and too closely linked to the pre-existing situation of environmental liability rules which were in force prior to the ELD.

The same criticism formulated at the beginning of the enactment of the Italian law of implementation of the ELD protracted until recently, in 2009. In order to partly address these criticisms, the Italian Government introduced a change which modifies some provisions[694] of the Italian law of implementation only. This change, is Article 5*bis* of the Decree n. 135/2009.[695]

Overall, several problems during the implementation process of the ELD in Italy surfaced, and the nature of these problems is still related to the formulation of the focal points at EU level, as this Italian law of implementation, was neither stringent nor clearly formulated, giving arise to many problems of 'misleading interpretation' of its formulation by the national courts during the application of the ELD in the Italian legal system.[696] In that respect, it is also worth noting that in parallel, to the Infringement Procedure n. 2007/4769 started against Italy,[697] there was also another type of procedure involving Italy which differs from an infringement procedure in terms of the nature and function. It is worth remembering that this procedure is the 'preliminary ruling procedure' and which started upon request from the Tribunale Amministrativo Regionale (TAR Sicilia),[698] in July 2007,[699] to the ECJ, to pronounce on 'preliminary ruling procedure' according to Article 234 of the EC Treaty, on the interpretation of the EU law and compatibility of the Italian Legislation with the EU law which lead the ECJ to give ruling of interpretation in the Cases C-379/08 and C-380/08 Raffinerie Mediterranee, which have been already object legal analysis in Chapter 5.[700]

These problems of confusion in the formulation of the Italian law of implementation of the ELD determined a grim implementation of the ELD in Italy, and further complicated the existence of public authorities, enterprises and insurers. Below, follows in more details, the problems of formulation by the Italian law of implementation of the ELD on the focal points originated at EU level, and increasingly returning and reflected in the transposition law, causing misunderstandings in the application of the ELD in the Italian national law due to the weak level of quality of elaboration of the Italian implementation law. More concretely, these

---

694. The provisions of the Italian law of implementation which have been modified will be identified and analysed in the next sub-section 6.1.3 titled '*Responses of Italy as to the Infringement procedure started by the Commission against its Government*'.
695. The changes to the Italian law of implementation, introduced with Art. 5-Bis, will be object of analysis of the last sub-section 6.1.3 of the present chapter
696. Alberton, M.C., '*Saint George and the Dragon: Transposing the Environmental Liability Directive in Italy*', 2007, Environmental Liability, Volume 15, Issue 6, pp. 235–241.
697. Infringement Procedure n. 2007/4679 against Italy (as previously introduced in the first section of the present chapter)
698. TAR is an Italian Administrative Court
699. Hence, in parallel with the notification of the Infringement Procedure 2007/4670 against Italy (as previously mentioned in the first section of the present chapter)
700. For an in depth analysis of the Cases C-379/08 and C-380/08 Raffinerie Mediterranee, see Chapter 5, sub-section 5.8.1

misunderstandings derived in elaborating the definition of environmental damage; the scope of application; compensation of environmental damage; and choice of the type of liability.

6.3.1.1 Definition of Environmental Damage

Article 300 of the Italian law of implementation indicates what has to be considered as 'environmental damage' both at general level and at specific level by listing the natural resources which have to be included into the notion of environmental damage.

The Italian definition of environmental damage is therefore reproducing the one furnished by the ELD[701] except that the Italian law add that the environmental damage has to be 'significant'[702] but excludes from the definition of environmental damage the damage caused by airborne,[703] in contrast to the ELD which includes into the definition of environmental damage, the airborne component too.

This means that the new provisions of the Italian law of implementation, as to the definition of environmental damage, shows a sign of regression on the protection accorded by Article 300.

The Italian law of implementation abrogates the Ronchi Decree which provide for a specific synoptical table of thresholds to be used as a parameter for determining the degree of pollution and the minimum and maximum acceptable degrees of pollution relevant to assign environmental liability on the operator, which is necessary for the evaluation of the risk each time that there is environmental damage.

6.3.1.2 Scope of Application

The Italian law of implementation is characterised by the absence of the activities determining environmental damage and which as a consequence establish liability for environmental damage. In substance, what is missing in Italian law, is the technical Annex III of the ELD, which selects those activities, in paragraph 2–7, which determine a significant potential or real risk to health and environment. The non-inclusion of the activities determining environmental damage mean that any kind of activities can be taken into consideration without differentiating those that determine a 'significant risk' for the environment and those that do not, as has

---

701. The definition of environmental damage in the ELD is reproduced in Chapter 5, section 5.5
702. The element of 'significance' in reference to the environmental damage was present in the 2002 Environmental liability proposal but was dropped out in the final text of the ELD
703. In contrast to the Italian definition of environment (as already explained in Chapter 3, sub-section 3.1.6.4.2, and reiterated, previously, in this chapter, in sub-section 6.3.1) where the Italian legislator adopts a broad and unitary notion of the environment which included: '*air, climate, surfacewater and groundwater, land, flora and fauna, ecosystem, health, landscape and noise*'. In reference to the definition of environment in Italy according the Law 349/86, in the situation *ex ante* the enactment of the ELD, see also Annex I of Ministerial Decree 27 December 1988, published in Official Journal of 5 January 1989 No. 4

been specified in the previous focal point, the definition of environmental damage.[704]

According to the Italian definition of environmental damage, the damage has to be 'significant' in order to put into function the mechanism of liability of the operator.

Hence, also in the Italian Law of implementation as regarding the scope of application, there is a sign of regression in the formulation of its provision as such a formulation, is clearly impeding the mechanism of liability as a consequence of environmental damage to start to function in time.

6.3.1.3   Compensation for Environmental Damage

The Italian law of implementation comprehends the criteria for reparation as a consequence of environmental damage from Articles 305–307. The Italian law of implementation did not correctly transpose the criteria for reparation as regards the respect of the 'hierarchy' provided in the technical Annex II of the ELD on the measures of reparations which are part of a separate Annex in the ELD titled 'Measures aimed at repairing environmental damage'.

The respect of the 'hierarchical' scheme of restorative measures, proposed by the EU legislator in the ELD, outlines the differences between Primary, Secondary and Compensatory Remediation'. However, it is worth remembering, as already explained in Chapter 5, section 5.8, that the scheme of restorative measures proposed by the EU legislator[705] does not outline clearly when environmental damage is compensable given that the EU legislator has distinguished incorrectly what the 'Secondary Remediation' is, which is aimed at compensating and what the 'Compensatory Remediation' is which actually does not compensate. The non-respect of such a described hierarchical scheme of restorative measure from Italy opened up the way for the Commission, to initiate, in 2008, an infringement procedure against the Italian government, precisely, due to this omission, from Italy, to integrate and respect the ELD hierarchical scheme of the measures of reparation.[706]

In that respect, the ELD place at the first level, Primary remediation, which means that it is not possible to adopt Secondary remediation or Compensatory remediation, without having expired, first, the 'chance' to repair the environmental damage through Primary remediation.[707] Thus, even though the Commission has

---

704. On the element of 'significance' in determining environmental damage, see the previous subsection.
705. The scheme of restorative measures provided by the EU legislator, in the ELD, is explained in Chapter 5, section 5.8 with a synotpical table outlining the differences between Primary, Secondary and Compensatory Remediation.
706. Infringement Procedure n. 2007/4679 against Italy (as previously introduced in the first section of the present chapter).
707. See for that point, Chapter 5, section 5.8.

defined the possibility to use techniques of monetary evaluation, the use of these techniques is only allowed to determine the extent of Secondary and Compensatory remediation, and not merely for substituting these two latter kinds of remediation, with pecuniary remediation.

Hence, the Commission admitted [708] that the provisions of the Italian law of implementation (specifically, from Articles 311 to 313) in its original version, were conceived and drafted in a way so as to allow the measures of reparation to be achieved with monetary remediation through the equivalency method, even though measures of Primary remediation were not previously adopted.

On the face of this latter argumentation, it is hard, now, to oppose the thesis exposed in Chapter 5, section 5.8, as regards the lack of clarity of the hierarchical scheme designed by the EU legislator, the misleading effect of which, is clearly reflected in the application of the ELD at national level, as the Italian example demonstrates.

Moreover, the ELD hierarchical disentanglement is not only reflected in the misleading use of the measures of reparation. The hierarchical disentanglement also has an impact on the misleading effect of the obligations of the operator as a passive subject restoring environmental damage.

Article 311, paragraph 2, states:

> whoever harms the environment, through fault or negligence, in violation of the provisions of the law or provisions adopted by law, causing damage to it, changing it, deteriorating it, or destroying it, totally or partially, is obliged to restore it as it was before the damage or when it is not possible to compensate the state for the damage.

The misleading effect on the operators' obligations is also aggravated by the unclear formulation of the scope of application. This is, as explained in section 6.1.2.2, because the selection of the activities is missing in the Italian law of implementation. Given that, the selection of activities is important for the attribution of liability as a consequence of environmental damage, there is, automatically, no liability as a consequence of environmental damage.

The lack of selection of activities in the Italian law of implementation is also a possible explanation as to why the Italian environmental liability system opted for a fault-based liability regime, instead of a strict-based liability regime. This will be addressed in the following sub-section, dedicated to the focal point 'choice of the type of liability'.

In that sense, it is worth noting that Article 311, paragraph 2, introduce a fault-based liability regime, which poses problems as to what kind of new liability emerges from a combined reading of Article 300 (on the focal point of the

---

708. The Commission opposed and still opposes, amongst its argumentations in the Infringement Procedure n. 2007/4679 against Italy (as previously introduced in the first section of the present chapter) the lack of existence, in the Italian law of implementation of the ELD, of the 'hierarchical scheme' of restorative measures, as explained previously.

'definition of environmental damage'),[709] and Article 311, paragraph 2 (on the focal point of the 'choice of the type of liability').[710] Whereby, in the Italian environmental liability system, there is coexistence between two different types of situations causing environmental damage, which are Articles 300 and 331, paragraph 2. The content of Article 331, paragraph 2, will be detailed in the following sub-section, where on the basis of which,[711] it will be possible to acknowledge the total absence of any kind of connection criteria between the two articles.[712]

6.3.1.4   Choice of the Type of Liability

Article 311, paragraph 2, of the Italian law of implementation, introducing a system of fault-based liability regime, is formulated in the same manner as the 'old' Article 18 of the law 349/1986[713] abrogated by Decree. The operator cannot be held liable if it is not proved that he/she/it was at fault and the environmental damaging event is caused by an emission or an event expressly allowed by authorisation.

In addition, the operator cannot be held liable for environmental damage as a consequence of a damaging event caused by an emission or activity or any manner of use of a product in the course of an activity which the operator demonstrates that was not considered likely to cause environmental damage according to the state of scientific and technical knowledge.

The Italian law of implementation apply, therefore, the two exemptions described in the ELD in letter a) Article 8 of the 'permit-defence'; and in letter b) Article 8 of the 'state-of-art'.[714] The Italian legislator, thus, continues to base the liability regime on fault-based liability, as recently demonstrated in the Joint Cases C-379/08 and C-380/08 Raffinerie Mediterranee which have been analysed in Chapter 5.[715]

According to the judgment of the Sicilian administrative Court (TAR Sicilia) of Catania in the above mentioned cases, the Italian law of implementation provides also for a retrospective system double based (fault-retrospective, and strict-retrospective based) in the case of land contamination. [716]

---

709. Article 300, as explained in sub-section 6.1.2.1, deals with the focal point of the definition of environmental damage which is, as explained in Chapter 2, the first focal point in the order of the chain of logical sequence explaining the key factors of the environmental liability regime and where the 1) definition of environmental damage, is the capital problem which reverberates over all the other six focal points (see Chapter 2).
710. Article 311, as will be explained in the next sub-section, deals with the focal point of the choice of the type of liability.
711. On the basis of the content of Article 331, para. 2.
712. Articles 300 and 331, para. 2 of the Italian law of implementation which are totally disconnected.
713. See the previous sub-section 6.1.2 of the present chapter.
714. See Chapter 5, sub-section 5.9.1.
715. See Chapter 5, sub-section 5.8.1.
716. See Tar Sicilia, Catania, Sez. I, 20 July 2007, No. 254/07.

6.3.2   RESPONSE OF ITALY AS TO THE INFRINGEMENT PROCEDURE STARTED
              BY THE COMMISSION AGAINST ITS GOVERNMENT

Italy has reacted to the action brought against its government[717], initiated by the Commission, providing immediately to rectify some parts of the Italian law of implementation, and also in clarifying some formulations in the provisions of this law of implementation, in order to render not only the implementation law but also the implementation, more effective. For these purposes, the Italian government has very recently introduced by Decree n.135 of 25 September 2009 converted with changes by the law no. 166 of 20 November 2009, the Article 5*bis* (which has been only briefly introduced at the beginning of this Chapter). This Article 5*bis* introduces some innovative aspects.[718]

In particular, Article 5*bis* introduces the following changes into the Italian law of implementation: (a) new criteria for the reparation of environmental damage which are more in line with those contained in the ELD; (b) re-introduction of individual-liability (and not joint and several liability) on the obligation of the passive subject that has to restore the environmental damage, and (c) the plan to set-up future enactments for criteria to quantify environmental damage.

With regards to point (a), new criteria for reparation of environmental damage, Article 311, paragraph 2, has been recently modified and clarified which means that Secondary and Compensatory Remediation has to be carried out in line with the hierarchical scheme of reparation of the ELD and only if remediation or the adoption of Secondary Remediation or Compensatory remediation turns out to be:

> in all or partly omitted, impossible or excessively expensive (Art. 2058 of the Italian Civil Code) or carried out in an incomplete way or differently as to what prescribed, the polluter is obliged, subsidiarily, to compensate and bring about remedial actions that should be able to render natural resources of the same kind equivalent both in term of quality and quantity which will have to be identified with further Decree by the Ministry of the Environment.

As to the point (b), re-introduction of individual liability (and not joint and several liability), some words have been added to the provision dealing with this issue which is Article 303, paragraph 1, letter f. The words added to the latter article of the Italian law of implementation are the following: 'criteria for determining the duty to repair in accordance with Art. 311, page 2, 3'.

---

717. Infringement Procedure n. 2007/4679 against Italy (as previously introduced in the first section of the present chapter)
718. The innovative aspects of Art. 5-Bis of the Italian law of implementation have been presented by Prof. Barbara Pozzo, during the course of a seminar organized by her-self and the Università degli Studi Milano-Facoltà di Giurisprudenza, the Camera di Commercio, in cooperation with other Partners, titled '*La responsabilità civile e penale delle imprese in campo ambientale alla luce delle novità comunitarie*', held on 8 February 2011 in Milan (Italy)

Lastly, with regards, to point (c) the plan to set-up future enactments for criteria to quantify environmental damage, the Italian legislator added to Article 311, paragraph 3, the following sentence:

through Decree of the Ministry of the Environment, Land and Sea to be enacted by sixty days from the date of enforcement of the present provision, in accordance with Art. 17, paragraph 3 of the law, n. 400 of 23 August 1988, are herby established, in conformity with what is provided for in point 1.2.3 of Annex II of Directive 2004/35/EC, the criteria for determination of remedy by equivalency and excessive expenses according to the estimated monetary values of natural resources and services in previous judgments at national and EU level of legislation. In cases of multi-parties, liable for environmental damage each party is responsible and shall be liable. The debts can be transmitted, according to legislation in force.

Overall, the last changes introduced into the Italian Law of implementation exposed in the aforementioned letters a) to c), are certainly to be estimated as 'promising' in terms of sources of inspiration for the design of future criteria for the quantification of the environmental damage to be understood as a good without a market price. Nevertheless, it is not yet sure what will be the future stand both of the Commission as to the Italian conduct in the infringement procedure,[719] and the future trends of the interpretation of the ECJ in the preliminary ruling procedures in the cases related to the emerging problems for national courts in interpreting provisions of the ELD in the process of implementation at national level, as the Sicilian case[720] which has been object of discussion in this book from Chapter 5 until now, shows.

However, it is difficult to cope with these parallels situations of uncertainties.[721] These uncertainties in the implementation phase of the ELD derive, on one hand, from problems of Member State's conduct in the correct application of the ELD; and on the other hand, from problems of interpretation of the ELD.

However, what is needed, especially in the prevention and remedying of environmental damage, is certainly not a permanent *status* of uncertainty in the

---

719. Infringement Procedure n. 2007/4679 against Italy (as previously introduced in the first section of the present chapter)
720. Cases C-379/08 and C-380/08 Raffinerie Mediterranee
721. The situation of uncertainty is due to the misunderstandings in the formulation of the focal points negotiated in the legal text of the ELD which has favoured the path for the opening of the too different and parallel procedures. On one hand, problems for Member States' conducts to respect the EU Treaty and implement adequately environmental directives (which open the path for the starting of several Infringement Procedures against Member States, *ex* Art. 226 of the EC Treaty, now Art. 258 TFEU), as the case n. 2007/4679 Infringement Procedure against Italy, demonstrates. On the other hand, problems emerging during the application of the ELD at national level which open the path for the emergence of problems of interpretation for national courts (and the starting of several Preliminary Ruling Procedures, *ex* Art. 234 of the EC Treaty), as the Cases C-379/08 and C-380/08 Raffinerie Mediterranee demonstrates

protection of the environment, as it is not possible to live forever without certainties.

6.4   CONCLUSION

In light of the analysis conducted on the problems of transposition in general, it can be adducted that the ELD represents a regression rather than advancement in terms of environmental protection goal achievements.

The ELD is ineffective due to the difficulties deriving from the political and compromising character which has distinguished the negotiation of its final text. In the final text of the ELD, it is more than evident that the focal points of the environmental liability regime have been 'negotiated', or even more 'traded' in order to reach agreements rather than reaching an effective environmental law. In doing so, the level of harmonisation appears quite low and certainly far from optimal.

Thus, ineffective, confused, and unclear, is also the Italian law of implementation. This ineffectiveness in the Italian law of implementation reverberates on the implementation because, as it has been proven in the Italian example, it also makes the implementation ineffective.

In fact the Italian implementation has been quite confused, often with problems of misunderstandings which are due to the low level of quality and clarity in the formulation of the focal points debated and negotiated during the decision-making of the ELD. Hence, the result of this 'political compromise' of the final legal text of the ELD is mirrored in the quality of the laws of implementation. Despite the attempts of the Italian legislator to address the difficulties in the design of the law of implementation of the ELD, there are still several problems in the formulation of the focal points of the environmental liability regime, starting with the definition of the environmental damage which is unclear. In the legal architecture of the Italian law of implementation the focal points are not interconnected and their sequential order does not respect the order of the chain of legal logical sequence necessary to create an effective environmental liability law. The unclear and too political formulations of the focal points in the Italian law of implementation are still pending solution, which creates several legal and jurisprudential uncertainties, and the impossibility to establish a future insurance mechanism. In particular, in Italy, the current implementation of the ELD is in the *status* of uncertainty and ineffectiveness, where:

(1) the definition of environmental damage is still unclear;
(2) the scope of application is still not defined;
(3) there is an absence of a clear definition on the choice of the type of liability;
(4) there is an absence of a Decree with regards to compensation of environmental damage, as well as a clearly defined, real, criteria for quantifying environmental damage.

Part IV

Recommendations, Amendments and Perspectives

Chapter 7
Overall Conclusions

7.1   CONCLUSION I, PART IV: HAS THE ELD ACHIEVED ITS GOALS AND AMBITIONS?

In light of the legal analysis conducted in the chapters of this book outlining an holistic perception of the focal points of the environmental liability regime in a chain of logical sequence operating in a multilevel context, it is possible to infer some conclusions.

The ELD leaves Member States with too many options for manoeuvring and adopting more stringent measures for the prevention and remedying of environmental damage. These measures include the identification of other activities subject to preventative and reparative actions, as established by the ELD, as well as the identification of other responsible parties.

The ELD should be up-dated, taking into account the lessons learned from past experiences, especially the circumstances under which the ELD has been developed since its inception.[722]

Drawing on the past in this way, suggests that the legal basis for the ELD should be reconsidered, and not be based solely on Article 192 of the TFEU; rather it should be dual-based. Dual-based means in terms of both based on Articles 114 and Article 192 of the TFEU.

Applying these articles would grant environmental legislation a certain degree of strength and rigour which would make it difficult for Member States to utilise their wide manoeuvrability in applying more stringent or less stringent legislation and favour harmonisation.[723] This dual basis for the legal foundation of the ELD is

---

722. See Chapter 3.
723. On the possibility of combining these two articles for legal basis for environmental legal acts, see also Chapter 3, especially the footnote which includes also the observations of Professor Jans on the same issue, but referred to environmental legal acts in general.

justified by the fact that the ELD has, at the present time, three main goals: (1) to harmonise environmental liability by establishing common criteria to which national legislators will have to conform when setting up an environmental liability regime; (2) to ensure the application of the Polluter-pays principle; and (3) to eliminate situations of internal market distortions and secure trade.[724]

By consequence, the ELD's objectives are related to economic reasons and not only to environmental protection aims. In order to bring the ELD in line with the concept of Sustainable Development and to face the new challenges of the political and legal globalisation of the environment, legal and economic environmental aspects should go hand-in-hand.

Hence, it is not possible to forget the context in which the ELD has been embedded since its inception. This context was, and still is, double-oriented: internal market goal achievement oriented and environmental protection oriented. The context is framed in a multilevel global perspective where the EU is also the carrier of environmental values based on the quality of environmental production, rather than on the quantity of goods produced.

In this perspective, even though Articles 114 and 192 of the TFEU have different purposes, the first, is aimed at harmonising national legislations in order to ensure the smooth functioning of the internal market of goods, services, workers and capitals; and the second, is aimed at protecting the environment in accordance of the objectives of the EU Treaty, they could be combined. This happens, in cases where a directive is designed to achieve both environmental protection and the functioning of the internal market. The purposes of these two articles are, therefore, overlapping and should be susceptible to being combined. The latter situation is precisely the case of the ELD.

Article 192 of the TFEU is generally applied to rules for industrial enterprises (which generally do not circulate, contrary to goods which circulate). Article 114 of the TFEU is normally applicable to goods that circulate (i.e.: rules related to emissions standards of the production of goods). Since those enterprises do not usually circulate but the products do, if a rule on environmental standards increases, this will have directly an effect on the costs of production and on competitiveness, and therefore it will have an impact on the functioning of the internal market.

That is why, the use of Article 114 of the TFEU, as a legal basis for the ELD, would render the law more effective since it would be more binding and stronger if the two articles were combined. The combination of these two articles would in fact, in the name of the internal market goal achievements, attenuate all the freedom given to Member States in applying stricter environmental rules, and avoid excessive flexibility being left to the Member States, to the competent authorities and to the enterprises willing to cut down the degree of environmental liability in order reduce their costs of production.

In other words, it is possible to reach a certain success in terms of environmental protection goal achievements results, even if the legal basis of a measure

---

724. See, for all three points, section 5.2 'Goals, Ambitions and Challenges of the ELD', in the present chapter.

is not necessarily based on Article 192 of the TFEU, but rather on Article 114 of the TFEU.

In substance, what is important is not the choice of the legal basis for the EU measures to be effective in terms of environmental goal achievement, rather the existence of a qualitative balance between economical and environmental protection goal achievements which must be stroked.

Nevertheless, the problem in this new formula harmonising environmental rules and combining simultaneously Articles 114 and 192 of the TFEU, consists of how to reconcile a total harmonisation directive with a minimum harmonisation directive.

Generally, a total harmonisation is encountered particularly frequently with measures based on Article 114 of the TFEU and is concerned with situations where there is a linkage between environmental protection and the free movement of goods, as for example the directives harmonising products' standards. A minimum harmonisation directive fixes common objectives and principles and leaves Member States free to adopt more stringent standards, but some degree of harmonisation is necessary if only to prevent Member States from using flawed environmental legislation as an instrument of industrial policy.

The problem of how to strike a balance between total and minimum harmonisation was exactly the same problem-situation that was also faced in the 'Battery Directive' 2006/66.[725] The problem was solved in the case of the Battery Directive with a dual-based approach. The dual-based approach of this directive was deemed to be appropriate as the legal basis to harmonise the laws of Member States as regards to product requirements by using Article 114 of the TFEU, but also to reduce the negative impacts on the environment by reducing the generation of batteries and accumulators on the basis of Article 192 of the TFEU. This same combination should be used in the ELD where: Article 192 individualises common criteria that the Member States' legislations have to comply with, and Article 114 of the TFEU which would be fully justified by the impact that the ELD is having on the functioning of the internal market since its inception.

In that sense, applying Article 114 of the TFEU means incorporating into the definition of environmental damage, the traditional damages also comprehensive of the economical damages or damage to goods or persons deriving from environmental damages and also those deriving from catastrophic events. The fact of keeping those damages out of the ELD increases disparities amongst legislations and, as it has been widely explained in Chapter 3 of this book, favours the persistence of unequal conditions as some Member States would include in the notion of environmental damage, the traditional damages, and others not.

That is why there is an urgent need to redraft the definition of environmental damage as if it remains as is, it will have a strong negative economic impact.

---

725. See Directive 2006/66 on Batteries and Accumulators and Waste Batteries and Accumulators, OJ 2006, L 66/1. Batteries and accumulators often contain dangerous substances such as heavy metals. The European legislator considered it necessary to have product rules and rules concerning their separate collection and safe treatment once the batteries become waste. For that reason, this directive contains rules based on Arts 114 and 192 of the TFEU.

In that sense, the economic component should not be considered as of minor importance compared to environmental protection needs, as if this was the case, it would not be possible to achieve a sustainable solution. In that perspective, the notion of environmental damage should include a real system of minimum threshold of graduation within the same threshold system which could be used, not only by Member States, but also by regions and public administrations. The graduation should also be susceptible to being regulated according to different uses of the different *media* (water, soil, air, etc.). The method of graduation should also guarantee the respect of the Polluter-pays principle and the Subsidiarity principle as well as the public participation of non-official actors.

The ELD is not concerned with the interesting and difficult cases of environmental damage. The ELD has become a legislative means for administrative issues; thus detaching its *raison d'être* from the original ambitions and goals set out. This shift in stance is paving the way for unseen challenges and is generating and keeping alive several shortcomings. These shortcomings must be addressed if the ELD is to become the piece of legislation it promised to be: effective in terms of environmental protection goal achievements.

The ELD ensures a strong administrative regime. However, this is too simplistic. In such a wrong direction, the ELD would not ensure the achievement of its original goals and ambitions which were laid down at the beginning. The ELD is suffocated with the concern to set up an 'administrative European legal model' for environmental protection instead of focusing on its original goals and ambitions. In that sense, the ELD will no longer deal with those difficult and interesting cases of catastrophic damages, and will regress and end up, silently, into a 'directive of ordinary banal administration' without exploiting the strong potential contained in it. In that sense, the ELD is paradoxically limited as should accept that the nature and human beings are constantly confronted with cases of severe and catastrophic damage to the environment resulting from human acts.[726]

The environmental liability regime of the ELD is not a true environmental liability regime; rather it is, in effect, an administrative regime aimed at implementing a public system defined by 'reference' to the definition of environmental damage.

7.2   CONCLUSION II, PART IV: WHAT IS THE OPTIMAL LEVEL OF HARMONISATION IN TERMS OF ENVIRONMENTAL PROTECTION GOAL ACHIEVEMENTS?

The definition of 'environmental damage' is the capital problem and the adjustment of its formulation would have a beneficial spill over effect reverberating on

---

726. Examples of environmental disasters are: the recent 2010 Louisiana Oil Spill Golf of Mexico Disaster, the 1989 Exxon Valdez Oil Release in Alaska; the accident of Erika in the South of Spain; as well as and numerous other examples.

all of the other focal points of the European environmental liability regime. Also, it is worth noting that in the five years since the ELD came into force, there were nine Member States which are still in the process of implementation.[727]

The ELD is not finding the right *formula* in order to realise environmental protection goal achievements. The degree of harmonisation reached with the ELD is far from being optimal as the ELD presents too many points of regression and shortcomings which impede the European environmental liability regime from working effectively and efficiently.

The aim of the ELD is to reach environmental protection goal achievements.

However, there are several shortcomings in the ELD which need to be addressed, in order to, effectively, attain for this law, environmental protection goal achievements.

On 30 April 2013, Member States shall report to the Commission, their experiences regarding their respective implementation. On the basis of this material presented by the Member States, the Commission will present some observations to the European Parliament and to the Council of the EU and shall forward by 30 April 2014, a proposal for amendments to the ELD. The shortcomings of the ELD lie in the focal points and the way in which they are designed and placed in a chain of logical sequence within the legal architecture of the ELD. The coverage of the shortcomings in the ELD can be considered as objects of future proposals for policy amendments.

In a more concrete way, the following key shortcomings are emerging from the ELD:

(1) The definition of environmental damage should be redrafted as it is too limited and too scientific-oriented. As presently drafted, the notion of damage in the ELD eliminates traditional types of damages and sets up a mechanism with a threshold principle that is too high and with no criteria to assess the significance of the damage. Hence, there are pending questions which are still without answers: what is meant by 'threshold' and 'scientific evidence' in the ELD? Is the notion of environmental damage strong enough for evaluating issues and bringing scientific evidence? It is not the scientific evidence which should dictate the legal terms since it is not the question which the EU legislator wants to address in the ELD, especially according to the original goals and ambitions of the directive. There is a need to separate the scientific point of view from the legal point of view in order to embrace traditional types of damage within the notion of 'environmental damage' and to outline guidance for assessing the

---

727. The Member States which did not implement the ELD in time have been the object of the procedure of enforcement actions brought by the Commission against Member States guilty of inadequate implementation of a directive, according to the Infringement Procedure under Arts 258–260 of the TFEU (previous Arts 226–228 of the EU Treaty). These Member States are: Austria, Belgium, Greece, Finland, France, Ireland, Luxembourg, Slovenia and the UK. See also Chapter 6.

significance of the damage, in particular so as to avoid the proliferation of orphan damages;

(2) The scope of application is clearly limitative as a consequence of the scientific definition of the notion of environmental damage. Consequently, also the scope of application needs to be extended;

(3) In investigating on the problem of who can claim for environmental damage the ELD outlines a top-down relationship between administrative authorities and operators with no duties for operators in the horizontal dimension. The triangular relationship (i.e. tortfeasor, victim and judge) which applies in a true environmental liability regime does not apply in the case of the ELD. The ELD abandons the triangular relationship with the purpose of creating a bipolar relationship between the operator and the competent authorities. The competent authorities play a strong role as 'guardians' of environmental protection with the effect of reinforcing their role and the bureaucratic machine of the regime instead of implementing a 'real liability regime' as a consequence of environmental damage. Significant discretion is left to the competent national authorities and this means extra hurdles for private enforcement;

(4) When the ELD treats compensation as a consequence of environmental damage and the problem of how to quantify environmental damage, especially in monetary terms, the ELD does not offer solutions. The legal *apparatus* put in place by the ELD completely avoids suggestions in that sense;

(5) With regard to the choice of liability, the ELD implemented a double system of fault based and strict based liability. Yet, it does not take into account the shift of the burden of proof, which would render the system of liability in the ELD much more rigorous. In addition, the choice of including optional exemptions from liability is weakening the environmental liability regime and accentuates the divergences in the way of rendering the tortfeasors liable. These exemptions leave too much room for Member States to decide whether to use them or not, and thus, instead of reinforcing harmonisation, this exacerbates differences among the national legislations of the Member States;

(6) With respect to the causality link, the ELD avoids the issue of diffuse pollution. The manifestation of the damage can occur at a long distance from the point where the activity causing damage occurred. A typical example of this situation is the phenomenon of acid rain. The ELD does not consider the long distance pollution, the different polluters and the phenomenon of multiple tortfeasors. The ELD does not consider either the situation of joint and several liabilities and the distinction between past and present pollution which would open up the path to new liability legal solutions which would include also the damage as a consequence of climate change events due to CO_2 emissions;

(7) With regards to the insurance mechanism, the ELD does not offers compulsory financial security products. The insurance mechanism, if

managed according to well established guidelines, can be combined with civil liability in the policy of prevention of environmental damage. However, it seems that the peculiarities of the environmental damage such as the long time period elapsed from the moment of the manifestation of the emissions of the polluting substances and the moment where the damage is manifested remain unsolved. This is the case where it is not possible to compensate the victims on the basis of the regular civil liability mechanism. Therefore, in that situation, the Compensation Funds,[728] especially the guarantee funds that permit claims with regards to potential polluters, seem to be the more appropriate solutions and could be coupled with civil liability and the policy of prevention of environmental damage. Thus, it is more than evident, as it has also been specified in the ELD,[729] that it is not possible to cover all the environmental risks through the insurance mechanism. In addition, has it has been pointed out along this study the ELD did not take a private approach to face the problems of the victims. In that sense, it should be appropriate to study a legal instrument which would couple mandatory insurance instruments (which should always be mandatory) with financial guarantees, such as for example, fidejussions. This solution could be a way to reach optimality as it would render the law much more homogeneous in all the Member States.

More concretely, the possible *formula* suitable in the case of the ELD could be represented not only by a combination of an insurance mechanism with financial guarantees but also with the set up of a maximum threshold to be determined together with a possibility that a part of the insurance *premiums* form a special compensation fund. Nevertheless, as regards to the insurance mechanism as a consequence of the environmental damage, the European experience has demonstrated that in general, European enterprises have the tendency of not stipulating voluntary and spontaneous insurance contracts. The only exception in this trend is the case of Germany, where it can be observed that the insurance contract's mechanism is quite developed. This means that the only plausible valid solution, for the time being, would remain the possibility to set-up a new *formula* based on the insurance mechanism. Without any doubt, this new proposed *formula* would always have to face both the problem of the identification of the author of the damage and the case of remoteness of the damage. Therefore, governments and the industry sector should set up a new legal-framework comprehensive also of a new *formula* for the insurance mechanism which should includes different scenarios of environmental damages able to predict incidents such as those related to GMOs and/or other unforeseeable and unpredictable environmental and health damages, such as those occurred as a consequence of nanotechnology.

Concluding, the shortcomings of the ELD need to be evaluated carefully in the light of the sequential order presented above. These are the focal points and are

---

728. See sub-section 5.11, Chapter 5 defining and categorizing 'Compensation Funds'.
729. See Art. 14, para. 1 of the ELD.

intertwined in this sequential order so as to reach an effective point of balance between law and policy. This balance must be struck to be effective in terms of environmental protection goal achievement. That said, the shortcomings represent a real challenge for the EU legislator who needs to also evaluate these points in the light of the historical political-legal multilevel context where this law has been and is being developed.

Thus, if the two aspects, the legal and the political, are not balanced there will be a barrier in the development of the environmental law, and consequently a regression of the regime-rules or provisions contained in environmental directives, since any attempt from the EU legislator to make use of the mechanism of interactions will have vanished.

From a substantive view, for the European environmental liability system to be effective and reach an optimal level of harmonisation it needs to link in a chain of logical sequence the focal points which are points of intersection between law and policy. Environmental regulations and environmental policies are complementary schemes and must be merged into a single, unique scheme including, simultaneous interactions in a three-levels: the EU, international and national levels. Nevertheless, the scheme shall also take into consideration and respect the Polluter-pays principle and the Subsidiarity principle.

In addition, such an evaluation scheme should include the avoidance of limiting public participation as this situation of limiting public participation is likely to lead to inadequate societal protection and inadequate environmental restoration. As such, the role of the non-official actors should be strengthened, including those representing the citizens' rights, as well as that of NGOs. In particular, the scheme should guarantee the enhancement of public participation as promised by the Aarhus Convention, but not achieved by the ELD.

From an ethical point of view, it is quite hard to admit that the effectiveness and the optimisation of environmental law are in the hands of the arbitrary political volition of human beings, where sometimes, what is more important is satisfying politico-materialistic egoistic interests obtained as result of a tremendous struggle for power, rather than genuinely protect the nature by trying to find true compromise on the eternal *dilemmas* between trade and environment.

The compromise is neither a black nor white, but reflects the *nuance* of the grey, where people from the business sector, are not always the 'bad black hatted people', and environmentalists, the 'good white hatted people'. Also, often, environmentalists or the greenest countries, hide using the technique of 'green environmental camouflage' and beyond their superior ideals of environmental protection, other interests more linked to national priorities which often have nothing to do with environmental protection.

This is why more work is needed to enhance the role of the EU as an actor through a stronger leadership role of the Commission by launching new intellectual and ethical environmental values or 'reformed values' integrating political, legal, sociological and economic elements that needs to lie on a common shared theoretical ground culminating in a new concept of environmental law.

References

BOOKS, JOURNAL ARTICLES AND REPORTS

Abraham K., 'Environmental Liability and the Limits of Insurance', 1988, Columbia Law Review, Vol. 88.

Alberton M.C., 'Saint George and the Dragon: Transposing the Environmental Liability Directive in Italy', 2007, Environmental Liability, Volume 15, Issue 6, pp. 235–241.

Alvaréz L., 'La responsabilidad civil por daños al medio ambiente' in Tratado de responsabilidad civil, Fernando Reglero Campos, 2008, Vol. 3 (parte especial segunda).

Amirante D., 'La forza normativa dei principi e il contributo del diritto ambientale alla teoria generale', 2006, Jovine Editore, pp. 93–156.

Amirante D., 'Diritto ambientale italiano e comparato – Principi', 2003, Quaderni della rivista Diritto e gestione dell'ambiente della seconda universtità degli studi di Napoli, Jovine Editore.

Anderson R., 'Natural Resource Damages, Superfund and the Courts', 16, Environmental Affairs, 1989, pp. 410–429.

Arnaud A.J., 'Legal Pluralism and the Building of Europe', in Petersen & Zahle, 'Legal Polycentricity: Consequences of Pluralism in Law', 1995, Dartmouth Publishing Company, pp. 149–169.

Askman D.F., 'The Role of Government Trustee in Recovering Compensation for Injury to Natural Resources', in Wettersteins 'Harm to the Environment – the Right to Compensation and the Assessment of Damages', 1997, Clarendon Press, Oxford, pp. 193–195.

Ashford N.A., 'Reflections on the Environmental Liability Scheme in the US and the EU: limitations and prospects for improvements', Paper Presented at the

Conference on Environmental Liability, Pireaus Bar Association, Pireaus, Greece, 26–27 June 2009.

Bernasconi C., 'Civil Liability resulting from Transfrontier Environmental Damage: a case for the Hague Conference?' Note drawn by Christophe Bernasconi, Secretary at the Permanent Bureau, pp. 10–12.

Berkamp L., 'The Proposed Environmental Liability Directive', Nov. 2002, Environmental Law Review, p. 1, footnote n. 6.

Berkamp L., 'Implementation of the Environmental Liability Directive in the EU Member State', 2005, ERA.

Berkgamp L., 'Liability and Environment: Private and Public Law Aspects of Civil Liability for Environmental Harm in an International Context', 2001, The Hague-London-New York.

Berlin Mc Cormick P. C., A., Professional Corporation, 'Obama's 2010 Budget: Becker's Iowa Environmental update published', April 2009.

Biergamann F., Brohm R. & Dingewerth R., 'Global Environmental Change and the Nation States – Proceedings of the 2001 Berlin Conference on the Human Dimension of Global Environmental Change', 2002, Potsdam: Potsdam Institute for Climate Impact Research, pp. 1-9.

Bitard F., 'Les mouvements transfrontaliers des déchets dangereux selon la Convention de Bale. Étude des regimes de responsabilité', Section 4 entitled 'Le champ d'application', 1997, Paris, Ed. Pedone.

Bretherton C. & Vogler, J., 'The European Union as Global Actor', 2003, Routledge.

Brighton W.D. & Askman D.F., 'The Role of Government Trustee in Recovering Compensation for Injury to Natural Resources', in Wettersteins 'Harm to the Environment – the Right to Compensation and the Assessment of Damages', 1997, Clarendon Press, Oxford, pp. 177–206.

Bryce 'Civil Liability for Environmental Damage and the UK government's response to the Green Paper', in Gazette du Palais, 5 mai 1994.

Calabresi G., 'The Cost of Accidents. A Legal and Economical Analysis', 1970, New Haven, Yale University Press.

Canadian, 'Responsabilià civile e assicurazione', 1993, Milano.

Canizzaro E., 'The European Union as an Actor in International Relations', 2002, Kluwer Law International-The Hague.

Carpentier R., 'Environment et indutrie', 1974, RMC, pp. 235–239.

Coroner F., 'Environmental Liability Directive: How well are Member States Handling Transposition?', Environmental Liability, 2006, Lawtext Publishing, Vol. 14, Issue 6, November – December, pp. 226–229.

Charalampidou N., 'The Protection of Land in Greece – before and after the implementation of the Environmental Liability Directive', August 2010, European Energy and Environmental Law Review, pp. 160–174.

Clarke C., 'The proposed EC liability Directive: Half-Way through Co-decision' 2003, RECIEL, p. 256, footnote n. 15.

Clifford C., 'Germany: update on the German Environmental Damages Act (Umweltschadensgesets) and its effects on insurance products', 11 September 2008, Global Environmental Group.

Cropper M.L., – Oates, W.E., 'Environmental Economics: a Survey', 1992, Journal of Economic Literature, 30, p. 678.

David R. & Spinosi Jauffret C., 'I grandi sistemi giuridici contemporanei', last edition, CEDAM.

Darpo, J. 'Komparation och Tradition', Abstract, Report of the Workshop, Comparative Environmental Law and Policy case studies and methodological perspectives, 15–17 August 2007, Finnish Environmental Institute (SYKE), NELN (Nordic Environmental Law Network).

De Burca Graig P., 'EU Law – Text, Cases and Materials', Third Edition, 2008, Oxford.

De Sadeleer N., 'Les Responsabilité environnementales dans l'espace européen – Point de vue Franco-Belge', 2006, Brulant- Bruxelles, p. 742.

De Sadeleer N., 'Environment et marché intérieur', 2010, Edition de l'Université de Bruxelles, p. 67.

De Sadeleer N., 'Polluter-Pays, Precautionary Principle and Liability' in Betlem G., Brans, E., 'Environmental Liability. The 2004 Directive compared with US and Member State Law', Cameron, 2006, pp. 89–101.

De Sadeleer N. & Born, C.H., 'Droit International et Communautaire de la biodiversité', 2004, Paris, Dalloz.

De Smedt K., 'Is Harmonisation always Effective'? The Implementation of the Environmental Liability Directive, 2009, European Energy Environmental Law Review.

D'Orta C., 'Ambiente e danno ambientale: dalla giurisrpudenza della Corte dei Conti alla legge sul Ministero dell'ambiente', 1987, Rivista Trimestrale di diritto pubblico, pp. 60–112.

Eco U., 'Dire presque la même chose. Expérience de traduction', 2003, Introduction, Milan, pp. 1–26.

Eeckhout P., 'External Relations of the European Union, Legal and Constitutional Foundations', 2009, Oxford EC Law.

Edward O.W., 'Biodiversity', 1988, National Academic Press.

Faure M., 'Deterrence, Insurability, and Compensation in Environmental Liability', 2003, Tort and Insurance Law, Wien/New York, p. 39.

Fajardo del Castillo T., 'La política exterior de la Unión Europea en materia de medio ambiente', Sectión IV 'los acuerdos mixtos', 2005, Editorial Tecnos, Madrid, pp. 76–82.

Findley R.W., and Faber D.A., 'Environmental Law', 1991, West Publishing Company, Minesota, pp. 240–266.

Fodella A., 'Il Protocollo di Basilea sulla responsabilità per i danni derivanti dal movimento tranfrontaliero di rifiuti pericolosi: il 'perfetto' è davvero 'nemico del buono?', a cura di Tullio Scovazzi, Osservatiorio Internazionale, 2000, Rivista Giuridica dell'Ambiente.

Fleming J.G., 'An Introduction to the Law of Torts', 2nd ed, 1985, Oxford Calderon Law Series.

Gambaro A. & Pozzo B., 'Responsabilità delle imprese in campo ambientale', pp. 88–140.

Gandolfi M.L., 'Profili del Trespass to land – il torts e gli improvements del trespasser', Studi di diritto comparato, 1979, Pubblicazioni della Facoltà di Giurisprudenza della università di Pisa, Milano–Giuffré Editore.

Giampietro F., 'La responsabilità per danno all'ambiente – l'attuazione della direttiva 2004/35 CE', 2006, Giuffré Editore.

Greene O., 'Environmental Regimes – Effectiveness and Implementation Review' in 'The Environment & International Relations', 1996 edited by Vogler, J., and Imber F., 1996, Routledge, pp. 114–196.

Hartkamp et al, 'Toward a Civil Code', 2004, Kluwer Law International, pp. 677–695.

Helleman G., 'The Forum: Are Dialogue and Synthesis Possible in International Relations?' Institut für Vergleichende Politikwissenschaft und Internationale Beziehungen, Johann Wolfgang Goethe-Universität Frankfurt am Main, 2003, International Studies Review, 5, pp. 123–153.

Jans J.H., 'European Environmental Law', 2008, European Law Publishing, p. 43; Krämer L., 'EC Environmental Law', 2007, Thomson Sweet & Maxell, pp. 27–29.

Jans, J.H., Squitani L., Aragao, A., Macrory R. & Wegener, B.W., 'Gold plating of European Environmental Measures?', 2009, Journal for European Environmental Planning Law, p. 417.

Jones B., 'Deterring, Compensating, and Remedying Environmental Damage: The Contribution of the Tort Liability' in Wettersteins 'Harm to the Environment – the Right to Compensation and the Assessment of the Damage', 1997, Clarendon Press, Oxford, pp. 11–27.

Jupille J., Caporaso, J. & Checkel, J.T., 'Integrating Institutions – Rationalims, Contructivism and the Study of European Union'; Comparative Political Studies, Vol., 36 No. $\frac{1}{2}$, February, March, pp. 1–40.

Jupille J., 'The European Union and International Outcomes', International Organisation 53, 2, Spring 1999, p. 410.

Kipnis S.A., 'The conflict between CERCLA and FIRREA: Environmental Liability of the Resolution Trust Corporation', 39, UCLA Law Review, 1996, pp. 439–456.

Kiss A. & Shelton D., 'Strict Liability in International Environmental Law', 2007, The George Washington University Law School Public Law and Theory Working Paper No. 345, Legal Studies Research Paper No. 345, p. 1136 (the paper can be downloaded at http://ssrn.com/abstract=1010478).

Krämer L., 'EC Environmental Law', 2007, Thomson Sweet & Maxell, pp. 27–28.

Krämer L., 'The Single European Act and environmental protection', 1987; n. 24 CMLR, pp. 659–688.

Krämer L., 'Focus on European Environmental Law', 1997, London, p. 143.

Krämer L., 'EEC Treaty and Environmental Protection', 1992, London.

Krämer L., 'Commentaires de l'Acte Unique Européen en matière de l'environnement', 1988, Revue juridique de l'environnement, p. 75.

Krasner S., 'Structural Causes and Regimes Consequences: Regimes and Intervening Variable', 1983, International Regimes, London: Cornell U. P, pp. 1–21.

Larsson M.L., 'The Law of Environmental Damage: Liability and Reparation', 1999, Kluwer Law International-The Hague.

Lawrence P., 'Negotiations of a Protocol on Liability and Compensation for Damage resulting from Transboundary movements of Hazardous Waste and their Disposal'; p. 251.

Lefevre J., 'Interactions of the EU Environmental Liability Regime', 2002, FIELD.

Levy A., 'Political Science and the Question of Effectiveness of International Environmental Institutions', 1993, International Challenges, Vol. 13, No. 2, pp. 17–35.

Lindross A. and Mehling M., 'Dispelling the Chimera of Self-Contained Regimes' International Law and the WTO', 2006, European Journal of International Law, pp. 857–877.

Louka E., 'International Environmental Law – Fairness, Effectiveness, and World Order', 2006, Cambridge University Press.

Lopatta H., 'ELD Report – Presentation for the EEB', 11 February 2011, Boulevard de Waterloo 34, Brussels, Belgium, DG Environment, Unit A.1.

Lopatta H., 'ELD Report – Presentation for EEB', 24 September 2010, Square de Meeûs 18, 1040 Brussels.

Meli, 'L'origine del principio chi inquina paga da parte della CEE', 1998, Rivista Giuridica dell'Ambiente.

Merryman J.H., 'The Civil Law Tradition. An Introduction to the Legal System of Western Europe and Latin America', last edition, Standford University Press, Stanford, California.

Miller P., Schzoeder Leape, 'Environmental regulation', 1996, Law, Science and Policy, Second Edition, Little, Brown and Company, pp. 279–399.

Monti A., 'Environmental Risk: a Comparative Law and Economics Approach to Liability and Insurance', 2001, European Review of Private Law, pp. 51–79.

Monti A., 'Environmental Risk and Insurance. A Comparative Analysis of the Role of Insurance in the Management of Environmental Related Risks', 2002, Environmental Risks and Insurance, OECD Report.

Mukakis, W.A., 'Hazardous Waste Regulations – Enforcement and Liabilities', 1999, Executives Entreprises Publications Co., Inc., pp. 75–113.

Oates W.E., 'Environmental Economics: a Survey', 1992, Journal of Economic Literature, 30, p. 678.

Olsen E.B. & Sørensen K.E., (eds), 'Regulation in the EU', 2006, Thomson A/S, pp. 38–39.

Petersen & Zahle 'Legal Polycentricity: Consequences of Pluralism in Law', 1995, Dartmouth Publishing Company.

Peterson J., 'Decision-Making in the European Union: Towards a Framework for Analysis', Journal of European Public Policy, 1995, Vol. 2, pp. 69–93.

Poli S., 'Shaping the EC Regime on Liability for Environmental Damage: Progress or Disillusionment?', 1999, European Environmental Law Review.

Pfennigsdorf 'L'assicurazione r.c Danni da inquinamento' – Considerazioni politiche per gli assicuratori, in Ass, 1991, p. 48.

Prebble A.L., 'Corporate Law Confines to Parent Liability under CERCLA', 67, University of Cincinnati Review, 1999, p. 1357.

Prieur M., 'Droit de l'environnement', 2001, Paris.

Ponzanelli G., 'American Tort Process', 1992, Pisa.

Posner R., 'Economic Analysis of law', 1998, Aspen Law and Business.

Pozzo B., 'Toward Civil Liability for Environmental Damage in Europe: The White Paper of the Commission of European Communities', 2001, Vol. 1, Issue 2, Article 2, Global Jurist Topics, pp. 1-34.

Pozzo B., 'Danno Ambientale ed imputazione della Responsabilità ', 1996, Milano Giuffré Editore.

Pozzo B., 'Responsabilità per i danni all'ambiente: valutazioni giuridiche ed economiche', 2003, Quaderni Crasl, S10/finale, p. 14.

Pozzo B., 'Liability Insurance and Environmental Risk', 2000, Revue Hellénique de Droit International, Athens, Vol.1, pp. 1-25.

Pozzo B., 'Danno ambientale ed imputazione della responsabilità', 1996, Milano, p. 251.

Pozzo B., 'Danno ambientale ed imputazione della responsabilità – esperienze giuridiche a confronto', 1996, Milano, Giuffré Editore, Chapter II, pp. 113–184.

Pozzo B, 'Danno ambientale ed imputazione della responsabilità – esperienze giuridiche a confronto', 1996, Milano, Giuffré Editore, p. 142.

Pozzo B., 'Towards Civil Liability for Environmental Damage in Europe: the "White Paper of the Commission of the European Communities"', 2001, Global Jurist, Vol. 1, Issue 2, p. 18.

Pozzo B., 'La responsabilità per danni all'ambiente in Germania' 1991, in Riv. dir. Civ.

Pozzo B., 'Towards Civil Liability for Environmental Damage in Europe: the White Paper of the Commission of the European Communities', 2001, Vol. 1, Issue 2, Global Jurist, p. 4.

Pozzo B., 'La nuova direttiva sulla prevenzione e il risarcimento del danno all'-ambiente', 2002, Quaderni della Rivista Giuridica dell'Ambiente, Giuffré Editore, pp. 273–292.

Pozzo B., Jacometti, V., 'Multilingualism and the Harmonisation of European Law', 2006, Kluwer Law International – The Hague, p. 13.

Pozzo B., 'Multilingualism, legal terminology and the problems of harmonising European private law' 2006, in Multilingualism and Harmonisation of European Law, ed. Pozzo, B., and Jacometti, V.

Rehbinder E., 'Implementation of the Environmental Liability Directive in Germany', 2007, Environmental Liability Directive, Vol. 5.

Ringleb A. & Wiggings S., 'Liability and Large-Scale, Long-Term Hazards', Journal of Political Economy, June, 1990, pp. 574–595.

Sand P., 'Principles of International Environmental Law', 2007, Cambridge University Press.

Santos De Sousa, in Wilhelmsson, T., 'Legal Integration and Disintegration of National Law', in 'Legal Polycentricity', 1995, p. 129.

Schoenbaum Thomas J., 'Environmental Damages: The Emerging Law in the United States' in Wettersteins, P., 'Harm to the Environment – the Right to Compensation and the Assessment of Damages', 1997, Clarendon Press, Oxford, pp. 159–174.

Silva Soares G.F. & Vieira Vargas E., 'The Basel Liability Protocol on Liability and Compensation for Damage resulting from Transboundary movement of Hazardous Wastes and their Disposal', 2001, in YIEL, p. 70.

Shavell S., 'Economic Analysis of Accident Law', 1987, Harvard University Press, Cambridge.

Snyder F., 'The Effectiveness European Community Law: Institutions, Process, Technique, Tools and Techniques', 1993, The Modern Law Review, Vol. 56, No. 1, pp. 19–54.

Tester P. & Whitehead M., 'The EC Directive on Civil Liability for Damage Caused by Waste: Lessons from the "Superfund Law"', 1992, EELR, Vol. 1, No 1 June, pp. 26–27.

Thieffry P., 'Environmental Liability in Europe: The European's Union Projects, and the Convention of the Council of Europe', 1994, in Int. Lawyers, p. 1083.

Thieme D., 'European Community External Relations in the Field of the Environment', 2001, August-September, European Environmental Law Review, p. 252.

Treves T., Pineschi L., Tanzi A., Pitea C., Ragni C. & Jacur F.R., 'Non-Compliance Procedures and Mechanism and the Effectiveness of International Environmental Agreements', 2009, T.M.C, Asser Press.

Ulfstein G., 'Effectiveness of International Environmental Law. Regulations, decision-making, participation and enforcement' in 'Environmental Law – From International Law too national law', 1999, Edited by Bass, E.M., pp. 345–363.

Van den Broek G.M., 'Environmental Liability and nature protection areas. Will the EU Environmental Liability Directive actually lead to the restoration of damaged natural resources?', 2009, Utrecht Law Review, Vol. 5, Issue 1 (June).

Vogler J. & Imber, M., 'The Environment & International Relations', 1996, Routledge.

Vogler J., 'The European Union as A Global Actor', 2003, Routledge.

Wetterstein P., 'Recent Trends in the Development of International Civil Liability', p. 32.

Winter G., Jans H, Macrory R. & Krämer L., 'Weighing up the EC Environmental Liability Directive', in section 2 titled: 'Terminological Disentanglement', 2008, Journal of Environmental Law, Vol. 20., N. 2.

Young O.R., 'Why is there No Unified Theory of Environmental Governance?' Essay for the 9th Biennial Conference of the International Association for the Study of Common Property, 2002, II EG/Darthmoth College.

Young O.R., 'Political Leadership and Regime Formation: on The Development of Institutions in International Society', 1991, International Organisation 45, 3, Summer, pp. 282–308.

Zweigert K. & Kötz H., 'An Introduction to Comparative Law', last Edition, Calderon Press.

Table of Cases

Index

ENERGY AND ENVIRONMENTAL LAW & POLICY SERIES

1. Stephen J. Turner, *A Substantive Environmental Right: An Examination of the Legal Obligations of Decision-makers towards the Environment*, 2009 (ISBN 978-90-411-2815-7).
2. Helle Tegner Anker, Birgitte Egelund Olsen & Anita Rønne (eds), *Legal Systems and Wind Energy: A Comparative Perspective*, 2009 (ISBN 978-90-411-2831-7).
3. David Langlet, *Prior Informed Consent and Hazardous Trade: Regulating Trade in Hazardous Goods at the Intersection of Sovereignty, Free Trade and Environmental Protection*, 2009 (ISBN 978-90-411-2821-8).
4. Louis J. Kotzé and Alexander R. Paterson (eds), *The Role of the Judiciary in Environmental Governance: Comparative Perspectives*, 2009 (ISBN 978-90-411-2708-2).
5. Tuula Honkonen, *The Common but Differentiated Responsibility Principle in Multilateral Environmental Agreement's: Regulatory and Policy Aspects*, 2009 (ISBN 978-90-411-3153-9).
6. Barbara Pozzo (ed.), *The Implementation of the Seveso Directives in an Enlarged Europe: A Look into the Past and a challenge for the Future*, 2009 (ISBN 978-90-411-2854-6).
7. Henrik M. Inadomi, *Independent Power Projects in Developing Countries: Legal Investment Protection and Consequences for Development*, 2010 (ISBN 978-90-411-3178-2).
8. Nahid Islam, *The Law of Non-Navigational Uses of International Watercourses: Options for Regional Regime-Building in Asia*, 2010 (ISBN 978-90-411-3196-6).
9. Yasuhiro Shigeta, *International Judicial Control of Environmental Protection: Standard Setting, Compliance Control and the Development of International Environmental Law by the International Judiciary*, 2010 (ISBN 978-90-411-3151-5).
10. Katleen Janssen, *The Availability of Spatial and Environmental Data in the European Union: At the Crossroads between Public and Economic Interests*, 2010 (ISBN 978-90-411-3287-1).
11. Henrik Bjørnebye, *Investing in EU Energy Security: Exploring the Regulatory Approach to Tomorrow's Electricity Production*, 2010 (ISBN 978-90-411-3118-8).
12. Véronique Bruggeman, *Compensating catastrophe victims: A Comparative Law and Economics Approach*, 2010 (ISBN 978-90-411-3263-5).
13. Michael G. Faure, Han Lixin & Shan Hongjun, *Maritime Pollution Liability and Policy: China, Europe and the US*, 2010 (ISBN 978-90-411-2869-0).
14. Anton Ming-Zhi Gao, *Regulating Gas Liberalization: A Comparative Study on Unbundling and Open Access Regimes in the US, Europe, Japan, South Korea and Taiwan*, 2010 (ISBN 978-90-411-3347-2).

15. Mustafa Erkan, *International Energy Investment Law: Stability through Contractual Clauses*, 2011 (ISBN 978-90-411-3411-0).
16. Levente Borzsák, *The Impact of Environmental Concerns on the Public Enforcement Mechanism under EU law: Environmental protection in the 25th hour*, 2011 (ISBN 978-90-411-3408-0).
17. Tarcísio Hardman Reis, *Compensation for Environmental Damages under International Law: The Role of the International Judge*, 2011 (ISBN 978-90-411-3437-0).
18. Kim Talus, *Vertical Natural Gas Transportation Capacity, Upstream Commodity Contracts and EU Competition Law*, 2011 (ISBN 978-90-411-3407-3).
19. Wang Hui, *Civil Liability for Marine Oil Pollution Damage: A Comparative and Economic Study of the International, US and Chinese Compensation Regime*, 2011 (ISBN 978-90-411-3672-5).
20. Chowdhury Ishrak Ahmed Siddiky, *Cross-Border Pipeline Arrangements: What Would a Single Regulatory Framework Look Like?*, 2012 (ISBN 978-90-411-3844-6).
21. Rozeta Karova, *Liberalization of Electricity Markets and Public Service Obligations in the Energy Community*, 2012 (ISBN 978-90-411-3849-1).
22. Sandra Cassotta, *Environmental Damage and Liability Problems in a Multilevel Context: The Case of the Environmental Liability Directive*, 2012 (ISBN 978-90-411-3830-9).